C. A. Strine
Sworn Enemies

Beihefte zur Zeitschrift für die alttestamentliche Wissenschaft

Herausgegeben von
John Barton · F. W. Dobbs-Allsopp
Reinhard G. Kratz · Markus Witte

Band 436

De Gruyter

C. A. Strine

Sworn Enemies

The Divine Oath, the Book of Ezekiel,
and the Polemics of Exile

De Gruyter

G

MIX
Papier aus verantwor-
tungsvollen Quellen
FSC
www.fsc.org   FSC® C016439

ISBN 978-3-11-029039-4
e-ISBN 978-3-11-029053-0
ISSN 0934-2575

Library of Congress Cataloging-in-Publication Data

A CIP catalog record for this book has been applied for at the Library of Congress.

Bibliographic information published by the Deutsche Nationalbibliothek

The Deutsche Nationalbibliothek lists this publication in the Deutsche
Nationalbibliografie; detailed bibliographic data are available in the Internet
at http://dnb.dnb.de.

© 2013 Walter de Gruyter GmbH, Berlin/Boston

Printing: Hubert & Co. GmbH & Co. KG, Göttingen
∞ Printed on acid-free paper

Printed in Germany

www.degruyter.com

pour Jacques; for Jack

Table of Contents

Acknowledgements

This book is a revised version of my doctoral thesis, for which I obtained the D.Phil. from the University of Oxford in 2011.

Dr Paul Joyce (now Professor of Hebrew Bible/Old Testament at King's College London) supervised my work. His guidance, critical insights, constant encouragement, and gracious mentoring went far beyond a supervisor's call of duty. I am very thankful that I can now call Paul a colleague, but I cherish most that he will be a friend and mentor for life. Sincere thanks are due to Prof. Hugh Williamson and Dr Andrew Mein, who examined the thesis, reading it with care and offering invaluable feedback. I am grateful to Dr Sue Gillingham, Prof. John Day, and Prof. John Barton for reading earlier drafts of the work. Special thanks are in order for Prof. Barton, who not only provided guidance and wisdom during my studies but also encouraged me to submit this manuscript to the editors of Beihefte zur Zeitschrift für die alttestamentliche Wissenschaft. Ben Edsall proofread this manuscript; for that work and for his friendship I am truly grateful. Finally, I wish to extend my thanks to the editors of BZAW for accepting this manuscript for publication and to the staff of Walter de Gruyter for their assistance. The contribution of all these people has made this a better book and I alone remain responsible for any mistakes or oversights in it.

I would never have pursued doctoral studies if it were not for the direction and support of my earlier teachers. I think especially of Bruce Waltke and Reggie Kidd, who believed in me when I doubted and celebrated with me when I succeeded. Perhaps the most important teachers I've had are my fellow students: at seminary, Scott Jones, Bill Fullilove, Christopher Caudle, and Scott Redd; in the Oxford Old Testament seminar, Carly Crouch, Jonathan Stökl, and Madhavi Nevader; and across Oxford, Chris Jones, Michael Burdett, Dave Lincicum, Christopher Hays, Bobby Ryu, Justin Hardin, and Syman Stevens. I appreciate that each one listened patiently, critiqued me graciously, and kept me grounded through the highs and lows of this project.

My doctoral studies and this book would not have been possible without the financial provision of the Seneff Family Foundation and the help of its staff, particularly Josh Benoit. I am eternally grateful for their support. The Foundation's vision to be a patron for young scholars literally changed my life. Thanks are also due to the American

Friends of Christ Church, who provided additional financial support during my doctoral studies.

The love and care of my family sustained me through this project. To Cathy Lang and to Jim Strine and Mary Jeane Strine I offer my heartfelt appreciation for their love and support. Mike and Vicky Pogue have not only been unwavering in their belief in me, they've never complained (too loudly) that my studies took their daughter so far away from them. The Pogue-Walters provided love and good laughs throughout my studies, even when they experienced tragic loss. With them, I wish John Walter were here to see this book in print; despite the certainty that his editor's eyes would have found numerous flaws, I know he would have applauded me for writing it.

While I am truly grateful to all those mentioned above, my greatest thanks go to Amanda, my wife. Without her I would have never dreamed this was possible, never taken the risk to pursue that dream, and most definitely not have persevered until it was reality. I wrote this book, but she gave this project life. I shall never be able to say thank you for that properly; I pray she will accept my love and devotion as an expression of my gratitude.

Finally, this book is jointly dedicated to my grandfather, Jacques Lang, and to my son who is named for him, Jack Strine. During five years with the book of Ezekiel, I recognized that I too had a vision that I want to impress upon a subsequent generation. I pray that many things will be true of Jack's life, but among the most important is that he will always love to learn. My model of life-long learning has always been Jacques Lang. For all the times that he wished me joy, happiness, and a good life, I offer this book in return. There will be, I am sure, few things that bring me as much joy and happiness as dedicating this work to him on his 93rd birthday.

C. A. Strine
Oxford
2 November 2012

Sigla and Abbreviations

AAeg	*Analecta Aegyptica*
AB	The Anchor Bible
AfO	Archiv für Orientforschung
AJSL	*Americal Journal of Semitic Languages and Literature*
AnBib	Analecta Biblica
ANET	*Ancient Near Eastern Texts Relating to the Old Testament.* Edited by J. B. Pritchard. 3rd ed. with supplement. Princeton: Princeton University Press, 1969
AnOr	Analecta orientalia
AOAT	Alter Orient und Altes Testament
AThANT	Abhandlungen zur Theologie des Alten und Neuen Testaments
BASOR	Bulletin of the American Schools of Oriental Research
BETL	Bibliotheca Ephemeridum Theologicarum Lovaniensium
Bib	*Biblica*
BibOr	Biblica et orientalia
BJS	Brown Judaic Studies
BO	*Bibliotheca orientalis*
BZAR	Beihefte zur Zeitschrift für Altorientalische und biblische Rechtsgeschichte
BZAW	Beihefte zur Zeitschrift für die alttestamentliche Wissenschaft
CAD	*The Assyrian Dictionary of the Oriental Insititue of the University of Chicago.* Edited by I. J. Gelb et al. Chicago: The Oriental Institute, 1956–
CBET	Contributions to Biblical Exegesis and Theology
CBQ	*Catholic Biblical Quarterly*
CHD	*The Hittite Dictionary of the Oriental Institute of the University of Chicago.* Edited by Hans Gustav Güterbock and Harry A. Hoffner. Chicago: The Oriental Institute, 1980–
COS	*The Context of Scripture.* Edited by William W. Hallo. 3 vols. Leiden: Brill, 1997-2002
CTH	*Catalogue des textes hittites.* Emmanuel Laroche. Paris: Klincksieck, 1971
DN	Divine Name

EBib	*Etudes bibliques*
ETL	*Ephemerides Theologicae Lovanienses*
FAT	Forschungen zum Alten Testament
FOTL	Forms of the Old Testament Literature
FRLANT	Forschungen zur Religion und Literatur des Alten und Neuen Testaments
HO	Hanbuch der Orientalisk
HUCA	*Hebrew Union College Annual*
IBHS	*Introduction to Biblical Hebrew Syntax.* Bruce K. Waltke and Michael P. O'Connor. Winona Lake, Ind., 1990
ICC	International Critical Commentary
Int	*Interpretation*
JANES	*Journal of the Ancient Near Eastern Society*
JAOS	*Journal of the American Oriental Society*
JDS	Judean Desert Studies
JSS	*Journal of Semitic Studies*
JNES	*Journal of Near Eastern Studies*
JNSL	*Journal of Northwest Semitic Languages*
JCS	*Journal of Cuneiform Studies*
JBL	*Journal of Biblical Literature*
JHS	*Journal of Hebrew Scriptures*
JSOT	*Journal for the Study of the Old Testament*
JSOTSup	Journal for the Study of the Old Testament: Supplement Series
KBo	Keilschrifttexte aus Boghazköi. Leipzig: J. C. Hinrichs, 1916–
KTU	Neue keilalphabetische Texte aus Ras Schamra-Ugarit
KUB	Keilschrifturkunden aus Boghazköi. Berlin: Akademie-Verlag, 1921–1990
LAE	*The Literature of Ancient Egypt.* Edited by William Kelley Simpson. New Haven: Yale University Press, 2003.
LHBOTS	Library of Hebrew Bible/Old Testament Studies
LXX	Septuagint
MT	Masoretic Text
NCB	New Century Bible
NICOT	New International Commentary on the Old Testament
OBO	Orbis Biblicus et Orientalis
OBT	Overtures to Biblical Theology
OG	Greek translation of the Prophets and the Writings

OIP	Oriental Institute Publications, University of Chicago Oriental Institute
OTL	Old Testament Library
OTM	Oxford Theological Monographs
OTS	Old Testament Studies
OtSt	Oudtestamentische Studiën
PRU	Le Palais Royal d'Ugarit
PTMS	Pittsburgh Theological Monograph Series
RHPR	*Revue d'histoire et de philosophie religieuses*
RN	Royal Name
RS	Ras Shamra
S	Peshitta
SAA	State Archives of Assyria
SBLDS	Society of Biblical Literature Dissertation Series
SBLMS	Society of Biblical Literature Monograph Series
SBLSP	Society of Biblical Literature Seminar Papers
SBLSymS	Society of Biblical Literature Symposium Series
SBLWAW	Society of Biblical Literature Writings from the Ancient World
SBTS	Sources for Biblical and Theological Study
SEL	*Studi Epigrafici e Linguistici*
TDOT	*Theological Dictionary of the Old Testament*
Tg	Targumim
TBü	Theologische Bücherei
UF	*Ugarit-Forschungen*
Vg	Vulgate
VT	*Vetus Testamentum*
VTSup	Supplements to Vetus Testamentum
WMANT	Wissenschaftliche Monographien zum Alten und Neuen Testament
WBC	Word Biblical Commentary
YOSR	Yale Oriental Series, Researches
ZAW	*Zeitschrift für die alttestamentliche Wissenschaft*

Chapter One: Introduction

The book of Ezekiel has no shortage of reproachful things to say about Jerusalem, Judah, and the Judahites that remain in the land after the initial deportation of 597 B.C.E. Condemnatory remarks fill the first 19 chapters of the book and reach a crescendo in Ezek 20, which leaves no generation in the history of Israel from Egypt to the Babylonian exile outside its negative evaluation. Ezekiel, it is plain, has no qualms rebuking ancestor or fellow Judahite.

Criticism is not restricted to Israel and Judah: seven foreign nations receive Ezekiel's censure too. The book is no respecter of size or strength in this matter either, taking to task both the small nations that surround Judah (Ezek 25–28) as well as Egypt, with that international power receiving particularly lengthy treatment for its various transgressions (Ezek 29–32).

It is, therefore, astonishing that the book of Ezekiel says almost nothing about the Babylonians among whom the exiles live. On one hand, Ezekiel portrays the Babylonians and their king in positive terms (e.g. Ezek 17 and 29), but this material falls short of an endorsement. The book of Ezekiel contains nothing comparable to Jeremiah's letter to the exiles that encourages them to settle down in Babylon and to seek the prosperity of that city in order that they themselves might benefit from the success of their Babylonian captors (Jer 29:4-7). On the other hand, there is a conspicuous lack of negative material about the Babylonians who are responsible for deporting Ezekiel and his community, stripping them of their social privilege, subjecting them to unenviable labor from which they gain no profit, and for destroying Jerusalem and its temple while appropriating the produce of their ancestral land for their own benefit. Although Marduk, patron deity of the Babylonians, and the rest of the Babylonian deities are represented in cult statues that receive worship and adoration, Ezekiel directs none of its condemnation of this practice (e.g. Ezek 8; 20:32-33) towards the Babylonians. This is a stark contrast to the openly critical language in Jeremiah and Deutero-Isaiah (e.g. Jer 10:1-10; Isa 46:1-11). These silences are conspicuous.

This book shall argue that both the vitriolic language directed at Ezekiel's fellow Judahites and also the apparent lack of critical speech about the Neo-Babylonians are the result of a single issue, namely the way in which asymmetric power structures influence the discourse of dominant and subordinate groups. The book of Ezekiel seeks to define the boundaries that mark off faithful Yahwism and legitimate Judahite nationalism over against both the Judahites that remain in the land and also their Babylonian captors. In order to succeed in this objective, the book disputes with both groups, arguing that their beliefs and behaviors are misguided. Even though this two-pronged polemic has a unified objective, the social situation demands that Ezekiel pursue its two sides in dissimilar ways. The book can speak openly and ostensibly authoritatively to other Judahites, but that mode of discourse is neither feasible nor shrewd when the Bablyonians are in view. To define the boundaries between its ideal Judahite community and their Babylonian overlords, Ezekiel depends upon implicit arguments, veiled language, and a disguised discourse of resistance.

Concealment, argues James C. Scott, is a fundamental feature of the way in which subordinate groups resist the dominant groups that exert control over them. Scott's model not only offers insight into the remarkable absence of overt criticism against the Babylonians, it explains why the book's critique of its fellow Judahites is so harsh: reproachful language like Ezekiel directs at its fellow Judahites is the privilege of the powerful, of dominant classes, of social groups that possess the power both to define what is acceptable and also the means to enforce its adoption. The content of Ezekiel's statements indicts his fellow Judahites for their role in bringing YHWH's judgment on Jerusalem, and its form serves as a weapon in the struggle over who will be the internally dominant group. Ezekiel, stripped of all other means by which to assert authority, possesses only words as a weapon in the fight to define the boundaries that mark off faithful Yahwism and authentic Judahite identity.

1. Formulaic Language in Ezekiel's Rhetoric

One of the most prominent features of Ezekiel is its fanciful visions. There is, of course, the intricate description of YHWH's chariot, which is filled with language that is constantly grasping for ways to portray the spectacular image (Ezek 1:4-28). YHWH's battle with Gog of Magog pits armies "like a cloud covering the earth" against a deity who makes even the fish in the sea tremble (Ezek 38–39). Jerusalem is portrayed as a blood-bathed baby, then as a grown woman whose sisters are the cities of Sodom and Samaria (Ezek 16). Judah's king is compared to a tree branch alongside the Babylonian ruler, pictured as an an eagle (Ezek 17). The book climaxes with a description of the restored land, marked by a river that grows deeper as it flows further away from its source, and a restored temple with simultaneously precise and mystifying measurements (Ezek 40–48). Ezekiel can be disorienting.

And yet, the book has an equal if not stronger propensity to use formulaic language, and to do so repetitively. There is the repeated address of the prophet as "son of man," which occurs 94 times. The divine word formula—"and the word of YHWH came to me"—appears 50 times too. Walther Zimmerli demonstrated that the repetitive use of formulaic language in Ezekiel possesses theological significance with his extended study on the formula of self introduction (*Selbstvorstellungsformel*) and its use in the recognition formula (*Erkenntnisformel*), "you shall know that I am YHWH."[1] There, Zimmerli concluded that "one cannot speak of Ezekiel's understanding of 'knowledge of God' without first considering the uniqueness and origin of this rigidly fixed formulation."[2] His conclusion emphasized the correlation between formulaic language and Ezekiel's central ideas.

Why mix these contrasting features in a single text? In the first place, the formulaic language serves as a signpost among the otherwise confusing landscape, directing the audience onwards towards a clear understanding of the book's key concepts. To an audience that might be wholly disoriented by the difficulties of the text, the potentially tedious formulae are indicators of its main concerns and theological ideas. In the second place, as the following study will demonstrate, formulaic language can carry various implicit connotations. Such implied meanings may only be evident to certain groups, insiders one might say, and enable a text to introduce themes under the cover of ambiguity.

Bearing in mind the importance of formulaic language for Ezekiel and the rhetorical possibilities it opens up, it is noteworthy that scholars have given so little attention to two key formulae: חי אני (commonly "as I live") and נשא יד (commonly "lifted hand"). Typically grouped

---

1   Walther Zimmerli, "Ich Bin Yahweh," in *Gottes Offenbarung: Gesammelte Aufsätze Zum Alten Testament* (TBü 19; Munich: C. Kaiser, 1963); ET in Walther Zimmerli, *I Am Yahweh* (Translated by D. Stott. Atlanta, Ga.: John Knox Press, 1982), 1-28. Walther Zimmerli, *Erkenntnis Gottes nach dem Buch Ezechiel: Eine theologische Studie* (ATANT 27; Zürich: Zwingli-Verlag, 1954); ET in Zimmerli, *I Am Yahweh*, 29-98.

2   Ibid., 31. Another important study of formulaic language in Ezekiel is Rolf Rendtorff, *The Covenant Formula: An Exegetical and Theological Investigation* (OTS; Translated by Margaret Kohl. Edinburgh: T & T Clark, 1998), 47. German original: Rolf Rendtorff, *Die Bundesformel* (Stuttgart: Verlag Katholisches Bibelwerk, 1995). Perhaps Rendtorff's most important contribution is to show how Ezekiel often relates one formula to another in order to amplify the meaning of each phrase and to drive home the larger message.

together as two ways in which YHWH swears and referred to under the
single heading of the divine oath, there are more occurrences of these
formulae in the book of Ezekiel than in the remainder of the Hebrew
Bible combined. For example, אני חי occurs 16 times in the book of
Ezekiel (Ezek 5:11; 14:16, 18, 20; 16:48; 17:16, 19; 18:3; 20:3, 31, 33; 33:11,
27; 34:8; 35:6, 11) and only seven times elsewhere (Num 14:21, 28; Deut
32:40; Isa 49:18; Jer 22:24; 46:18; Zeph 2:9). The נשא יד formula exhibits
a similar distribution: it appears 10 times in Ezekiel (Ezek 20:5 [twice],
6, 15, 23, 28, 42; 36:7; 44:12; 47:14) and only seven times with YHWH as its
subject outside the book (Exod 6:8; Num 14:30; Deut 32:40; Isa 49:22;
Pss 10:12, 106:26; Neh 9:15). The overlap between this distribution and
Zimmerli's analysis of the recognition formula suggests these formulae
may possess a similar importance for understanding Ezekiel's message.

Frequency alone does not demonstrate importance, but it is a contributing factor. To it one can add the first-person nature of both statements. Ezekiel is known for its radical theocentricity, so this is not
entirely surprising. Yet, scholars generally miss that the solemnity of
YHWH's oaths enhances this sense of theocentricity. Swearing constitutes the most elevated, earnest statement of belief or intent an individual can make. When a person swears they indicate something about
what is most important to them and invite anyone who hears the oath
to evaluate their character based on their faithfulness to it. When
YHWH, the central figure in Ezekiel, swears the undivided attention of
the audience, both ancient and modern, is demanded.

The first part of this study analyzes the formulae אני חי and נשא יד
and may be summarized in one question: why does the book of Ezekiel
employ the divine oath so often? In order to adequately answer this
broad query, the study will focus on the meaning of both the אני חי and
the נשא יד formula. This is more than merely asking how to translate
them. Given their use in Ezekiel, the Hebrew Bible, and the broader
ancient Near East, what connotations does each formula possess?
What other texts, inside and outside the Hebrew Bible, use similar
phraseology? How does the book of Ezekiel draw on this context and
use it in its presentation of YHWH's oaths?

Answering these questions involves drawing conclusions on the
use of the divine oath throughout the ancient Near East, its role as a
genre marker, and the connections each formula has to the theological
traditions contained in the Hebrew Bible. Attending to those issues,
this study will provide greater clarity about how the book of Ezekiel is

related to the Priestly[3] and Deuteronomistic[4] theological traditions, make plain that the whole book of Ezekiel is argumentative in tone, and reinforce Ezekiel's connection to the exodus tradition as the legitimate account of Israel's origin.[5]

At this stage it is necessary to provide context to the detailed study of chapters two through four by offering a brief overview of previous work on the divine oath.

---

3   Henceforth P. The present study will also use the term priestly writings on occasion to refer to a broader group of texts that exhibit priestly concerns, primarily P, the Holiness Code (Lev 17–26), and Ezekiel, but also texts in other books that exhibit the same theological profile.

4   Hereafter, DTR.

5   Because "exodus tradition" is a key concept for this study, a brief note about what it does and does not mean is required. Firstly, the term comprises what Martin Noth called the "guidance out of Egypt" and "guidance into the arable land" themes (Martin Noth, *Überlieferungsgeschichte des Pentateuch* [Stuttgart: Kohlhammer, 1948]; ET Martin Noth, *A History of Pentateuchal Traditions* [Translated by Anderson, Bernard W. Englewood Cliffs, N. J.: Prentice Hall, 1972]). It is evident that Ezekiel knows and presumes that its audience shares his knowledge of a tradition that the community YHWH guided out of Egypt, through the wilderness, and into the land of Canaan represents Judah's ancestors (e.g. Ezek 20:1-31). Secondly, the contents of Ezekiel's "exodus tradition" overlap with events narrated in Exodus through Joshua. Whether or not the authors and tradents of Ezekiel knew those texts and whether or not the tradition that Ezekiel knows agrees with those books on all points, is not obvious. Observe that Ezekiel never mentions Moses. This omission necessitates adopting "exodus tradition" instead of "the Moses story," preferred by Schmid (Konrad Schmid, *Erzväter und Exodus. Untersuchungen zur doppelten Begründung der Ursprünge Israels innerhalb der Geschichtsbücher des Alten Testaments* [WMANT 81; Neukirchner-Vluyn: Neukirchner Verlag, 1999.]; ET Konrad Schmid, *Genesis and the Moses Story: Israel's Dual Origins in the Hebrew Bible* [Siphrut 3; Translated by James D. Nogalski. Winona Lake, Ind.: Eisenbrauns, 2010]) and Carr (David M. Carr, "Genesis in Relation to the Moses Story: Diachronic and Synchronic Perspectives," in *Studies in the Book of Genesis: Literature, Redaction and History* [ed. A. Wénin; Betl 155; Leuven: Peeters, 2001], 273-95). Perhaps Ezekiel knows an exodus tradition without Moses as the pivotal figure; perhaps Ezekiel deems it unnecessary to mention Moses; perhaps Ezekiel omits Moses in order to place himself in that role and to raise his own profile. Resolving such issues—if they can even be resolved—lies beyond the scope of this work. As the argument unfolds, evidence will show that Ezekiel does indeed know some of the texts that make up the final form of Exodus–Deuteronomy, but no attempt is made to be comprehensive in addressing that issue. In sum, "exodus tradition" is a shorthand way to distinguish a communal memory

2. Forms of the Divine Oath

Blane Conklin explores the syntax of oath formulae in Hebrew and its cognate languages in his book *Oath Formulas in Biblical Hebrew*.[6] The precise terminology that Conklin suggests for speaking about oaths is one of his most significant contributions. He separates each oath into two parts: the authenticating element and the content of the oath. An authenticating element may invoke any number of things like a precious entity, a witness, or a divine power to guarantee its content. Irrespective of what is invoked to authenticate the oath, in its content "[o]ne may affirm or deny a present or past state of affairs (assertory), or one may affirm or deny a future course of action (promissory)."[7] This terminology will be used throughout the present study for the clarity it brings to the topic.

For instance, Conklin's terminology encapsulates the criterion for placing some passages outside the scope of the present study. The Hebrew Bible contains many texts indicating that an oath was sworn without actually recording the oath. An easy way to determine the presence or absence of an oath is to look for an authenticating element. When it is absent, so too is the oath. Genesis 15 includes an account of YHWH making a covenant with Abram. Contrary to many statements, the passage does not include a divine oath. So, when Sweeney writes that "YHWH's statement in verse 18, 'To your descendants I have given this land from the River of Egypt to the great river, the River Euphrates,' constitutes a standard oath, in which a treaty party binds itself to certain obligations,"[8] he lacks the necessary rigor. The text certainly does contain obligations to which YHWH commits, but it does not contain an oath because there is no authenticating element. In this case, the commitment is guaranteed through an elaborate covenant ceremony symbolizing a self-curse. Genesis 15 and similar passages are certainly relevant to this study, but only insofar as one can reconstruct the oath that

---

about the journey out of Egypt and into the land from the complex of stories about Abraham, Isaac, Jacob, and Joseph that appear in Genesis. For Ezekiel, the history of YHWH's people begins in Egypt. Israel and Judah originate there, not in the land of Canaan.

6   Blane W. Conklin, *Oath Formulas in Biblical Hebrew* (Linguistic Studies in Ancient West Semitic 5; Winona Lake, Ind.: Eisenbrauns, 2011).

7   B. W. Conklin, "Oath Formulae in Classical Hebrew and Other Semitic Languages" (Ph.D., The University of Chicago, 2005), 1; cf. Conklin, *Oath Formulas*, 2.

8   Marvin A. Sweeney, "Form Criticism," in *To Each Its Own Meaning: Biblical Criticisms and Their Application* (eds. S. L. McKenzie and S. R. Haynes; Louisville, Ky.: Westminster John Knox, 1999), 78.

any particular text implies. On this account, it is important to highlight Ezekiel's custom: YHWH always explicitly expresses the authenticating element by which the divine oath is guaranteed. Thus, while Gen 15 and other covenant passages will be drawn into the discussion at relevant points, they are not part of the core group of passages under investigation.

Humans authenticate their oaths in various fashions in the Hebrew Bible. Four forms are prominent: using the verbal root "to swear" (שׁבע); speaking the authenticating element "as YHWH lives" (חי יהוה); authenticating an oath "by YHWH's name" (בשׁם יהוה); and accompanying an oath with the symbolic gesture of lifting the hand or hands (רום יד). Human oaths most frequently employ a form of the verb "to swear" (usually נשׁבע). This verb generally authenticates the oath on its own, but occasionally it occurs in conjunction with another authenticating element.[9] Both Israelites and foreigners, those who do and do not worship YHWH, use this form.

The second most frequent form utilizes the authenticating element "as YHWH lives" (חי יהוה). This formula appears 43 times in the Hebrew Bible,[10] but also outside it in texts such as the book of Judith[11] and the Lachish Letters.[12] There are three variations to the חי יהוה formula in the Hebrew Bible. In one variation, Joseph swears, "as Pharaoh lives" (חי פרעה),[13] a fitting change to its Egyptian setting. The second variation includes Joab declaring to Abner, "As God lives (חי האלהים), if you had not spoken, the people would have continued to pursue their kins-

---

9   1 Sam 19:6; 20:3; 20:42; 28:10; 2 Sam 3:35; 1 Kgs 1:29; 2:23; Isa 48:1; 65:16; Jer 4:2; 12:16; 38:16; Hos 4:15; Amos 8:14; Zeph 1:5; Zech 5:4; Dan 12:7; Neh 13:25; 2 Chr 36:13.

10   Judg 8:19; 1 Sam 14:39, 45; 19:6; 20:3, 21; 25:26, 34; 26:10, 16; 28:10; 29:6; 2 Sam 4:9; 12:5; 14:11; 15:21; 22:47; 1 Kgs 1:29; 2:24; 17:1, 12; 18:10, 15; 22:14; 2 Kgs 2:2, 4, 6; 3:14; 4:30; 5:16, 20; 2 Chr 18:13; Jer 4:2; 5:2; 12:16; 16:14, 15; 23:7, 8; 38:16; Hos 4:15; Ps 18:47; Ruth 3:13.

11   Judith 13:16: "As the Lord lives, who has protected me in the way I went, I swear that it was my face that seduced him to his destruction, and that he committed no sin with me, to defile and shame me" (NRSV).

12   Lachish 3 and 6; see F. W. Dobbs-Allsopp et al., *Hebrew Inscriptions: Texts from the Biblical Period of the Monarchy with Concordance* (New Haven, Conn.: Yale University Press, 2005), 322-24; cf. "Lachish 6: Reactions to Forwarded Correspondence," translated by Dennis Pardee (*COS* 3.42E:80-1); "Lachish 3: Complaints and Information," translated by Dennis Pardee (*COS* 3.42B:79); cf. Lachish 12, line 3, for a similar but very fragmented example. Another possible instance can be found in the ostraca from Tel Arad; see Yohanan Aharoni, *Arad Inscriptions* (JDS; Jerusalem: Israel Exploration Society, 1981), 42-43.

13   D.B. Redford, *A Study of the Story of Joseph (Genesis 37–50)* (VTSup 20; Leiden: Brill, 1970), 233, especially note 2.

men, not stopping until morning" (2 Sam 2:27; cf. Amos 8:14).   The
third variation appears in one of Job's speeches:

> Job again took up his discourse and said:
> "As God lives (חי־אל), who has driven away my justice,
> El Shaddai has made my soul bitter;
> As long as my breath is in me
> and the breath of God is in my nostrils,
> my lips will not speak falsehood,
> my tongue will not speak deceit.
>
> Job 27:2-4

The third way in which humans authenticate an oath is "in YHWH's
name" (בשם יהוה), a formula that appears only three times in the Hebrew Bible (Exod 20:7; Josh 23:6-8), in each case connecting swearing in
YHWH's name with proper religious conduct.

Fourth and finally, there is some evidence for connecting the symbolic gesture of raising a hand (רום יד) with an oath.   The occurrence of
this formula at Gen 14:22 and Dan 12:7 will be considered later in this
section.

The forms of human oaths are relevant because there is significant
overlap between them and the forms of the divine oath.   The Hebrew
Bible uses the verbal root שבע in the Niphal stem most frequently to authenticate the divine oath.   Its 67 appearances span the Hebrew Bible
but, notably, do not include the book of Ezekiel.[14]   This authenticating
element will be given further attention later, primarily with respect to
how it correlates to the חי אני formula.

As noted above, the חי אני formula occurs 16 times in the book of
Ezekiel (Ezek 5:11; 14:16, 18, 20; 16:48; 17:16, 19; 18:3; 20:3, 31, 33; 33:11,
27; 34:8; 35:6, 11) and only seven times elsewhere (Num 14:21, 28; Deut
32:40; Isa 49:18; Jer 22:24; 46:18; Zeph 2:9).   On every occasion the formula is the authenticating element in YHWH's oath.   Some ambiguity remains as to the best translation of this formula because of the rather
odd Masoretic vocalization of חַי as opposed to the expected חֵי.   Both
Greenberg and Conklin argue that this is influenced by the human au-

---

14   This authenticating element occurs fourteen times in YHWH's assertory oath: Gen
     22:16, 26:3; 1 Sam 3:14; Isa 14:24; 45:23; 54:9; 62:8; Jer 22:5; 44:26; 49:13; 51:14; Amos
     4:2, 6:8; 8:7. It occurs 53 times in recollections of those oaths: Gen 24:7; 50:24; Exod
     13:5; 32:13; 33:1; Num 11:12; 14:16, 23; 32:10, 11; Deut 1:8, 34, 35; 2:14; 4:21; 6:10, 18,
     23; 7:13; 8:1; 9:5; 10:11; 11:9, 21; 13:18; 19:8; 26:3, 15; 28:9, 11; 29:12 [ET 13]; 30:20; 31:7,
     20, 21, 23; 34:4; Josh 1:6; 5:6; 21:43, 44; Judg 2:1; 2 Sam 3:9; Jer 11:5; 32:22; Mic 7:20; Pss
     89:4 [ET 3], 36 [ET 35], 50 [ET 49]; 95:11; 110:4; 132:11.

thenticating element יהוה חי, where חי is collocated with the divine
name. Perhaps they are correct, but there is no direct evidence. The
lack of evidence, combined with a phrase that contains several
gutturals and weak consonants, means that a clear resolution lies beyond present reach.

Both scholars observe about חי אני, furthermore, that "[i]n ordinary
circumstances the phrase would unhesitatingly be rendered 'living am
I,' 'I live' – in an oath, possibly 'as I live.'"[15]   Conklin, however, advocates the translation 'by my life' based on an Ugaritic cognate.[16]   Although his grammatical arguments do have some merit they ultimately
fail to convince, a situation illustrated by the forced way he renders
Deut 32:40: "I raise my hand to heaven and say, (by) my life forever [I
swear that,] if I sharpen my sword..."[17]   The preferable resolution is actually what both Greenberg and Conklin note initially as the appropriate translation, "as I live." In this study, therefore, חי אני will be called
the "as I live" authenticating element.

The נשא יד formula is used 10 times in Ezekiel with Yhwh as the
subject (Ezek 20:5 [twice], 6, 15, 23, 28, 42; 36:7; 44:12; 47:14) and seven
times elsewhere (Exod 6:8; Num 14:30; Deut 32:40; Isa 49:22; Pss 10:12,
106:26; Neh 9:15). It is immediately necessary to explain the absence of
two passages often mentioned with these texts: Gen 14:22 and Dan 12:7.
Those two passages will not be part of the core group of texts discussed
for two reasons. First, in neither case is Yhwh the subject. On its own
this does not mean those passages are irrelevant, but it is an important
distinction from Ezekiel. Second, and more importantly, in both cases
the verb employed is רום and not נשא. This distinction is generally obscured in English translations, and even for those working with the Hebrew text the variation is sometimes ignored.[18]   Still, this variation distinguishes the two phrases and suggests they are not directly related.
Both Gen 14 and Dan 12 are discussed later as part of answering a central question for the present study: is the נשא יד formula actually an authenticating element for any oath, let alone a divine oath? Although
the affirmative answer to this question remains the consensus position,
evidence will be presented against that interpretation. Thus, through-

---

15   Moshe Greenberg, "The Hebrew Oath Particle Ḥay/Ḥē," *JBL* 76 (1957): , 38; Conklin,
     Oath Formulas, 24-26.

16   Ibid., 25. He also mentions Nah 2:9, 2 Kgs 9:18, and Isa 18:2 as support.

17   Ibid., 15.

18   This is one of the main problems with Eugene McGarry's position in "The Ambidex-
     trious Angel (Daniel 12:7 and Deuteronomy 32:40): Inner-Biblical Exegesis and Tex-
     tual Criticism in Counterpoint," *JBL* 124 [2005]: , 216-24.

out this study נשא יד will be referred to with the neutral phrase "lifted hand" formula.

3. History of Research

In seeking to situate the present research within previous work, the list of relevant studies is rather more limited than one might expect. The literature on covenants is extensive, but this material remains tangential to Ezekiel's use of the divine oath. Now, then, a brief review of those studies relevant to the present question.

(a) Johannes Pedersen, *Der Eid bei den Semiten*

Nearly a century old, Pedersen's *Der Eid bei den Semiten* is one of the most extensive studies on the oath. Methodologically, his concern is to reconstruct the actual practices humans employed when swearing oaths. Pedersen's ultimate goal is to use the biblical material to help explain the role of oaths in Islam. Thus, while he does mention the various biblical authenticating elements,[19] this is in service of establishing cognates for Arabic oath formulae. Pedersen is keen to explore the etymology of various formulae, prompting him to draw a connection between Akkadian *nīšu* and Hebrew נשא.[20] When he does discuss the biblical texts in their own right, it is almost exclusively to attempt the reconstruction of human practices. For him the biblical text is merely a window, darkly tinted though it may be, into rites and practices used in the ancient Near East. Because they mention ritual acts such as animal sacrifice and celebratory meals, Pedersen focuses on biblical passages about covenant-making.[21] When he does touch on the divine oath briefly, it is to distinguish YHWH's practice of swearing only by himself with the evidence from Mesopotamia, where lesser gods may swear by higher gods. Albeit made in passing, Pedersen's insight here remains important.

---

19   Johannes Pedersen, *Der Eid bei den Semiten: in seinem Verhältnis zu verwandten Erscheinungen sowie die Stellung des Eides im Islam* (Strassburg: K. J. Trübner, 1914), 2-3, 16-18.

20   Ibid., 2.

21   Ibid., 21-102.

(b) Samuel Mercer, *The Oath in Babylonian and*
Assyrian Literature

Appearing at nearly the same time as Pedersen's work, Mercer offered a study of the oath in Mesopotamian texts, suggesting that "the literature most fruitful for the study of the character of the Babylonian and Assyrian oath is that which contains legal and business contracts."[22] Like Pedersen, Mercer wanted to establish the rites and procedures that accompanied swearing. He, therefore, focuses on human oaths and largely ignores the accounts of deities swearing. Mercer also was interested to catalogue the various ways humans swore and to explain the etymology of what he believed were the key Akkadian terms: *mamītu*, *tamû*, and *nīšu*. He, like Pedersen, connects Akkadian *nīšu* with Hebrew נשׁא, a finding which prompted him to assert that the taking of an oath "involved especially the almost universal ritual of raising the hand."[23] Although both this etymological connection and the ubiquity of this symbolic gesture are now known to be erroneous, Mercer was correct to correlate the Akkadian and Hebrew formulae. Further, his conclusion that "the taking of an oath was essentially a religious ceremony"[24] is accurate and remains relevant for interpreting Jer 4:1-2, 5:1-2, and 12:16. This will be given more attention in chapter four.

(c) Friedrich Horst, "Der Eid im Alten Testament"

Horst addresses the areas of use (*Verwendungsbereich*) and the concept (*Vorstellung*) of the oath in his helpful overview of the topic. In the first section, he identifies four settings for the oath: the promissory oath as the guarantor of future action; the oath in the legal sphere; the oath in the religious sphere; and the divine oath. When discussing the fourth setting, Horst deals with Yhwh's oath by speaking of the three topics it addresses: the promise of the land to the ancestors; the promise of the Davidic monarchy; and the divine oath in prophetic announcements. Albeit mostly descriptive, Horst offers two shrewd pieces of analysis here. First, he notes the DTR texts include a large number of instances

---

22 Samuel A. B. Mercer, *The Oath in Babylonian and Assyrian Literature, with an Appendix [in Germ.] on the Goddess Esch-Ghanna* (Paris: Librarie Paul Geuthner, 1912), 1; see also Samuel A. B. Mercer, "The Oath in Cuneiform Inscriptions III: The Oath Since the Time of the Hammurabi Dynasty," *The American Journal of Semitic Languages and Literatures* 30 (1914): , 196-211.

23 Mercer, *The Oath in Babylonian and Assyrian Literature*, 29, 42.

24 Ibid., 42.

where the divine oath appears in the land promise (e.g. Num 14:23; 32:10; Deut 1:34ff, 2:14; Jos 5:6),[25] though he leaves this observation without any further discussion. Second, Horst observes what he believes are strong differences between this DTR inclination and that of Ezekiel:

> As the cumulative occurrences indicate, the divine oath plays a special role in the DTR and Ezekielian theology. However, what the divine oath has in its substance here and there is capable of illustrating, in order, how differently the two developing movements were operating successively and in parallel with one another.[26]

One may question Horst's interpretation, but his sense that the relationship between DTR and Ezekiel is crucial remains correct.

The second section of the article discusses the concept of the oath under four headings: the correlation between oaths and curses; the various formulae, gestures and rites associated with the oath; the setting of a curse against an unknown person; and, finally, the termination of an oath. Relevant here is his second heading, dealing with the various formulae, gestures and rites associated with the oath. Horst alludes to the similarities with Egyptian and Mesopotamian practice, once again pointing to an important line of inquiry but leaving it unexplored. Furthermore, Horst asserts the common view that "[t]he oath is usually accompanied by a gesture of swearing. The most common gesture is the raising of the right hand."[27]

Horst's work is an advance on Pedersen and Mercer because it not only has interest in reconstructing ancient practice but because it also gives attention to how the oath functions on the literary level. The latter allows Horst to identify connections between the divine oath and various theological traditions, a line of investigation that he appears to be the first to pursue.

---

25   Friedrich Horst, "Der Eid im Alten Testament," in *Gottes Recht: Gesammelte Studien Zum Recht Im Alten Testament* (TBü 12; Munich: Kaiser, 1961), 298-300.

26   Ibid., 301. "Wie das gehäufte Vorkommen zeigt, spielt der Gottesschwur eine besondere Rolle in der deuteronomischen und in der hesekielischen Theologie. Aber was hier wie dort der Gotteseid zum Inhalt hat, vermag seinerseits auch zu veranschaulichen, wie unterschiedlich die beiden nach und nebeneinander wirksam werdenden Bewegungen gewesen sind."

27   Ibid., 308. "Das Schwurwort wird gewöhnlich begleitet vom Schwurgestus. Der geläuftigste Gestus ist das Erheben der rechten Hand."

(d) Suzanne Boorer, *The Promise of the Land as Oath*

Boorer's monograph is an extended study of the so-called "primary oath texts," that is those texts where Yhwh swears (נשׁבע) to give the land to the ancestors of Israel (Gen 50:24; Exod 13:5, 11; 32:13; 33:1; Num 11:12; 14:23; 32:11). She evaluates various models for the composition and redaction of the Pentateuch based upon the relative dating of those texts .

Because Boorer focuses almost entirely on the divine oath with נשׁבע, a form not employed in Ezekiel, the relevance of her work is limited. This need not have been the case. Note, for instance, that her analysis of Num 14:11-25 never mentions the "as I live" or "lifted hand" formulae,[28] which occur there. Boorer's primary contribution to the present work is methodological: in her excellent historical review of the interpretation of the land promise, she identifies a methodological shift in the consideration of these texts, ca. 1970, when scholars moved from assigning the land promise texts to their pre-existing sources towards using these texts as evidence for "discerning relative redaction levels in the Pentateuch."[29] The present study adopts this approach. Only after sustained analysis of the meaning and function of the divine oath is complete will the potential implications for the composition and redaction of both Ezekiel and also the Pentateuch receive attention.[30]

(e) David Seely, "The Raised Hand of God as Oath Gesture"

Seely's contribution to the David Noel Freedman *Festschrift* is the most extended discussion of the "lifted hand" formula to date. He begins by describing its context, noting the deep connection between this idiom and the divine promise of the land to the fathers. Furthermore, he states, "It is clear that in the context of the promise of the land the phrase *nśʾ yd* is synonymous with the more frequent verb 'to swear,' *nšbʿ*."[31] Seely also suggests that Ezekiel's omission of "the more common *nšbʿ*" is "another case where Ezekiel avoids Deuteronomic lan-

---

28 Suzanne Boorer, *The Promise of the Land as Oath: A Key to the Formation of the Pentateuch* (BZAW 205; Berlin: Walter de Gruyter, 1992), 327-402.

29 Ibid., 97.

30 See below, ch. 5, §3.

31 David Rolph Seely, "The Raised Hand of God as an Oath Gesture," in *Fortunate the Eyes That See: Essays in Honor of David Noel Freedman in Celebration of His Seventieth Birthday* (ed. Astrid B. Beck; Grand Rapids, Mich.: Eerdmans, 1995), 412.

guage and relies on other traditions."[32] Although he astutely notes the
correlation between formulae and the DTR and P traditions, Seely fails
to pursue the issue in any detail, just as Horst before him. In the second major portion of the essay, Seely seeks the origin and significance
of the raised hand as an oath gesture.[33] He offers several plausible origins, but settles on "a gesture pointing [YHWH's] hand toward heaven to
symbolize swearing the oath 'by the heavens' – as the guarantee, or as a
witness, or by circumlocution that God is swearing by himself, pointing
to his heavenly abode."[34] The ambiguity in this assessment is an early
indication of the weaknesses in Seely's position, a topic that will be addressed in detail later.

(f) Johan Lust

The primary, if not lone, dissenting voice to the prevailing position on
the "lifted hand" formula is Johan Lust. His opposition to interpreting
the "lifted hand" formula as part of a divine oath goes back to his earliest work,[35] where it shaped his argument that Ezek 20 views the actual
realization of YHWH's promise to give Israel the land as a still future
event. Lust re-presented the main points of his argument in an essay
that deals with the appearance of the "lifted hand" formula in Deut
32:40.[36] In total, Lust puts forward five main arguments against the
consensus position.

First, Lust gives evidence that refutes claims that the Akkadian *nīšu*
is derived from *našû*, to lift, the cognate to Hebrew נשא; it is actually related to Akkadian *nēšu*, life.[37] This means the Akkadian *nīš ilim* is actually related to the "as I live" authenticating element and not the "lifted
hand" formula. Second, he demonstrates that the gesture of raising a
hand symbolizes force, sometimes in the act of protection, but always

32   Ibid., 413.
33   Ibid., 411.
34   Ibid., 421.
35   J. Lust, "Ez., Xx, 4-26 une parodie de l'histoire religieuse d'Israel," *ETL* 43 (1967):
     488-527.
36   J. Lust, "For I Lift Up My Hand to Heaven and Swear: Deut 32:40," in *Studies in
     Deuteronomy: In Honour of C.J. Labuschagne on the Occasion of His 65th Birthday* (VTSup
     53; Leiden: Brill, 1994).
37   Lust, "Ez., Xx, 4-26," 518. In support of his argument Lust cites a personal commu-
     nication from Leo Oppenheim in which he says that this phrase "has nothing to do
     with *našu*, «to lift»."

as an act of intervention.[38] In support of this position Lust shows that
in Ps 10:12, Isa 49:22, and Ezek 36:7, 44:12 the raised hand functions "to
point in the direction of an active intervention by the Lord."[39] Third,
Lust argues that the "lifted hand" formula is preferred in P, H, and especially Ezekiel, and that its appearance constitutes a systematic replacement of the DTR use of נשבע: "when [the priestly writers] replaced
נשבע with נשא יד, they probably did so because of theological reasons."[40] He further suggests that this theological reason is an aversion
to YHWH needing to confirm his statements in the same way a human
might need to do.

Lust's fourth argument comes from a detailed analysis of the colon
division of Deut 32:40, in which a comparison of the MT, Greek text,
and 4QDeut[q] demonstrates that the phrase "for I lift up my hand to
heaven" is related to the preceding colon, "none delivers from my
hand,"[41] and not the following colon, "and I say, 'as I live forever,'"
removing its link to YHWH's oath. Fifth and finally, he draws a distinction between the temporal horizon of the two formulae: the divine oath
with the verbal root שבע is used to make a promise to a future generation whereas the "lifted hand" formula "does not necessarily include a
promise for future times."[42]

Lust's evidence for the Akkadian etymology, the connotation of the
lifted hand gesture, and the colon division of Deut 32:40 is strong. His
argument that P, H, and Ezekiel replace the divine oath with שבע by
using the "lifted hand" formula is correct in concept, but his view that
they are essentially synonymous will be challenged in due course. Finally, Lust's desire to draw a distinction in the temporal horizon of שבע
and the "lifted hand" formula fails to convince because the evidence is
too vague to support the argument.

To date the majority of scholars have rejected Lust's case despite
the positive evidence he does marshall against the oath interpretation.
This study will explore his argument at length, an effort that recognizes
the strength of his evidence and refuses to accept the consensus interpretation without good reason for disregarding Lust's substantial
objections.

---

38   Ibid., 519.

39   Lust, "For I Lift," 161; cf. Lust, "Ez., Xx, 4-26," 523-24.

40   Ibid., 521-22; Lust, "For I Lift," 162.

41   Ibid., 160; Lust, "Ez., Xx, 4-26," 523.

42   Lust, "For I Lift," 162. This seems to soften Lust's earlier position: "Autrement dit,
     nāśāʾ jād n'implique pas une promesse pour les temps à venir, mais partout une ac-
     tion actuelle" (Lust, "Ez., Xx, 4-26," 524).

(g) Yael Ziegler, *Promises to Keep*

Yael Ziegler's recent monograph concerning the role of oaths in biblical narrative with particular attention to their place in the books of Samuel and Kings focuses on the use of three oath formulae: חַי יה, כֹּה יֵעֶשֶׂה, and חָלִילָה.[43] In each case, she finds that the small but noticeable variations in the phrasing of oaths are carefully crafted and work to highlight the central themes and ideas of the narrative in which they reside.[44] Oaths are not incidental to their context, but rather they work in conjunction with other features to construct that context.

Subsequently, Ziegler turns her attention to the characters of Saul and David, because the oaths in the narratives about them "can be regarded as an especially effective literary indicator which can be mined to reveal different aspects of the narrative."[45] For example, David's oaths reflect the arc of his life, revealing his changing attitude towards power and violence. When their various formulations are given careful attention, these oaths point towards David's move from pious restraint in his rise to rash injudiciousness during and after his fateful sin with Bathsheba. Ziegler concludes that "[b]y examining the oaths in David's career, it emerges that the conflict regarding David's use or abuse of power looms large as the subject upon which his career turns, ultimately determining its success and failures."[46]

Because Ziegler selects the narrative of Samuel and Kings, two texts that include only human oaths, she offers little direct insight into the meaning and function of the divine oath. What she does conclusively demonstrate, however, is the important role that oaths play on a literary level. She writes:

> It appears, then, that oaths do not appear arbitrarily in biblical narratives. Instead, oaths are artfully placed in order to underscore different aspects of the literary work. In this way, oaths function as textual indicators which shed light on a character's inner life, intentions, aspirations or traits. More

---

43   Yael Ziegler, *Promises to Keep: The Oath in Biblical Narrative* (VTSup 120; Leiden: Brill, 2008).

44   Ibid., 79-80, 122, 147.

45   Ibid., 149.

46   Ibid., 263. This insight is pursued further in Yael Ziegler, ""So Shall God Do.": Variations of an Oath Formula and Its Literary Meaning," *JBL* 126 (2007): 59-81, and Yael Ziegler, ""As the Lord Lives and as Your Soul Lives": An Oath of Conscious Deference," *VT* 58 (2008): 117-30.

over, the oaths in a story may be seen as an index to the underlying meaning of a narrative, revealing its internal dynamics, the tensions and solutions at its core.[47]

This insight provides one of the pillars upon which the present study is built: oaths are not incidental to the message of the passages in which they occur. Rather, as elevated speech representing the most solemn statements of an individual, they are indicators of the central message and concerns of the texts in which they appear.

4. Methodological Guidelines

With some context about the work that has been done on the divine oath, it is now possible to discuss the working methods of this book. This study will draw from various methods, selecting them in a pragmatic manner based upon their likelihood to help explain the meaning and function of the divine oath. None of the methods are selected because of a prior methodological commitment, nor is their relative value to the present study an indication of their general utility.

(a) Comparative Analysis

This study begins broadly with comparative analysis of the divine oath in the ancient Near East. There are at least three reasons for employing this method and for giving it priority in the research.

First, the book of Ezekiel is known for its wide-ranging familiarity with other ancient Near Eastern cultures and literature. Greenberg suggests that "one who aspires to be an interpreter to another age of such a polymath in his historical setting should possess a correspondingly wide range of antiquarian knowledge."[48] Such thorough knowledge is impossible to achieve given both the temporal distance between contemporary interpreters and the book and also due to the limited evidence available. The effort is, nonetheless, worthwhile.

This is confirmed by the second reason, the fruitfulness of past studies on Ezekiel employing comparative analysis. Daniel Bodi demonstrated the importance of YHWH's departure from the Jerusalem

---

47 Ziegler, *Promises to Keep*, 269.

48 Moshe Greenberg, *Ezekiel 21–37: A New Translation with Introduction and Commentary* (AB 22A; New York: Doubleday & Co., 1997), 395-96.

temple in the book of Ezekiel by comparing it to the same theme in the
Mesopotamian poem *Erra and Ishum*.[49]   Daniel Block expanded upon
these insights to explain similarities about how gods relate to their people and their land in *Gods of the Nations*.[50]   Most recently, John Kutsko
has suggested that the book of Ezekiel employs the metaphor of humans as the image of god in a polemic against idol worship.[51]   This
polemic is perceptible when Ezekiel is compared to Assyrian texts on
idol spoilation and the mouth opening (*mīs pî*) ritual used in Assyria
and Babylonia. All three studies show how important the Mesopotamian intellectual context is for understanding Ezekiel's message. Like-
wise, exploring the divine oath outside the Hebrew Bible, with particular attention to its Mesopotamian context, will assist in understanding
Ezekiel.

Third and finally, comparative study of this sort takes seriously the
book's self-attested Babylonian provenance. This origin has not gone
unchallenged by scholars who often cite the book's concern for
Jerusalem as an indication that significant parts of it must have originated there. But, addressing a speech to Jerusalem is no more determinative of provenance than is addressing an oracle to Egypt (e.g Ezek
29) or Tyre (e.g. Ezek 26).[52]   Greenberg is correct to explain this dynamic through the simultaneous existence of two "Jerusalemite"
communities:

> But what of his appearance of addressing an audience (Jerusalem)
> hundreds of miles away? Here appearances can mislead. Prophecies
> against foreign nations—an established prophetic genre—always involve
> an incongruity between the ostensible audience (the foreign nation, ad-
> dressed as "you") and the real audience (the Israelites, for whose ears the
> prophecy is intended, and for whom it bears an important message). In the
> same way we may suppose than an exiled prophet's address to Jerusalem
> would really have been aimed at the ears of his proximate audience. In
> Ezekiel's case, little contrast would be felt between the ostensible and the

---

49   Daniel Bodi, *The Book of Ezekiel and the Poem of Erra* (OBO 104; Göttingen: Vanden-
     hoeck & Ruprecht, 1991). For an English translation of the poem see "Erra and
     Ishum," translated by Stephanie Dalley (*COS* 1.113:404-16).

50   Daniel I. Block, *Gods of the Nations: Studies in Ancient Near Eastern National Theology*
     (Evangelical Theological Society Monograph Series 2; Jackson, Miss.: Evangelical
     Theological Society, 1988).

51   John F. Kutsko, *Between Heaven and Earth: Divine Presence and Absence in the Book of
     Ezekiel* (Biblical and Judaic Studies from the University of California, San Diego 7;
     Winona Lake, Ind.: Eisenbrauns, 2000).

52   See Andrew Mein, *Ezekiel and the Ethics of Exile* (OTM; Oxford: Oxford University
     Press, 2001), 44-48, for a discussion of Jerusalem's role in the book's provenance.

real audience, since the hearers of the prophet were, in fact, Jerusalemites
who identified themselves with their fellow citizens in the homeland in
every way. If there is any anomaly in Ezekiel's addressing Jerusalem from
the exile, it is no greater than the anomalous contemporaneity of two
Jerusalemite communities hundreds of miles apart at this juncture of
history.[53]

In addition to the book's provenance, establishing the date of the
material is also relevant for comparative study. This question is, of
course, inextricably tied to authorship. A comprehensive review of an
issue addressed thoroughly elsewhere is unnecessary, but a brief summary of the most important turns in the debate is appropriate.[54]

The book of Ezekiel was viewed as a unified composition far longer
than Isaiah and Jeremiah. There were antecedents to Gustav Hölscher's
work, but his 1924 study presented the first substantial challenge to
Ezekiel's unity. He argued the prophet's work appeared only in the
book's poetic passages, a mere 170 verses in total.[55] Hölscher was by no
means alone, and a few years later the fracturing process reached its
apogee when C. C. Torrey suggested the prophet was actually a late
historical fiction.[56]

These issues remained in debate for nearly 40 years until a consensus emerged around the work of Walther Zimmerli.[57] Zimmerli believed a substantial amount of the book's material went back to the
prophet himself. The originally oral speeches of Ezekiel were recorded
after the fact and underwent an initial editing and arranging, perhaps
the work of the prophet himself or maybe of others under his direc-

---

53 Moshe Greenberg, *Ezekiel 1–20: A New Translation with Introduction and Commentary*
    (AB 22; Garden City, N.Y.: Doubleday & Co., 1983), 17; cf. Mein, *Ezekiel and the Ethics
    of Exile*, 46-47.

54 For a recent and extended discussion of this question see Paul M. Joyce, *Ezekiel: A
    Commentary* (LHBOTS 482; London: T & T Clark International, 2007), 7-16.

55 Gustav Hölscher, *Hesekiel, der Dichter und das Buch: eine literarkritische Untersuchung*
    (BZAW 39; Giessen: Töpelmann, 1924).

56 C. C. Torrey, *Pseudo-Ezekiel and the Original Prophecy* (Yale Oriental Series 18; New
    Haven, Conn.: Yale University Press, 1930).

57 Walther Zimmerli, *Ezechiel 1: Ezechiel 1–24* (BKAT 13.1; Neukirchen-Vluyn: Neukir-
    chener Verlag, 1969); Walther Zimmerli, *Ezechiel 2: Ezechiel 25–48* (BKAT 13.2;
    Nuekirchen-Vluyn: Neukirchener Verlag, 1969). ET Walther Zimmerli, *A Commen-
    tary on the Book of the Prophet Ezekiel, Chapters 1–24* (Hermeneia 1; Translated by Ro-
    nald E. Clements. Minneapolis, Minn.: Fortress, 1979); Walther Zimmerli, *A Commen-
    tary on the Book of the Prophet of Ezekiel, Chapters 25–48* (Hermeneia 2; Translated by
    James D. Martin. Philadelphia: Fortress, 1983).

tion.[58] This material was then interpreted and expanded (*Fortschreibung*) by a "school" of the prophet's disciples, a process that accounts for the homogeneity of the book's message.

In the wake of Zimmerli's work, two trends of interpretation have prevailed. On the one hand, the identification of multiple redactional layers has characterized the work of Jörg Garscha[59] and Karl-Friedrich Pohlmann.[60] Even though each scholar dates a small core of material to the sixth-century B.C.E., both argue that the majority of the text is a product of the Persian period. On the other hand, a move towards even greater unity in the text has emerged, largely due to the influential contributions of Moshe Greenberg.[61] Greenberg advocates a "holistic" interpretation that emphasizes the artistry and intelligent design of the text. This has certainly enabled him to contribute substantial insights about the message of the book, and it has spurred a number of studies that basically accept his viewpoint.[62]

Both trends are susceptible to exaggerating their position, either splintering the text into an unmanageable number of layers or falling into an implicit attribution of the entire book to the prophet himself. The actual historical development most likely lies somewhere in between, as Clements argues:

58 Zimmerli, *Ezekiel 1–24*, 68-74, especially p. 71. Ellen Davis has presented a contrasting view, arguing that the book of Ezekiel shows signs of being an originally written, not oral, composition (Ellen F. Davis, *Swallowing the Scroll: Textuality and the Dynamics of Discrouse in Ezekiel's Prophecy* [JSOTSup 78; Sheffield: The Almond Press, 1989]).

59 Jörg Garscha, *Studien zum Ezechielbuch: eine redaktionskritische Untersuchung von 1–39* (Europäische Hochschulschriften 23; Bern: Herbert Lang, 1974).

60 Karl-Friedrich Pohlmann, *Der Prophet Hesekiel/Ezechiel Kapitel 1–19* (ATD 22.1; Göttingen: Vandenhoeck & Ruprecht, 1996); Karl-Friedrich Pohlmann, *Der Prophet Hesekiel/Ezechiel Kapitel 20–48* (ATD 22.2; Göttingen: Vandenhoeck & Ruprecht, 2001); cf. Karl-Friedrich Pohlmann, *Ezechielstudien: zur Redaktionsgeschichte des Buches und zur Frage nach den ältesten Texten* (BZAW 202; Berlin: Walter de Gruyter, 1992).

61 Greenberg, *Ezekiel 1-20*; Greenberg, *Ezekiel 21-37*; cf. Moshe Greenberg, "The Design and Themes of Ezekiel's Program of Restoration," *Int* 38 (1984): 181-208; Moshe Greenberg, "Notes on the Influence of Tradition on Ezekiel," *Journal of the Ancient Near Eastern Society* 22 (1993): 29-37.

62 Lawrence Boadt, *Ezekiel's Oracles against Egypt: A Literary and Philological Study of Ezekiel 29–32* (BibOr 37; Rome: Biblical Institute Press, 1980); Gordon H. Matties, *Ezekiel 18 and the Rhetoric of Moral Discourse* (SBLDS 126; Atlanta, Ga.: Scholars Press, 1990); Jacqueline Lapsley, *Can These Bones Live? The Problem of the Moral Self in the Book of Ezekiel* (BZAW 301; Berlin: Walter de Gruyter, 2000); Thomas Renz, *The Rhetorical Function of the Book of Ezekiel* (VTSup 76; Leiden: Brill, 2002).

So far as the chronological aspects of this transition from the time when the original prophet had been active until the time when a fixed book of his prophecies came into being no wholly definitive criteria appear to be available. Yet all the indications are that the main part of such a task was completed within a space of no more than two generations from the time of the original prophet's death. There is little reason therefore for allocating this part of the formation of the book of Ezekiel beyond the end of the sixth century, by which time most of the material contained in it can be satisfactorily explained.[63]

Space must remain for arguments that selected parts of the text did receive further editing or expansion in the fifth century B.C.E. or later.[64] Granting this possibility, there is a solid foundation of evidence that the majority of the book, arranged largely in its final shape, is a product of the Neo-Babylonian period.[65]

Upon this rationale, the study will proceed by observing the principles for comparison laid out by William Hallo and Tremper Longman in order to observe similarities and differences between Ezekiel, and more broadly the Hebrew Bible, and the other ancient Near Eastern evidence.[66] Adopting these principles does not bring "scientific precision" to the process, as Longman remarks, "but adherence to them in-

---

63 R. E Clements, "The Chronology of Redaction in Ez 1–24," in *Ezekiel and His Book: Textual and Literary Criticism and Their Interrelation* (ed. J. Lust; BETL 74; Leuven: Peeters, 1986), 294; cf. Joyce, *Ezekiel*, 16.

64 This is necessitated by the evidence of P967, an Old Greek manuscript that indicates the content and arrangement of at least chs. 36–39 was still not settled at the time of this translation. For details, see J. Lust, "The Use of Textual Witnesses for the Establishment of the Text. the Shorter and Longer Texts of Ezekiel," in *Ezekiel and His Book: Textual and Literary Criticism and Their Interrelation* (ed. J. Lust; BETL 74; Leuven: Peeters, 1986) and Ashley S. Crane, *Israel's Restoration: A Textual-Comparative Exploration of Ezekiel 36–39* (VTSup 122; Leiden: Brill, 2008).

65 One might add to the evidence discussed here indications that the language of Ezekiel represents a transitional stage that can be located in the sixth-century B.C.E. See Avi Hurvitz, *A Linguistic Study of the Relationship between the Priestly Source and the Book of Ezekiel: A New Approach to an Old Problem* (CahRB 20; Paris: Gabalda, 1982) and Mark F. Rooker, *Biblical Hebrew in Transition: The Language of the Book of Ezekiel* (JSOTSup 90; Sheffield: Sheffield Academic Press, 1990) for details.

66 William W. Hallo, "Biblical History in Its Near Eastern Setting: The Contextual Approach," in *Essays on the Comparative Method* (eds. C.D. Evans, William W. Hallo and John B. White; PTMS 34; Pittsburgh, Pa.: Pickwick, 1980), 1-26; Tremper Longman, *Fictional Akkadian Autobiography: A Generic and Comparative Study* (Winona Lake, Ind.: Eisenbrauns, 1991), 23 36; Tremper Longman, "Israelite Genres in Their Ancient Near Eastern Context," in *The Changing Face of Form Criticism for the Twenty-First Century* (eds. Marvin A. Sweeney and Ehud Ben Zvi; Grand Rapids, Mich.: Eerdmans, 2003), 177-95. Further discussion of Hallo and Longman's method appears at the beginning of ch. 2.

creases the probability of a valid comparison."[67] Texts that are close
geographically, temporally, linguistically, and generically—as is the
case with the Egyptian, Akkadian, and Ugaritic evidence discussed in
chapter two—remain the best evidence available for reconstructing the
non-biblical resonances that Ezekiel's formulaic language carried.

(b) Form Critical Analysis

After the comparative study, the basic components of form-critical
analysis are used in order to guide the remaining discussion concerning the meaning of the divine oath formulae. Form criticism as a
method has come under much scrutiny; while these criticisms must be
noted and taken into account, a revised version of form criticism remains a relevant and beneficial approach for many reasons, two of
which are worthy of mention here.

First, the form critical method suits the object of study, namely a set
of phrases that appear in multiple biblical books from various authors
with varying dates and places of authorship. By definition, these texts
will exhibit particularity, having differences from each of the others.
Yet, even a brief overview of their content, such as that given at the
opening of this chapter, shows that they share features. For instance,
each passage in which these formulae appear can be characterized as a
prophetic speech, that is a direct word from YHWH or a report of first-
person speech by YHWH to the prophet. This initial observation about
genre will need to be tested, and indeed it will receive significant revision in chapter three. The theme of judgment is also immediately evident in many of these passages. Again, this notion will need evaluation
and refinement. Nonetheless, it suggests that a form critical approach
is appropriate because its tools enable the interpreter to find the shared
attributes among disparate texts.

Second, the form critical method provides a clear structure for research while also leaving the desired space for drawing in other methods. "Insofar as it provides the tools by which to assess the overall linguistic form and content of a biblical text while continuing to interact
with other critical methods," remarks Marvin Sweeney, "form criticism
is well positioned to serve as a fundamental method of biblical exegesis."[68] This flexibility enables rhetorical criticism, redaction criticism,
and insights from inner-biblical exegesis to be used at various points.

---

67   Longman, *Fictional Akkadian Autobiography*, 31.

68   Sweeney, "Form Criticism," 85.

Because the form critical method has changed much in the last 40 years, it is necessary to specify how it is conceived in this study.[69] The original concern of form critics to establish the oral prehistory of a text has come under heavy criticism. The tendency to atomize texts, breaking them into their smallest units, has also been disparaged. And rightly so. The work of Hermann Gunkel, Sigmund Mowinckel, Albrecht Alt, Gerhard von Rad, and Martin Noth is no less valuable because of these critiques, but scholars can no longer employ the method in the same fashion they did. However, the critiques that have made the earlier application of form criticism outmoded have not brought about the method's death. Rather, they have spurred its practitioners to refine and modify the methodology to create something more useful. Two of the most notable contributors to this evolution have been James Muilenburg and Rolf Knierim.

Muilenberg, in his 1968 Presidential Address to the Society of Biblical Literature,[70] called for greater attention to the individuality of texts and to the communicative goals of those texts. His critique paved the way for rhetorical criticism, now a widely accepted method in its own right. Notwithstanding this development, one of Muilenburg's lasting contributions was to increase the attention form critics give to the particularity of texts.[71]

Rolf Knierim has advocated for greater attention to the final form of the text.[72] This is often characterized as an emphasis on synchronic concerns prior to diachronic ones. Furthermore, Knierim promotes taking a wider view of the text, moving beyond short, self-contained units and looking at the larger text. His proposal has been widely accepted and in the study of biblical prophets has even prompted scholars to accept the prophetic book as an important genre.[73] Knierim's concern for larger contexts has been further advanced by Sweeney,

---

69   Sweeney provides an excellent review, with much greater detail than can be given here, in his essay (Ibid., 58-89). See also John Barton, *Reading the Old Testament: Method in Biblical Study* (2nd ed. London: Darton, Longman and Todd, 1996), 30-44.

70   James Muilenburg, "Form Criticism and Beyond," *JBL* 88 (1969): 1-18.

71   Sweeney, "Form Criticism," 66-67.

72   Rolf Knierim, "Old Testament Form Criticism Reconsidered," *Int* 27 (1973): 435-60; Rolf Knierim, "Criticism of Literary Features, Form, Tradition, and Redaction," in *The Hebrew Bible and Its Modern Interpreters* (eds. Douglas A. Knight and Gene M. Tucker; Philadelphia: Fortress, 1985), 123-65; Rolf Knierim, *Text and Concept in Leviticus 1:1-9: A Case in Exegetical Method* (FAT/I 2; Tübingen: Mohr Siebeck, 1992).

73   Ehud Ben Zvi, "The Prophetic Book: A Key Form of Prophetic Literature," in *The Changing Face of Form Criticism for the Twenty-First Century* (eds. Marvin A. Sweeney and Ehud Ben Zvi; Grand Rapids, Mich.: Eerdmans, 2003), 276-97.

who suggests that "interpreters must begin with the largest literary unit available,"[74] that is the final form of a biblical book.

That process is well warranted, and Sweeney has certainly demonstrated its fruitfulness in his work.[75] Yet, rigidly suggesting that form critics "must" begin with the final form of a biblical book is as problematic as the earlier proclivity of form critics to endorse the atomization of texts. Rather, the present study adopts Knierim's assertion that interpreters should "conceptualize the methodology less ideologically than in the past"[76] and "set up a framework within which the specific form-critical tools can be applied flexibly."[77]

In keeping with the recognition that form criticism has valuable insights to offer on entire prophetic books and other intermediate size units, the present study will always have an eye towards these contexts. However, the evaluation of particular formulae occurring in multiple books, as opposed to commentary on a single book, necessitates attention be given to what some will consider small, self-contained units. The intention will never be to atomize these texts, for instance by breaking the "as I live" or "lifted hand" formulae away from the prophetic speeches in which they are found. But opportunities to engage in analysis of the whole of the book of Ezekiel, or even a smaller selection of chapters within it, will arise very rarely in the present study.[78] On balance, paying attention to the *Sitz in der Literatur* in this way will avoid "the literary dissection of a prophetic book" and the creation of an "artificial text"[79] even as it acknowledges the particular selection criteria necessary to investigate two formulae.

---

74 Marvin A. Sweeney, "Formation and Form in Prophetic Literature," in *Old Testament Interpretation: Past, Present, and Future* (eds. James Luther Mays, David L. Petersen and Kent Harold Richards; Edinburgh: T & T Clark, 1995), 115.

75 One may see representative examples of the results in the following works: Marvin A. Sweeney, "A Form-Critical Reassessment of the Book of Zephaniah," *CBQ* 53 (1991): 388-408; Marvin A. Sweeney, "Structure, Genre, and Intent in the Book of Habakkuk," *VT* 41 (1991): 63-83; Marvin A. Sweeney, "Concerning the Structure and Generic Character of the Book of Nahum," *ZAW* 104 (1992): 364-77; Marvin A. Sweeney, "A Form-Critical Reading of Hosea," *JHebS* 2 (1998): 1-16. More recently, he has applied the same method to Ezekiel in Marvin A. Sweeney, "The Assertion of Divine Power in Ezekiel 33:21-39:29," in *Form and Intertextuality in Prophetic and Apocalyptic Literature* (FAT/I 45; Tübingen: Mohr Siebeck, 2005), 156-72.

76 Knierim, "Old Testament Form Criticism Reconsidered," 459. Emphasis original.

77 Ibid. Emphasis original.

78 An effort of this scale has recently been undertaken by Tyler D. Mayfield, *Literary Structure and Setting in Ezekiel* (FAT II/43; Tübingen: Mohr Siebeck, 2010).

79 Both phrases used by Sweeney in his defense of beginning with the biblical book (Sweeney, "Formation and Form," 115).

In what follows, then, the four main steps of analyzing structure (*Form*), genre (*Gattung*), social setting (*Sitz im Leben*) and function are evident. The detailed structural analysis of the relevant texts—defining their limits and outlining their content—is grouped together in appendix one for brevity and ease of reference. The consideration of genre constitutes chapter three, and particular methodological questions relevant to that topic are discussed at its outset. The study of social setting (*Sitz im Leben*) and literary setting (*Sitz in der Literatur*) comprises chapter four, again with further methodological issues addressed therein.

The second part of this study will take the findings gained from the comparative analysis and the first three steps of form critical investigation and utilize them in answering the question that encapsulates the second part of this book: What function does the divine oath play in the book of Ezekiel? This question is the logical pair and continuation of the question that guides the first part: Why does the book of Ezekiel employ the divine oath so often?

In order to answer this second guiding question, the second part of the book draws on the fourth and final step of form criticism, namely investigating the function or intention of a genre.[80] There is a limit to the similarities in this final step: instead of exploring intention with relation to a single genre or text, the question addresses texts that employ a range of genres and are united by their location in Ezekiel. This approach emphasizes the exegetical contribution of form criticism, that is the way in which its detailed findings can have a "direct implication for exegesis and interpretation."[81] Employing the method in this manner has the benefit of de-emphasizing the now suspect attempts to establish the oral pre-history of a text without losing the still beneficial way in which form criticism promotes close readings of the text.[82]

To address the question of the divine oath's function fully, it will be necessary to supplement form criticism with relevant social scientific work.

---

80   Gene M Tucker, *Form Criticism of the Old Testament* (Guides to Biblical Scholarship: Old Testament Series; Philadelphia: Fortress, 1971), 16-17.

81   Ibid., 17.

82   On dividing form criticism into these two areas, see Renz, *The Rhetorical Function*, 12-13.

(c) Public and Hidden Transcripts

James C. Scott offers a model that has proved influential regarding the ways power relations affect discourse that builds on a simple observation: people carefully measure their words when speaking to those who have power over them in a way that they don't when speaking to peers or subordinates.[83] This insight allows Scott to make sense of the "divergent accounts" he heard among the Malay villagers where he did field work[84] and to explain instances where "the same villagers were occasionally contradicting themselves!"[85] Scott combines his own work with a survey of subaltern groups across time and place that substantiates his theory that "[e]very subordinate group creates, out of its ordeal, a 'hidden transcript' that represents a critique of power spoken behind the back of the dominant."[86] When this "offstage" discourse is compared with the public performance of the oppressed group, Scott argues that it "offers a substantially new way of understanding resistance to domination."[87] In this way, he establishes that the absence of explicit, visible resistance to power is not an indication that it is accepted. Scott's model also recognizes the pragmatism of subaltern groups, who speak openly about their retaliatory desires among their peers but shrewdly disguise their subversive efforts when expressing them in an open context where they might incite disciplinary action.

The importance of Scott's model to the second part of this study necessitates a discussion of its main concepts and a brief review of key critiques leveled against it before finally setting out how this study will utilize the model.

(i) The Public Transcript

One of Scott's most important contributions is to provide a straightforward vocabulary for the various types of discourse that occur in every society: public transcript and hidden transcript.

---

83   James C. Scott, *Domination and the Arts of Resistance: Hidden Transcripts* (New Haven, Conn.: Yale University Press, 1990), ix-x.

84   James C. Scott, *Weapons of the Weak: Everyday Forms of Peasant Resistance* (New Haven, Conn.: Yale University Press, 1985); chapters six and seven (pp. 184-303) are especially foundational for his later work on this subject.

85   Scott, *Domination*, ix.

86   Ibid., xii.

87   Ibid.

The public transcript is not simply speech broadcast to a large group, but:

> to put it crudely, the self-portrait of dominant elites as they would have themselves seen. Given the usual power of dominant elites to compel performances from others, the discourse of the public transcript is a decidely lopsided discussion. While it is unlikely to be merely a skein of lies and misrepresentations, it is, on the other hand, a highly partisan and partial narrative. It is designed to be impressive, to affirm and naturalize the power of dominant elites, and to conceal or euphemize the dirty linen of their rule.[88]

The dominant class that defines the public transcript possesses the capacity to propagate and disseminate its contents, but that is not a one-time process. "Once established, domination does not persist of its own momentum,"[89] remarks Scott. In order to maintain the supremacy of the public transcript the dominant class adopts four strategies to reinforce its prominence.

Affirmation, the first strategy, includes "discursive affirmations of a particular pattern of domination."[90] Public events such as parades are often the site for affirmation, but it also occurs in the routine forms of address and deference that are required of subordinates. Concealment, the second strategy, entails using control of the public stage to create an ideal persona and to "hide whatever might detract from their grandeur and authority."[91] Unanimity, Scott's third category, denotes a variety of actions that dominant classes use to keep whatever practical resistance may exist offstage out of public view. "Patterns of domination can," he argues, "accommodate a reasonably high level of practical resistance so long as that resistance is not publicly and unambiguously acknowledged."[92] If and when resistance does move into open view an immediate reply is necessary. Thus the importance of public apologies for insubordinate acts, even when those apologies are inescapably hollow. The very ability to compel the apology, sincere or insincere, underscores that the dominant class possesses the social, political, and religious power necessary to coerce acceptable behavior.

---

88   Ibid., 18.
89   Ibid., 45.
90   Ibid., 46.
91   Ibid., 50.
92   Ibid., 57.

Though all three of these strategies provide insight into asymmetric power relations, Scott's fourth strategy is most important for this study, specifically the paired acts of euphemization and stigmatization. The former, which Scott borrows from Pierre Bourdieu,[93] describes the numerous ways in which dominant groups use language to mask "the many nasty facts of domination."[94] By describing their own actions in a "harmless or sanitized" manner, language obscures the coercive force that compels subordinates to act or speak in ways not of their choosing.[95] Stigmatization is the other side of the same coin, a strategy that labels subordinate actions that might have a positive connotation in dangerous or subversive terms. Scott summarizes it memorably:

> the power to call a cabbage a rose and to make it stick in the public sphere implies the power to do the opposite, to stigmatize activities or persons that seem to call into question official realities.[96]

Stigmatization includes, for example, the dominant class calling reform groups "revolutionaries," authorizing "aggressive interrogation tactics" and not torture, or employing "capital punishment" instead of state sponsored execution.

Euphemization and stigmatization amount to something very much like the "spin" that characterizes contemporary political discourse. Indeed, the tactic is visible even here: "spin" serves as a euphemism for the intentional, ideological, and potentially unsubstantiated (re)interpretation of events or words in order to support one's own viewpoint. To be sure, not all acts of euphemization and stigmatization are insidious, but the strategy is ubiquitous.

This pair of tactics are inherently rhetorical in character and, therefore, among the most directly applicable of Scott's concepts to the predominantly textual sources from the ancient Near East. Indeed, a central argument of chapter five will be that the book of Ezekiel repeatedly seeks to stigmatize the Judahite community left in Jerusalem in an effort to demonstrate that it possesses the power necessary to define the public transcript and the authority to compel others to reproduce it.

---

93   Pierre Bourdieu, *Outline of a Theory of Practice* (Cambridge Studies in Social Anthropology 16; Translated by Richard Nice. Cambridge: Cambridge University Press, 1977), 159-97; see in particular "Modes of Domination" on pp. 183-97.

94   Scott, *Domination*, 53.

95   Ibid., 52-55, especially p. 53.

96   Ibid., 55.

(ii) The Hidden Transcript

On the subordinate side of the power structure, a hidden transcript develops. Scott defines it as a:

> discourse that takes place "offstage," beyond direct observation by power-holders. The hidden transcript is thus derivative in the sense that it consists of those offstage speeches, gestures, and practices that confirm, contradict, or inflect what appears in the public transcript.[97]

The subordinate class is able to develop this discourse because it often dwells apart from the dominant class. This setting creates:

> the audience (one might say "the public") for the hidden transcript... subject to the same terms of subordination, they have a shared interest in jointly creating a discourse of dignity, of negation, and of justice. They have, in addition, a shared interest in concealing a social site apart from domination where such a hidden transcript can be elaborated in comparative safety.[98]

Although this safe space enables subordinates to voice their views, the hidden transcript is not merely a collection of unconnected retaliatory statements. It is, according to Scott, a discourse that forms over time and through a process of refinement.

> If then [an expression of resistance against the dominant] is to become the social property of a whole category of subordinates it must carry effective meaning for them and reflect the cultural meanings and distribution of power among them. In this hypothetical progression from "raw" anger to what we might call "cooked" indignation, sentiments that are idiosyncratic, unrepresentative, or have only weak resonance within the group are likely to be selected against or censored.[99]

In sum, the hidden transcript is a communal possession that becomes the unifying expression of resistance for a subordinate group against the dominant class and, more specifically, the public transcript that the powerful demand subordinates adopt without choice.

Recognizing the differences in scholarly opinion on the dating of Ezekiel, it remains true that its authors and tradents were members of a subordinate class with strong similarities to those Scott draws from in

---

97   Ibid., 4-5.
98   Ibid., 114.
99   Ibid., 119.

order to develop his model. There are, in fact, two strong indicators that the social dynamics Scott describes were at work in the Judahite exilic community.

First, the book includes evidence that the Judahite exiles actively considered and debated the relative merits of various views about their situation with an eye towards developing a communal narrative about the predicament. Perhaps the best example of this is Ezek 33:30-33, in which the book records that its eponymous character draws an audience that listens to his message before selecting against it as an authentic interpretation of their situation. There are, in addition, three section-heading statements that explain the elders came to hear what Ezekiel had to say (Ezek 8:1; 14:1; 20:1). The elders' agreement or disagreement with Ezekiel is never discussed, though the book's description of the resistance that Ezekiel's message encountered suggests they were not often persuaded to agree with the prophet. These texts indicate, nevertheless, that the Judahite exiles' leaders, perhaps the whole community, adjudicated between different assessments of their situation in an effort to develop a coherent outlook on their predicament.

Second, the very fact that the book of Ezekiel exists indicates that it was adopted as a legitimate expression of the community's experience by some not insignificant portion of the Judahite exilic community. If this were not true, the material would not have been transmitted, in oral or written form, and then reproduced for successive generations. Ezekiel is *an* expression of the hidden transcript, though this cannot be confused with it being *the* expression of the hidden transcript.[100] It remains necessary to account for the possibility that Ezekiel contains an idiosyncratic record of what the exiles thought, but the conditions required for it to eventually obtain canonical status makes it important evidence about the ways in which the Judahite exiles voiced their resistance against their Babylonian captors.

Returning to the structure of Scott's argument, after establishing what the public and hidden transcripts are, he turns his attention to the ways in which the two transcripts interact. This discussion includes a central argument of the book, namely that the hidden discourse that develops beyond the gaze of the dominant class emerges in a disguised form within the public performance of the subaltern class.

To contextualize this point, Scott divides the way subordinates speak into four categories on a spectrum. At one end of the spectrum is the hidden transcript itself, that discourse that stands outside the hearing and gaze of the powerful. At the opposite end is flattery. Flattery is

---

100 On this, see the discussion of Charles Tilly's critique of Scott below.

not mindless acquiescence to the dominant class, but is a discourse that contains none of the content of the hidden transcript. Often, Scott contends, oppressed groups adopt the language of the public transcript in order to use it against the dominant group. If the public transcript includes notions of benevolent paternalism, for instance, subordinates are likely to adopt this language unaltered and use it to petition their oppressors for improved conditions.[101]

In between these two ends of the spectrum lie two further categories: a disguised discourse of resistance and the open declaration of the hidden transcript. The latter designates the socially explosive act when a previously unarticulated expression of anger and dignity receives a full-throated declaration. This is the utopian notion of "speaking truth to power." Rupturing the norm, directly challenging the dominant class, this type of speech is rare, though its potent nature means that such instances often find a prominent place in communal memory.

Memorable as the latter may be, far more common and relevant to the book of Ezekiel is the former category, namely the inclusion of a disguised form of the hidden transcript within the public performance of the subordinate. Or, in other words, a resistant discourse camouflaged so that it escapes discipline from the powerful.[102]

---

101 Ibid., 18; cf. Jan Palmowski, *Inventing a Socialist Nation: Heimat and the Politics of Everyday Life in the GDR, 1945-1990* (New Studies in European History; Cambridge: Cambridge University Press, 2009), especially chs. 7 and 8. The example of the resistance to power in Holungen in ch. 7 has numerous analogies to the argument about Ezekiel in ch. 6 of this book.

102 The work of Yairah Amit, *Hidden Polemics in Biblical Narrative* (Biblical Interpretation Series 25; Translated by Jonathan Chipman. Leiden: Brill, 2000) must be distinguished from Scott's model. Amit identifies three kids of polemics: open, indirect and hidden. For her, the controlling issue is whether the contested issue is explicitly mentioned: whereas an indirect polemic makes its subject explicit, but hides its view, a hidden polemic neither explicitly mentions its topic nor its view on it. This makes it difficult to identify, so Amit correctly argues that one needs a more explicit example of the issue elsewhere to substantiate it is possible. She also recommends that a hidden polemic be discussed explicitly in subsequent reception of the text.

Amit's approach is fruitful, and she points out several instance in the Hebrew Bible where hidden polemics do occur. Those strengths notwithstanding, her work is limited in two significant ways. First, it deals only with issues in debate among Israel and Judah, and not with external parties as will be the case in this study. Second, her model fails to account for the impact that asymmetric power relations have on these polemics in any detail (cf. Ibid., 97-8) and to interact with the relevant social scientific contributions, like Scott, that would allow her to address this issue.

Her model is, ultimately, undertheorized and limited by not considering the international dimension of the issue.

Scott explains that this activity lies strategically between flattery and the hidden transcript and represents the low-level struggle that happens on a daily basis between the dominant and the subordinate. This realm of activity contains "a politics of disguise and anonymity that takes place in public view but is designed to have a double meaning or to shield the identity of the actors."[103] Scott does not give this category a name, though some refer to is as a private transcript.[104] Its lack of designation seems appropriate: Scott does not describe a separate discourse, which a unique term might connote, but emphasizes that this is a way of speaking and acting that gives voice to the hidden transcript within the confines of public performance. By that very act it resists domination because one of the ways in which the powerful attempt to impose their will is by winning the ongoing struggle to define "what counts as the public transcript and what counts as offstage."[105]

Potential disguises divide into two categories: anonymity and ambiguity. The former cloaks the messenger under the premise that insubordination from an unknown source cannot be punished. The latter camouflages the message: it presents some aspect of the hidden transcript in images, metaphors, or polysemous language that engenders enough ambiguity into the meaning so that an innocuous interpretation is possible. In other words, it deprives the powerful of the evidence needed to determine that their authorized view is being subverted. These techniques explain a recurring evaluation of subaltern groups, writes Scott:

> If subordinate groups have typically won a reputation for subtlety—a subtlety their superiors often regard as cunning and deception—this is surely because their vulnerability has rarely permitted them the luxury of direct confrontation.[106]

Because this study concerns the book of Ezekiel it shall focus on the ways in which the message, not the messenger, is masked. The possible ways of accomplishing this are only limited by the imaginative capacity of those speaking. That is, with one exception: even the masked discourse of resistance remains connected to the public transcript be-

---

103 Scott, *Domination*, 10.

104 Palmowski, *Socialist Nation*, 145-46.

105 Scott, *Domination*, 14; it is worth noting Scott's point that "[t]he capacity of dominant groups to prevail—though never totally—in defining what counts as the public transcript and what counts as offstage is... no small measure of their power."

106 Ibid., 136.

cause it must interact with its symbols and language. Still, the ways in
which those symbols and terms might be creatively transformed is co-
pious, such that Scott cautions it is "impossible to overestimate the subtlety of this manipulation."[107]   In order to identify the glimpses of the
hidden transcript that emerge in this camouflaged form "we shall have
to learn its dialect and codes."[108]

That process is a key objective of the first part of this study—the
comparative analysis and form critical evaluation of the oath formulae.
The findings there will point to the many layers of meaning contained
in and the various allusions evoked by each phrase.   Furthermore,
those findings open contemporary eyes to the possible ways this language provides camouflage for the hidden transcript as Ezekiel knows
it. The comparative analysis, which is supplemented in the second part
of the study with further investigation of Ezekiel's relationship to Neo-
Babylonian sources, is particularly illuminating, pointing out several
ways that Ezekiel works with the public transcript authorized by its
Neo-Babylonian captors to disguise its resistant discourse.

To be sure, the findings offered here are far from a full directory of
Ezekiel's dialect and codes of disguise. Still, insofar as this study does
describe that dialect and break those codes, it grants access to a previously inaudible broadcast of the Judahite exiles' hidden transcript.

(iii) The Infrapolitics of Subordinates

Scott concludes his argument by outlining the "infrapolitics" of subordinates, a neo-logism that draws on two separate metaphors simultaneously.   The resistance of subordinate groups is, on the one hand,
comparable to an infrared light, something that is "beyond the visible
end of the spectrum"[109] for the dominant classes.   On the other hand,
the concealed actions of resistance, no matter how small or large, ultimately form the foundation for any public protest or resistance that
does materialize. Scott draws an analogy to roads, banks, and telecom-
munications networks, the *infra*structure that makes commerce possible. In a similar fashion, Scott argues that open, direct resistance is not
an *ex nihilo* action, but intimately connected to and based upon camouflaged resistance already in progress.

---

107 Ibid., 139.
108 Ibid., 138.
109 Ibid., 183.

For Scott, then, the hidden transcript is not only a means of resistance, it is the fuel for resistance. The hidden transcript both sheds light on daily, low-level insubordinate behavior and, by gathering the community around a unifying message, encourages the members of the subordinate community to persist in these forms of resistance.[110] "Far from being a relief-valve taking the place of actual resistance," comments Scott, "the discursive practices offstage sustain resistance."[111]

Returning to an earlier theme, that of the subaltern social space, Scott concludes by outlining how subordinate groups remain unified. Subordinates reside in two overlapping worlds: the one controlled by the dominant and the offstage world controlled by their peers. Like the powerful have the capacity to sanction behavior, so too does the subaltern social structure. Indeed, there is overwhelming evidence that oppressed groups successfully police the behavior of their members.

Scott draws his various lines of argument together by writing:

> We can, in this respect, view the social side of the hidden transcript as a political domain striving to enforce, against great odds, certain forms of conduct and resistance in relations with the dominant. It would be more accurate, in short, to think of the hidden transcript as a condition of practical resistance rather than a substitute for it.[112]

The final sentence encapsulates the most often noted contribution of Scott's book, but the preceding statement is fundamental for this study. When the various lines of argument in this book are drawn together, they will demonstrate that Ezekiel's open polemic against the non-exiled Judahites and disguised resistance against its Neo-Babylonian overlords are united by a concern to define and enforce the forms of speech, conduct, and resistance that it believes exemplify faithful Yahwism. Ezekiel's definition of authentic Judahite identity is justified and defended by connecting it to the exodus tradition, a communal memory of a previous occasion when YHWH redeemed an elect community living outside Judah in order to demonstrate that he is an exceptionally powerfully deity that is uniquely worthy of allegiance and worship.

---

110 Ibid., 188.
111 Ibid., 191.
112 Ibid.

(iv) Critiques of Scott's Model

Domination and the Arts of Resistance has made a broad impact in the so-cial sciences, though not without criticism. In biblical studies, the model has been well received, though New Testament scholars have made far more use of it than those working on the Hebrew Bible.[113] A short discussion of four social scientist's critiques is thus necessary to establish how Scott's model may be appropriated.

Susan Gal concentrates on two deficiencies in Scott's model: first, she argues that Scott presumes an "authentic self that is necessarily betrayed by performance" and, second, that he overdetermines the relationship between rhetorical strategies and social class.[114] Regarding the first point, Gal maintains that Scott fails to allow for sufficient variability in the way emotion is expressed in different cultures. Restraining one's speech, which Scott associates with subordinates, might also be

---

113 The two most extensive studies are the edited volumes Richard A. Horsley, ed. *Hidden Transcripts and the Arts of Resistance: Applying the Work of James C. Scott to Jesus and Paul* (Semeia Studies 48. Leiden: Brill, 2004) and idem. *Oral Performance, Popular Tradition, and Hidden Transcript in Q* (Semeia Studies 60. Leiden: Brill, 2006). Horsley also employs Scott's model in his volume *Jesus and Empire: The Kingdom of God and the New World Disorder* (Minneapolis, Minn.: Fortress, 2003). David Reed, "Rethinking John's Social Setting: Hidden Transcript, Anti-Language, and the Negotiation of Empire," *BTB* 36 (2006): 93-106, uses the concept of hidden transcripts as part of a proposal about the Jewish motivations for expelling the Christians from the synagogue in John's gospel. This list is illustrative of work in the New Testament, and by no means exhaustive, but shows the popularity of Scott's model there.

Gerald O. West has applied Scott's model to biblical studies as a whole; see "And the Dumb Do Speak: Articulating Incipient Readings of the Bible in Marginalized Communities," in *The Bible in Ethics: The Second Sheffield Colloquium* (eds. John W. Rogerson, Margaret Davies and M. Daniel Carroll R.; The Bible in Ethics: The Second Sheffield Colloquium; London: Continuum, 1995), 174-92, and "Gauging the Grain in a More Nuanced Literary Manner: A Cautionary Tale Concerning the Contribution of the Social Sciences to Biblical Interpretation," in *Rethinking Contexts, Rereading Texts: Contributions from the Social Sciences to Biblical Interpretation* (ed. M. Daniel Carroll R.; Rethinking Contexts, Rereading Texts: Contributions From the Social Sciences to Biblical Interpretation; London: Continuum, 2000), 75-105.

In one of the few studies concerning the Hebrew Bible, Anathea Portier-Young, *Apocalypse Against Empire: Theologies of Resistance in Early Judaism* (Grand Rapids, Mich.: Eerdmans, 2011) takes account of Scott's work, including a thoughtful critique of his model. Portier-Young finds Scott's model inappropriate to her object of study and, therefore, does not interact with Scott much after her discussion on method. That section is, nevertheless, a helpful discussion of the issues in applying Scott in an ancient context.

114 Susan Gal, "Language and the 'Arts of Resistance,'" *Cultural Anthropology* 10 (1995): 411-21; quote from p. 411.

adopted by the dominant as a sign of their self-control, something that substantiates their power. Gal is correct on this point, and it emphasizes that each culture's distinctive traits need to be taken into account. With respect to ancient Israel and Judah, there is strong evidence that "speaking truth to power" and resisting foreign domination were valued as part of faithful Yahwism and appropriate nationalism.[115] Thus, keeping Gal's point in mind, it seems reasonable to work with Scott's model nonetheless.

Gal's second point problematizes Scott's attribution of certain rhetorical techniques to only the dominant or subordinate classes. The point is well made and shows that Scott's taxonomy of disguise remains only illustrative. Scott's own observation that sudordinates' methods of concealment are limited only by their imaginative capacity must be broadened, for the dominant are no less clever. It will be important to bear in mind this cautionary point at all times, but it does not preclude applying Scott's model to Ezekiel.

Alexei Yurchak builds on Gal's critique, contending that Scott adopts an inadequate set of binary oppositions, particularly public performance as either real or false support of an established position. Though there are reasons to think that Scott has room in his model to account for substantial parts of Yurchak's critique,[116] Yurchak's synthesis of J. L. Austin's speech-act theory with Jacques Derrida's and Bourdieu's discussions of it does advance on Scott.[117] In particular, when he draws on Austin's categories of constative and performative speech, which occur in every speech act, Yurchak provides a way to explain how an utterance may perform an act that it does not endorse. An oath illustrates the matter succinctly: when one swears in a court of law to tell the truth they obligate themselves to do so by nature of the performative aspect of the utterance; at the same time, the person may know they will subsequently lie, but this does not invalidate the oath. The si-

---

115 Daniel, for instance, expresses this view. Historically earlier, one might note the way Isaiah of Jerusalem encourages Ahaz to resist multiple foreign powers and (Isa 6–9), of particular relevance, how he endorses Hezekiah's resilience in the face of Assyrian propaganda (Isa 36–39). The prominence of the oracles against the nations, especially those against Assyria, Egypt, and Babylonia reinforce this idea.

116 For instance, Scott does recognize the limits of binary classifications about speech as true and false (Scott, *Domination*, 5), which could logically be extended to account for some of Yurchak's points, although perhaps not all of them.

117 Alexei Yurchak, *Everything Was Forever, Until It Was No More: The Last Soviet Generation* (Princeton, N.J.: Princeton University Press, 2006), 18-26; cf. Scott, *Domination*, 57, where the discussion of public apologies appears particularly hospitable to the way in which Yurchak speaks about performative and constative dimensions of speech.

multaneity of the performative and constative dimensions allows for dominant groups to expand their control of the performative dimension at the same time that the constative dimension becomes "increasingly open or even irrelevant."[118] Yurchak's approach aids immensely in explaining how acts of hollow obedience work. Furthermore, recognizing that the constative meaning of every performative utterance is determined by its context provides a theoretical basis to explain the occasions when a dominant group interprets an action as obedient while a subaltern group simultaneously understands it as resistant.

Charles Tilly offers a largely positive evaluation of *Domination and the Arts of Resistance*, but he recognizes shortcomings in the way Scott conceives subordinate communities as cooperative entities. Tilly's problem is that Scott nowhere accounts for discord within the subaltern group, a situation in which multiple hidden transcripts exists and may even be in conflict with one another.[119] A knock on effect of this omission is that Scott cannot explain why some groups openly rebel and others do not.[120] Tilly's critique is more pertinent to theories of hegemony, but he raises an issue that is relevant here. Scott's assumption of uniformity must be tested against what is known about the community in question, particularly when evidence of factions or sectarianism exists. Where there is evidence of discord among subordinates, as there is in Ezekiel, it is necessary to account for it.[121] At a minimum, the evidence that Ezekiel represents a portion, perhaps even a small portion, of those in the Judahite exilic community must guide discussion about how it uses the hidden transcript.

Finally, Timothy Mitchell has proffered a widely cited criticism about Scott's conception of hegemony. Mitchell's central point is that the very idea of a different sphere for thought and action requires a mind-body dualism that is itself a creation of the dominant class. This binary opposition is not only created by the powerful, the dominant class employs it to drive any potential resistance underground and to inculcate a metaphysical view that makes its power structures look unassailable. Granting that Mitchell's assessment raises an important issue and that behavior does indeed shape ideas and identities in important ways, his suggestion runs the risk of equating any conscious

---

118 Yurchak, *Everything Was Forever*, 24.

119 Charles Tilly, "Domination, Resistance, Compliance. Discourse," *Sociological Forum* 6 (1991): 598-601.

120 Ibid., 599.

121 Scott, *Domination*, 119, appears open to a process of debate and refinement in the development of the hidden transcript, but fails to expand on this possibility sufficiently.

deliberation, grumbling against power, or thoughtful discourse about how one might resist into acquiescing to the powerful.[122] That is a step too far.

Mitchell shows that Scott gives insufficient attention to the ways in which metaphysics and epistemology might themselves be tools of domination, an issue that all must be alert to and seek to incorporate when examining a particular instance of domination or resistance. Be that as it may, Mitchell hardly invalidates the evidence, ubiquitous in history and personal experience, that people do resist power in subtle, disguised ways.

Each of these four critiques provides a cautionary note, identifying ways in which Scott's model may be deficient. *"Caveat emptor"* they correctly declare. But, this is no more or less than what any social scientific model faces. Philip Esler summarizes the issue well:

> [Social-Scientific] Models are essentially simplifications, exemplifications, and systematizations of data used for comparative purposes. Those who employ them in exegesis know they are merely tools available to enable comparison. It is senseless, therefore, to ask if models are "true" or "false"... Rather, one must judge a model by whether or not it is helpful.[123]

The various critiques of Scott's model point out places where he has oversimplified or overemphasized something in his systematizing. They also raise cases where the model is not helpful, or at least not as helpful as other models.

With those caveats in mind, this study adopts Esler's recommendation to use social scientific models as a heuristic approach, not ignorant of potential lacuna or anachronisms, but focused primarily on the exegetical benefit achieved. The subsequent analysis shows that the model Scott develops in *Domination and the Arts of Resistance* provides a lens through which the book of Ezekiel can be seen in a new way, one that provides significant new exegetical insights and highlights how it seeks to define and impose its view of Judahite identity and faithful Yahwism.

To anticipate the argument that follows, this study maintains that the book of Ezekiel employs the "as I live" authenticating element and the "lifted hand" formula as structuring devices in shaping its message. That message is a two-pronged polemic: on one side, the book denies

---

122 Cf. Tilly, "Domination," 595.

123 Philip Esler, "Social-Scientific Models in Biblical Interpretation," in *Ancient Israel: The Old Testament in Its Social Context* (Philadelphia, Pa.: Fortress, 2006), 3-4.

the appeals of the Judahites left in the land to a combined Abraham-Jacob tradition for social, political, and religious legitimacy, symbolized in their right to possess YHWH's land; on the other side, the book utilizes the prominent affiliation of these formulae with the exodus tradition as part of a disguised polemic against the claims to political and religious dominance of their Babylonian captors.   Through the intra-Judahite and inter-national polemics in the book of Ezekiel the text defines what it believes are the boundary markers of legitimate Yahwism and Judahite nationalism.   To remain faithful to YHWH according to Ezekiel, one must trace one's lineage to the ancestors in Egypt, reject all forms of image-based worship, and interpret both history and contemporary events through the lens of the exodus tradition.   The exodus tradition is central because it testifies that YHWH chooses a faithful community outside the land and under foreign oppression to illustrate his sovereignty over nations, history, and other deities.   As YHWH acted on behalf of the ancestors in Egypt who remained faithful despite the obvious challenges, so YHWH will do for the Judahite exiles in Babylon.   If, that is, they remain faithful as well.

Part One: The Meaning of the "As I Live" and "Lifted Hand" Formulae

Part one of this study will explore the meaning of the "as I live" and "lifted hand" formulae in an attempt to bring greater clarity to their role in the book of Ezekiel and the Hebrew Bible as a whole. The first step is to review the relevant parallels from throughout the ancient Near East, which indicates that the "as I live" formula is used when deities swear to judge their own people. Furthermore, the previously noted absence of a parallel for the "lifted hand" formula in oaths is explained by identifying its counterpart in Akkadian legal documents authorizing the transfer of land.

The second step is a genre analysis that demonstrates both that the "as I live" authenticating element is employed in prophetic announcements of judgment, which are often constructed as disputation speeches, and also that the "lifted hand" formula is used in two conventions, with one relating to land transfers and the other defining the punishment for a guilty party.

The third and final step analyzes the literary setting (*Sitz in der Literatur*) and suggests a potential social setting (*Sitz im Leben*) for the three formulae. The evidence demonstrates that the "as I live" authenticating element is characteristic of the DTR theological tradition while the "lifted hand" land transfer formula features in texts written and edited by the authors of the Holiness Code. The "lifted hand" punishment formula is rare, appearing only in the book of Ezekiel.

These findings about the connotations, inner-biblical allusions, genre, and literary setting of the formulae significantly enhance the contemporary understanding of their meaning. Providing texture and depth to Ezekiel's dialect, this knowledge exposes otherwise disguised messages made through coded language, and is, therefore, foundational to the second part of the book in which Ezekiel's explicit polemic against the non-exiled Judahites and disguised polemic against its Babylonian captors is analyzed.

Chapter Two: The Ancient Near Eastern Context for the Divine Oath

Moshe Greenberg's observation about Ezekiel that "one who aspires to be an interpreter... of such a polymath in his historical setting should possess a correspondingly wide range of antiquarian knowledge"[1] was noted earlier. Achieving such knowledge is challenging with the available evidence, but further analysis can enhance the present knowledge base. This chapter, therefore, focuses on a lacuna in Ezekiel scholarship, specifically a detailed, contextual analysis of the various forms of the divine oath in the Hebrew Bible.

The analysis will focus on three questions. First, what phrases are employed in the ancient Near East as authenticating elements for swearing oaths? In particular, are there parallels to the phrases חי אני and נשא יד which are so prevalent in Ezekiel? Second, which of these authenticating elements do deities employ? And, third, in what context do deities swear and what intent do their oaths reveal?

Answering these three questions establishes three findings. Firstly, there are parallels to the biblical "as I live" authenticating element in Egyptian, Akkadian, and Ugaritic texts. Secondly, there is no parallel to the biblical "lifted hand" formula as an authenticating element for an oath.[2] Thirdly, the presence of fewer than ten examples of deities swearing in the comparative literature shows that the divine oath is far more frequent in the Hebrew Bible than in its ancient counterparts.

Prior to beginning the analysis, it is necessary to say a few words on the parameters of the comparative analysis.

---

1   Greenberg, *Ezekiel 21-37*, 395-96.

2   The absence of a parallel to this phrase as an oath is resolved in the following excursus, which argues that the parallel is found in the Akkadian legal formula *našû-nadānu* that authorizes land transfers.

1. Ancient Near Eastern Comparative Study and the Book of Ezekiel

Comparative study, by its very nature, can expand far and wide.[3] Limitations of scope require making decisions about where to place the boundaries on the study, and what to include in the discussion of results. In general, this means looking at texts that are linguistically, generically, temporally, and geographically close to those of primary interest.[4]

A model in which potential parallels are placed in one of two concentric circles guides this study. The most central and most directly comparable circle contains instances of divine oaths in the ancient Near East. This evidence, where available, offers the most direct comparison to the divine oath in the Hebrew Bible generally and Ezekiel in particular. Although there are few texts that fit within this category, they enrich the present understanding of the divine oath substantially.

The second, larger concentric circle comprises human oaths that use authenticating elements closely related to those employed by deities. The Hebrew Bible indicates that human authenticating elements—like 'as YHWH lives'—are related to the divine oath formulae and, therefore, can be instructive. Of particular help are instances when kings swear in this fashion. Due to the limited number of divine oaths outside the Hebrew Bible, this evidence increases in value. Beliefs about how the king is related to a deity or deities in the ancient Near East are not uniform, to be sure, likely the result of a plurality of views on that topic in antiquity. Thus, while it is certain that royal rhetoric is a near counterpart to divine language, it will always have to be considered with attention to distinctions between divine and human speech.

While these two concentric circles account for genre and chronology, geography and language also guide the selection of texts from Egypt, Mesopotamia, Anatolia, and Ugarit.[5] Though alternately ene-

---

3   On the enterprise in general, see Meir Malul, *The Comparative Method in Ancient Near Eastern and Biblical Legal Studies* (AOAT 227; Neukirchen-Vluyn: Neukirchener Verlag, 1990), 13-21, Hallo, "Biblical History," 1-26, and Longman, *Fictional Akkadian Autobiography*, 23-36.

4   Ibid.; cf. Peter C. Craigie, "The Poetry of Ugarit and Israel," *TynBul* 22 (1971): 4-10.

5   The lack of a separate section on Aramaic texts, surely relevant for comparative study of the Hebrew Bible, is a result of two factors. First, despite a thorough search, there was no evidence of a deity swearing in any extant Aramaic text. Second, though there are examples of humans swearing in Aramaic, including the phrase *ḥy lyhh* (TAD D7.16.3), they add no substantial insight to the others already

mies and allies throughout history, there is no question about the political interaction between Egypt, Israel, and Judah. There is, furthermore, little doubt that biblical literature is influenced by Egyptian texts.[6] Because the book of Ezekiel presents itself as originating from Babylonia, Mesopotamian thought, literature, and practice furnish pertinent comparisons.[7] Previously, Bodi demonstrated the book's familiarity with *Erra and Ishum*[8] and others revealed how Mesopotamian views on divine presence and absence are deeply imbedded within the theology of the book of Ezekiel.[9] Prominent among the evidence available from Anatolia is Hittite practice. The twentieth century produced an ongoing discussion of the role Hittite vassal treaties played in determining the form of biblical covenants. Although opinion has vacillated on whether there is a direct influence from Hittite to biblical forms, or if the influence comes via Assyrian treaties, there is little denying their resemblance and at least an anecdotal connection between them and the Hebrew Bible.[10] Finally, Ugarit is the best known precursor to Canaan-

---

included. The Aramaic inscriptions of Sefire do offer some important context nonetheless; see pp. 88-9 below..

6   Donald B. Redford, *Egypt, Canaan, and Israel in Ancient Times* (Princeton, N.J.: Princeton University Press, 1992), 333; Ronald J. Williams, "Egypt and Israel," in *The Legacy of Egypt* (ed. J.R. Harris; Oxford: Oxford University Press, 1971), 262-69. Egypt dominates in Ezek 29–32; for a detailed analysis, see Boadt, *Ezekiel's Oracles against Egypt.*

7   Although one must remain cognizant of the differences between Neo-Assyrian and Neo-Babylonian culture and thought, both offer a rich assortment of comparative material for the book of Ezekiel and are relevant to this study.

8   Bodi, *Ezekiel and the Poem of Erra.*; cf. Stephanie Dalley, *Myths from Mesopotamia: Creation, the Flood, Gilgamesh, and Others* (Oxford: Oxford University Press, 1989), 282-315, and Benjamin R. Foster, *Before the Muses: An Anthology of Akkadian literature* (3rd ed. Bethesda, Md.: CDL Press, 2005), 880-911.

9   Morton Cogan, *Imperialism and Religion: Assyria, Judah, and Israel in the Eighth and Seventh Centuries B.C.E* (SBLMS 19; Missoula, Mont.: Scholars Press, 1974), opened this line of study for biblical scholars. Recently, Block (Block, *Gods of the Nations.*; Daniel I. Block, "Divine Abandonment: Ezekiel's Adaptation of an Ancient Near Eastern Motif," in *The Book of Ezekiel: Theological and Anthropological Perspectives* [eds. Margaret S. Odell and John T. Strong; SBLSyms 9; Atlanta, Ga.: Society of Biblical Literature, 2000], 15-42) and Kutsko (Kutsko, *Between Heaven and Earth*) have extended this line of argument.

10   The question of Hittite treaty forms was opened by Viktor Korošec, *Hethitische Staatsverträge: ein Beitrag zu ihrer juristischen Wertung* (Leipziger rechtswissenschaftliche Studien 60; Leipzig: T. Weicher, 1931). In biblical studies, George E. Mendenhall was the first to demonstrate the similarities (*Law and Covenant in Israel and the Ancient Near East* [Pittsburgh, Pa.: The Presbyterian Board of Colportage of Western Pennsylvania, 1955]). He was followed by many scholars; a small selection of the notable treatments includes Delbert R. Hillers, *Treaty-curses and the Old Testament Prophets* (BibOr 16; Rome: Pontifical Biblical Institute, 1964), Dennis J. Mc-

ite culture, a prominent foil to Israel and Judah in the Hebrew Bible.
There is no question Ugarit's religious beliefs as expressed in *The Baal
Cycle*, *The Legend of Keret*, *The Story of Aqhat*, and other texts influenced
the authors and editors of the Hebrew Bible,[11] although one must be
sensitive to the many unknowns about how and when they encountered these ideas.

The evidence is organized by language for ease of presentation. Although this is straightforward for Egypt and Ugarit, where language
and geography coincide, it also produces a section that combines the
Akkadian texts that originate in Assyria, Babylonia, and Hatti, cultures
that cross geographical boundaries between Mesopotamia and Anatolia. This could blur cultural and geographic distinctions, but care will
be taken to avoid such reductionism and to draw positively from the
significant interaction between these cultures that is reflected by their
shared language.

2. The Divine Oath in Egyptian Texts

The classic study on Egyptian oaths is a 1948 article by John A. Wilson[12]
that catalogued over 130 examples. Indeed, oaths are so prevalent as to
have a role even in ancient Egyptian satirical works.[13] Although schol-

---

Carthy, *Treaty and Covenant: A Study in Form in the Ancient Oriental Documents and in
the Old Testament* (AnBib 21; Rome: Pontifical Biblical Institute, 1963), Ernest W.
Nicholson, *God and His People: Covenant and Theology in the Old Testament* (Oxford:
Clarendon Press, 1986), and various contributions by Moshe Weinfeld, including
"The Covenant of Grant in the Old Testament and in the Ancient Near East," *JAOS*
90 (1970): 184-203, and also "Covenant Terminology in the Ancient Near East and Its
Influence on the West," *JAOS* 93 (1973): 190-99.

The exact identity of the "Hittites" in the book of Ezekiel remains an open question
(Ezek 16:3, 45). Were they a transient remnant of the thirteenth century Anatolian
people in the Levant? Or, did the term Hittite merely denote a subset of the people
known as Canaanites with no direct relation to the state in Anatolia? This question
cannot be resolved here, and in this section the term Hittite will refer exclusively to
the thirteenth century Anatolian state ruled from Hatti. Later, when discussing the
text of Ezek 16, the term Hittite will be used to represent the identification made in
the text without judgment to its historical referent.

11   John Day, *Yahweh and the Gods and Goddesses of Canaan* (JSOTSup 265; Sheffield:
     Sheffield Academic Press, 2000), 13-41, offers a thorough discussion of the
     connection.
12   John A. Wilson, "The Oath in Ancient Egypt," *JNES* 7 (1948): , 129-56.
13   Ibid. cases 19-21. See also Hans-Werner Fischer-Elfert, *Die satirische Streitschrift des
     Papyrus Anastasi I: Übersetzung und Kommentar* (Ägyptologische Abhandlungen 44;
     Wiesbaden: Otto Harrassowitz, 1986), 82-4, and "The Contending of Horus and

ars have added to and nuanced Wilson's findings in the ensuing sixty years, the central details of his research remain the standard, and his discussion will serve as the starting point here.

(a) The Egyptian Authenticating Elements

In his foundational article, Wilson identified three authenticating elements in Egyptian oaths. The first employs the verb ꜥnḫ, which means "to live." Wilson explains that "[t]he translation 'oath' derives from the use of this word as the first element in a customary form of the oath: 'As truly as lives for me the God (or King) X...'"[14] Often referred to as "the oath of the God,"[15] it appears continually from the Old Kingdom (late third millennium B.C.E.)[16] through the eighth century B.C.E.[17] Wilson notes 27 instances where this authenticating element is used,[18] which span the spectrum of genres from myths to legal documents and appear in the speech of both gods and humans.

The second Egyptian authenticating element utilizes the verb wꜣḥ, which means "to endure."[19] The earliest recorded use of the wꜣḥ authenticating element is from the New Kingdom,[20] and it continues to appear at least through the eighth century B.C.E.[21] The primary use of the wꜣḥ authenticating element was in Egyptian legal proceedings. Wilson comments: "in the Late Empire the normal verbal formula for a le-

---

Seth," translated by Edward F. Wente (*LAE*, 91-103). Among the many maledictions cited for breaking an oath, it was not uncommon for an oath-breaker to be threatened with sexual violation by an ass, an act certainly meant to defame by its indecency (Scott Morschauser, *Threat-formulae in Ancient Egypt: A Study of the History, Structure, and Use of Threats and Curses in Ancient Egypt* [Baltimore, Md.: Halgo, 1991], 198-99).

14 Wilson, "The Oath in Ancient Egypt," 130. This synecdoche indicates the prevalence of this oath formula in ancient Egypt.

15 Ibid., 153-56.

16 Ibid., 129-56. See case 22.

17 Ibid.. See cases 26 and 69 which date to the reign of Piankhy, also known as Piye, 747-716 B.C.E. (Amélie Kuhrt, *The Ancient Near East: c. 3000-330 B.C.* [2 vols. Routledge History of the Ancient World; London: Routledge, 1995], II:624).

18 Wilson, "The Oath in Ancient Egypt," 151, table 1. Among the examples, cases 6, 14, 26, 65, and 69 include a self-referential form of the ꜥnḫ authenticating element.

19 Ibid., 130.

20 Ibid., 133, case 12. The earliest example dates to the reign of Amose, which Kuhrt places ca. 1550-1525 B.C.E. (Kuhrt, *The Ancient Near East: c. 3000-330 B.C*, I:186).

21 Wilson, "The Oath in Ancient Egypt," 134-35, cases 27 and 30. By comparison, this formula appears later and disappears sooner than the ꜥnḫ authenticating element.

gal oath began with the words, 'As Amon endures and as the Ruler endures.'"[22] E. D. Bedell furthered Wilson's analysis by parsing these oaths into two categories:[23] those which were assertory, used to deny that a crime had been committed in the past,[24] and those which were promissory, used to ensure true testimony would be given in the legal proceeding at hand.[25] Even though the *w3h* authenticating element is more frequent than *'nh*, it is never used by a deity, although there is a noteworthy instance in the tale of *Truth and Falsehood*, where Falsehood is taken to court for wrongly accusing Truth and having him blinded. Truth retorts: "Falsehood took an oath by the Lord, saying: 'As Amun lives, as the Ruler lives, if Truth is found alive, I shall be blinded in both eyes and made door-keeper of the house of Truth!'"[26] In this tale, Truth and Falsehood are more than average humans, appearing before the Ennead (a divine counsel) and representing timeless virtues. Nonetheless, they are presented as thoroughly anthropomorphic in the tale and the *w3h* authenticating element appears to be one way of portraying them in human terms. Resolving whether these two figures are divine or not is not determinative for this analysis, and the *Tale of Truth and Falsehood* evokes the important role oaths play in defining a figure's character.

The third phrase Wilson understood as an authenticating element, *sdf(3)-tr(yt)*, is the most difficult to interpret. With only six instances, evidence for its meaning is sparse.[27] Wilson believed *sdf(3)-tr(yt)* meant "to undertake fealty,"[28] but conceded that the phrase "cannot be translated with any confidence."[29] Most scholars have followed Wilson's suggestion to the point that "the interpretation of *sdf(3)-tr(yt)* as a loyal-

---

22   Ibid., 153.

23   E. D. Bedell, "Criminal Law in the Egyptian Ramesside Period" Brandeis University, 1973), 129.

24   For instance, Wilson, "The Oath in Ancient Egypt," 136 cases 36, 38.

25   For instance, Ibid., 135, cases 31, 33-35. See Michael A. Green, "A Means of Discouraging Perjury," *Göttinger Miszellen* 39 (1980): 33-39, for a detailed discussion of the oath as a measure to reduce perjury. In a few cases, a promissory oath might be used to promise compensation to atone for a previous crime.

26   Miriam Lichtheim, *Ancient Egyptian Literature: A Book of Readings* (3 vols. ; Berkeley, Calif.: University of California Press, 2006), II:213.

27   See Scott Morschauser, "The End of the *sdf(3)-tr(yt)* "Oath"," *Journal of the American Research Center in Egypt* 25 (1988): 93-103, for details of these six instances. Cf. Wilson, "The Oath in Ancient Egypt," 129-56, cases 39-41, 78, 79. The Eighteenth Dynasty appearance is in the Gebel Barkal stela of Thutmose III.

28   Ibid., 130.

29   Ibid.

ty or fealty oath has achieved something of a consensus."[30] However, Scott Morschauser has now demonstrated the phrase means "the expunging of sin."[31] He explains:

> Although it may be accompanied by a reference to "swearing," *sdf(3)-tr(yt)* is not itself an oath. The suggestion that the compound refers to the standard form of Egyptian loyalty oath should be dismissed on etymological and contextual grounds. The etymology of *sdf(3)-tr(yt)* as the "expunging of sin" is both satisfactory in and of itself and suits the legal and religious contexts in which it is used. Thus, we would assert that *sdf(«)-tr(yt)* is a technical expression referring to the issue of a legal pardon for a crime.[32]

Morschauser's work underscores that care must be taken in identifying formulaic speech as an oath without strong evidence for that use.

In view of this evidence, further discussion of the ꜥnḥ authenticating element is merited. There are three germane examples to review.

(b) ꜥnḥ — "To Live"

First, the mythological tale *The Destruction of Mankind*,[33] which comprises one part of a larger myth called *The Book of the Heavenly Cow*, includes two instances of the ꜥnḥ authenticating element. This tale "relates how the sun-god Re set out to destroy the human race because mankind was plotting rebellion against him."[34] Re enlists the goddess Hathor to destroy humanity on his behalf. After completing a portion of her assignment, she returns to the council of the gods and reports "[a]s you [Re] live for me, I have overpowered mankind, and it was

---

30   Morschauser, *sdf(3)-tr(yt)* "Oath," 94. A.G. McDowell, *Jurisdiction in the Workmen's Community of Deir El-Medîna* (Egytologische uitgaven 5; Leiden: Nederlands Instituut voor het Nabije Oosten, 1990), 202-08, gives a brief history of scholarship on the question before resolving that it is an oath of office, essentially a specific type of fealty.

31   Morschauser, *sdf(3)-tr(yt)* "Oath," 96-97.

32   Ibid., 103.

33   "The Destruction of Mankind," translated by Miriam Lichtheim, (*COS* 1.24:36); "The Book of the Heavenly Cow," translated by Edward F. Wente (*LAE*, 289); David Lorton, "God's Beneficent Creation: Coffin Texts Spell 1130, the Instructions for Merikare, and the Great Hymn to the Aten," *Studien zur altägzptischen Kultur* 20 (1993): 141.

34   "The Destruction of Mankind," (*COS* 1.24:36).

balm to my heart."[35] But Re unanticipatedly chooses to relent from the further destruction of humanity and devises a ruse to stop Hathor from completing the onslaught.[36] The sun-god has seven thousand jars of red beer made and poured out to simulate a lake of blood. The beer draws the goddess' attention, and after drinking it Hathor is so drunk she does not recognize humanity and fails to destroy them. Having successfully averted further destruction, Re declares his intent to withdraw from interaction with humanity altogether: "As I live for myself, my heart is too weary to remain with them, that I should slay them to the very last one."[37] The remainder of the myth explains how the sun-god places the other great gods in various roles in his stead.

Second, *The Instructions for Merikare* offer the wisdom of a royal father to his young son Merikare, a king of the Ninth or Tenth Dynasty.[38] A prominent theme of the text is how to deal with the Asiatics, a frequent military threat to Egypt. Merikare's father remarks:

> But as I live and shall be what I am,
> When the Bowmen were a sealed wall,
> I breached [their strongholds],
> I made Lower Egypt attack them,
> I captured their inhabitants,
> I seized their cattle,
> until the Asiatics abhorred Egypt.
> Do not concern yourself with him,

---

35 "The Destruction of Mankind," (*COS* 1.24:36); cf. Wilson, "The Oath in Ancient Egypt," 135.

36 "The Destruction of Mankind," (*COS* 1.24:36).

37 "The Book of the Heavenly Cow," translated by Edward F. Wente (*LAE*, 293); cf. Wilson, "The Oath in Ancient Egypt," 135, note 31.

38 Most scholars believe the text is pseudepigraphic, although many still date the text to the period of Merikare, for instance Lichtheim, "The Destruction of Mankind," *COS* 1.24:36. *The Instructions for Merikare* exhibit other connections with the Hebrew Bible. Around line 130, the text says, "Well tended is mankind—god's cattle, he made sky and earth for their sake, he subdued the water monster, he made breath for their noses to live. They are his images, who came from his body." Beyond the obvious connection to Gen 2, Perdue has shown similarities between Merikare and the so-called succession narrative (2 Sam 9–20, 1 Kgs 1–2; Leo G. Perdue, "The Testament of David and Egyptian Royal Instructions," in *Scripture in Context Ii: More Essays on the Comparative Method* [eds. William W. Hallo, James C. Moyer and Leo G. Perdue; Winona Lake, Ind.: Eisenbrauns, 1983], 93-95). Another intriguing connection is the phrase "and I shall be what I am," which invites comparisons to Exod 3:14, the etiology for the divine name YHWH; see Albrecht Alt, "Ein ägyptisches Gegenstück zu Ex 3 14," *ZAW* 35 (1940): 160, on this question.

the Asiatic is a crocodile on its shore,
it snatches from a lonely road,
it cannot seize from a populous town.[39]

The use the ʿnḫ authenticating element in this self-referential oath
demonstrates that Egyptian humans as well as deities swore in this
fashion.[40] There is no human usage of the comparable authenticating
element in the Hebrew Bible.

The third and final example from Egypt is the stereotypical response to the report of an enemy attack or rebellion in which the ruler
swears an oath to annihilate the foe, often employing the self-referential ʿnḫ authenticating element. This formulaic interchange constitutes
an important component of the Egyptian *Königsnovelle*, "a specific literary form describing a unique event in the life of the king—a single, simple, great deed."[41] For instance, Thutmosis II receives the news of a rebellion in Nubia and responds, "As I live, as Re loves me, as my father,
the Lord of the Gods, Amon, Lord of the Thrones of the Two Lands favors me, I will certainly not let (any) of their males live; I will certainly
leave death among them!"[42] In another text, Piankhy (747-716 B.C.E.) is
told of a threat to his conquest of Egypt:

> Then his majesty was furious threat, like a panther. "Have they let a sur-
> vivor from the army of the Northland remain, permitting a goer-forth of
> them to go forth, to tell of his campaign, not causing them to die, to destroy
> the end of them? As I live, as Re loves me, as my father Amon favors me, I
> will go north myself, that I may overthrow what he has done, that I may
> make him turn back from fighting forever!"[43]

39 "Merikare," translated by Miriam Lichtheim, (*COS* 1.35:64); cf. "The Teaching for
King Merikare," translated by Vincent A. Tobin [*LAE*, 161-2]; "The Instruction for
King Meri-ka-re," translated by John A. Wilson (*ANET*, 416); Aksel Volten, *Zwei altä-
gyptische politische Schriften: Die Lehre für König Merikarê (Pap. Carlsberg VI) und die
Lehre des Königs Amenemhet* (AAeg 4; Copenhagen: E. Munksgaard, 1945), 48;
Joachim Friedrich Quack, *Studien zur Lehre für Merikare* (Göttinger Orientforschun-
gen Ägypten, 23; Wiesbaden: Harrassowitz, 1992), 56-57.

40 Although the question of the king's deification in Egypt remains debatable, in
Merikare there remains a strong distinction between the gods and the king, justifying
the attribution of this oath to a human.

41 Anthony J. Spalinger, *Aspects of the Military Documents of the Ancient Egyptians* (Yale
Near Eastern Researches 9; New Haven, Conn.: Yale University Press, 1982), 102.
Spalinger's section on the *Königsnovelle* in ch. 4 describes this form and its function
in greater detail.

42 Wilson, "The Oath in Ancient Egypt," 140, case 65.

43 Ibid., 141, case 69.

This Egyptian evidence indicates that deities employ the ʿnḫ authenticating element to swear upon one's own life, a feature clearest in the *Destruction of Mankind*. The texts show, furthermore, that human kings and deities both use this form of oath, though it is notable that such language consistently announces the use of violence or military power against a group of adversaries. This theme will repeat elsewhere, suggesting it is intertwined with this form of swearing.

3. The Divine Oath in Akkadian Texts

The large and ever growing corpus of Akkadian texts has provided numerous important insights on ancient thought and practice. Samuel Mercer, as noted in the scholarship review, has dedicated a whole study just to the role of oaths in Assyrian and Babylonian legal texts with helpful results, even if some of his conclusions are now questionable in light of additional evidence. Oaths occur frequently in Akkadian texts and, as it was in Egypt, even have a role in satirical pieces.[44] Therefore, the following discussion will range widely, dealing with well known religious texts as well as lesser known legal agreements. Along the way, it will corroborate the evidence from Egypt that deities swear by using an authenticating element similar to the self-referential "as I live" formula found in the Hebrew Bible.

(a) The Akkadian Authenticating Elements

The Akkadian evidence relating to oaths is most helpfully divided into four categories by authenticating element:[45] the invocation of a precious entity, verbs of swearing, mention of deities as witnesses, and wishing

---

44   For instance, a letter entitled "Do Not Sit on a Chair!", humorous in intent, exclaims: "By Ishtar and Ilaba, Ashgi, and Ninhursag, by the king's life and the queen's life you must swear it! So long as you have not seen my eyes, may you swallow neither food nor drink! Also, so long as you do not come to me, do not sit on a chair!" (Foster, *Muses*, 69). For another example of the oath in a parody, see the explicit "Lackey of a Dead God" (Foster, *Muses*, 1021-2).

45   Notable discussions of the oath formulae in Akkadian are Conklin, *Oath Formulas*, 81-92, Hayim Tadmor's 1980 address to the Society of Biblical Literature ("Treaty and Oath in the Ancient Near East: A Historian's Approach," in *Humanizing America's Iconic Book: Society of Biblical Literature Centennial Addresses 1980* [eds. Gene M. Tucker and Douglas A. Knight; Society of Biblical Literature Centennial Publications 6; Chico, Calif.: Scholars Press, 1982]), and the *Reallexikon der Assyriologie* (Erich Ebeling et al., *Reallexikon der Assyriologie* [11 vols. ; Berlin: Walter de Gruyter, 1928]).

the gods to strike the swearer for infidelity to the oath. Of these four, the latter two are sparsely attested and offer no substantial insight into the biblical material, so they will not be discussed here.[46] The invocation of precious entities and verbs of swearing, however, provide key parallels to the biblical material. Finally, it will be necessary to address the role and content of the so-called *adê* loyalty oaths.

(b) *nīš* X — "By the Life of X"

Although different types of precious entities can be invoked to authenticate an oath,[47] the most common[48] uses the noun *nīšu*, which literally means life,[49] in the phrase *nīš* X, "the life of X."[50] In oaths with the authenticating element *nīš* X, the variable element most often refers to a deity. Another frequently used phrase is "by the life of the king," but this phrase appears approximately one-quarter as often as those with

---

46   For information on these two categories, see Conklin, *Oath Formulas*, 85-86.

47   As examples, "by the city Assur" and by local rulers ("*nīšu A*," *CAD* 11.2:292-4). In the category of precious entities, it is also worth mentioning *šum X šūlû*, "raise the name of X," where the variable element can be a king, a celestial object, and a deity ("*elû*," *CAD* 4:135, entry 12). The phrase is found in Middle Babylonian, Neo-Babylonian, and Neo-Assyrian texts. It is used by various persons in taking an oath, although there is presently no indication of a deity using this authenticating element, making it practically, if not totally, irrelevant.

48   According to "*nīšu A*," *CAD* 11.2:292-4, there are over sixty instances of this authenticating element. This phrase is approximately four times more likely to appear than the second most frequent, *nīš šarrim*.

49   "*nīšu A*," *CAD* 11.2:290-4.

50   As with all cuneiform writing, a certain amount of uncertainty persists in translation. In this case, the Akkadian word for life (*nīšu*) shares the logogram mu with the word for name (*šum*). As such, a case can be made that this phrase is actually *šum X*, "the name of X." However, the scholarly consensus is for interpreting the phrase as *nīš* X. Recently, Conklin provided a thorough grammatical and syntactical analysis of oaths which supports this interpretation (Conklin, *Oath Formulas*, 79-92). Furthermore, he notes the Akkadian text of a letter from the King of Carchemish to Ugarit (RS 8.333) which includes the oath:

na-na-a na[p-]ša-ta ša šarri li-it-ma-a-mi

Nana should swear (by) the life of the king

This phrasing follows the typical use of the Akkadian *nīš* X authenticating element, here invoking the King's life. Conklin comments: "Note that the word for life used here is not *nīš*, as in mainstream Akkadian, but *napšata*, the cognate to the Ugaritic *npš*" (Ibid., 80). In view of this text, it appears certain the Akkadian phrase should be taken to reference "life" and not "name."

deities.[51] In some occasions, the two are joined to yield "by the life of god and king."[52]

Nīš X occurs as the object of the verbs to swear (*tamû*) and declare (*zakāru*). Conklin summarizes the historical distribution of *nīš* X with these two verbs:

> In Old Assyrian (OAs), the verb *tamû* is also used, but X may be a mixture of human and divine figures, or even non-animate precious entities... In Old Babylonian (OB) texts, as well as Middle Babylonian (MB) texts from Alalakh, and Neo-Babylonian (NB) and Neo-Assyrian (NA) texts, the verb generally used is *zakāru*, and X is a deity.[53]

Alongside Conklin's observation about the distribution of the *nīš* X authenticating element with these verbs, Tadmor has shown that there is a preference for the *nīš* X authenticating element in Babylonia during the first and second millennia, a feature that distinguishes Babylonian practice from the concurrent Assyrian inclination to specify imprecations in oath taking.[54] Because the Neo-Babylonians favored the *nīš* X authenticating element, it provides valuable context for the book of Ezekiel.

Perhaps the most informative use of *nīš* X occurs in *The Descent of Ishtar to the Underworld*.[55] Ishtar, goddess of fertility, descends to the underworld in hopes of extending her power. But, like all who enter the domain of Ereshkigal, queen of the netherworld, Ishtar dies. The resulting lack of fertility on earth[56] prompts the god Ea to craft a ploy for resurrecting Ishtar. Ea creates a special being, neither male nor female, who can descend to the netherworld without dying. Ea, furthermore, instructs this unique being to elicit an oath of hospitality from Ereshkigal:

---

51   According to *CAD*, there are seventeen instances of this authenticating element with šarrum ("*nīšu* A," *CAD* 11.2:292-4).

52   "*nīšu* A," *CAD* 11.2:292-4. On occasion, proper names are used in this phrase.

53   Ibid., 83-84.

54   Tadmor, , 127-52. On page 134 he writes: "we are entitled to conclude that in Assyria as well as in the lands west of the Euphrates, the imprecation element of the treaty-oath played a major role, whereas in Babylonia, so it seems, curses were not invoked. There, an oath sworn by the life of the gods, although followed by certain symbolic actions, was sufficient to guarantee the implementation of the treaty."

55   "The Descent of Ishtar to the Underworld," translated by Stephanie Dalley (*COS* 1.108:381-4). This myth likely finds its origin in an earlier Sumerian text called *The Descent of Inanna*, but it is attested in the Late Bronze age in both Assyria and Babylonia.

56   "The Descent of Ishtar to the Underworld," (*COS* 1.108:381-4), lines 76-80.

Ereškigal līmurkama ina pānika liḫdu
Ereshkigal shall look at you and be glad to see you

ultu libbaša inuḫḫu kabtassa ippereddû
When she is relaxed, her mood will lighten.

tummēšima nīš ilāni rabûti
Get her to swear the oath by the great gods.[57]

"[T]he motif used here is well known from folktales where the hero, having obtained the promise that one wish of his would be granted, asks for the only thing that he is not supposed to ask for,"[58] explains Erica Reiner. The messenger successfully deceives Ereshkigal, receives Ishtar's body and she is summarily revived, restoring fertility.

This is, at present, the only instance that indicates a deity can swear using the *nīš X* authenticating element, so one must proceed cautiously. Be that as it may, the text indicates that Ereshkigal invoked the life of the great gods in order to authenticate her oath. The precise phrasing of it remains uncertain since it is only implied in the text. One indication that the text implies some form of *nīš X* is its departure from the Sumerian *Descent of Inanna* at this point, which indicates the precious entities of heaven and earth were invoked.[59] Given the tendency in *The Descent of Ishtar to the Underworld* to follow the *Descent of Inanna*, the divergence is significant. Recalling the Neo-Babylonian preference for *nīš X*, the departure suggests an effort to update the text with material more familiar to a Babylonian audience.

Exemplary for human use of the *nīš X* authenticating element is the text of the Bavian Rock inscription detailing Sennacherib's (705-681 B.C.E.) military and building accomplishments:[60]

---

57 "The Descent of Ishtar to the Underworld," (*COS* 1.108:381-4), lines 95-7. The transliteration is taken from Anne D. Kilmer, "How Was Queen Ereshkigal Tricked? a New Interpretation of the Descent of Ishtar," *UF* 3 (1971): 303. In light of Conklin's detailed study of the formula *nīš X* in Akkadian (Conklin, *Oath Formulas*, 85-87), I would propose translating line 97 as, "Get her to swear by the life of the great gods."

58 Erica Reiner, *Your Thwarts in Pieces, Your Mooring Rope Cut: Poetry from Babylonia and Assyria* (Michigan Studies in the Humanities 5; Ann Arbor, Mich.: Horace H. Rackham School of Graduate Studies at the University of Michigan, 1985), 43.

59 S. N. Kramer, *The Sacred Marriage Rite: Aspects of Faith, Myth, and Ritual in Ancient Sumer* (Bloomington, Ind.: Indiana University Press, 1969), 116.

60 Cogan dates the inscription to ca. 689 B.C.E ("Sennacherib: The Capture and Destruction of Babylon," translated by M. Cogan [*COS* 2.119E:305]).

among the kings my sons, whoever reflects... and cannot bring himself to believe that with these few people I had dug that canal:— *by the life of Assur my god,*[61] if with these men I did not dig that canal, and in a year not complete its construction, then [its construction] was not finished [nor] its excavation brought to completion.[62]

Sennacherib's attempt to secure credit for his accomplishments is only one of the ways humans use this authenticating element. A Babylonian marriage agreement, precisely dated to 564 B.C.E., reads: "They swore[63] by the life of Nabû and Marduk their gods,[64] and by the life of Nebuchadnezzar, the king, their lord, not to contravene (this agreement)."[65] Evidence of wide and varied use of the *nīš X* authenticating element underscores its prominence in the Neo-Babylonian period.

Finally, it is necessary to note that there is a symbolic gesture related to the *nīš X* authenticating element, namely touching the throat. In *Enūma Eliš* (Tablet VI, lines 95-100), Marduk is enthroned as king of the gods: "They made Marduk's destiny highest, they prostrated themselves. They laid upon themselves a curse (if they broke the oath), with water and oil they swore,[66] they touched their throats."[67] Foster calls this "[a] symbolic gesture meaning that they may die if they break the oath."[68] Paul Hoskisson demonstrated that there is a connection between the gesture and the corresponding authenticating element at Mari, and he argues it was also used in the Old Babylonian empire based on several pieces of correspondence.[69] This evidence will be in-

---

61 Here I follow Conklin's translation of the Akkadian text "*ni-iš ᵈAššur DINGIR-ia*" as "(by) the life of Ashur my god..." (Conklin, *Oath Formulas*, 85).

62 Translation by Daniel David Luckenbill, *The Annals of Sennacherib* (OIP 2; Chicago: The University of Chicago Press, 1924), 80-81, except for the italicized portion which follows Conklin's findings on the *nīš X* authenticating element. Luckenbill's classic work has been reviewed and updated by Eckhart Frahm, *Einleitung in die Sanherib-Inschriften* (AfO 26; Vienna: Oriental Institute University of Vienna, 1997), 151-54; in this section, Frahm offers no correction to Luckenbill's earlier work.

63 The verb is *tamû* (Martha T. Roth, *Babylonian Marriage Agreements 7th – 3rd Centuries B.C.* [AOAT 222; Neukirchen-Vluyn: Neukirchener Verlag, 1989], 48).

64 I follow Roth's (Ibid.), excepting the phrases "niš ᵈAG u ᵈAMAR+UD DINGIR.MEŠ-šú-nu" and "niš ᵈAG-NIG₂.DU-URU₃" which I render as "by the life of X.".

65 Ibid., 47-48.

66 The verb is *tamû* (Conklin, *Oath Formulas*, 84).

67 Foster, *Muses*, 436-86. For other instances, see the entry for "*lapātu*" in *CAD* 9:82-5.

68 Foster, *Muses*, 472.

69 Paul Hoskisson, "The *Nīšum* 'Oath' in Mari," in *Mari in Retrospect: Fifty Years of Mari and Mari Studies* (ed. Gordon D. Young; Winona Lake, Ind.: Eisenbrauns, 1992), 203-10.

structive at a later stage in the argument (ch. 5), but for now it is sufficient to note that the Hebrew Bible lacks any corresponding evidence
for this gesture accompanying an oath.

(c) *NĪŠ DINGIR^{LIM}* — "By the Life of the Thousand Gods"

The tablets discovered in the ancient Hittite capital (modern Bog-
hazköy) are best known to biblical scholars because of the numerous
treaties they include. Those texts also indicate the Hittites were fond of
ritualistic ceremonies, often sacrificing animals or employing wax fig-
urines in symbolic actions. Hittite texts include the noun *lingai*,
meaning "oath," and its related verbal form based on the root *link–* to
describe Hittite practice.[70] Characteristic of Hittite, *lingai* is often
written with Akkadograms, in this case two different ones: *NĪŠ* and
MĀMĪTU.[71] The Akkadogram *MĀMĪTU*, which appears in at least sixteen texts,[72] is not an authenticating element but a general term for a
sworn agreement, so it will not be discussed in detail. *NĪŠ*, however,
appears in two combinations with unmistakable similarities to the
Akkadian formula *nīš ilāni*:[73] *NĪŠ DINGIR^{LIM}* and *NĪŠ DINGIR.MEŠ*.
The Chicago Hittite Dictionary summarizes the distinction in meaning:

---

70 Hans Gustav Güterbock and Harry A. Hoffner, eds. *The Hittite Dictionary of the Ori-*
    ental Institute of the University of Chicago (6 vols. Chicago: The Oriental Institute of the
    University of Chicago, 1980), L–N: 62-69.

71 *"lingai-" CHD* L–N:64. Although the *CHD* evidence on the verbal form is not ex-
    haustive, it does not indicate the verbal form is written with Akkadograms, only syl-
    labically (Ibid., 69-71). Furthermore, there is no extant Hittite text recording a deity
    swearing with this form.

    For examples of the verbal form see *CHD* (Ibid.). An illustrative text, *Indictment of*
    Madduwatta by Amuwanda I of Hatti, can be found in Gary M. Beckman and Harry A.
    Hoffner, *Hittite Diplomatic Texts* (2nd ed. Atlanta, Ga.: Society of Biblical Literature,
    1999), 153-60; critical edition is Albrecht Götze, *Madduwattaš* (Leipzig: J.C. Hinrichs,
    1928).

72 CTH 61.II.10, 62.II, 66, 123, 126, 212, 255, 316, 401.II, 420, 569, 570, 584, 585, 782; KUB
    18.28; KBo 13.131.

73 Oettinger makes this point also: "Ab mittelheth. Zeit erscheint dann *NI-IŠ DINGIR^{LIM}*,
    wofür KUB XIV 1 und KUB XXIII 72 zu vergleichen sind. Auch dieses Nebeneinan-
    der hat im Akkadischen seine Entsprechung, wo allerdings der Wechsel von Sg. *nīš*
    ilim zu Pl. *nīš ilī* bzw. *nīš ilāni* (s. AHW a.a.O.) funktional begründet ist" (Norbert
    Oettinger, *Die Militärischen Eide der Hethiter* [Studien zu den Bogazköy-Texten 22;
    Wiesbaden: Harrassowitz, 1976], 28, note 27). Cf. Johann Tischler, *Hethitisches Hand-*
    wörterbuch (Innsbrucker Beiträge zur Sprachwissenschaft 102; Innsbruck: Institute
    for Language and Literature and the University of Innsbruck, 2001), 287, who makes
    the connection with Akkadian *nêšu*.

even in the NH or in pre-NH/NS careful scribes tended to distinguish between *NĪŠ DINGIR^LIM* (for syll. *lingain/lingauš*, the oath as object of the verb
šarra-) from *NĪŠ DINGIR.MEŠ* (for syll. *linkiyanteš* or *linkiyaš šiuneš*, the
oath deities as agents)... When NH scribes began to abandon the distinction, *NĪŠ DINGIR.MEŠ* was used for both...[74]

Thus, *NĪŠ DINGIR^LIM* is usually glossed "oath of the gods" and *NĪŠ
DINGIR.MEŠ* is commonly glossed "gods of the oath."[75]

The *Treaty between Muwattalli of Hatti and Alaksandu of Wilusa* (CTH
76)[76] highlights the critical distinction between these two phrases. The
treaty contains seven instances of *NĪŠ DINGIR.MEŠ*[77] and six appearances of *NĪŠ DINGIR^LIM*.[78] The phrase *NĪŠ DINGIR.MEŠ* reflects that
the Hittites believed their gods would visit punishment upon anyone
violating an oath:

> If someone speaks an evil word concerning My Majesty before you, Alak-
> sandu, and you conceal it from My Majesty, and act rashly and commit
> some evil against My Majesty, then you, Alaksandu, will have offended be-
> fore the oath gods (*NĪŠ DINGIR.MEŠ*). The oath gods (*NĪŠ DINGIR.MEŠ*)
> shall pursue you unrelentingly.[79]

NĪŠ DINGIR^LIM occurs at the end of a list of stipulations as part of the
phrase "this too shall be placed under oath (*ŠAPAL NĪŠ DINGIR^LIM*)."[80]
The final two instances come in the long section invoking the divine
witnesses to the treaty, which includes "the Moon-god, Lord of the

---

74   "*lingai-*" *CHD* L–N:64-9.

75   An unnamed treaty from the pre-empire period (CTH 28) contains this use of *NĪŠ
     DINGIR^LIM*, giving a *terminus a quo* for this use of Akkadian terminology to at least the
     middle of the second millennium B.C.E. See Heinrich Otten, "Ein hethitischer Vertrag
     aus dem 15./14. Jahrhundert v. Chr. (KBo XVI 47)," *Istanbuler Mitteilungen* 17 (1967):
     57, for this text.

76   This text dates to approximately 1300 B.C.E. and closely follows the well-known
     Hittite vassal treaty form. For a brief overview, see Beckman and Hoffner, *Hittite
     Diplomatic Texts*, 2-4.

77   In Friedrich's transcription these come at the following locations: §9, 56; §13, 2
     (twice); §16, 30 (twice); §17, 56, 60; §18, 61, 72 (Johannes Friedrich, *Staatsverträge des
     Ḫatti-Reiches in hethitischer Sprache* [Leipzig: J.C. Hinrichs'sche, 1930], 50-83). See
     Beckman and Hoffner, *Hittite Diplomatic Texts*, 87-95, for a translation of this text.

78   In Friedrich's transcription these come at the following locations: §17, 55, 59; §18, 61,
     72; §20, 12, 14.

79   Translation is by Beckman (Ibid., 90, §13). The transcription is taken from Friedrich,
     Staatsverträge, 70, §16, line 30.

80   In Friedrich's edition, these occur at: §17, lines 55, 59; §18, lines 61, 72 (Ibid., 74-77).

Oath (*SIN EN NĪŠ DINGIR^LIM*)"[81] and "Ishhara, Queen of the Oath (*IŠḤARA SAL.LUGAL NĪŠ DINGIR^LIM*)."[82] Thus, it is clear the two phrases fill different purposes: *NĪŠ DINGIR.MEŠ* refers to the multiplicity of gods that would pursue an oath violator and visit punishment upon them; *NĪŠ DINGIR^LIM* indicates the precious entity invoked to authenticate the oath. The *Indictment of Madduwatta by Amuwanda I of Hatti* (CTH 147) further clarifies this distinction. This text includes no less than seven instances of *NĪŠ DINGIR^LIM*,[83] for instance in section 8:

> The father of My Majesty [gave] you the land of Mount Zippasla to occupy. Then he made you swear an oath,[84] and placed the following under [oath] (*ŠAPAL NĪŠ DINGIR^LIM*) for you: I have now given you the land [of Mount] Zippasla, [so] occupy [it alone]. You shall not occupy another land or [another] river valley in addition [on your own authority].[85]

Here, the Hittite verb of swearing is used with *ŠAPAL NĪŠ DINGIR^LIM* as its object, which is directly analogous to how the Akkadian verbs to swear (*tamû*) and to declare (*zakāru*) employ *nīš ilāni* as their object. This corresponding syntax implies that the phrase *NĪŠ DINGIR^LIM* plays the equivalent role, specifying the precious entity by which the oath is authenticated: the life of the god or gods. Indeed, given the use of *DINGIR^LIM* one might conclude that it is the life of the thousand gods of Hatti that are invoked.[86]

---

81 Translation from Beckman and Hoffner, *Hittite Diplomatic Texts*, 92; transcription from Friedrich, *Staatsverträge*, 78.

82 Translation from Beckman and Hoffner, *Hittite Diplomatic Texts*, 92; transcription from Friedrich, *Staatsverträge*, 78.

83 Götze, *Madduwattaš*.: §5, 27; §6, 28; §8, 43; §21, 15; §27, 44; §28, 48; §31, 63. Götze also proposes this same form in his reconstruction of the broken text at §9, 51, which is certainly possible. But, given the context—"gegen den Göttereid [gefrevelt] hatten"—one would expect *NĪŠ DINGIR.MEŠ* and not *NIŠ DINGIR^LIM* in this instance.

84 This is the verb of swearing *link-* (here as *li-in-ga-nu-ut*), which is from the same root as *lingai* (Ibid., 10); see "*link-, linka-?*" *CHD* L–N:62-4, for further details.

85 Translation from Beckman and Hoffner, *Hittite Diplomatic Texts*, 155-56. Transcription from Götze, *Madduwattaš*., 10.

86 Charles Burney, *Historical Dictionary of the Hittites* (Historical Dictionaries of Ancient Civilizations and Historical Eras 14; Lanham, Md.: Scarecrow Press, 2004), 223-24.

The *Treaty between Hattusili III of Hatti and Ulmi-Teshshup of Tarhun-tassa*[87] (CTH 106),[88] demonstrates that this practice was not merely an international accommodation but became an internal Hittite custom. This text concerns Hattusili's dominion over southern Anatolia after he had usurped the Great Kingship of Hatti from Uhri-Teshshup.[89] Beckman observes that Ulmi-Teshshup was "ruler of an appanage kingdom in Tarhuntassa. As head of a parallel, if junior, line of the Hitite royal family... [he] was preceded in rank only by the Great King of Hatti himself, and by the latter's heir apparent."[90] Because this text treats an intra-Hittite matter one would anticipate it to use the native Hittite language.[91] Nevertheless, the Akkadogram *NĪŠ DINGIR^{LIM}* appears in section 12:

> If My Majesty requests a city or some locality from Ulmi-Teshshup, he must give it to him with good grace. It is not a matter for coercion. This shall be exempted from the oath (*NĪŠ DINGIR^{LIM}*). Or if Ulmi-Teshshup requests something from My Majesty, My Majesty will give it to him. This shall also be exempted from the oath (*NĪŠ DINGIR^{LIM}*).[92]

By referring specifically to items left out of the solemn agreement, this section underscores that the sworn stipulations are specifically those things guaranteed by *NĪŠ DINGIR^{LIM}*, the life of the gods.

Additional evidence comes from the *Treaty between Hattusili III of Hatti and Ramses II of Egypt* (CTH 91). The Hittite copy of this treaty, written in Akkadian, and the Egyptian copy are both still extant. When placed side-by-side, the texts make explicit the connection between *NĪŠ DINGIR^{LIM}* and the Akkadian *nīš ilāni*:

---

87 Tarhuntassa is also known as Kurunta (Beckman and Hoffner, *Hittite Diplomatic Texts*, 107-08).

88 This text can be dated to ca. 1250 B.C.E.

89 Ibid., 107.

90 Ibid.

91 Throughout this document *NĪŠ DINGIR.MEŠ* refers to the "oath gods," as Beckman translates. For example, "If he (His Majesty) does not wish to give some city or some locality to Ulmi-Teshshup, and the latter exerts himself and takes it by force, then these oath gods (*NĪŠ DINGIR.MEŠ*) shall eradicate him from the Dark Earth, together with his progeny" (Ibid., 113, §13). See also §10, 11 of the treaty for this usage.

92 Ibid., §12.

Hittite Text	Egyptian Text	Translation
^{d}XXX bēl nīš ilim	n<ỉ> -ntrw nbw ʿnḫ	the moon god, lord of the oath
^{d}ereš.ki.gal	t3-ntrt t3-hnwt p3-jwtn	Ereškigal
{šarrat māmīti}	{t3-hnwt n {ʿnḫ}	queen of the oath
^{d}Išḫara šarrat nīš ilim	Išḫr^k t3-ḥnwt <n ʿnḫ>	Išḫara queen of the oath[93]

The relationship between the two phrases suggests that the Egyptians and Hittites used these authenticating elements in a similar fashion.

In light of the preceding evidence, it seems likely that oaths of both Hittite vassal treaties and domestic agreements were authenticated "by the life of the god(s)." Although those gods are never specified, the phrase NĪŠ DINGIR^{LIM} suggests that all of the "thousand gods of Hatti" are invoked.

(d) Verbs of Swearing

The second category of authenticating elements in Akkadian is verbs of swearing. Two verbs fill this role: tamû and zakāru. The first verb, tamû, means specifically "to swear;"[94] the second verb, zakāru, is more general term connoting "to declare."[95] These two verbs typically occur in a narrative or discursive context, rather than in the actual pronouncement of an oath, though they do both fill the latter role. Tamû, in particular, occurs in two pertinent examples where deities swear.

The first example is in the Babylonian flood story Atra-ḫasīs; the same material recurs in Tablet XI of The Babylonian Gilgamesh Epic. In Atra-ḫasīs, the longer and more detailed of the two stories, Enlil determines to destroy humanity because their noise makes it impossible for him to sleep. After failing twice, Enlil convenes the divine counsel in order to take sweeping action:

93 Elmar Edel, Der Vertrag zwischen Ramses II. von Ägyten und Ḫattušili III. von Ḫatti (Wissenschaftliche Veröffentlichung der Deutschen Orient-Gesellschaft 95; Berlin: Gebr. Mann, 1997), 70-73; Edel assumes the unreadable text is Sin, the moon god.

94 "tamû" CAD 18:159-68. This verb has a cognate noun, māmītu, which can mean either oath or curse. In some cases where it means curse, māmītu is the personified demon of the oath who pursues those who do not show fidelity to the oath ("māmītu" CAD 10:189-95).

95 "zakāru" CAD XXI:16-20.

[a]l-ka-ni ka-la-ni a-na ma-mi-tú a-bu-bi
"Come, all of us, and take an oath to bring a flood."

ᵈa-nam i-na pa-ni ⌜ta⌝-mu-ni
Anu swore first,

ᵈen-líl it-ta-mi māréᵐᵉˢ-šú it-ti-šú ta-mu-ni
Enlil swore, his son swore with him...[96]

However, Enki, the crafty god who controls the watery regions below the earth, informs Atra-ḫasīs of the plan and instructs him to build a reed boat in order to survive the flood. When Enlil realizes Atra-ḫasīs has survived the flood as a result of Enki's actions, he is filled with anger and declares: "All we great Anunnaki decided together on an oath.[97] Where did life escape? How did man survive in the destruction?"[98] The parallel text in *The Babylonian Gilgamesh Epic* has Enlil swear (*tamû*) to bring the flood (Tablet XI, line15), but does not include the second recollection of the oath indicting Ea. The second example appears in *Erra and Ishum*,[99] Tablet III:

ᵈen-líl ù⌐-a [iq-ta]bi lìb-ba-šú iṣ-ṣa-bat
Ellil has cried "woe!" and clutched at his heart.

[i-n]a! ⌜šub⌝-ti-[šú ....]
[He has risen up from] his dwelling.

[ar-rat l]a nap-[šu-ri iš-ša-kin ina pi-i-šú]
An irredeemable curse is set in his mouth,

[it-m]a-ma šá n[āri ul i-šat-ti mêᵐᵉˢ-šá]
He has sworn not to drink the river's waters

---

96 x rev ii 46-8 in W.G. Lambert and A.R. Millard, *Atra-Ḫasis: The Babylonian Story of the Flood* (Oxford: Clarendon Press, 1969), 120-21; cf. Foster, *Muses*, 267.

97 The term here is *māmītu*.

98 Tablet III, column vi 7-10; Lambert and Millard, *Atra-Ḫasis: The Babylonian Story of the Flood*, 100-1).

99 Dalley proposes an eighth-century B.C.E. date for composition of the extant version and suggests the reign of Nabonassar or Merodach-Baladan II as its backdrop. The dating is strongly supported by the identification of the scribe, Kabti-ilani-Marduk of the Dabibi clan, whose family is first attested around 765 B.C.E. (Dalley, *Myths from Mesopotamia*, 282-84).

dāmē^{meš}-šú-nu i^{!}(=E)-d

He shuns their blood

[ur^{!}-ma ul ir-ru-ub ana]^{!} [é-kur]^{??}
and will not enter into Ekur.[100]

This text also records a deity swearing using the verb *tamû*, but it too lacks an authenticating element. This example is especially suggestive of the milieu in which Ezekiel was written, a point demonstrated in Daniel Bodi's persuasive argument that the book of Ezekiel knows *Erra and Ishum* and mirrors some of its beliefs about the results of divine absence.[101]

(e) The *adê* Loyalty Oath

The *adê* loyalty oaths were a pivotal tool in the administration of the Neo-Assyrian and Neo-Babylonian empires, part of what makes them well-known and debated texts.[102] Mario Liverani summarizes their role: "It is by now clear that the term is wide enough to designate a variety of legal and political conditions, including both proper vassal-treaties... as well as loyalty oaths sworn on special occasions such as the succession to the Assyrian throne."[103]

---

100 *Erra and Ishum*, Tablet III. Transliteration by Luigi Cagni, *L'Epopea di Erra* (Studi Semitici 34; Rome: Institute for the Study of the Near East, 1969), 96; translation by Dalley, *Myths from Mesopotamia*, 300; cf. Foster, *Muses*, 898.

101 See Bodi, *Ezekiel and the Poem of Erra* for a thorough analysis of the correlation. Of further interest, Foster notes: "While some of the narrative is in the third person, in one long passage... Erra narrates his own actions. This represents, in modern critical terms, an attempt to fuse narrative and narrated, discourse and event" (Foster, *Muses*, 880). This "fusion" is striking when considered against the book of Ezekiel which draws on the first person accounts of the prophet and the first person speeches of YHWH to fashion a similar profile.

102 The term derives from Gelb's assessment of the texts. He writes: "What the *adê* texts are concerned with mainly are matters of loyalty by the obligated person or persons to a sovereign party. Both the *riksu* and *rikiltu* and *adê* texts are sworn documents, but while the oath plays a secondary and supplementary role in the former texts, it plays a primary and paramount role in the latter. This is what we might call a 'loyalty oath' in modern parlance. The interpretation which I would like to propose for the *adê* texts in general is that they represent sworn pacts of loyalty imposed by a sovereign party upon one or more subordinate parties" (I.J. Gelb, review of D.J. Wiseman, *The Vassal Treaties of Esarhaddon*, BO 19 [1962]: 162).

103 Mario Liverani, "The Medes At Esarhaddon's Court," *JCS* 47 (1995): 58. In fact, Liverani argues persuasively that the text famously known as The Vassal Treaties of

In this study, it is important to stress that *adê* is not an authenticating element for an oath. Tadmor remarks that "*adê* is almost synonymous with *māmītu*,"[104] appears in the construction "oath of the king (*adê ša šarri*)," and refers either to treaties or loyalty oaths in narrative contexts. The *adê* texts focus on the curses for breaking the agreements rather than the swearing of the oath. This is part of the evidence upon which Tadmor supports his distinction between Assyrian and Babylonian tendencies in swearing oaths. One might add to it that when *adê* texts do actually address oaths, they typically employ the verb *tamû*.[105]

There is, nevertheless, evidence in two inscriptions of Esarhaddon to indicate that the *nīš X* authenticating element was the authenticating element used to swear an *adê* loyalty oath. An inscription from Nineveh, which records Esarhaddon's accession to the throne and his campaign against Ḫanigalbat, includes the intriguing phrase "*adê nīš ilâni rabûti*."[106] This "treaty by the life of the great gods" points towards the lives of a group of gods as the precious entities by which the agreement is authenticated.

A second inscription, entitled *Esarhaddon's Treaty Inscription*, supports this reading.[107] A. K. Grayson argues that text represents "a fragment of a treaty which may have been the agreement imposed by Esarhaddon on the citizens of Sippar early in 672 B.C. to respect the right to succession of Ashurbanipal and Shamash-shuma-ukin."[108] Near the end of column I, the inscription specifies that "[Esarhaddon]

Esarhaddon is actually a domestic loyalty oath between the King of Assyria and his Median palace guards and not an international suzerain-vassal treaty.

104 Tadmor, "Treaty and Oath," 142.

105 For instance, see the "Treaty of Assur-Nerrari V" (Simo Parpola and Kazuko Watanabe, *Neo-Assyrian Treaties and Loyalty Oaths* [State Archives of Assyria 2; Helsinki: Helsinki University Press, 1988], 13) and "Esarhaddon's Succession Treaty" §3, line 25ff (Ibid., 30; Kazuko Watanabe, *Der adê-Vereidigung anlässlich der Thronfolgeregelung Asarhaddons* [Baghdader Mitteilungen 3; Berlin: Gebr. Mann Verlag, 1987], 144-45). In total, there are 12 uses of *tamû* in the *SAA* collection of *adê* documents.

106 Riekele Borger, *Die Inschriften Asarhaddons, Königs von Assyrien* (AfO 9; Graz: Im Selbstverlage des Herausgebers, 1956), 44. Borger translates the relevant text as, "Der Assyrer, die mir bei den grossen Göttern Treue geschworen hatten, kamen mir entgegen und küssten meine Füsse." He further notes on this phrase that MU, the logogram which *nīš* and *šum* share is here specifically not to be read as *šum*, further evidence for interpreting the *nīš X* authenticating element as "by the life of X."

107 A. K. Grayson, "Akkadian Treaties of the Seventh Century B.C," *JCS* 39 (1987): 135-38. Parpola and Watanabe are able to join Grayson's fragments with others to expand the text (SAA 2 14; cf. the explanation in the notes on the treaty corpus at page L), though it remains fragmentary with many lacunae.

108 Ibid., 135.

made all of the [people] take an oath by the life of the gods (*ina nīš DINGIR.MEŠ*)."[109] The broken lines that follow at the end of column I and the beginning of column II list the deities invoked in a series of five statements of the form "*ina nīš DN*,"[110] that is "by the life of DN." This also indicates that the *adê* loyalty oaths were authenticated by invoking the life of the god(s).

Thus, while it remains possible that other authenticating elements were employed in the *adê* loyalty oaths, these inscriptions are ample evidence to conclude that the *nīš X* authenticating element did play this role. This finding offers new and important context for interpreting Ezek 17, a text that concerns a loyalty oath sworn by Zedekiah, king of Judah, to Nebuchadnezzar, king of Babylon.[111]

4. The Divine Oath in Ugaritic Texts

The finds from the ancient city of Ugarit and its surrounding areas have provided an ever growing understanding of life and belief in this important ancient city. Indeed, the texts which have emerged from there are some of the most helpful pieces available for understanding ancient West Semitic language, belief, and religious practice and are a tremendous resource for comparative study with the Hebrew Bible.

(a) The Ugaritic Authenticating Element *ḥy npš*

The large corpus of extant Ugaritic texts yields only one Ugaritic authenticating element: *ḥy npš*.[112] This phrase is attested in three Ugaritic texts. First, there is a personal letter entitled *ʾAbniya isn't Happy* (RS 94.2284).[113] In this letter, ʾAbniya declares to ʾUrtētub:

---

109 Ibid., 137.

110 Grayson: Col I 13′, 14′, 17′, 18′; Col II 1′, 2′ (Ibid., 136); cf. SAA 2 14:I.26′, 28′, 31′, 32′ and 14:II.1′, 2′.

111 See ch. 6, §2 for the discussion of Ezek 17.

112 Conklin, *Oath Formulas*, 79-80, discusses the evidence. However, Conklin goes too far when he states RS 94.2284 is the only spoken oath attested in Ugaritic.

113 "*ʾAbniya isn't Happy*," translated by Dennis Pardee (*COS* 3.45 LL:113-4).

ḥnpšk . wḥn[pšy?]   (By) your life and (by) [my li]fe
hm ᵓyṯ d ytn l[y]   if there was (anyone) who gave (anything)
                              to me, (may I be cursed)[114]

Conklin comments on this text that "[w]hile the combination *ḥy npš* is
not attested in any of the biblical oaths, it is difficult to suggest another
alternative here... In all other respects this single oath conforms closely
to what we have found in Classical Hebrew."[115]

The second text confirms this connection. In a draft of a letter between the king of Ugarit and the Egyptian Pharaoh (RS 16.117)[116] there
are details of an exchange between messengers in which the Ugaritic
king's desires to send "blessings for the life of Pharaoh."[117]

(17) *mlk . r[b] . p . l .*	Great King, be well(?)![118]
(18) *ḥy . np[š? a?]rš*	By my life,[119] I send greetings
(19) *l . pn. bʿ[l] ṣpn(?) . bʿly*	from before Baal Zaphon (to) my lord
(20) *w. urk. ym. bʿly*	and long days (for) my lord
(21) *l . pn . amn. w . l . pn*	before Amon and before
(22) *il . mṣrm . dt . tǵrn*	the gods of Egypt who may protect
(23) *npš . špš . mlk .*	the life of the sun, the Great King,
(24) *rb . bʿly*	my lord.[120]

---

114 Ibid., 79. In Pardee's earlier translation of the text he gives this portion as follows:
     "As you live, and as do [I], (I swear that) nobody gave [me (any)] and my heart is
     very sick [...]" ("*ᵓAbniya isn't Happy*," *COS* 3.45 LL:113-4).

115 Ibid., 79-80 notes 1 Kgs 18:10 as the nearest biblical text to this Ugaritic example.

116 This text corresponds to PRU II 18 (Charles Virolleaud and Claude F-A Schaeffer, *Le
     palais royal d'Ugarit* [Mission de Ras Shamra 7; Paris: Imprimerie Nationale, 1957],
     33-34) and UT 1018 (Cyrus H. Gordon, *Ugaritic Textbook: Grammar, Texts in Translit-
     eration, Cuneiform Selections, Glossary, Indices* [AnOr 38; Rome: Pontifical Biblical In-
     stitute, 1998], 219).

117 Itamar Singer, "A Political History of Ugarit," in *Handbook of Ugaritic Studies* (eds.
     Wilfred G.E. Watson and Nicolas Wyatt; Handbuch der Orientalistik, nahe und der
     mittlere Osten 39; Leiden: Brill, 1999), 713. The identification of the precise king and
     Pharaoh are debatable; Singer argues for Ammurapi of Ugarit and Merneptah in
     Egypt (the thirteenth-century B.C.E.) though others have dated it to the Amarna age.

118 Based upon Virolleaud's proposal, "Eh bien!" (Virolleaud and Schaeffer, *Le palais
     royal d'Ugarit*, 34).

119 Alternately, "as I live." See Pardee's translation of "*ᵓAbniya isn't Happy*" where he
     construes this phrase in this way. However, in "Part of a Letter Addressed to the
     King of Egypt," translated by Dennis Pardee (*COS* 3.45N:99-100), the phrase is trans-
     lated as "[I add]ress requests for [his] lif[e]..."

120 Transliteration from Gordon, *Ugaritic Textbook*, 219. This translation is mine; cf. Vi-
     rolleaud and Schaeffer, *Le palais royal d'Ugarit*, 33-34, Gordon, *Ugaritic Textbook*, 219,

Although it is speculative, the Ugaritic *ḥy npš* authenticating element may be meant to evoke the Egyptian "as DN/RN lives for me" authenticating element. Itamar Singer suggests this draft would be translated into Akkadian and then sent,[121] with the likely translation mirroring RS 8.333, a letter from the King of Carchemish to the King of Ugarit dating from the same era:[122]

na-na-a na[p-]ša-ta ša šarri li-it-ma-a-mi
Nana should swear (by) the life of the king

This text follows the typical use of the Akkadian *nīš X* authenticating element, here invoking the King's life.[123] Conklin notes that the text uses *napšata*, a less common Akkadian term than *nīšu*, but the closest cognate to the Ugaritic *npš*. All this points to an equivalence between Akkadian *nīš X* and Ugaritic *ḥy npš* and indicates the self-referential, life-invoking authenticating element found in Egypt, Babylonia, and Ugarit are conceptual equals. The cognate form and similar usage of the Hebrew phrase אני חי justifies including it in this group too.

A third and final example from *The Story of Aqhat* (KTU 1.17-19) adds texture to the comparison. Nicolas Wyatt observes that the traditional tale, whose central characters are Danel and his son Aqhat, deals with the "theme of childlessness (in this case, perhaps, specifically sonlessness…)."[124] He summarizes the action which precedes the oath:

Danel has no son and so performs devotions to obtain divine assistance. For six days he sacrifices to the gods, apparently spending every night in the temple. On the seventh day Baal intercedes for him, asking El to provide a son who will perform all the filial duties necessary for a father to be blessed. El blesses Danel and promises a son.[125]

---

and Otto Eissfeldt, "The Alphabetical Cuneiform Texts From Ras Shamra Published in 'Le palais royal d'Ugarit,' Vol. II, 1957," *JSS* 5 (1960): 9.

121 Singer, "Political History," 713. Indeed, that the letter would be sent in Akkadian seems natural based upon the evidence of the El-Amarna letters.

122 The letter has been dated to the reign of Amiṯṯamru II in the mid-thirteenth century B.C.E. (Conklin, *Oath Formulas*, 80).

123 The selection of *napšata* where *nīš* is expected eliminates any lingering uncertainty that the Akkadian formula *nīš X* invokes the life of a deity or king.

124 Nicolas Wyatt, *Religious Texts from Ugarit* (Biblical Seminar 53; 2nd ed. London: Sheffield Academic Press, 2002), 246-47.

125 Nicolas Wyatt, "The Ugaritic Poem of Aqht: Text, Translation, Commentary," in *Handbook of Ugaritic Studies* (eds. Wilfred G.E. Watson and Nicolas Wyatt; Handbuch der Orientalistik, nahe und der mittlere Osten 39; Leiden: Brill, 1999), 235-36.

This promise is where the relevant oath occurs (KTU 1.17 i 34-43):

(34) [ks .]yiḫd . il . <bdh	Il took [the cup] ‹in his hand,
krpn . bm . ymn	the flagon in (his) right hand.
brkm . ybrk .> ˤbdh .	He blessed his› servant,
ybrk (35) [dni]l . mt . rpi .	he blessed [Daniʾi]l, the Rapiʾan,
ymr . ǵzr (36) [mt . h]rnmy .	he benefited the hero, the Harnamiyyan.
npš . yḫ . dnil (37) [mt . rp]i .	"By my life, may Daniʾil, [the Rapiʾ]an, live
brlt . ǵzr . mt . hrnmy	by my soul, the hero, the Harnamiyyan,
(38) [w? (.) r]ḫ? . ḫw . mḫ .	[and(?) by] my(?) [bre]ath, (that) is my(?) vitality!¹²⁶

In line thirty-six the author uses only *npš* and omits *ḥy*, in essence a
short form of the authenticating element;[127] the parallel, "by my soul"
(*brlt*), substantiates this translation. El's oath is decidedly reminiscent
of Yhwh's use of the "as I live" authenticating element in Ezekiel, a correspondence heightened by the many features shared by El and

---

126 Translation and transcription by David P. Wright, *Ritual in Narrative: The Dynamics of Feasting, Mourning, and Retaliation Rites in the Ugaritic Tale of Aqhat* (Winona Lake, Ind.: Eisenbrauns, 2001), 70.

A second oath is taken in Aqhat when Danel encourages his daughter, Pughat, to
find and kill Yatipan as revenge for his involvement in Aqhat's death. The text
closely corresponds to El's blessing of Danel (KTU 1.19 iv 35-39):

w yˤn . dn(36)il . mt . rpi .	Daniˤil, the Rapiˤan, answered:
npš . tḥ [.] pǵ[t] (37) tkmt . mym .	"By my life, may Pughat, who shoulders water, live,
ḥspt . l šˤr (38) tl .	who extracts dew from the fleece,
ydˤt [.] hlk . kbkbm	who knows the course of the stars!
[w(?) (.)] (39) npš . ḥy . mḫ	[And(?) by my(?)] life, (that) is my(?) vitality!

Once more, the author has written the oath with the shortened form, using only *npš*,
in line thirty-six. Thus, Danel takes the same oath in blessing his daughter which El
used in blessing him. Because of the repetition in the two passages, the final line
here (1.19 iv 39) provides some insight into the less clear final line from El's blessing
(1.17 i 38). Wright cogently argues for the reconstructed text cited above, which restores *rḥ* in 1.17 i 38 as a parallel to *npš* as attested in 1.19 iv 39. In each blessing,
those terms are expounded through a metaphorical understanding of the final word:
mḫ, literally meaning marrow, and expressed dynamically as vitality.

127 Wyatt, *Religious Texts*, 260-61, corroborates Wright's translation; Baruch Margalit offers "By-my-soul (I swear): Dan'el [the Rap]ian shall live (on), By-my-vitality, the Hero, the devotee of the 'Rainmaker' (shall endure)" (*The Ugaritic Poem of Aqht: Text, Translation, Commentary* [BZAW 182; Berlin: Walter de Gruyter, 1989]).

Y[HWH][128] and enhanced further by the links between Ugaritic Danel and Daniel who appears in the refrain of Ezek 14: "even if Noah, Daniel, and Job, these three, were in it, they would save only their own lives by their righteousness, says the Lord Y[HWH]."[129]

One notable difference in El's oath is its positive tone and its offer of blessing and not judgment. In this respect, El's oath is a departure from every other comparable text. This feature will be helpful for interpreting Isa 49:14-21 in due course. Despite this difference, the Ugaritic evidence agrees with the relevant Egyptian and Akkadian texts, showing the central role that the authenticating element that invoked the life of the gods played in ancient oaths.

5. Summary

The evidence surveyed in this chapter has demonstrated many similarities and differences between the broader ancient Near Eastern and biblical practices concerning oaths and, in particular, the divine oath. A brief summary of those similarities and differences is offered prior to mentioning the key implications of these observations.

(a) Similarities between the Ancient Near East and the Hebrew Bible

The evidence in the central concentric circle, comprised of divine oaths, shows that deities in Egypt, Mesopotamia, and Ugarit swear oaths. The context for these divine oaths is hostility between the divine and human realm, specifically mythological texts where one or more deities intends to destroy one or more humans. There is one departure from this profile: El swears to bless Danel with a son in the Ugaritic *Tale of Aqhat*. The judgment of humanity is the dominant theme of the ancient Near Eastern divine oath, but it is not the only one.

Although the divine oath is not always recorded in the texts, in both Egypt and Ugarit there is one recorded case of a deity swearing with a self-referential authenticating element that invokes their own

---

128 See Day, *Yahweh and the Gods and Goddesses of Canaan*, 13-41; for its presence in Ezekiel see pp. 26-32.

129 John Day, "The Daniel of Ugarit and Ezekiel and the Hero of the Book of Daniel," *VT* 30 (1980): 174-84, argues for this position. For the other option, see Daniel I. Block, *The Book of Ezekiel: Chapters 1–24* (NICOT; Grand Rapids, Mich.: Eerdmans, 1997), 447-49.

life. This closely parallels the biblical "as I live" authenticating element employed by YHWH. There is no corresponding divine oath documented in Akkadian, but *The Descent of Ishtar to the Underworld* implies that Ereshkigal invokes the life of the gods to authenticate an oath.

This form of the authenticating element also appears frequently in human oaths, the second concentric circle for comparison. Examples are extant in various genres, including myths, international treaties, domestic loyalty oaths, legal documents, and royal inscriptions.

More often than not the human swearing is a king. Perhaps this situation is predictable given both the strong similarities in divine and royal rhetoric and also the preponderance of texts found in royal precincts. These texts demonstrate that humans did swear by the life of their gods, and in exceptional text by their own life. This evidence largely parallels human use of the authenticating element חי יהוה, "by the life of YHWH" and demonstrates further continuity between the the Hebrew Bible and its ancient Near Eastern counterparts.

(b) Differences between the Ancient Near East and the Hebrew Bible

The first and most striking difference between the ancient Near Eastern and biblical material is the disparity in frequency with which the divine oath occurs. Investigation uncovered at most eight instances of deities swearing outside the Hebrew Bible.[130] By contrast, the book of Ezekiel alone has 16 occurrences of the divine oath with the "as I live" authenticating element. This collection of evidence gains another seven examples in the remainder of the Hebrew Bible. If one adds a conservative count of cases where YHWH employs verbs of swearing, another twenty-five examples are accumulated. This means the divine oath occurs approximately six times as often in the Hebrew Bible as compared to the rest of the ancient Near East combined. It remains possible that this disparity results from unintended textual selection; to be sure, the extant texts may not reflect the actual frequency of the formulae in ancient usage. However, the magnitude of the difference is conspicuous and underscores the prominent role the divine oath has in the book of Ezekiel.

---

130 (1) Re in the Egyptian *Destruction of Mankind*; (2) Hathor in the Egyptian *Destruction of Mankind*; (3) Falsehood in the Egyptian tale *Truth and Falsehood*; (4) Ereshkigal in the Akkadian *The Descent of Ishtar*; (5) Ereshkigal in the Sumerian *Descent of Innana*; (6) Enlil and the gods in the Akkadian *Atra-ḥasis Epic*; (7) Enlil and the gods in the Babylonian *Enūma Eliš*; (8) El in the Ugaritic *Tale of Aqhat*.

A second difference concerns the parties involved in the oaths. In Egypt, Re and Hathor's oaths are made amongst the gods and for the gods. The same is true of Ereshkigal's oath in the *Descent of Ishtar to the Underworld*. The *intra*-divine nature of the divine oath is most clear in *Enūma Eliš*, where Enlil's is furious because the gods have defied their sworn obligations to one another: "All we great Anunnaki decided together on an oath. Where did life escape? How did man survive in the destruction?"[131] The divine oath in the ancient Near East governs relationships between the gods.

Contrast that to Yhwh's oaths, which are made with humanity and govern the divine-human relationship. For example, there is the ubiquitous phrase "the land I [Yhwh] swore to your ancestors," which occurs five times in Deuteronomy alone.[132] This accords with a monolatrous attitude, a view prominent, if not dominant, in Israelite and Judahite thought and characteristic of both Ezekiel and the theological traditions with which it identifies.[133]

Finally, there is a notable absence of any evidence in either concentric circle for a parallel to the "lifted hand" formula that argues in favor of it being an authenticating element for swearing an oath. This issue, because of its importance and complexity, is treated in the following excursus.

---

131 Tablet III, column vi, lines 7-10 (Lambert and Millard, *Atra-Ḫasis*, 100-1).

132 Deut 1:35; 10:11; 31:21, 23; 34:4.

133 For more on this issue, see ch. 4, where the "as I live" authenticating element is demonstrated to be characteristic of the Dᴛʀ tradition, which is known for its monolatrous attitude; see, e.g., Juha Pakkala, *Intolerant Monolatry in the Deuteronomistic History* (Publications of the Finnish Exegetical Society 76; Göttingen: Vandenhoeck & Ruprecht, 1999); Nathan MacDonald, *Deuteronomy and the Meaning of 'Monotheism'* (FAT/II 1; 2nd ed. Tübingen: Mohr Siebeck, 2012).

Excursus One: The Lifted Hand Formula and Akkadian *našû-nadānu*

At this juncture it is necessary to explore in detail the absence of a parallel to the biblical hebrew idiom נשׂא יד as part of an oath in the extant ancient Near Eastern texts. Based on the strong evidence for a relationship between symbolic gestures and oral forms,[1] many have posited an association between the gesture of raising a hand and swearing an oath.[2] There is, without doubt, evidence to associate hand gestures with oath taking outside Israel and Judah. Hoskisson establishes a link between the phrase *lipit napištim* in Mari, where "they no doubt refer to touching or seizing the throat, and connote the seriousness of the commitment undertaken by reciting the oath,"[3] and the authenticating element *nīš ilāni*, "by the life of the god," found in Mesopotamia.[4] This practice appears far different from the biblical phrase נשׂא יד, "I lifted (my) hand," which offers no indication of being a symbolic gesture.[5]

---

1   See Meir Malul, *Studies in Mesopotamian Legal Symbolism* (AOAT 221; Kevelaer: Butzon & Bercker, 1988) for a discussion of the intertwining of the two ideas in Mesopotamian legal practices.

2   Ibid., 272-76; Pedersen, *Der Eid bei den Semiten*, 2; Mercer, *The Oath in Babylonian and Assyrian Literature*, 29, 42. The major commentators on Ezekiel are similar. Zimmerli, *Ezekiel 1–24*, 399, commenting on Ezek 20:5 (note c) accepts this viewpoint without discussion; Greenberg, *Ezekiel 1-20*, 363, agrees; Block, *Ezekiel 1–24*, 626, claims that "Yahweh bound himself by oath to the Israelites... The idiom derives from the hand gesture that accompanied ancient oath ceremonies; by metonomy the gesture refers to the oath itself."

3   Hoskisson, "*Nīšum*," 204.

4   Ibid., 204-10.

5   In the past, many scholars have proposed an etymological connection between Akkadian *nīšu* and Hebrew *nāśāʾ* to support this view. However, *nīšu*, like many Akkadian words, is a homonym. *Nīšu* A (oath, lit. life) shares a logogram with *nīšu* B (raising, lifting; *CAD* 11.2:290-6). Though homonyms, they derive from different roots: *nīšu* A from *nêšu* (to live) and *nīšu* B from *našû* (to lift). Scholars now agree that the etymological link is between Akkadian *našû* and Hebrew *nāśāʾ*, eliminating any connection with the *nīš* X authenticating element discussed at length here. Indeed, Akkadian *našû* does not appear connected to swearing or oaths in any fashion. For a full discussion of the etymological questions see Tikva Frymer-Kensky, "Suprarational Legal Procedures in Elam and Nuzi," in *Studies on the Civilizations and Culture of Nuzi and the Hurrians: In Honor of Ernest R. Lacheman on His Seventy-Fifth Birthday April 21, 1981* (eds. M.A. Morrison and D.I. Owen; Winona Lake, Ind.: Eisenbrauns, 1981), 120-21.

The lack of evidence is all the more relevant because the other two biblical formulae for the divine oath do have clear ancient Near Eastern counterparts. The absence of a parallel is not the only oddity; others will be detailed in this excursus. When combined, these various points highlight significant barriers to accepting the consensus view that נשׂא יד is an oath formula.

The analysis will proceed in three stages: first, the strongest argument for the consensus position will be summarized; second, difficulties with that position are raised; third, and finally, a new and different ancient Near Eastern parallel to נשׂא יד is offered.

1. Evidence for the "Lifted Hand" Formula as a Divine Oath

The most extensive argument for interpreting נשׂא יד as an authenticating element for the divine oath comes from David Seely. His argument includes several noteworthy points: first, he contends that the "lifted hand" formula "is synonymous with the more frequent verb 'to swear' nšb'"[6] because in ten cases the "lifted hand" formula appears in a promise of the land to the fathers that is expressed 49 other times with the verb nšb'; second, he asserts that "[t]his is another case where Ezekiel avoids Deuteronomic language and relies on other traditions,"[7] either for "poetic variation" or simply because "[Ezekiel] prefers other traditions to Deuteronomy;"[8] the remainder of Seely's argument relies upon Mayer Gruber's analysis of non-verbal acts in the ancient Near East.[9] In lieu of a clear parallel to lifting a hand in an oath, Seely proposes five possible "explanations as to the origin and significance of the raised hand as an oath gesture:"[10] one, that it represents YHWH pointing to the divine heavenly abode by which the heavens are invoked as a witness, and which by metonymy "may be tantamount to the Lord swearing by himself;"[11] two, with reference to Isa 62:8, the hand is a metonymy for YHWH's arm, denoting God's power; three, by analogy to raising a hand to demonstrate it is not holding a weapon, YHWH raises

---

6   Seely, "Raised Hand," 412.

7   Ibid., 413.

8   Ibid., 420.

9   M.I. Gruber, *Aspects of Non-Verbal Communication in the Ancient Near East* (Rome: Biblical Institute Press, 1980).

10 Seely, "Raised Hand," 416.

11 Ibid., 417.

his hand to demonstrate he is swearing in good faith; four, Seely invokes a number of passages where hand gestures symbolize some sort of pledge, notably Gen 14:22, to suggest that this "is another such gesture whose exact significance is obscure;"[12] five, with reference to Job 13:14, Seely suggests that the gesture may represent a self-curse. Seely prefers the first option, where YHWH points to a divine heavenly abode, but he remains unwilling to rule out the other possibilities.

2. Difficulties Internal to the Hebrew Bible

There are numerous issues with Seely's argument. It is logical to begin with one that he himself recognizes.

(a) Instances Where נשא יד Cannot Be an Oath

Seely himself admits that the "lifted hand" formula cannot be an oath gesture in some cases. He notes Ps 10:12,[13] about which Adrian Curtis comments that the psalmists petition—"Arise YHWH, God raise your hand, do not forget the afflicted!"—appeals to YHWH "to arise... and take action (vv. 12-13)... it can also convey a more negative sense of seeking recompense (Gen. 9.5), and some such sense is appropriate here."[14] It is hardly conceivable that YHWH swearing an oath against the psalmist's enemy would fulfill this request. Peter Craigie affirms that active divine intervention, not an oath, is in view, offering Ps 7:6-7 as a parallel case that implores YHWH to rise up against his enemies.[15]

Isaiah 49:22 exhibits similar features. This text indicates by synonymous parallelism that YHWH's intent to raise his hand is equivalent with raising a banner (ואל־עמים ארים נסי) to the peoples. John Goldingay and David Payne observe that "YHWH is now acting as a general, summoning nations/peoples," with the meaning of the raised hand clarified because "YHWH's words are neatly parallel, with the word order verb-indirect object-object, indirect object-verb-object."[16] This tight literary

---

12   Ibid., 418.

13   Ibid., 411.

14   Adrain Curtis, *Psalms* (Epworth Commentaries; Peterborough: Epworth, 2004), 22.

15   Peter C. Craigie, *Psalms 1–50* (WBC 19; Waco, Tex.: Word Books, 1983), 101, 125.

16   John Goldingay, *The Message of Isaiah 40–55: A Literary-Theological Commentary* (2 vols.; London: T & T Clark, 2005), 2:194.

arrangement rules out the possibility that אשא אל גוים ידי, "I raise my hand to the nations," is an oath formula.

Very similar to Isa 49:22 is Deut 32:40. This occurrence provides an important test case because Seely uses it as the key passage to demonstrate that the "lifted hand" idiom is in "juxtaposition with a *verbum dicendi*,"[17] the main criteria of Gruber's schema to which Seely appeals in order to substantiate that נשא יד is an oath formula. There are numerous problems with interpreting the raised hand of YHWH in Deut 32:40 as an oath.

First and foremost, the hand is an image for power and active intervention in Deut 32. Three times prior to v. 40 it serves this role (vv. 27, 36, and 39). The first two occasions refer to human hands: in v. 27 the hands belong to YHWH's adversaries and in v. 36 to YHWH's people. The sense of the image is well represented in the English translations of כי יראה כי אזלת יד as "when he sees that their power is gone."[18] Finally, in v. 39 the hand belongs to YHWH: when the god of Israel decides to move in judgment "there is none that can deliver from his hand" (ואין מידי מציל). The same image occurs immediately after v. 40, when in v. 41 YHWH's hand seizes judgment and executes it against god's adversaries. Deuteronomy 32 corresponds to the way the image functions elsewhere in Deuteronomy, where it occurs no less than a dozen times carrying this connotation.[19]

If, then, the image of YHWH lifting up a hand in v. 40 connotes an oath it is not only exceptional within Deuteronomy but also intrudes directly between two verses where the image represents divine power and intervention. Though this is possible, it is odd that after using the hand to deal death and to heal that the next line changes it into a sign that accompanies the speech-act of swearing, only for it to immediately return as a weapon in the following line. Further evidence that this oscillation was not how ancient audiences understood the text comes from the versions, about which more in a moment.

Second, it is important to bear in mind the theme of Deut 32, namely the faithfulness of YHWH to Israel despite her trust in other gods that cannot save. Nathan MacDonald is correct to remark that "[i]n this speech YHWH derides the other gods for their powerlessness (vv. 37-38) and affirms his own ability to act on behalf of his people in salvation and judgment (vv. 39-42)."[20] It follows logically that Deut 32:40 should

17 Seely, "Raised Hand," 419.
18 NRSV; cf. JPS, "when He sees that their might is gone."
19 Deut 2:15; 3:24; 4:34; 5:15; 6:21; 7:8, 19; 9:26; 11:2; 13:10; 17:7; 26:8; 34:12; cf. 8:17.
20 MacDonald, *Deuteronomy*, 85; cf. 176-80.

support this larger theme. If YHWH's hand expresses YHWH's power and active intervention, then this rhetorical intention is served by the language. If, however, it is a symbolic gesture for an oath, it is hard to see how the larger intention is achieved.

One potential objection to this point is that the phrase חי אנכי לעלם is an oath, which is not in dispute. Is this language not equally susceptible to the point that it does not advance the overall theme of Deut 32? In a word, no. It is crucial to recognize why the text invokes YHWH's life, one might say vitality, at this point. Life and vitality are an attribute denied to other gods, the group with which Deut 32 seeks to contrast YHWH. Within the Song of Moses this is not stated explicitly, but the reference to other deities as "no gods" (לא אלה, v. 17; לא אל, v. 21) implies that they lack vitality. Direct evidence of this contrast occurs in Deut 5:26: in context with the command for Israel to eschew other deities (v. 7), the text characterizes YHWH as the "living god" (אלהים חיים), a title that highlights YHWH's vitality over against the powerlessness of other deities. The "as I live" authenticating element picks up on this notion and, therefore, alludes to YHWH's power and ability to actively intervene. This connotation distinguishes the "as I live" authenticating element from the "lifted hand" formula and connects it directly to the larger intent of Deut 32 to differentiate YHWH's vitality from the lifelessness of the other gods.

A third problem for reading the "lifted hand" formula as part of an oath is the grammar of Deut 32:40. Blane Conklin's thorough analysis of the relevant texts enumerates all the variations in syntax for swearing an oath in Biblical Hebrew. If Deut 32:40 is read together as an oath, it begins with the particle כי, so one expects it to be discussed in his chapter on "oaths marked with *ky*," specifically in the section on full or partial conditional clauses "within a *ky* clause."[21] This text is, nevertheless, conspicuously absent despite the fact that Conklin refers the reader here for further remarks on Deut 32:40.[22] Indeed, there is not a single passage covered in this section that reflects the combination of protasis introduced with כי and apodosis beginning with אם in an oath.

There is a knock on effect from this purported structure: scholars struggle to explain why אם cannot perform its usual function in an oath. Typically, אם negates the thought that follows, suggesting that vv. 40-41a should read "for I lift my hand to heaven and I say 'as I live forever, I will not sharpen my flashing blade.'" But, this meaning is impossible in context. Commentators take the particle in a temporal

---

21   Conklin, *Oath Formulas*, 54-56.

22   He specifically points to this section as the relevant explanation on p. 63.

sense, rendering "when" in their translations, but recognize this is an extraordinary situation with no clear logic.[23]

Conklin encounters another problem with the syntax of v. 40. He notes that Deut 32:40 differs from the other texts that employ the "lifted hand" formula. "With the exception of Deut 32," he observes, "in each of the texts... the essential content of the oath is spelled out in an infinitival construct phrase."[24] Rather than an exception to a larger pattern for the divine oath, this is further evidence that something else is present.

To summarize, reading Deut 32:40a as a symbolic gesture accompanying an oath requires one to accept that the phrase employs imagery otherwise anomalous in Deuteronomy, relates only tangentially to the theme of the poem, and defies the grammar and syntax exhibited by oaths in the remainder of the Hebrew Bible. That is too much to ask.

A first step towards a more suitable interpretation comes from the ancient versions, namely 4QDeut[q] and LXX. Lust shows that both 4QDeut[q] and LXX pair the "lifted hand" formula with the preceding phrase "none delivers from my hand" (v. 39b), not the following oath authenticated by YHWH's life.[25] The strongest evidence of this is the textual arrangement in 4QDeut[q]:[26] that text places MT v. 40b on its own line, with MT v. 40a standing on the previous line alongside "there is none who can deliver from my hand."[27] The result is that the "lifted hand" formula concludes a series of statements that emphasize YHWH's power by invoking the divine hand as an image of judgment (vv. 36-39). The LXX points towards a similar arrangement, demonstrated by the notable plus καὶ ὀμοῦμαι τῇ δεξιᾷ μου, "I swear by my right hand." Sanders suggests that this phrase is added because the meaning of MT v. 40a "was no longer clear to the intended readers;"[28] Lust believes this plus arose to fill in a perceived gap in v. 40, specifically that

23 Paul D. Sanders, *The Provenance of Deuteronomy 32* (OtSt; Leiden: Brill, 1996), 242-43, especially n. 812.

24 Conklin, *Oath Formulas*, 15.

25 Lust, "For I Lift,"; cf. J. Lust, "The Raised Hand of the Lord in Deut. 32:40 According to MT, 4QDeut[q], and LXX," *Text* 18 (1995). The introductory phrase "and I say 'as I live forever'" (ואמרתי חי אנכי לעלם) could also be an anacrusis. This is supported by Skehan (Patrick W. Skehan, "A Fragment of the 'Song of Moses' (Deut. 32) From Qumran," *BASOR* 136 [1954]: 12-15) and Lust's reconstruction of 4QDeut[q].

26 Ibid., 12-15; Patrick W. Skehan, "The Structure of the Song of Moses," in *A Song of Power and the Power of Song: Essays on the Book of Deuteronomy* (ed. Duane L. Christensen; Winona Lake, Ind.: Eisenbrauns, 1993), 156-68.

27 Lust, "Raised Hand," 34-35.

28 Sanders, *The Provenance of Deuteronomy 32*, 242.

the translator thought a parallel with v. 40b was necessary. The translator created this parallel by synthesizing the preceding and following ideas into a new phrase that balanced with ἐρῶ ζῶ ἐγὼ εἰς τὸν αἰῶνα, "I said 'as I live forever.'" The plus, though it balanced the line and mimicked the form that dominates the poem, confused the images.

That there is this sort of fluidity in the transmission of the poem is undeniable: it is well-documented that MT, 4QDeut^q, and LXX vary significantly on the content of Deut 32:43.[29] Though not unanimous, the tendency is to regard the text of 4QDeut^q as an earlier version of the poem than MT and LXX.[30] It is likely, furthermore, that MT has shaped the poem with specific theological concerns in mind.[31] For instance, v. 8 replaces the division of the nations according to the polytheistic sounding "sons of god" with the less problematic "sons of Israel."[32] More holistic editing is evident too: Arie van der Kooij illustrates how the whole poem is worked into 70 lines, an effort "to bring the composition of the poem in line with 'the number of the sons of Israel'" (cf. Gen 46:20; Exod 1:5).[33] Just that sort of overarching goal would explain why a phrase originally connected with vv. 36-39 was displaced and paired with material that was previously separate.

If one follows this logic there is also an explanation for the syntactical and grammatical issues noted above. Taking 4QDeut^q to indicate the original arrangement of the text, thus reading MT v. 40b as a monocolon,[34] results in the following text:

---

29 MT is the shortest text, with 4 lines; 4QDeut^q is next longest, with 6 lines; LXX is the longest, with 8 lines in total. Further evidence that the text varied is the Samaritan Pentateuch, which generally follows MT but diverges with 4QDeut^q in at least one place (Arie van der Kooij, "The Ending of the Song of Moses: On the Pre-Masoretic Version of Deut 32:43," in *Studies in Deuteronomy: In Honour of C. J. Labuschange on the Occassion of His 65th Birthday* [eds. F. García Martinez, A. Hilhorst, J.T.A.G.M. van Ruiten and A.S. van der Woude; VTSup 53; Leiden: Brill, 1994], 95).

30 Carmel McCarthy, *Deuteronomy* (Biblia Hebraica Quinta 5; Stuttgart: Deutsche Bibelgesellschaft, 2007), 152.

31 Carmel McCarthy, *The Tiqqune Sopherim and other Theological Corrections in the Masoretic Text of the Old Testament* (OBO 36; Göttingen: Vandehoeck & Ruprecht, 1981), 211-14.

32 Ibid.; cf. MacDonald, *Deuteronomy*, 176-80.

33 van der Kooij,"The Ending ", 100.

34 Sanders, *The Provenance of Deuteronomy 32*, 242, n. 809 and Åke Viberg, *Symbols of Law: A Contextual Analysis of Legal Symbolic Acts in the Old Testament* (Coniectanea Biblica: Old Testament Series 34; Stockholm: Almqvist & Wiksell International, 1992), 29-31, demonstrate that Lust is incorrect to take the LXX reading as evidence for an earlier, longer Hebrew *Vorlage*.

רְאוּ עַתָּה כִּי אֲנִי אֲנִי הוּא וְאֵין אֱלֹהִים עִמָּדִי
אֲנִי אָמִית וַאֲחַיֶּה מָחַצְתִּי וַאֲנִי אֶרְפָּא
וְאֵין מִיָּדִי מַצִּיל כִּי־אֶשָּׂא אֶל־שָׁמַיִם יָדִי

וְאָמַרְתִּי חַי אָנֹכִי לְעֹלָם
אִם־שַׁנּוֹתִי בְּרַק חַרְבִּי וְתֹאחֵז בְּמִשְׁפָּט יָדִי־[35]
אָשִׁיב נָקָם לְצָרָי וְלִמְשַׂנְאַי אֲשַׁלֵּם
אַשְׁכִּיר חִצַּי מִדָּם וְחַרְבִּי תֹּאכַל בָּשָׂר
מִדַּם חָלָל וְשִׁבְיָה מֵרֹאשׁ פַּרְעוֹת אוֹיֵב

"See now that I indeed am he, and there is none like me;
I kill and I give life; I smite and I myself heal;
none can deliver from my hand when I lift my hand to heaven."

I said "as I live forever:
when I sharpen my flashing sword and my hand seizes judgment,
I shall return vengeance on my enemies, and those who hate me I
    will annihilate,
I shall drench my arrows in blood and my sword will devour flesh;
from the blood of the slain and captives, from the head of the
    leaders of the enemy."

This arrangement addresses the problems with imagery and, by resolving the syntactical problems, shows how it corresponds to the overall logic of the poem.

First, when the "lifted hand" formula is connected with MT v. 39
the image of Yhwh's hand as a weapon is maintained throughout the
poem. The lack of an infinitival explanatory phrase is no longer a problem either because, in this arrangement, Deut 32:40 is clearly not a parallel to the other instances of the "lifted hand" formula that uniformly
include this clause.

Second, standing on its own, in something like an anacrusis, the "as
I live" authenticating element becomes more prominent and establishes
an even stronger allusion to Yhwh's identity as the living god. This fits
well in a poem so concerned to emphasize Yhwh's unique character.

---

35 There may be enough space at the beginning of this line in 4QDeut^q for another
    word, which Lust suggests is לְעֹלָם. This is possible, but speculation. Indeed, any
    proposal is conjectural, but another logical one would be the presence of כִּי, which
    would produce both a more standard syntax for an oath in which the apodosis be-
    gins with כִּי אִם and also allow for the contextually necessary translation of v. 41 as
    an affirmative statement about Yhwh's course of action.

Third, this textual arrangement resolves the syntactical problems related to כִּי and אִם. The particle כִּי simply functions in its temporal meaning, contextualizing the thought of v. 39. Separating the phrases also eliminates the question of how to explain an oath that contains a protasis introduced by כִּי and continues with an apodosis that opens with אִם, precluding its typical negative meaning. The opening statement of MT v. 40b, וְאָמַרְתִּי, is then read as the conjunction plus a perfective verb denoting completed action. The sense of completed action is important within the logic of the Song of Moses: vv. 40b-42 describe what will happen in the future when YHWH finally brings the judgment that was postponed in vv. 26-27. Recall that YHWH delays the divine judgment "lest [his adversaries] say our hand is exalted" (v. 27). This announcement is the turning point between the first and second halves of the poem,[36] and it informs everything that follows. Although YHWH holds off judgment, it has not receded entirely. The divine wrath is, rather, stored up for a future day (v. 35) when it will be poured out. The oath in v. 40b is the assurance that the delay will not be infinite, that a time of reckoning will come because YHWH has sworn by his own life that it will come. Thus, the description of divine judgment in vv. 40b-42 "expresses Yahweh's determination to execute judgment"[37] in such a way that "the Song... may confront them as a witness" (Deut 31:19) when these things happen.[38]

In sum, Seely's position, supported by Conklin and many others, is problematic for at least five reasons: Isa 49:22, the closest parallel to Deut 32:40, is not an oath; the use of hand imagery in Deuteronomy as a whole and throughout ch. 32 indicates it is a metonymy for power and active intervention; v. 40 better serves the overall theme of the Song of Moses, contrasting YHWH's power with other gods powerlessness, if MT v. 40a is a companion to MT v. 39b; the various grammatical problems with reading vv. 40-41 together as an oath suggest another interpretation is needed; and, finally, the different division of the text supported by the versions, especially 4QDeutq, points towards reading v. 40a with v. 39b. This is a comprehensive case against Seely's view that allows, furthermore, for a different interpretation that accounts for its inherent difficulties. Psalm 10:12, Isa 49:22, and Deut 32:40, there-

---

36 A. D. H. Mayes, *Deuteronomy* (NCB; Grand Rapids, Mich.: Eerdmans, 1981), 381.

37 C. J. Labuschagne, "The Song of Moses: Its Framework and Structure," in *De Fructu Oris Sui: Essays in Honour of Adrianus Van Selms* (eds. I. H. Eybers et al.; Pretoria Oriental Series 9; Leiden: Brill, 1971), 97.

38 Ibid., 91

fore, all correlate the "lifted hand" formula with YHWH's active intervention, not an oath.

(b) LXX translation of the "Lifted Hand" Formula

Another indication that נשׂא יד was not understood as an oath formula in antiquity is that LXX never translates the idiom with a word that means "to swear." The translators typically selected verbs expressing the literal act: most common is αἴρω (to lift, raise; Deut 32:40; Ezek 20:28, 42; 36:7; 44:12; 47:14), with its related compounds ἐξαίρω (Ezek 20:15, 23) and ἐπαίρω (Ps 106:26); ἐκτείνω (to stretch out; Exod 6:8; Num 14:30; Neh 9:15) also appears widely. Ezekiel 20:5-6 is an important case that departs from the norm: for the first instance of נשׂא יד the translator provides ἐγνωρίσθην (to make known; v. 5a), and for the second and third instances he uses ἀντελαβόμην (to help; vv. 5b, 6). The translator obviously had difficulty rendering the formula, but in neither case was his solution to choose ὄμνυμι or a similar verb meaning "to swear."[39] If the idiom was recognized as an oath formula, it is logical that the translator would have adopted this meaning in at least one case to handle such difficulties, making its absence significant. For now it is sufficient to note that even when the translator interprets the idiom he avoids using terms that indicate the swearing of an oath.[40]

In sum, the evidence from at least four, perhaps as many as six, different ancient translators indicates that Biblical Hebrew נשׂא יד was not understood as a divine oath formula.

(c) The idiom רום יד

A final issue to address is the meaning of the idiom רום יד (Gen 14:22; Dan 12:7), which Seely and others take as a human equivalent to a divine oath with נשׂא יד.[41] An obvious, albeit often overlooked concern, is its asymmetry with the other divine oath formula: whereas both the "as I live" authenticating element and the verbal root שׁבע have a human

---

39 Further attention is given to the Hebrew text of Ezek 20:5-6 below in ch. 3, section 3.b.

40 See Lust, "Ez., XX, 4-26," 523. Regarding Deut 32:39-41 he writes, "Jahvé lève la main non pas en signe de serment, mais en guise de punition."

41 Cf. Viberg, *Symbols of Law*, 19-31.

counterpart that employs the same terms as the divine oath, רוּם יד
would be anomalous in having different divine and human forms.

A second difficulty arises in Dan 12:7, where it remains ambiguous
what the mysterious man clothed in linen intends when he raises his
right and left hands.[42] Even Seely brackets this text from his argument:

> Daniel 12:7 mentions a man, or divine messenger, raising (hrym) both
> hands to heaven and then swearing an oath. It is difficult to tell whether
> an oath gesture or a prayer is intended. Although the verb hrym is never
> used as a gesture of prayer elsewhere (usually nś² ydym), because the ges-
> ture includes both hands raised—which is never attested in oath gestures—
> I assume that the intended image was one of prayer or supplication done
> in conjunction with an oath.[43]

Excluding Dan 12:7 leaves only Gen 14:22 to consider. In this account of Abram's interaction with Melchizedek and the king of
Sodom,[44] Abram lifts his hand "to YHWH, El Elyon, creator of heaven
and earth" as a symbolic gesture. Nothing in vv. 22-23 is explicit in
making this idiom an oath, though it must be said that the syntax of
these verses does point in that direction. Still, like נשׂא יד, LXX translates with ἐκτείνω, "to stretch out," leaving the meaning ambiguous.
There is also some uncertainty in the form ידי , which can either be singular, as most commentators suggest and LXX translates, or plural, as it
is in Dan 3:15. The latter scenario would bring Gen 14:22 into line with
the well known ancient Near Eastern idiom for prayer in which both
hands are raised to a deity.

Because Gen 14:22 is the only evidence to consider when deciding
whether רוּם יד represents a symbolic gesture used by humans to swear
and oath, it is logical to set it aside as anomalous and not to allow it to
obscure the other evidence concerning what נשׂא יד means in divine
speech.

---

42 It is worth noting that Dan 12:7 actually lacks the word יד, containing instead
    ימינו ושׂמאלו.

43 Seely,"Raised Hand ", 411-2; Pace Conklin, Oath Formulas, 80-1, the same issue—the
    raising of two hands in an ambiguous gesture—necessitates bracketing out the Old
    Aramaic example from the Hadad inscription as well; cf. Paul-Eugène Dion, La
    langue de Ya'udi: description et classement de l'ancien parler de Zencirli dans les cadres des
    langues sémitiques du nord-ouest (Waterloo: Editions SR, 1974), 34, 384 n. 21, who
    connects the gesture to prayer, not the oath.

44 For details on this chapter, see the various studies by J. A. Emerton: "Some False
    Clues in the Study of Genesis XIV," VT 21 (1971): 24-47; "The Riddle of Genesis
    XIV," VT 21 (1971): 403-39; "The Site of Salem, the City of Melchizedek (Gen 14:18),"
    in Studies in the Pentateuch (VTSup 41; Leiden: Brill, 1990), 45-71.

(d) A Precedent for Priestly Theology Determining Formulaic Language

Seely argues that the consistent substitution of the "lifted hand" formula for the divine oath with the verbal root שׁבע, the preferred language of DTR, is "another case where Ezekiel avoids Deuteronomic language and relies on other traditions."[45] This conclusion is not in debate. However, Seely's correlated assertion that this situation indicates semantic equivalence between the two phrases is problematic.

The first weaknesses in this argument is Seely's inability to offer a firm reason for the persistent avoidance of the DTR language. He raises two possibilities: either a desire for "poetic variation" or that "[Ezekiel] prefers other traditions to Deuteronomy."[46] Poetic variation, though not impossible, is a rather weak reason for wholesale avoidance of a term. That Ezekiel's language is closely related to the the priestly tradition is indisputable, but that fact remains far too general to explain what Ezekiel found problematic with the divine oath employing the verbal root שׁבע.

Compounding these issues is the strong evidence that Ezekiel does adopt a substantial number of DTR terms,[47] even preferring DTR language in some cases where the priestly tradition offered different vocabulary. This rules out the logic that Ezekiel excluded a form of the divine oath common to the DTR tradition as part of a larger program.

There is a precedent that Ezekiel's does indeed choose to avoid certain phrases because of a theological conviction that made a particular expression unacceptable. John Day argues that P consciously and consistently substitutes קומ ברית for the more common כרת ברית in order to avoid the close connection with sacrifice. "[S]ince the usual expression 'cut a covenant' was redolent of making a covenant by cutting up an animal in sacrifice," Day remarks, "it behooved P to avoid the expression 'cut a covenant' and find an alternative phrase which avoided sacrificial overtones, and for this purpose the phrase 'establish a covenant' was entirely satisfactory."[48] It is significant to note that this preference, although identified in P, is also characteristic of the Holi-

---

45   Seely,"Raised Hand ", 413.

46   Ibid., 420.

47   Risa Levitt Kohn, *A New Heart and a New Soul: Ezekiel, the Exile and the Torah* (JSOTSup 358; London: Sheffield Academic Press, 2002), 86-95.

48   John Day, "Why Does God 'Establish' Rather Than 'Cut' Covenants in the Priestly Source?," in *Covenant as Context: Essays in Honour of E. W. Nicholson* (eds. A. D. H. Mayes and Robert B. Salters; Oxford: Oxford University Press, 2003), 92.

ness Code (Lev 26:9) and Ezekiel (Ezek 16:60, 62),[49] precisely the same texts where the "lifted hand" formula is substituted for the divine oath with the verbal root שבע.

Day states the underlying rationale for his position thus:

Certainly when one reflects on the thoroughness and consistency with which P has avoided the phrase which was almost universal elsewhere in earlier Old Testament works and substituted his own expression, one can only conclude that this was the result of a deliberate and self-conscious policy, so presumably he had some reason for doing so.

Mutatis mutandis, the same is true about P, H, and Ezekiel's use of the "lifted hand" formula and suggests that a theological conviction may also underly the substitution of נשא יד for שבע. In order to substantiate this view it will be necessary both to identify the theological issue in question and also to explain how the "lifted hand" formula eludes its problematic connotations.

To begin, the DTR language—the divine oath with the verbal root שבע plus נתן—supports the land theology that characterizes Deuteronomy. Twenty-one of the 23 times YHWH swears in Deuteronomy, the divine oath specifies YHWH's promise to give the land to the ancestors (only Deut 2:14; 28:9 deal with other issues). Jan Joosten and Christophe Nihan, among others, have demonstrated that a key concept that separates P, H, and Ezekiel from Deuteronomy is the way that human disobedience affects the sanctuary and the land.[50] Joosten encapsulates the situation concisely by warning scholars "not to view H in the light of Deuteronomy, even where both codes contain elements that at first sight may be thought to be identical."[51]

The DTR tradition connects the divine oath with שבע to the verbal root ירש and its derivatives. Lohfink states that "the qal of *yrš* with the conquered land as its object became a key theological concept in a

49   Ibid., 99.

50   Jan Joosten, *People and Land in the Holiness Code: An Exegetical Study of the Ideational Framework of the Law in Leviticus 17–26* (VTSup 67; Leiden: Brill, 1996), 169-92; Christophe Nihan, *From Priestly Torah to Pentateuch* (FAT II/25; Tübingen: Mohr Siebeck, 2007), 395-575; cf. Jacob Milgrom, *Leviticus 17–22: A New Translation with Introduction and Commentary* (AB 3A; New York: Doubleday, 2000), 1404-05; Norman C. Habel, *The Land is Mine: Six Biblical Land Ideologies* (Minneapolis, Minn.: Fortress, 1995).

51   Joosten, *People and Land*, 176.

Deuteronomistic narrative structure."[52] This central role is highlighted by the three instances of ירשׁ in Deut 1: v. 8 indicates that YHWH reasserted at Horeb an oath made to Abraham, Isaac, and Jacob to possess the land; v. 21 portrays Moses recalling YHWH's sworn promise in order to encourage the first exodus generation in their military incursion to capture the land; finally, v. 39 depicts YHWH transferring the sworn promise to possess the land to the second exodus generation after the rebellion of the first exodus generation. Lohfink concludes that "the various strata and recensions of the entire Deuteronomistic history build on these texts, using the qal and hiphil of *yrš* (with the land or peoples inhabiting it as the object) as a cliche in the stereotyped Deuteronomistic vocabulary."[53]

P, H, and Ezekiel differ considerably on this point. This is reflected by the terms they choose for the land: where DTR uses ירשׁ, ירשׁה, and מרשׁה, these three texts favor נחלה and אחזה.[54] Greater attention will be given to this issue later, and it will demonstrate the deep rift that this terminological difference only hints at. For now it is sufficient to note that this can explain why P, H, and Ezekiel select formulaic language that avoids unwanted links with DTR's theology.

When P, H, and Ezekiel wanted to describe the same episodes as DTR without either adopting its theological perspective or permitting its audience to equate its view with DTR, they judiciously selected their language. Rather than avoiding the idea of covenant for the relationship between YHWH and Israel, P selects a phrase that does not possess the sacrificial undertones with which it was uncomfortable. P, therefore, speaks of a covenant being established, not cut. In the same way, it is reasonable to propose that P, H, and Ezekiel select נשׂא יד because it can be used in a parallel manner to the DTR divine oath with שׁבע without being synonymous with it. The two phrases, despite appearing in the same context, need not be semantic equivalents. They are interchanged, but they are not interchangeable in meaning.

---

52   Norbert F. Lohfink, "ירשׁ" in *Theological Dictionary of the Old Testament* (eds. G. Johannes Botterwerk and Helmer Ringgren; Grand Rapids, Mich.: Eerdmans, 1990), 6: 383.

53   Ibid.

54   See ch. 5, §2.

3. *Našû-nadānu*: A New Potential Parallel

This final section argues that the "lifted hand" formula eludes the problematic concepts implied by the divine oath with שׁבע through its connection to a widely-known Akkadian legal formula for royal authorization of land transfers.

Seely concedes early on in his essay the lack of any parallel for the "lifted hand" formula outside the Hebrew Bible:

> The expression *nśʾ yd* as an oath gesture is unique to Biblical Hebrew. The linguistic equivalent of Hebrew *nśʾ yd* is well attested in Akkadian *qāta našû*, Aramaic *nśʾ yd*, as well as in Ugaritic *nśʾ yd*. But there is no semantic equivalent of *nśʾ yd*—as a gesture accompanying an oath—outside Hebrew. In these other languages the phrase is almost always used with mortals and signifies gestures of worship or prayer, and is usually associated with mortals rather than deities.[55]

Seely is correct in his evaluation of the non-biblical evidence insofar as he goes, but he does not go far enough.[56] Upon further analysis, the evidence indicates the proper parallel to the נשׂא יד formula is the Akkadian formula *našû-nadānu* along with *ištu qâti* that is used for the royal endorsement of land transfers.

(a) The "Lifted Hand" as Active Intervention

The lifted hand gesture is a metonymy for active intervention, typically with hostile intent, against another party. Evidence from Assyria, Ugarit, and the Sefire Inscriptions illustrates this usage. The Assyrian text *Erra and Ishum* contains a clear example. In Tablet IV, Erra instructs Ishum to attack:

---

55 Seely,"Raised Hand ", 414.

56 Another theme related to the use of the hand is the transfer of kingship in Baal and Yam (KTU 1.1 iv 19-20: "Over my hands I pronounce.... Your name is Beloved of El..." [Wyatt, *Religious Texts*, 49]). Furthermore, in Assyria, a call for military assistance can be symbolized by the raising of a hand: "Now the whole country has raised its hand towards the king. May the army come and take its hand!" (*May the Army Come Quickly!* in Manfried Dietrich, *The Babylonian Correspondence of Sargon and Sennacherib* [State Archives of Assyria 17; Helsinki: Helsinki University Press, 2003], 134).

The warrior Erra said these words to Ishum his vanguard,
"Go Ishum, the matter you spoke of, do as you wish."
Ishum set out for the mountain Sharshar,
The Seven, warriors unrivalled, fell in behind him.
When the warriors reached the mountain Sharhar,
He raised his hand and destroyed the mountain,
He reckoned the mountain Sharshar as level ground.
He cut away the trunks of the cedar forest,
The thicket looked as if the deluge had passed over,
He laid waste cities and turned them into open spaces...[57]

The connection between raising the hand and Ishum's aggressive act is plain. Indeed, the imagery here reflects the land being completely destroyed to the point of reverting into chaos. A second Assyrian text supporting this relationship is Assurbanipal's inscription recounting his attack against Elam: "Kudurnanhundi, the Elamite, who did not fear the oath (sworn) by the great gods, who in (his) madness [trusted] in his own strength, brought his hand against the sanctuaries of Akkad and ruined the land of Akkad..."[58] Although this inscription lacks the hyperbolic imagery of *Erra and Ishum*, the hand remains a symbol for an aggressive, military action which "ruins" Akkad.[59]

The strongest evidence for this meaning in Ugarit comes from *The Story of King Keret* (KTU 1.14-16). When Yasib, the eldest son of Keret, believes his father is dying and should allow him to immediately ascend the throne, he declares (KTU 1.16 vi 40-45):

He came in to his father.
He lifted up his voice and cried:
"Listen, I pray, O Keret the votary,
listen, and let your ear be alert!
Like a warrior can you command warriors,
and give orders to those under your command?
You have lowered your hand in weakness![60]

---

57 Foster, *Muses*, 908. Italics are mine. See also Dalley, *Myths from Mesopotamia*, 309 and the transcription in Cagni, *Erra*, 120-21.

58 Daniel David Luckenbill, *Ancient Records of Assyria and Babylonia: Volume II, Historical Records of Assyria from Sargon to the End* (Ancient Records 2; Chicago: University of Chicago Press, 1927), 356-57, text 923.

59 Cf. "The Murder of Sennacherib," translated by William W. Hallo (*COS* 3.95: 244).

60 Translation by Wyatt, *Religious Texts*, 239-42; italics are mine. Cf. KTU 1.16 iv 25-39, especially line 33: Yasib makes the same speech alone and then to Keret in public.

The point of Yasib's speech is unmistakable: Keret's credentials as a warrior have been impugned. This is articulated with the image of lowering the hand, an image that only makes sense if one assumes the opposite indicates the strength associated with a victorious warrior.

Finally, the *Aramaic Inscriptions of Sefire* directly connect the raised hand and active, hostile intervention.[61] A treaty (Aramaic עדי)[62] between Mati'ilu and Bar-Ga'yah stipulates:

> [But if you obey and car]ry out this treaty and say, "[I] am an ally," [I shall not be able to raise a hand] (*šlḥ yd*) against you; nor will my son be able to raise a hand (*lyšlḥ yd*) against [your] son, or my offspring against [your] off[spring. And if] one of (the) kings [should speak a word] against me or one of my enemies (should so speak) and you say to any king, "What are you [going to do?" and he should raise a hand (*lḥ yd*) against] my son and kill him and raise his hand (*wyšlḥ ydh*) to take some of my land or some of my possessions, you will have been unfaith[ful] to the trea]ty which is in this inscription.[63]

Further on, in the second tablet, the text says (Sefire II, Face B, lines 5-7a):

> [And] if you say in your soul and think in your mind, ["I am an ally, and I shall obey Bar-Ga'yah] and his sons and his offspring," then I shall not be able to raise a ha[nd (*lašlḥ yd*) against you, nor my son against your son, nor my offspring against your offspring], either to rout them, or to destroy their name.[64]

These texts are only anecdotal since they employ the verb *šlḥ* and not a direct cognate to נשׁא, but they remain instructive about the wide currency this image had in the ancient Near East.

---

61   The full text and translation of these inscriptions is found in Joseph A. Fitzmyer, *The Aramaic Inscriptions of Sefire* (BibOr 19/A; Rome: Pontifical Biblical Institute, 1995).

62   This term, familiar from the Neo-Assyrian *adê* loyalty oaths, is in those cases borrowed from Aramaic, as Fitzmeyer notes (Ibid., 58; cf. Tadmor, , 127-52). For the opposing position see Simo Parpola, "Neo-Assyrian Treaties From the Royal Archives of Nineveh," *JCS* 39 (1987): 180-83.

In a notable turn of phrase at Tablet I, Face B, line 41, the agreement is called "a living pact" (עדן חין). Although it is entirely speculation, the mention of life along with treaty calls to mind the Hittite treaties and their use of the NĪŠ DINGIR[LIM] authenticating element. One wonders if the custom of authenticating treaties by the life of the god(s) doesn't lie somewhere in the background.

63   Sefire I, Face B, lines 23-28a (Fitzmyer, *The Aramaic Inscriptions of Sefire*, 48-51).

64   Ibid., 122-23.

More evidence for this meaning across the ancient world could be offered, stretching as far as the oath ceremonies in Homer's *Iliad*,[65] but these examples are sufficient to establish the point. The same meaning is present in the Hebrew Bible, as the discussion of Ps 10:12, Isa 49:22, and especially Deut 32 above pointed out. Recall, for instance, that the adversaries of YHWH represent their military power by saying "[o]ur hand was high, YHWH has not done all this" (Deut 32:27b).[66]

In sum, all this evidence supports the position that Johan Lust has advanced, namely that the symbolic gesture of lifting a hand is often a metonymy for the active, hostile intervention of one party against another. Lust's argument is limited to biblical evidence, and is not supported by the ancient Near Eastern parallels discussed here. Thus, this survey adds weight to his proposal for reading the Biblical Hebrew idiom "as a reference to an active intervention and not to an oath."[67]

Even though this evidence supports Lust's position and shows that it is a definitive advance over reading the phrase as a symbolic gesture for taking an oath, it only addresses one of two ways in which the "lifted hand" formula is employed in the Hebrew Bible, so it omits another critical ancient Near Eastern parallel to נשא יד.

(b) The Meaning of the Akkadian Formula *našû-nadānu*

Isaac Gottlieb, in an article on the legal background to the verbs in Exod 6:6-8,[68] opens a fruitful line of investigation by proposing a connection between the Akkadian *našû-nadānu* plus *ištu qâti* formula and Biblical Hebrew נשא יד. The context and function of the *našû-*

---

65 Margo Kitts shows that in the *Iliad* Poseidon and Athene confirm an oath with Achilles when "taking his hand in theirs they bound themselves with words" (Margo Kitts, *Sanctified Violence in Homeric society: Oath-making Rituals in the Iliad* [Cambridge: Cambridge University Press, 2005], 79-80, 101).

66 Sanders, *The Provenance of Deuteronomy 32*, 206.

67 Lust, "For I Lift," 164.

68 Isaac B. Gottlieb, "Law, Love, and Redemption: Legal Connotations in the Language of Exodus 6:6–8," *Journal of the Ancient Near Eastern Society* 26 (1998): 54-57. His proposal for a connection between the two will be adopted here, but with important differences. For instance, Gottlieb misses the implications of his own position when he states, "*nāśā'tī*, whose obvious meaning is 'swore'" (Ibid., 56). Moreover, his attempts to connect all the verbs in Exod 6:6-8 to ancient marriage practices is programmatic and causes him to stretch the evidence, nowhere more notably than in connection with the *našû-nadānu* formula.

nadānu formula, widely attested in the Akkadian legal texts from Ras Shamra,[69] is aptly summarized by Labuschagne:

> The documents falling in the third category, viz. royal transactions, are particularly interesting. They bear ample witness to the royal prerogatives with regard to property and to the king's authoritative disposal in these matters. They picture him as administrator and controller of the land and estates, in fact as the real owner of land. The actions of the king, who takes the initiative, seem to be unilateral, for there is no question of any kind of agreement between the persons concerned. He takes property away from the one and gives it to the other. The formula used to express such an action is as a rule *našû-nadānu*. The monarch 'lifts up' or 'takes away' the house and land of A and 'gives' it to B, that is, he 'transfers' property from one to the other. The conditions of such a conveyance are clearly stated, whether it is a hereditary grant or a personal one or a sale represented as a grant, and there are also clear stipulations about feudal services and payments. In one instance only the *našû-nadānu* formula is used not of property but of a document of purchase... Elsewhere in these documents, however, the formula is used exclusively in connection with conveyance of property.[70]

In this summary, Labuschagne adopts a proposal originally made by E. A. Speiser to read the formula as a hendiadys with the combined meaning of "transfer,"[71] a position accepted widely despite variable views on precisely why the scribes at Ras Shamra preferred this formula.[72] The text of RS 16.247 is illustrative of the usage:

iš-tu ₂ûmi an-ni-i-im	From today
¹*niq-maᶦˡadu mâr am-mi-iš-tam-ri*	Niqmadu, son of Ammistamru,
šàr ᵃˡu-gar-it	King of Ugarit,
it-ta-ši bît-šu eqilᴴ-šu	produced the house and the land

---

69   Jean Nougayrol, *Textes Accadiens et Hourrites des archives est, ouest et centrales: avec des études de G. Boyer et E. Laroche* (PRU 3; Paris: Imprimerie Nationale, 1955).

70   C. J. Labuschagne, "The Našû-Nadānu Formula and Its Biblical Equivalent," in *Travels in the World of the Old Testament: Studies Presented to Professor M. A. Beek on the Occasion of His 65th Birthday* (eds. G. Heerma van Voss, H. J. Houwink ten Cate and N. A. Van Uchelen; Assen: Van Gorcum, 1974), 177.

71   E. A. Speiser, "Akkadian Documents From Ras Shamra," *JAOS* 75 (1955): 160.

72   Nougayrol, *PRU 3*, 288; Burkhart Kienast, "Rechtsurkunden in Ugaritischer Sprache," *UF* 11 (1979): 431-52; Jonas C. Greenfield, "Našû-Nadānu and Its Congeners," in *Essays on the Ancient Near East in Memory of Jacob Joel Finkelstein* (ed. Maria de Jong Ellis; Memoirs of the Connecticut Academy of Arts & Sciences 19; 1977), 87-91; Ignacio Márquez Rowe, *The Royal Deeds of Ugarit: A Study of Ancient Near Eastern Diplomatics* (AOAT 335; Munster: Ugarit-Verlag, 2006), 213-18.

ša [1]*sí-na-ra-na*	of Sinaranu
ina [al]*ma-ra-pa*[K]	in Maʿrabu
ú it-din-šu	and he transferred it
a-na [1]*ibri-šarru* [amil]*ardi-šu*	to Ibrisûarru, his servant,
a-na da-ri -du-ri	forever
ú-ra-am sĕ-ra-am	In the future
ma-am-ma-an la i-le-qì-šu	no one will take it
iš-tu qâti[ti] [1]*ibri-šarru*	from the hands of Ibrisûarru
a-na da-ri du-ri	forever
ni-id-ni šarri	(It is) a gift of the king.[73]

This text shows that the three component parts of the idiom—the verbs *našû* and *nadānu* and the phrase *ištu qâti*—are separated in the text but work together to connote that a property has been taken from one party (*našû*; line 4 above) and transferred to another party (*nadānu*; line 7 above) from whose hands it cannot be removed (*ištu qâti*).[74]

The practice at Ugarit is corroborated, and its importance augmented, by the use of the same formula in Hittite land grants.[75] Kaspar Riemschneider related its interpretation to Speiser's earlier work and noted that at Hatti "the hendiadys of both verbs *našû* and *nadānu* does not generally express the handover of an item from one man to another, but means the transfer of an object through a third [person]."[76] The close connection to land possession is clarified by a notable variant: one Hittite land grant uses *našû-šakānu*, emphasizing the right to dwell in that land, instead of the otherwise standard *našû-nadānu* formula.[77] This particular variation is also seen in the biblical material, on which more discussion follows momentarily.

---

73   Transliteration from Nougayrol, *PRU 3*, 65. The English translation is mine.

74   CAD describes the *ištu qâti* as a phrase that "complements a verb expressing movement away—with such meanings as... take away from."

75   See Hans Gustav Güterbock, *Siegel aus Boğazköy: Erster Tiel. Die Königssiegel der Grabungen bis 1938* (AfO 5,7; Berlin: 1940) and Kaspar K. Riemschneider, "Die Hethitischen Landschenkungsurkunden," *Mitteilungen des Instituts für Orientforscung* 6 (1958): 321-81.

76   Ibid., 332: "Wie E. A. Speiser in einer ausführlichen Studie festgestellt hat drückt die Verbindung der beiden Verben *našû* und *nadānu* nicht allgemein die Übergabe eines Gegenstandes von einem Manne an einen andern aus, sondern meint die Übertragung einer Sache durch einen Dritten."

77   LS 3, rev 30-32, Güterbock, *Siegel aus Boğazköy*, 48; cf. Márquez Rowe, *The Royal Deeds of Ugarit*, 283, note 87.

As early as 1955, Speiser identified that "[t]he combined use of *nśʾ* and *ntn*, the respective Hebrew cognates of Akk. *našû* and *nadānu*, is amply attested in Middle Hebrew and has survived into Modern Hebrew. The resulting phrase appears both as *maśśā(ʾ)-umattān* and as *lāśē(ʾ)ṯ-wᵉlātēṯ*."[78] The logical bridge between these idioms is, of course, Biblical Hebrew. Scholars have put forward various proposals for what constitutes that bridge. For instance, Labuschagne offers *lqḥ-ntn* as an equivalent and provides numerous biblical examples,[79] but he fails to persuade. In only two out of some twenty examples does *lqḥ-ntn* describe a third party overseeing the transfer of property between two other parties, the standard meaning in Ugarit and Hatti. In both of those cases (2 Sam 12:11-12; 1 Kgs 11:35-37) it is YHWH, and notably not a human king, who fills the role played by the monarch at Ugarit and Hatti. Elsewhere, Labuschagne's examples simply describe one party giving a portion of its possessions to a second party, an arrangement never explained by the *našû-nadānu* formula. Labuschagne also presents "a synonymous phrase, *hiṣṣíl-ntn*... that occurs twice in the Old Testament where both instances tell of Yahweh's authoritative disposal: Gen [31:9] 'God has *taken away* your father's cattle and has *given* it to me' and Num [11:25] 'Yahweh *took away* some of the spirit that was on him (scil. Moses) and *conferred* it on the seventy elders.'"[80]

Greenfield agrees with Labuschagne's suggestion and notes its bridging role to Mishnaic Hebrew where, "*nṭl* has replaced *lqḥ*... in most of the common usages of 'to take.'"[81] Albeit impossible to deny some conceptual relationship between these idioms and the *našû-nadānu* formula, Ignacio Márquez Rowe is correct in his recent evaluation of these attempts:

> I believe there can be little doubt about "the antique flavour" of the Hebrew and Aramaic terms pointed out by these scholars. Nevertheless, I would hesitate to take all of them as "true" cognates, not only on the basis of the different verbs (or etymologies) adduced but also on account of their

---

78 Speiser, "Akkadian Documents From Ras Shamra," 161. Greenfield, "Congeners," 91, argued for a further parallel in Aramaic that he found attested in two documents from Elephantine. The texts are CAP 8 and 9, published in Bezalel Porten and Jonas C. Greenfield, *Jews of Elephantine and Arameans of Syria: Fifty Aramaic Texts with Hebrew and English Translations* (Jerusalem: Hebrew University of Jerusalem, 1984).

79 Labuschagne, "Formula," 179-80. He includes solemn occasions (Gen 18:7ff; 21:14; Ex 12:7; Num 6:18ff; 19:17; Judg 17:4; 1 Sam 6:8; 2 Sam 21:8ff; Ezek 4:1, 3, 9; 45:19), royal actions (1 Sam 8:10-18; 2 Sam 9:9; 16:4; 19:29) and divine actions (2 Sam 12:11; 1 Kgs 11:35; Job 1:21).

80 Ibid., 180. Emphasis original.

81 Greenfield, "Congeners," 91.

meaning and the context in which they appear. Indeed, although the verb denoting the transfer of property is *ntn* like *nadānu* in the deeds of Ugarit, the verbs *lqḥ*, *nṭl*, and *ḥnṣl*... are not strictly speaking cognates of Akkadian *našû*, the particular term of the Akkadian formula.[82]

Despite this balanced assessment, Márquez Rowe embraces Biblical Hebrew *lqḥ-ntn* as the closest parallel to the *našû-nadānu* formula, all the while wanting to affirm Speiser's connection between Talmudic *maśśā(ʾ)-umattān* and Mishnaic *lāśē(ʾ)t-wᵉlātēt*, two formulae without *lqḥ*. Can both positions really be held together? They appear contradictory, and one must surmise Márquez Rowe attempts to do so out of a desire to find *some* bridge in Biblical Hebrew.

(c) The Connection between *našû-nadānu* and נשׂא יד

In spite of this tension, no one has made a detailed effort to defend the Biblical Hebrew idiom נשׂא יד as a semantic equivalent to the *našû-nadānu* formula. Yet, there are several strong arguments for this proposal. To begin, it is important to note that the key features of the *našû-nadānu* formula are (1) a three party arrangement with (2) royal authorization for (3) the transfer of property, most often in the form of land. The same concerns appear in Exod 6:6-8, particularly in v. 8, the passage that originally suggested a potential relationship between the two idioms:

> Therefore, say to the Israelites, 'I am YHWH and I will bring you out from under the burdens of the Egyptians and I will deliver you from slavery to them. I will redeem you with an outstretched arm and with mighty acts of judgment. I will take you as my people, and I will be your God. You shall know that I am YHWH your God, who has brought you out from under the burdens of the Egyptians. I will bring you to the land that I lifted my hand to give it to Abraham, Isaac, and Jacob; I will give it to you as a possession. I am YHWH'"
>
> Exod 6:6-8

Taking the three criteria in order, the three parties involved are YHWH, the Israelites and the implied, but undeniably present, inhabitants of the land that YHWH promises to Israel. Secondly, although YHWH is not specifically called king in this passage, it is clearly in that role that Is-

---

82 Ignacio Márquez Rowe, *The Royal Deeds of Ugarit: A Study of Ancient Near Eastern Diplomatics* (AOAT 335; Münster: Ugarit-Verlag, 2006), 284.

rael's god is portrayed here. Thirdly, the passage specifies that Yhwh will transfer (נשׂאתי את־ידי) the land (הארץ), giving it (לתת אתה) to Israel. Thus, all three distinctive themes are present in a passage that does use the cognate verbs נשׂא and נתן.

Four additional passages demonstrate the same three themes in conjunction with נשׂא יד continued by נתן: Ezek 20:28, 42; 47:14; and Neh 9:15. The three features are perhaps most visible in Ezek 47:14, in which Yhwh raises his hand (נשׂאתי את ידי) to give the land (לתתה) to the people who will return from exile in the same way it was given to their ancestors (לאבתיכם) in the past. This demonstrates that the three-fold combination of (1) a three party arrangement with (2) royal authorization for (3) the transfer of property, most often in the form of land, is not an isolated feature of Exod 6:6-8 but one that repeats in other instances of the "lifted hand" formula.

Numbers 14:30 is an especially helpful case because it uniquely employs the נשׂא יד formula in connection with the verb שׁכן instead of נתן. This difference argues for, rather than against, the connection with the našû-nadānu formula: recall that one Hittite document used našû-šakānu to express the right of a group to dwell in their land.[83] Numbers 14:30 revokes the right to dwell in Yhwh's land from one group—the first exodus generation, called a wicked congregation (העדה הרעה)—and transfers that right to another group, the second exodus generation. Consistency across these variations of usage is a strong indicator that there is a relationship between the two formulae.

One issue remains for discussion: how does the phrase "my hand" in the Biblical Hebrew נשׂאתי את־ידי לתת expression relate to the našû-nadānu formula? Whereas in the Akkadian formula the object of našû is the land, in Hebrew the object of נשׂא is Yhwh's hand.[84] The issue relates to the phrase ištu qâti that expresses the idea of control in the Akkadian idiom. The phrase ištu qâti is part of the so-called warranty clause that follows the našû-nadānu formula. It creates a metonymy between the hand or hands of one party in the transaction and control of the item in question. It indicates that when the transaction is complete the property is in the hands of a new party, who the king has promised may control the land "in the future" (urram šeram).[85] Márquez Rowe

---

83 LS 3, rev 30-32 (Güterbock, *Siegel aus Boğazköy*, 48); cf. Márquez Rowe, *The Royal Deeds of Ugarit*, 283, n. 87.

84 The land is the object of both *nadānu* and נתן.

85 This future may be specified as forever (*ana dari duri*): this is likely to be hyperbolic rhetoric that has the legal function of allowing the land to remain in the control of the receiving party upon the enthronement of a new king.

proposes a very similar concept for the "original action" that the *našû-nadānu* formula preserves:

> Our conjecture would then be whether the formula *našû-nadānu* could not reflect the traditional physical or rather ceremonial act of 'producing' and 'giving' the title deed (in an irreversible temporal sequence), and with it of course the transfer of ownership to the transferee...[86]

Meir Malul investigated the function of symbolic actions at length. He takes pains to explain that the actual symbolic act underlying an idiom is elusive, and he counsels that "the scholar must consider the legal meaning... to be of primary importance."[87] His study lends credence to the present argument: from the evidence of four formulae related to property rights, Malul concludes that "[t]he use of the hand... in legal expressions and acts of claiming a right or taking possession of something is, thus, another expression of these organs' function as power instruments."[88] The emphasis on the power represented by the hand diminishes the necessity to clearly link its role in the "lifted hand" formula to a particular act and emphasizes the sense of the expression. "This metaphor of control underlying these expressions and acts fits the concept of ownership as defined above," writes Malul, prior to concluding that "[o]ne's ownership of an object was his physical control of it."[89] The "lifted hand" formula when used to state YHWH's land promise produces the same sense.

Furthermore, C. J. Labuschange and Jonas Greenfield have both suggested that the scribes at Ras Shamra who used the formula might not have understood its original connection to a sign-act, making the language a "frozen formula" to them.[90] If Labuschange and Greenfield are correct, then it is very easy to imagine that this image was freely adapted when crossing into Biblical Hebrew in order to emphasize a particular theological concept, namely that the item in question is in YHWH's hand and, therefore, belongs to the divine king. YHWH retains possession of the land even while transferring the right to dwell in it to one group or another. This agrees with Márquez Rowe's proposal that in Ugarit "the property was [the king's], and that accordingly his was

---

86   Rowe, *Royal Deeds of Ugarit*, 218.

87   Malul, *Studies in Mesopotamian Legal Symbolism*, 33.

88   Ibid., 405

89   Ibid.

90   Labuschagne,"Formula," 178-79; Greenfield, , 88-89; Seely,"Raised Hand,", 419 considers the same possibility for different reasons; cf. Malul, *Studies in Mesopotamian Legal Symbolism*, 397-98.

first and ultimately the right to give it."[91]   The shift is from a human king to a divine one, something that emphasizes Yhwh's continual control over the land even as the right to live on it and use it is given to a chosen group. That theology reflects precisely how H and the book of Ezekiel, the two theological traditions in which the "lifted hand" formula appears most often, explain Yhwh's relationship to the land.

A final and further point to bear in mind is that this proposal offers a simple logic to connect Biblical Hebrew נשׂאתי את־ידי לתת and the arhcaizing Mishnaic formula lāśē(ʾ)t-wᵉlātēt. No longer is the use of an infinitive, specifically a Biblical Hebrew form of the infinitive, unexplained. It is, rather, a logical outgrowth of its biblical antecedent, a precursor that contains both נשׂא and נתן, which provides an unbroken, if not unmodified, chain of usage throughout the various historical periods.

The absence of an expression employing a raised hand to authenticate oaths elsewhere in the ancient Near East does not, in itself, disprove that the Biblical Hebrew idiom נשׂא יד is used in the divine oath. Each culture, and its textual record, must be allowed to speak for itself. Perhaps evidence will come to light in the future that does indicate a raised hand supported oath taking in the ancient Near East. Still, the lack of any corroboration for this custom contrasts with the abundant parallels for the "as I live" authenticating element and increases the burden of proof for this argument. The presumption that "the idiom derives from the hand gesture that accompanied ancient oath ceremonies"[92] is no longer valid and represents an instance of assuming that modern practice reflects ancient habit.

This excursus has demonstrated that there are problems both internal and external to the Hebrew Bible to interpreting the "lifted hand" formula as a divine oath. Furthermore, this excursus has shown that prior suggestions for alternate meanings may be synthesized with previously unnoticed evidence for the ancient legal context of the "lifted hand" formula in such a way that it accounts for the way in which Exod 6, Ezek 20 and 47, and Neh 9 use the idiom.

---

91   Rowe, *Royal Deeds of Ugarit*, 233. "But it is also possible that the king's promise of non-interference... did not mean so much that he or a successor of his would not interfere, but that the property was his, and that accordingly his was first and ultimately the right to give it. It is significant in this regard that tenants did not seem to have the right to covey property presumably given by the king without the latter's consent or due authorisation."

92   Block, *Ezekiel 1–24*, 626.

All this must be kept in mind while further evidence is gleaned from a study of the genre and social setting of the passages in which the "lifted hand" formula appears. Only then, with all the evidence available, can a conclusion about the meaning of נשׂא יד be drawn.

Chapter Three:
Genre Analysis of the "As I Live" and "Lifted Hand" Formulae

This chapter examines the "as I live" and "lifted hand" formulae in order to identify the genre or genres in which they appear and to determine if there is a pattern in their usage. This analysis leads to several conclusions. With respect to the "as I live" formula, it demonstrates that the formula is employed in prophetic announcements of judgment, frequently structured as disputation speeches. The "lifted hand" formula, upon further investigation, is employed in two distinct ways: the first convention uniformly speaks of Yhwh's role in authorizing the transfer of the land promised to Israel in oracles of salvation or theological reflections; the second convention is an idiom used to assign punishment upon a guilty party that occurs, somewhat unexpectedly, within oracles of salvation.

1. The Concept of Genre

The criteria for establishing a genre (*Gattung*) or categorizing the genre of a particular passage remains notoriously difficult to define, despite frequent attempts to do so. This chapter is not the proper place for an extended discussion of conceptual questions about genre,[1] but it is necessary to state a few principles that will guide how genre is understood and applied in the present study.

In the first place, this analysis takes on board the observation of John Barton that "unless we can read a text as something—unless we can assign it to some genre, however ill-defined and in need of subsequent refinement—we cannot really read it at all."[2] This insight, not simply a detached commitment to the series of form-critical steps, supports discussing the question of genre at this stage. Barton further argues that "[o]ur initial judgement about genre and our initial attempt at exegesis play back and forth on each other and are mutually correc-

---

1   A brief overview of the main issues in debate can be found in Knierim, "Criticism," 136-46.

2   Barton, *Reading the Old Testament*, 24.

tive."[3] Indeed, this chapter will reflect precisely that journey from an initial genre assessment to a more exact, and hopefully more valuable, understanding of what the passages in question should be "read as."[4] This chapter, therefore, documents the outcomes of an interpretive heuristic; that is, it does not guarantee a single, indubitable answer but limits the possibilities and presents the most plausible option(s) for genre classification.

The essential insight that Barton foregrounds also informs the communicative-semiotic approach taken by Tremper Longman III.[5] Recognizing that "[i]n the act of reading, a transaction takes place between author and reader" in which genre directs the reader "how to take what is written" and guides the author without precluding their ability to stretch and expand an existing form, Longman argues persuasively for the continued benefit of genre analysis, despite the need to move away from the trajectory set by Herman Gunkel. Gunkel's neoclassical approach to genre was too rigid even for its day, and it over emphasized genre classification as the critical step in reconstructing the original, oral *Sitz im Leben* from which a text developed at a chronologically subsequent stage.[6] Recent research into orality and the transmission of texts in primarily oral cultures has undermined this linear conception of textual development and proven that literature goes through a series of oral and written stages that feedback on one another in a fluid, often unpredictable, process.[7] This variability problematizes the use of genre in an effort to reconstruct the pre-literary history of a text and to define a single social setting from which it emerged. These effects are more evident in the next stage of the form critical process, discussed in the following chapter, and while they are accounted for here, they do not nullify the benefit of careful attention to genre.

Based upon the recognition that Gunkel and others employed genre analysis in a flawed manner, scholars have reoriented the way in which genre is considered, giving more attention to the final form of the text. This is clear, for instance, when David Damrosch remarks that "genre is the narrative covenant between author and reader, the framework of norms and expectations shaping both the composition and the

---

3   Ibid., 18; cf. Longman, *Fictional Akkadian Autobiography*, 15-17.

4   This is Barton's terminology for the hermeneutical posture required for informed interpretation in *Reading the Old Testament*.

5   Longman, *Fictional Akkadian Autobiography*; Longman, "Israelite Genres."

6   Susan Niditch, *Oral World and Written Word: Orality and Literacy in Ancient Israel* (London: SPCK, 1997), 108-30; David M. Carr, *Writing on the Tablet of the Heart: Origins of Scripture and Literature* (Oxford: Oxford University Press, 2005).

7   Longman, "Israelite Genres," 181-82.

reception of a text."[8] By foregrounding the text in this way, Damrosch, like Longman, underscores the lasting importance of genre for exegesis.

Damrosch, furthermore, offers evidence that there was a concept of genre in ancient Israel and Judah.[9] The book of Ezekiel is a good example of this observation: the book classifies its own material as proverbs (מָשָׁל; Ezek 12:22–23; 14:8; 16:44; 17:2; 18:2–3; 19:11, 14; 21:5; 24:3) and even includes a riddle (חִידָה; Ezek 17:2). Although such terms are not proof of a concern for genre at a theoretical level, they indicate that the authors of these texts classified texts and applied those categories to their own writing. Real theoretical questions about genre and genre classification remain, but those unanswered questions should not obscure evidence within the Hebrew Bible that argues in favor of genre analysis and classification as a legitimate tool in exegesis.[10]

"A genre," concludes Longman, "is defined by the critic based on a series of similar traits found in texts,"[11] albeit not without difficulty. Caution is necessary in an etic analysis of literature meant to delineate genres. Yet, Longman is also correct to observe that "benefits abound" from careful attempts to do so.[12] Bearing these cautionary notes in mind, the following three points guide the genre analysis of this study and are intended to mitigate against common errors and potential problems that arise from the challenge of bridging the chronological and cultural distance between the contemporary West and the ancient Near East.

Firstly, this study concedes that a passage can resist allocation into a single genre and may legitimately be placed in multiple categories. In his programmatic article "Old Testament Form Criticism Reconsidered," Knierim addressed this quandary:

> The entirety of a text may be governed by more than one typical structure. A psalm can follow a rhetorical pattern (acrostic, strophe, verse) and at the same time the typical structure of a traditional theme, or a liturgical event. The question is, therefore, how these structural types interact. What is the

---

8   David Damrosch, *The Narrative Covenant: Transformations of Genre in the Growth of Biblical Literature* (San Francisco: Harper & Row, 1987), 2.

9   Longman, "Israelite Genres," 179-81; Longman, *Fictional Akkadian Autobiography*, 14-15; cf. Damrosch, *Narrative Covenant*, 37-39.

10   Longman, *Fictional Akkadian Autobiography*, 14-15.

11   Ibid., 11.

12   Ibid., 14.

hierarchy of their relations to each other? And then, which of them governs the others and ultimately the structural type of the text?[13]

Some subjectivity is, therefore, inherent in the categorization process. Although one seeks irrefutable proof, it is frequently necessary to make judgments on cumulative arguments that offer plausible and probable conclusions.[14] Barton affirms that "all decisions about genre rest on informed intuition, rather than on knock-down proof, but some are more plausible than others."[15] The observations about genres in which the "as I live" and "lifted hand" formulae appear will be seen to have sufficient, if not definitive, evidence that provides new and illuminating background for their interpretation.

Secondly, this study takes into account the content of passages in making genre classifications. Knierim argues for this position as follows:

> [A] problem arises when genre is defined strictly on such morphological grounds, to the exclusion of "content" as one of its inherent elements. This problem would be less complicated if one could show that in many cases definitions of genres on the basis of content were simply acts of methodological oversight and neglect. However, there is a broad chorus of voices stating explicitly either that form, content, and setting, or that form and content together are the factors that constitute a genre.[16]

A main opponent to this view is Wolfgang Richter,[17] who attempts to define form by contrast to content. Erhard Blum has demonstrated the weaknesses in Richter's position, in particular showing that his catego-

---

13 Knierim, "Old Testament Form Criticism Reconsidered," 462.

14 Longman, *Fictional Akkadian Autobiography*, 18-19, notes that some genre theorists have invoked analogies to probability theory in how genre classifications work.

15 Barton, *Reading the Old Testament*, 42.

16 Knierim, "Old Testament Form Criticism Reconsidered," 451; cf.: "Such findings may occasionally show that a text is governed by factors beyond those asked for by the form-critical method, for example, by a thematic concern or a motif. Even so, the form-critical tools will be indispensable for the understanding of the texts wherever the texts are predisposed to their application" (Ibid., 468).

17 Wolfgang Richter, *Exegese als Literaturwissenschaft: Entwurf einer alttestamentlichen Literaturtheorie und Methodologie* (Göttingen: Vandenhoeck & Ruprecht, 1971), particularly pp. 72-152.

ry "inner form" is "substantially content-related."[18] In practice, Rich-
er's distinction breaks down.

Thirdly, the present study seeks to understand the particularities of
each text first and then to assess the typicality among them. This is especially important since the passages examined here are selected not
based upon their collocation in a particular biblical book but because
they contain a particular formula. Falling prey to the easy temptation
to focus on only their typicality would be both methodologically care-
less and likely to exclude relevant findings.[19] This underscores the importance of completing a structural analysis of each passage prior to
the genre analysis. Detailed outlines of each passage that resulted from
such structural analysis are included in appendix one. For brevity, the
current chapter will emphasize the commonalities among the passages
that emerged at the end of the genre analysis. This is not meant to
minimize the differences that do exist between the passages, but it is
necessitated by the focus of the present study.

In sum, though it is no longer tenable to pursue genre classification
as form criticism originally advocated, there is sufficient evidence at
both a theoretical level and within the Hebrew Bible to retain genre
analysis as a key step in the exegetical process. To do so, one must recognize the potential pitfalls and proceed in a manner that seeks to mitigate those errors. Cautionary notices notwithstanding, the positive
contributions of careful genre analysis to interpretation are manifold.

2. Genre and the "As I Live" Formula

The most extensive discussion of genre in relation to the "as I live" authenticating element appears in Zimmerli's commentary on Ezekiel.
Discussing its role in Ezek 20 he observes:

---

18 Erhard Blum, "*Formgeschichte*—a Misleading Category? Some Critical Remarks," in
    The Changing Face of Form Criticism for the Twenty-First Century (eds. Marvin A.
    Sweeney and Ehud Ben Zvi; Grand Rapids, Mich.: Eerdmans, 2003), 38-43, especially
    pp. 38-40; cf. Barton, *Reading the Old Testament*, 22-24. See Richter, *Exegese*, 82-98, for
    his argument on inner and outer form.

19 Knierim states this plainly: "Form criticism has been interested in typical structures
    and has generally tended to relegate the interpretation of the uniqueness of texts to
    subsequent exegesis. However, it seems necessary to reverse this approach: *Not only
    must the structural analysis of the individuality of texts be included into the form-critical
    method, it must, in fact, precede the analysis of the typical structure if the claim that such a
    typicality inherently determines an individual text is to be substantiated*" (Knierim, "Old
    Testament Form Criticism Reconsidered," 461). Emphasis original.

The oath formula חי אני, which is found sixteen times in the book of Ezekiel, never introduces a prophecy. In 16:48 it gives an element of emphasis into reproach that has already been set out. More frequently it marks the transition from reproach to declaration of judgement (cf. in the double declaration of judgment in 17:16, 19, which answers the accusing account of Zedekiah's sin in 17:12-15; further 14:16, 18, 20; 34:8; in 5:11; 35:6, 11 it is introduced directly with לכן). In the remaining passages it introduces the divine antithesis to an assumption (20:3, 31), or a saying of the people being addressed set out in the form of a quotation, so 18:3 after 18:2; 33:11 after 33:10; 33:27 slightly removed from 33:24.[20]

Zimmerli's brief sketch intimates two genres: the judgment speech and the disputation. Even so, he offers only this abbreviated statement and fails to investigate whether the evidence outside of Ezekiel confirms his view. Further study of Ezekiel, and more significantly those passages outside of Ezekiel, confirms and extends Zimmerli's observations.

(a) Prophetic Judgment Speeches

Zimmerli's initial observation that the "as I live" authenticating element marks "the transition from reproach to judgment" in Ezekiel is supported strongly by its usage in the Pentateuch and other prophets.

Numbers 14 has two instances of "as I live." The composite nature of this text is well known and, indeed, the two occurrences of the formula serve as evidence for such a view: the first instance[21] introduces Yhwh's mediated judgment as a response to Moses' intercession (Num 14:11-25) while the second instance,[22] seemingly redundant in the final form of the text, begins Yhwh's pronouncement of a *lex talionis* punishment for the rebellion of the exodus generation (Num 14:26-35). Even though the two uses of "as I live" are attributed to different authors, it remains the introductory phrase for the divine punishment in both cases. Deuteronomy 32:40 similarly introduces Yhwh's promise to take vengeance on an undefined group of enemies. Mayes describes the message of vv. 26-44 as "[t]he declaration of punishment and destruction."[23] Within this section, it is at v. 40 that the pronouncement of

---

20 Zimmerli, *Ezekiel 1–24*, 404.

21 Rolf P. Knierim and George W. Coats, *Numbers* (FOTL 4; Grand Rapids, Mich.: Eerdmans, 2005), 190, assign this to the Yahwist, but others have argued there is a DTR insertion here. This matter is addressed in more detail as part of ch. 4.

22 Knierim and Coats assign this to P (Ibid., 188-89).

23 Mayes, *Deuteronomy*, 381.

judgment actually begins, opening with the "as I live" authenticating element.[24]

In the other prophetic books, Jer 22:24, the final decree in a collection of prophecies against the Judahite monarchy, makes a biting statement against Jehoiachin, here referred to by his personal name Coniah, not his more familiar throne name. The direct address to Coniah, unmistakably switching the focus from his father Jehoiakim (cf. vv. 11-17, 18-23), marks off vv. 24-30 as a new section and places the "as I live" authenticating element at the opening of yet another pronouncement of judgment. Later in Jeremiah the "as I live" formula appears in the oracles against Egypt. Occurring midway through the material concerning Egypt (Jer 46:2-26), it facilitates the transition from reproach to judgment: a new section, marked by the word of Yʜwʜ formula, begins at 46:13 and is followed by a series of rhetorical questions and mocking comments[25] that finally yield to the divine oath with "as I live," which commences a statement of judgment by exile and desolation. Finally, there is Zeph 2:9, part of the oracle against Moab and Ammon in Zeph 2:8-11. Sweeney comments: "The introductory particle, לָכֵן, 'therefore,'" which immediately precedes חַי אָנִי, "is a characteristic feature of the prophetic judgment speeches that typically introduces the announcement of punishment in the prophetic judgment speech form."[26]

In sum, despite the various concerns of Num 14, Deut 32, Jer 22 and 46, and Zeph 2, the "as I live" authenticating element occupies the same position throughout: it introduces a divine punishment.

Zimmerli's observations can be extended when further attention is given to the introductory role of the "as I live" authenticating element. First, Zimmerli speaks of Ezek 16:48 providing "an element of emphasis into a reproach that has already been set out."[27] This is certainly true of the role Ezek 16:44-58 plays within Ezek 16:1-63, but Zimmerli himself, along with other commentators, notes that there are strong signs that vv. 44-58 constitute a later expansion.[28] Verses 44-58, regardless of their authorship, is a distinct section: v. 44 opens with a proverb and is followed by a recollection of Jerusalem's relationship to her metaphorical sisters, Samaria and Sodom, whose sinfulness she has ex-

---

24   In this instance, appearing as חַי אָנֹכִי.

25   William Holladay, *Jeremiah: A Commentary on the Book of the Prophet Jeremiah* (2 vols. Hermeneia; Minneapolis, Minn.: Fortress, 1989), II:326-27.

26   Marvin A. Sweeney, *Zephaniah: A Commentary* (Hermeneia; Minneapolis, Minn.: Fortress, 2003), 138.

27   Zimmerli, *Ezekiel 1–24*, 404.

28   Ibid., 349-52; Pohlmann, *Ezechiel 1–19*, 221; Those arguing for unity include Block, *Ezekiel 1–24*, 462-65; Greenberg, *Ezekiel 1-20*, 295; and Joyce, *Ezekiel*, 133.

ceeded so that YHWH is inclined to punish her. The announcement of
that punishment begins in v. 48 with the "as I live" authenticating element, is subsequently interrupted by a description of the sisters' behavior and, finally, resumes with the announcement in v. 52:

> Now, you, bear your disgrace with which you have brought about for your
> sisters a more favorable judgment; because of your sins in which you acted
> more abominably than they, they are more in the right than you. So, you,
> be ashamed and bear your disgrace, for you have made your sisters appear
> righteous.

Bearing disgrace, the main topic of vv. 44-58, is not a *product* of YHWH's
judgment, it *is* YHWH's punishment.[29] Thus, even though vv. 44-58 echo
the judgment described in vv. 37-43 in the final form of ch. 16, when
read as a unit vv. 44-58 employ the "as I live" authenticating element to
introduce judgment.[30]

Second, note the element of judgment associated with each usage of
"as I live" in Ezek 20. Although Zimmerli correctly recognizes that vv.
3, 31, and 33 each introduce the "divine antithesis" to an assumption
the implied audience holds—in vv. 3 and 31 the people believe they
will be able to consult YHWH and in v. 33 they desire to be like the nations who "worship wood and stone" (Ezek 20:32)—more can be said.
YHWH's response introduces an element of judgment as well. The refusal to be consulted in vv. 3 and 31 indicates a fracture in the relationship between deity and people. This divine silence, produced by the
peoples' sinfulness, certainly implies reprimand. This meaning is all
the more clear because vv. 1-31 indict Israel specifically for remaining
unrepentant in the face of previous divine prompts to abandon idolatry. Furthermore, YHWH's promise that "surely with a mighty hand and
an outstretched arm, and with wrath poured out, I will be king over
you" (Ezek 20:33) also connotes judgment. Block observes, "Since the
prophet never applies the expression [with outpoured fury] to Yahweh's treatment of Israel's enemies, it can only signify his anger to-

---

29 Compare with Jacqueline E. Lapsley, "Shame and Self-Knowledge: The Positive Role
    of Shame in Ezekiel's View of the Moral Self," in *The Book of Ezekiel: Theological and
    Anthropological Perspectives* (eds. Margaret S. Odell and John T. Strong; SBLSyms 9;
    Atlanta, Ga.: Society of Biblical Literature, 2000), 160-68, especially p. 163.

30 "Verse 58, formulated analogously to v 52, concludes the events of vv 44-52 and ex-
    presses the final judgment... The statement about the connection between guilt and
    punishment becomes quite clear in its synthetic character: in carrying its punish-
    ment Jerusalem is carrying its own trespasses and its abomination" (Zimmerli,
    Ezekiel 1–24, 352).

wards his own people. The force of divine wrath that Pharaoh once experienced will now be felt by Israel."[31]

In view of the evidence from outside Ezekiel, and the refinement of Zimmerli's observations about Ezek 16 and 20, it is possible to conclude that in the Hebrew Bible the "as I live" authenticating element introduces prophetic announcements of punishment (*prophetische Gerichtsankündigungen*) within prophetic judgment speeches (*prophetische Urteilsreden*).[32] It is important to stress both the prophetic and the judgment components of this designation.

In the first place, they are *prophetic* judgment speeches: even when "as I live" occurs in a narrative context (Deut 32:40; Num 14:21, 28) it also exhibits a prophetic character. Paul Sanders, in his detailed study of the Song of Moses (Deut 32:1-43), underlines the "song's relationship with the prophetic literature of the Hebrew Bible."[33] Moreover, although most scholars now reject the view that the Song of Moses is a *rîb*, the number that advocated that position at one time is indicative of its prophetic character.[34] Numbers 14 has prophetic features too. After Yʜᴡʜ's double declaration of judgment the non-priestly source indicates that "[w]hen Moses told these words to all the Israelites, the people mourned greatly" (Num 14:39); in the priestly account, v. 28 indicates specifically that Moses is to אמר אלהם the punishment that follows. Both statements place Moses in the role of prophetic messenger transmitting Yʜᴡʜ's speech to the people.

Equally important, these passages are prophetic *judgment* speeches. Judgment may be directed at Israel, Judah, the nations who are their enemies, groups within Judah or, as its lone individual addressee, against Judah's king. But in each case the "as I live" authenticating element introduces judgment. This feature, and its importance for interpretation, receives further attention in the following chapter, where the literary setting of the "as I live" authenticating element is discussed.[35]

31   Block, *Ezekiel 1–24*, 650.
32   Marvin A. Sweeney, *Isaiah 1–39 with an Introduction to the Prophetic Literature* (FOTL 16; Grand Rapids, Mich.: Eerdmans, 1996), 530-1, 533-4.
33   Sanders, *The Provenance of Deuteronomy 32*, 58; cf. his entire section on this question, pp. 58-68.
34   Ibid., 88-94.
35   See below, ch. 4, §2.

(b) Disputation Speeches

The perceptive reader will have noticed that Isa 49:18, Ezek 18:3 and Ezek 33:11, 27 have been omitted in the discussion of prophetic judgment speeches. Zimmerli judiciously noted that in these cases the defining characteristic of the "as I live" authenticating element is to open Y<small>HWH</small>'s response to a quotation of the people, in his view a different function than introducing judgment. He only treated this function briefly and with respect to his division of Ezek 20, so the insight requires further development.

Additional study indicates that all four examples appear in disputation speeches (*Disputationswörter*).[36] Adrian Graffy's monograph, *A Prophet Confronts His People*, establishes very specific criteria for what constitutes a disputation speech:[37] an introduction, a quotation, the refutation and, in a few cases, a rejoinder. Based upon these criteria he identifies Isa 49:14-25, Ezek 18:1-20, 33:10-20, and 33:23-29 among the sixteen disputation speeches in the prophetic books.[38] Graffy's criteria for what constitutes a disputation speech are rather complex and D. F. Murray has demonstrated they "unnecessarily restrict the scope of the genre, and imperfectly represent its essential elements."[39] Murray's position that "where the elements thesis, counter-thesis, dispute, are present or clearly implied in the text is use of the term appropriate"[40] allows for the requisite freedom that any author may take in constructing a particular passage while recognizing that certain constituent parts must be identifiable.[41] While Murray's view shall guide the additional analysis here, the more restrictive nature of Graffy's criteria demonstrates the basic point: even by this more constrained definition, the "as I live" authenticating element has a place in disputation speeches.

---

36   Sweeney, *Isaiah 1-39*, 519.

37   Adrian Graffy, *A Prophet Confronts His People: The Disputation Speech in the Prophets* (AnBib 104; Rome: Biblical Institute Press, 1984).

38   Others he identifies in Ezekiel are Ezek 11:2-12, 14-17; 12:21-25, 26-28; 20:32-44; 37:11b-13.

39   D. F. Murray, "The Rhetoric of Disputation: Re-Examination of a Prophetic Genre," *JSOT* 38 (1987): 114.

40   Ibid.

41   Murray continues: "But it is the presence, be it noted, of these three in the logical deep structure which is essential to disputation, and not necessarily their direct representation in the rhetorical surface structure, though the latter will, understandably, frequently be the case" (Ibid., 99).

Taking this evidence into account, it is logical to re-examine the entire corpus of "as I live" passages to see if the disputation speech genre is a more prevalent aspect than previously perceived. Ezekiel 20:32-44, for instance, is a passage widely agreed to be a disputation[42] that can be added to those already discussed. Comparing the other passages to Murray's three-fold criteria, looking for the presence of a thesis, counter-thesis, and argument,[43] identifies six additional passages: four from the book of Ezekiel (16:44-58; 17:11-21; 20:1-31; 35:1–36:15) and two outside that book (Deut 32:26-43; Zeph 2:8-11).

Ezekiel 16:44-58 is a distinct unit within the longer allegory about Jerusalem that can, as argued above, be read as a judgment speech. Moreover, one can identify a thesis in the proverb "'[l]ike mother, like daughter.' You are the daughter of your mother, who loathed her husband and her children" (Ezek 16:44b-45a). At least two other times in the book of Ezekiel a proverb constitutes the thesis in a disputation (Ezek 12:21-28; 18:1-32).[44] In this case, vv. 44-46 provide context for the proverb and reveal that the underlying contention is that Jerusalem was not like its metaphorical Hittite mother or its sisters, Samaria and Sodom, who constitute a paradigm of sinfulness. YHWH's counter-thesis follows in v. 47 and not only inverts Jerusalem's contention but magnifies it by accusing the city of behavior surpassing the lewdness of Samaria and Sodom. The third component, that is the argument, is introduced by the "as I live" formula in v. 48 and continues through the end of the section in v. 52. This passage indicates, among other things, that "as I live" may introduce a component of the disputation speech and open a pronouncement of judgment simultaneously.

The interpretation of Ezekiel's allegory about the eagle and vine in Ezek 17:11-21 also exhibits the three features of the disputation speech. After briefly clarifying the meaning of the allegory (vv. 11-15a), the thesis of the dispute is implied in the rhetorical questions of v. 15b: Zedekiah believes he can rebel against Babylon, escaping the conse-

---

42   Graffy, *A Prophet Confronts His People*, 65-72; Zimmerli, *Ezekiel 1–24*, 404-05; Block, *Ezekiel 1–24*, 648 (who notes this arrangement but expresses reservations); Joyce, *Ezekiel*, 152.

43   Murray's criteria are understood as follows. A thesis is the proposition that the "opposing" group—that is from the perspective of the author or editor—puts forward. The counter-thesis, or counter-theses, are the propositions that characterize the author's or editors' position. The dispute is the evidence presented or argument constructed to prove that the counter-thesis is the proper view. Unfortunately, at this point Murray's terminology creates more confusion than is necessary. Thus, the term "argument," understood in its plain rhetorical and not antagonistic sense, rather than "disputation" will be adopted here.

44   Block, *Ezekiel 1–24*, 387, 554.

quences of the covenant (ברית, v. 13) he has made. Verses 16-21 divide into two parallel sections,[45] each beginning with a counter-thesis introduced by the "as I live" authenticating element. The counter-thesis of section one (vv. 11-18) focuses on Zedekiah's disregard for the human partner of the covenant and specifies that his failure will be demonstrated by his death at the king's hands in Babylon. Its argument contends that this will happen because "Egyptian help will be denied at the decisive moment, when the war reaches its climax in the siege of Jerusalem."[46] In section two (vv. 19-21), the counter-thesis focuses on Zedekiah's responsibility to the divine partner in the covenant, YHWH,[47] stipulating that Zedekiah will be caught in YHWH's net. The related argument, found in v. 20, presents Zedekiah's death in Babylon as YHWH's doing.

Ezekiel 20:1-31, despite strong similarities to Ezek 20:32-44, is not recognized as a disputation speech. But, that description is suggested by the opening quotation of the elders: their approach to the prophet comprises the thesis of the disputation and expresses their belief that YHWH will hear their inquiry (Ezek 20:3a). YHWH's counter-thesis immediately follows and begins with the "as I live" authenticating element: "As I live, says the Lord YHWH, I will not be consulted by you" (Ezek 20:3b). The argument follows in the form of the historical reflection on the house of Israel's rebellion. Verses 5b-30 recall Israel's habitual sinfulness, which persists to the present day, and precludes YHWH from considering the elders' inquiry. The passage closes with a second occurrence of the counter-thesis, once more introduced with "as I live," forming an inclusio around this section.

The last passage within the book of Ezekiel to consider is the speech to Mt Seir and the mountains of Israel in Ezek 35:1–36:15.[48] Commentators generally regard this passage as composite and Greenberg divides it into four sections: after an opening command to prophesy, he marks off 35:3aβ-4, 5-9, 10-15, and 36:1-15.[49] The "as I live" formula occurs in Ezek 35:10-15, which opens with a quote attributed to Mt Seir, a metaphorical depiction of Edom. This quotation comprises

---

45 Greenberg, *Ezekiel 1-20*, 318-19.

46 Zimmerli, *Ezekiel 1–24*, 365.

47 For details, see the discussion in Block, *Ezekiel 1–24*, 547.

48 Although this was understood as two separate sections in antiquity, modern commentators have recognized their coherence. See Zimmerli, *Ezekiel 25–48*, 232; Greenberg, *Ezekiel 21-37*, 722-25; Daniel I. Block, *The Book of Ezekiel: Chapters 25–48* (NICOT; Grand Rapids, Mich.: Eerdmans, 1998), 309-10; Pohlmann, *Ezechiel 20–48*, 473.

49 Greenberg, *Ezekiel 21-37*, 722-25.

the thesis: "These two nations and these two countries shall be mine, and we will take possession of them" (Ezek 35:10). In the argument that follows, which again opens with "as I live," YHWH characterizes Edom as angry, envious, and abusive and swears to deal with it accordingly. The thesis ascribed to Edom is echoed in v. 12b-13 and rejoined by YHWH's counter-thesis in vv. 14-15:

> Thus says Lord YHWH, "as the whole world rejoices, I will make you a desolation. Just as you rejoiced over the inheritance of the house of Israel, which was a desolation, therefore I will do to you: you will be a desolation, Mt Seir and all Edom, all of it, and you will know that I am YHWH."

The disputational character of this passage has also been recognized by Lust and Sweeney, confirming the view taken here.[50]

Outside of the book of Ezekiel, one may first consider Deut 32:1-43. The Song of Moses, as a whole, has defied genre classification and no attempt will be made here to resolve that issue.[51] Nonetheless, vv. 26-42 exhibit the three criteria of a disputation speech. Mayes notes that vv. 26-27 "represent the turning point in the whole Song, from a threat of destruction to a promise of vindication,"[52] evidence that supports considering these verses as a section within the whole. Verses 26-27 also contain the thesis of the disputation: if YHWH destroys Israel then their enemies would conclude "[o]ur hand is triumphant; it was not YHWH who did all this" (Deut 32:27b). Rather than being immediately followed by the counter-thesis, the argument ensues in vv. 28-36. Therein, "the enemy is characterized as lacking wisdom when it imagines that it has defeated Israel by its own strength,"[53] and it asserts, "Israel's disasters are due only to Jehovah's alienation, occasioned by Israel's sin."[54] The counter-thesis, alluded to in v. 31, is announced plainly in v. 39:

---

50   J. Lust, "Edom – Adam in Ezekiel, in the MT and LXX," in *Studies in the Hebrew Bible, Qumran, and the Septuagint Presented to Eugene Ulrich* (eds. Peter W. Flint, Emmanuel Tov and James C. VanderKam; VTSup 101; Leiden: Brill, 2006), 393-94; Sweeney, "Assertion of Divine Power," 156-72, especially p. 166.

51   For a full discussion of this matter see Sanders, *The Provenance of Deuteronomy 32*, 84-96. For a recent proposal for the Song's liturgical role see Matthew Thiessen, "The Form and Function of the Song of Moses (Deuteronomy 32:1-43)," *JBL* 123 (2004): 401-24.

52   Mayes, *Deuteronomy*, 389.

53   J. G. McConville, *Deuteronomy* (Apollos Old Testament Commentary 5; Leicester, England: Apollos, 2002), 457.

54   S. R. Driver, *A Critical and Exegetical Commentary on Deuteronomy* (ICC; 3d ed. Edinburgh: T & T Clark, 1902), 371.

See now that I, I am he;
> there is no god beside me.

I kill and I cause to live;
> I wound and I heal;

None delivers from my hand.

It is noteworthy that the אני הוא formula is found elsewhere only in Deutero-Isaiah, at least once in a disputation speech.[55] The counter-thesis is followed by a description of the adversary's punishment introduced with "as I live." That punishment is, in the context, also an expansion of Yhwh's argument and serves to confirm the assertion that vengeance belongs to God (v. 35). Deuteronomy 32:26-42 appears, in the end, to be a hybrid of many genres and it is doubtable that the disputation speech governs the whole unit. Nevertheless, the three features of the disputation speech are part of its logical structure.

Finally, then, there is the oracle against Moab and Ammon in Zeph 2:8-11. This text does not plainly present itself as a disputation speech, but there is evidence for all three criteria. The oracle begins by recalling that Yhwh has heeded Moab and Ammon:

I have heard the taunt of Moab
> and the revilings of the Ammonites,

how they have taunted my people
> and made boasts against their territory.

Zeph 2:8

The characterization of the words as a taunt (חרף) and revilings (גדפים) indicates a polemical tone. Although a thesis cannot be securely reconstructed from this statement, its content may be surmised from v. 9b: the promise that the remnant of Yhwh's people will plunder and possess Moab and Ammon suggests their thesis was to impose just that fate on Judah. It is notable that precisely this logic underlies Ezek 35:10-15, another oracle that includes the features of the disputation speech. Working from this proposed thesis, vv. 9b-10 constitute Yhwh's counter-thesis. The argument, once more introduced by the "as I live" formula, appears between the thesis and counter-thesis in v. 9a.

---

55   אני הוא occurs at Isa 41:4; 43:10, 13; 46:4; 48:12; and 52:6. Isaiah 48:12-15 is generally agreed to be a disputation (Antoon Schoors, *I Am God Your Saviour: A Form-Critical Study of the Main Genres in Is. XL-LV* [VTSup 24; Leiden: Brill, 1973], 278-83).

In summary, there is substantial evidence for adding these six passages to the four previously identified disputation speeches, indicating that as many as 10 of the 18 passages employing the "as I live" authenticating element have the basic characteristics of the disputation speech. Within those speeches, the "as I live" formula can introduce either a counter-thesis or an argument, but it always occupies the lead position in the section to which it belongs.

It remains to detail the similarities between the disputation speeches and the judgment speeches. The evidence demonstrates that, among the disputation speeches, the element of judgment usually remains apparent (Deut 32:26-42; Ezek 16:44-52; 17:11-21; 20:1-31; 20:32-44; 35:10-15; Zeph 2:9), though this feature seems to be absent in Ezek 18:1-32, 33:10-20, and Isa 49:14-21. However, the immediate context of Ezek 18:1-32 suggests that judgment remains imminent (see Ezek 18:30-32) and the wider context, particularly in relation to the message of Ezek 20:32-44, indicates that the author and editors of the book saw this casuistic principle resulting in the punishment of a significant portion of the exilic community. Similarly, Ezek 33:10-20 insinuates the judgment of its addressees. This comes to the fore in vv. 17-20 where, even after a second exposition about the possibility of repentance and life, the people once more exclaim "[t]he way of the Lord is not proper," only to be reminded "I will judge you according to your ways house of Israel!" (Ezek 33:20).

Isaiah 49:14-21 is the only instance that truly lacks an element of judgment, a fact represented by its consistent classification as an oracle of salvation.[56] This exception accords with Deutero-Isaiah's "skill in adapting the genre to his own purposes."[57] It is unsurprising that Deutero-Isaiah intentionally contravenes the typical rhetorical function of the disputation in order to emphasize its message. Further details explaining why Isa 49:14-21 differs from the other "as I live" passages is offered in chapter five.

---

56 Graffy, *A Prophet Confronts His People*, 91-98; Schoors, *I Am God Your Saviour*, 105-06;
    Claus Westermann, *Isaiah 40–66* (OTL; Translated by David M.G. Stalker. Philadelphia: Westminster, 1969), 218.

57 Graffy, *A Prophet Confronts His People*, 98.

(c) The "As I Live" Authenticating Element and the Land Theme

Before ending this discussion of the "as I live" authenticating element, it is necessary to remark on the thematic continuity of the relevant passages, namely an overriding concern for the land promised by Yнwн to his people. More specifically, the "as I live" authenticating element occurs in passages that address the question "who will inhabit Yнwн's land?" A brief review of the passages outside and then inside Ezekiel will demonstrate this feature.

The spies narrative in Num 13–14, from beginning to end, deals with the question of who will inhabit the land of Canaan. The spies' report indicates it will be the current occupants who are too powerful for the Israelites to defeat. Yнwн's response, mediated by Moses' intercession, indicates that the first exodus generation will not inhabit the land. That privilege will fall to their children, the second exodus generation who will dispossess the current occupants of the land.

Deuteronomy 32:26-43 opens with Yнwн's intention to exile the people from the land, a plan Yнwн aborts in order to preserve his reputation. The passage continues on by describing Yнwн's judgment, but ends in v. 43 with the declaration that Yнwн's judgment has "cleansed the land for his people."

Isaiah 49:14-21 portrays the magnitude of Israel's restoration by describing the people as too numerous to live within the borders of the land. The people are the primary interest of this passage, and some will conclude that this means it is less directly connected to the overall theme. Yet, the people are the potential inhabitants of the land, so the theme is hardly absent.

In Jeremiah's prophecies about the capture and exile of Jehoiachin from Judah (Jer 22:24-27), it is said that the deposed king and his mother will never again see Jerusalem or Judah, "the land to which they cherish false hopes of returning."[58] Jeremiah 46:13-26 describes Nebuchadrezzar's assault on Egypt that will leave that land decimated and its people exiled. The interest in the residents of a foreign land seems out of place—but, this oracle against Egypt is immediately followed by an oracle of salvation for Israel:

---

58 William McKane, *A Critical and Exegetical Commentary on Jeremiah* (2 vols. ICC; Edinburgh: T & T Clark, 1986), I:540.

But you, do not fear, my servant Jacob,
      do not be dismayed, O Israel;
for I am going to save you from far away,
      and your offspring from the land of their captivity.
Jacob will return and have quiet and ease,
      and no one shall make him afraid.

You, have no fear, my servant Jacob—declaration of YHWH
      —for I am with you.
I will make an end of all the nations
      among which I have banished you,
      but I will not make an end of you!
I will chastise you in just measure,
      and I will by no means leave you unpunished.

Jer 46:27-28

This passage seems out of place, situated between an oracle against Egypt and one against Philistia. That is, unless a compiler was motivated to place it after an oracle that uses the "as I live" authenticating element precisely because of its larger correlation to the question of who will inhabit YHWH's land.

The final passage outside Ezekiel, Zeph 2:8-11, parallels Jer 46's interest in foreign territory. When YHWH hears the taunts of Moab and Ammon he is motivated to use Israel to desolate their land, allowing his people to inherit (נחל) it.

In sum, the concern for who will inhabit the land in these passages is not uniform, and the theme is definitely more prevalent in some passages than others. Yet, in no case is the theme absent. This evidence on its own would sustain the proposed correlation between the "as I live" authenticating element and the question of who will inhabit the land, but there is still additional evidence from Ezekiel.

The "as I live" authenticating element occurs for the first time in the book of Ezekiel in chapter five. Ezekiel 5:5-17 announces YHWH's intent to overwhelm Jerusalem with judgment. The result of YHWH's assault will be the death of two-thirds of the population in the land and the death of the final third after it has been scattered from the land. It is unclear whether this is envisioned as leaving the land empty, but it certainly indicates that the present inhabitants of Jerusalem will no longer live there.

Ezekiel 14:12-23 is structured as a casuistic legal text, but its particular case asks whether a righteous individual can prevent YHWH from
destroying all humans and animals (והכרתי ממנה אדם ובהמה; Ezek
14:13), leaving the land so desolate that no one can pass through it
(Ezek 14:15).

Ezekiel 16:44-58 is primarily concerned to show Jerusalem's sins as
even more heinous than those of Samaria or Sodom. Jerusalem will
recognize this when the three sisters are returned to their "former
state" (קדמה). The precise features of this restoration are unclear,[59] but
in the context of Ezek 16's interest in Jerusalem's defeat and exile (vv.
35-43), a return to their land seems certain to be part of its substance.

Ezekiel 18 is most familiar for its opening proverb and the possibility that it defends a theology of individual responsibility. There is no
doubt the possession of the land is not the dominant theme in the chapter. However, if Joyce is correct about the real referents of the grandfather, father and child as generations, then his suggestion that "[t]he
proverb is used by the exiles 'concerning' the fate of 'the land of Israel'
(i.e. defeat at the hands of the Babylonians)"[60] means the underlying
premise for the entire casuistic discussion is the exiles' deportation
from the land.

The next three instances of the "as I live" authenticating element
come in Ezek 20. In this passage the question about who will inhabit
the land is front and center: vv. 1-31 recounts the events from Israel's
time in Egypt, in the wilderness, occupying Canaan, and into exile; vv.
32-44 explain that YHWH will bring a community of cleansed people out
of exile and back to "my holy mountain."

The test case in Ezek 33:10-20 must be read in the broader context
of Ezek 32:17–33:20.[61] The thread running through the three sections
that make up this larger unit (32:17-32, 33:1-9, 33:10-20) is the death of
nations, a fate envisioned as their descent into the "pit" (בור), better
known as *Sheol*. In view of this, there is a connection between "life" in
33:10-20 and the continued existence of the house of Israel.

The remaining three instances in the book of Ezekiel are unambiguously reflective of the proposed relationship. The disputation between
the non-exiles and the exiles in Ezek 33:23-29 is perhaps the clearest indication of a link between the "as I live" authenticating element and the
inhabitants of YHWH's land. It is, in fact, the "as I live" formula that in-

---

59 For instance, Block can only be as specific as suggesting they will return to a state of
    "well being" (Block, *Ezekiel 1–24*, 514).

60 Joyce, *Ezekiel*, 140.

61 Sweeney, "Assertion of Divine Power," 156-72; Mayfield, *Literary Structure*, 182-87.

troduces Yʜᴡʜ's categorical repudiation of the non-exiles claim to Judah and Jerusalem. Ezekiel 34:1-10 details the failures of Israel's leaders, portrayed as shepherds. The passage continues on in vv. 11-22 to explain that Yʜᴡʜ will replace these failed leaders and exclude them from the community of people he will gather from amongst the nations in order to return them to the mountains of Israel. Finally, Ezek 35:1–36:15 details Edom's animosity towards Israel and its ambition to possess their land (35:10). The passage ends with a description of how Yʜᴡʜ will re-fructify the land and inhabit it with "my people Israel" (עַמִּי יִשְׂרָאֵל; 36:12).

Neither the book of Ezekiel nor the other texts that include the "as I live" authenticating element use it exclusively to identify who will inhabit Yʜᴡʜ's land, but that concern is at least obliquely present in each passage. In many instances—such as Ezek 20, 33:23-29, and 35:1–36:15—it is the dominant theme. Combining this evidence with the support shown in the passages outside Ezekiel, it is well substantiated to conclude there is a correlation between the "as I live" authenticating element and the question of who will inhabit Yʜᴡʜ's land.

3. Genre and the "Lifted Hand" Formula

In the preceding excursus evidence was presented to challenge the prevailing consensus that the "lifted hand" formula is a symbolic gesture employed by both humans and Yʜᴡʜ in swearing an oath. The evidence from the remainder of the ancient Near East suggested, by contrast, that the formula is related to the royal authorization of land transfer agreements.

Yet another objection to the majority view is necessary: the "lifted hand" formula is actually used in two distinct conventions. The following argument demonstrates the differences between these two conventions and employs this new understanding to make genre classifications for both uses.[62]

The first indication of the two separate conventions is the difference in syntax across the instances of the "lifted hand" formula. On the one hand, there are eleven passages where the phrase נָשָׂא יָד is continued by לְ plus the infinitive construct. The remaining four cases follow נָשָׂא יָד by a prepositional phrase indicating direction and a finite verb

---

62 Seely, for instance, briefly notes the thematic differences but ultimately considers all the instances of נָשָׂא יָד as a single entity (Seely, "Raised Hand," 411-21).

denoting Yʜᴡʜ's action. Although there is variability in the prepositional phrase, the continuation by finite verb is consistent.

The passages continued by ל plus infinitive construct are:

Citation	Infinitive Construct
Exodus 6:8	לתת
Numbers 14:30	לשׁכן
Ezekiel 20:5b	לאמר
Ezekiel 20:6	להוציאם
Ezekiel 20:15	ל[63] ... הביא
Ezekiel 20:23	להפיץ ... לזרות
Ezekiel 20:28	לתת
Ezekiel 20:42	לתת
Ezekiel 47:14	לתתה[64]
Psalm 106:26	להפיל
Nehemiah 9:15	לתת

Table 3.1: נשׂא יד with ל plus Infinitive Construct

Those passages fitting the second convention are:

---

63 In this case the verbal idea is negated, thus the ל appears prior to the particle בלתי
    and not directly prior to the infinitive construct.

64 Here with third person feminine singular suffix, referring back to ארץ in the previ-
    ous verse.

Citation	Prepositional Phrase	Finite Verb(s)
Deuteronomy 32:40	אל־שׁמים	אשׁלם, אשׁיב
Ezekiel 20:5a	לזרע בית יעקב	ואודע
Ezekiel 36:7	—	ישׁאו
Ezekiel 44:12	עליהם	ונשׁאו

Table 3.2: נשׂא יד plus Prepositional Phrase and Finite Verb

Once a distinction has been made based upon this syntactical difference, the thematic coherence among the passages within each group is
striking. The first group of eleven passages addresses Israel's possession of the promised land; the second group of four passages addresses
the bearing of guilt by a specified group.

It is necessary to recall, at this juncture, the methodological approach set out at the beginning of this chapter regarding the interplay
of content and genre. Knierim observed, "that form and content together are the factors that constitute a genre."[65] Distinguishing between
the themes dealt with by these two conventions *is* the first statement
about genre that can and should be made. This distinction substantiates handling them separately in what follows as well.

(a) The "Lifted Hand" Formula and the Land Theme

The initial observation about the use of the "lifted hand" plus infinitive
construct noted its concern with Israel's possession of the land. Canon-
ically, this formula occurs first at Exod 6:8: "I will bring you into the
land that I lifted my hand to give it, to Abraham, to Isaac, and to Jacob."[66] Precisely the same matter is addressed as part of the spy narrative at Num 14:30, which in the final arrangement of the Pentateuch explains why the promise of Exod 6:8 is revoked from the first exodus
generation:

---

65   Knierim, "Old Testament Form Criticism Reconsidered," 451.

66   The wooden English phrasing is intentional, highlighting the asyndetic position of
     the patriarchal triad in this verse. For further discussion, see ch. 4, §3 and 4.

Say to them: "As I live—declaration of YHWH—according to what you said in my hearing, thus I will do to you. In this wilderness your corpses will fall, all of your arrays, all of your number, twenty-years old and upward, which grumbled against me. You will not come to the land that I lifted my hand in order to cause you to dwell in it, except for Caleb, son of Jephunah, and Joshua, son of Nun. But your little ones that you said would be plunder, I will bring them in and they will know the land that you rejected.

Num 14:28-31

The next six occurrences are in Ezek 20. Five times the "lifted hand" formula appears in the first disputation speech (vv. 1-31), each instance helping to structure this extended argument for YHWH's refusal to consult with the elders. Seeing the connection between these examples and Israel's possession of the land depends upon the proposal that this formula is derived from the royal authorization of land transfers (see chapter two, section five). With that connotation in mind, one can see a thread running through the passage: the "lifted hand" formula is used to depict the series of decisions YHWH made about who will dwell in the land.

The first convention of the "lifted hand" formula appears in Ezek 20:5b, 6, 15, 23, and 28 (for details see table 3.3 on p. 120). The first occurrence, which refers to the divine self-introduction described in Exod 6:2, is the least clear of all the instances. Its primary intent is to recall the divine self-introduction, but in Exod 6:2-8 that introduction is an integral part of YHWH taking possession of the people, i.e. taking them away from Pharaoh's control. The use of the Akkadian našû-nadānu formula for the transfer of possessions other than land is well-attested, and it seems this instance of the "lifted hand" formula draws on that usage. Even though the focus of this statement is not directly on the land, it prepares for the theme that dominates the rest of the passage: the "lifted hand" formula explains how YHWH has changed Israel's status vis-à-vis the land throughout history.

The first change YHWH makes to their status is to elect them (בחר) and free them from slavery. In Ezek 20:6 YHWH declares his intent to bring the people to the land that "I spied out for them, a land flowing with milk and honey, the best of all lands." This allusion to the spy account in Num 13–14 brings into the audience's mind that the promised land is already occupied, meaning YHWH's statement requires the transfer of the territory from one group to another. Ezekiel 20:15, yet another echo of Num 13–14, indicates the transfer of the land from the first, rebellious exodus generation to their children. Ezekiel 20:23 indicates that the further rebellion of the second exodus generation motivated YHWH to determine, even before bringing the people into the land, that

Citation	Infinitive Construct	Action
Ezekiel 20:5b	לֵאמֹר	to say, 'I am YHWH'
Ezekiel 20:6	לְהוֹצִיאָם	to bring them out of the land of Egypt
Ezekiel 20:15	לְבִלְתִּי הָבִיא	to not bring them into the land
Ezekiel 20:23	לְהָפִיץ ... לְזָרוֹת	to scatter them in the nations and to disperse them in the lands
Ezekiel 20:28	לָתֵת	to give it [the land] to them

Table 3.3: נָשָׂא יד in Ezek 20:1-31

in the future they would be exiled. That is, in the future YHWH would transfer control of the land from Israel to another nation. Ezekiel 20:28, the final instance of the formula in the *Unheilsgeschichte*, recalls Israel's actions once they were in the land. The syntax requires that the "lifted hand" formula refer to YHWH's having transferred the land to the people,[67] indicating within the final form of Ezek 20:1-31 the realization of the decision taken in v. 6. The final instance of נָשָׂא יד (Ezek 20:42), part of the disputation speech of vv. 32-44, asserts that YHWH has decided to once again transfer control of the land to his people: "You shall know that I am YHWH, when I bring you into the land of Israel, the land that I lifted my hand to transfer it to your ancestors." The final instance of the formula in Ezekiel, Ezek 47:14, also employs the land transfer connotation, in that case as a preamble to the book's revised tribal allotments.

There is a salient correspondence between the verbs that continue the "lifted hand" formula in Ezek 20:1-31 and the verbs of Exod 6:2-8. Isaac Gottlieb demonstrates Exod 6:6-8 is crafted around three series of three verbs and draws on the land transfer connotation of the Akkadian

---

67   This is the only occasion where a past tense translation is necessary for this convention of the "lifted hand" formula, adding to the evidence scholars have presented that vv. 27-29 may be secondary (Zimmerli, *Ezekiel 1–24*, 412; Dalit Rom-Shiloni, "Ezekiel as the Voice of the Exiles and Constructor of Exilic Ideology," *HUCA* 76 [2005]: 24).

našû-nadānu formula in order to describe the promise of land to Israel.[68]
The following chart shows the overlap between the two passages:

Citation	Infinitive Construct	Action	Referent
Ezekiel 20:5b	לאמר	to speak	Exod 6:2
Ezekiel 20:6	להוציאם	to bring out	Exod 6:6
Ezekiel 20:15	הביא	to (not) bring (in)	Exod 6:8 (cf. Num 14:30-31)
Ezekiel 20:23	להפיץ ... לזרות	to scatter	—
Ezekiel 20:28	לתת	to give	Exod 6:8

Table 3.4: נשא יד in Ezek 20:1-31 and Exod 6:2-8

Given the tight literary structure of both Exod 6:2-8 and Ezek 20:1-31, this similarity hardly seems coincidental. It is true that בוא, יצא, אמר, and נתן are common verbs, and their recurrence alone does not prove any correlation. Still, Ezek 20 employs the verbs in precisely the same order as Exod 6:2-8. Perhaps this seems the only logical possibility, but the author and editors of Ezek 20:1-31 certainly had various options available for structuring their material and yet, over more than 20 verses, maintained this scheme. Furthermore, though יצא is a common verbal root, Jacques Pons explains that its use in Ezek 20:6 is rare among the prophets,[69] its only parallels appearing in the DTR passages of Jeremiah (Jer 7:22, 11:4, 31:32, 32:21, 34:13; cf. Ezek 34:13). All five passages in Jeremiah—precisely like Ezek 20:6—refer to YHWH bringing his people out of Egypt. That thematic consistency further supports the link between Ezek 20 and Exod 6. Even though many studies have observed the strong similarities in formulaic language between these two

---

68 Gottlieb, "Law, Love, and Redemption," 54-57.

69 J. Pons, "Le vocabulaire d'Ez 20. Le prophète s'oppose à la vision deutéronomiste de l'histoire," in *Ezekiel and His Book: Textual and Literary Criticism and Their Interrelation* (ed. J. Lust; Betl 74; Leuven: Peeters, 1986), 219.

passages,[70] for instance highlighting the presence of the formula of self-introduction (אני יהוה)[71] and the covenant formula,[72] none has perceived this overlap in language. This evidence suggests that the author of Ezek 20 is working with knowledge of the tradition preserved in Exod 6:2-8. Determining whether that knowledge is based upon a written text or an oral tradition later recorded in Exodus is beyond the scope of this study, but is a line of inquiry that deserves further attention.[73]

The combined effect of Ezek 20 utilizing the land transfer connotations of the "lifted hand" formula and various allusions to the exodus tradition is to explain YHWH's power over Israel vis-à-vis the land.[74] That jurisdiction is applied analogously in YHWH's counter-thesis: just as in each phase of the historical account Israel's rebellion provoked YHWH to prevent the transfer of the land to them, for the same reason the elders' present appeal to consult YHWH will be rejected. That is to say, the pattern of rebellion that has prevented the transfer of the land to the people is exactly what precludes YHWH from listening to the elders' inquiry.

Continuing the review of passages relevant to the נשא יד formula and the theme of the land, Psalm 106:26 is part of another account of YHWH's historical interaction with Israel where these appear together. This instance is nearly identical to Ezek 20:23, and it presents the parallel point that YHWH decided to exile the people from the land while they were still in the wilderness.

The final example, Neh 9:15, is close to Ezek 20:28 in that it recalls YHWH's initial statement of intent to transfer the land in Exod 6, remarking, "you [YHWH] told them to go and to possess the land which you lifted your hand to give to them."

---

70 A longer discussion is available in J. Lust, "Exodus 6,2-8 and Ezekiel," in *Studies in the Book of Exodus: Redaction-Reception-Interpretation* (ed. Marc Vervenne; BETL 126; Leuven: Peeters, 1996).

71 Zimmerli, *I Am Yahweh*, 7-13.

72 Rendtorff, *The Covenant Formula*, 11-37.

73 For instance, this appears to be an ideal case for applying David Carr's "empirical criteria" for establishing the direction of dependence (David M. Carr, "Method in Determination of Dependence: An Empirical Test of Criteria Applied to Exodus 34:11-26 and Its Parallels," in *Gottes Volk am Sinai: Untersuchungen zu Ex 32–34 und Dt 9–10* [eds. Matthias Köckert and Erhard Blum; Veröffentlichungen Der Wissenschaftlichen Gesellschaft Für Theologie 18; Gütersloh: Kaiser Gütersloher, 2001]).

74 Michael Lyons has recently demonstrated the book of Ezekiel's capacity for such intricate rhetorical transformations (*From Law to Prophecy: Ezekiel's Use of the Holiness Code* [LHBOTS 507; New York: T & T Clark, 2009], especially pp. 114-45).

In view of this evidence, it is logical to conclude the following: rather than interpreting the first convention of the lifted hand formula as a symbolic gesture for authenticating an oath it is, in reality, an expression that draws on the meaning of the Akkadian *našû-nadānu* formula, used for royal authorization of land transfers, to present YHWH as the royal authority who ultimately decides who will control the land. The preceding review of the relevant passages demonstrates that this meaning fits into each passage where the formula appears. Therefore, this convention of usage for יד נשׂא can be called the *"lifted hand" land transfer formula*.

Broadening the scope to consider all of the instances of the "lifted hand" land transfer formula, two genres emerge. The first genre accounts for Exod 6:2-8 and Ezek 47:13–48:35, which are oracles of salvation (*Heilsorakel*).[75] The remaining passages fall into a second genre that might be called a "historical review,"[76] drawing on their concern for Israel's and Judah's past actions. However Hals is nearer the intention of the texts when he calls Ezek 20 a theological reflection (*theologische Überlegung*), that is "a type of relatively abstract thinking which categorizes the concrete realities of human experience and formulates them as parts of a standardized, overarching theological structure."[77] The historical reality, at least as reflected in the texts, includes the first exodus generation's prohibition from entering the land (Num 14), the elders rebuff by YHWH (Ezek 20), and communal lament about past and present disobedience (Ps 106, Neh 9); in each case, the overarching theological structure characterizes human disobedience as the basis for YHWH bringing about these historical realities.

(b) The "Lifted Hand" Formula and the Punishment Theme

In addition to the syntactical and thematic evidence indicated there is a second usage of the "lifted hand" formula, these texts share a concern for the bearing of guilt by a specified group. A brief review of the four relevant passages demonstrates this feature.

---

75 George W. Coats, *Exodus 1–18* (FOTL 2A; Grand Rapids, Mich.: Eerdmans, 1999), 58-59. For details of this genre see Sweeney, *Isaiah 1-39*, 526.

76 Ibid., 521.

77 Ronald M. Hals, *Ezekiel* (FOTL 19; Grand Rapids, Mich.: Eerdmans, 1989), 357.

The two clearest cases are Ezek 36:7 and 44:12. The first instance, part of the longer passage in Ezek 35:1–36:15 directed against Mt Seir and the mountains of Israel, describes the intent of Edom to take Israel's land while it suffers in the Babylonian exile. It promises, subsequently, a reversal of fortune: "Therefore, thus says the Lord Yнwн, I lifted my hand against the nations that are all around you; they shall bear their disgrace" (Ezek 36:7b). The second example appears in Ezek 44:9-14, a passage that indicts "the Levites who went far from me, going astray from me after their idols when Israel went astray" (Ezek 44:10a). The Levites' conduct prompts Yнwн's judgment: "Because they ministered before their idols and became a stumbling block of iniquity to the house of Israel, therefore I will lift my hand over them— declaration of Yнwн—and they will bear their guilt." (Ezek 44:12). In each case the formula is expanded by a finite verb, a syntactical observation made above. Significantly, in both cases in Ezekiel the continuing verb is נשׂא—used in the priestly guilt bearing formula.[78]

The third occurrence is in the Song of Moses:

I say, "as I live forever,
> when I whet my flashing sword, and my hand takes hold of
> judgment;
I will take vengeance on my adversaries,
> and will repay those who hate me."

                                               Deut 32:40b-41

This passage continues the "lifted hand" formula by specifying that Yнwн will return (שׁוב) vengeance on his enemies and repay (שׁלם) his adversaries.

The remaining case, Ezek 20:5a, stands at some remove from the other three examples, a situation that requires explanation. To begin, this instance demonstrates no connection to the guilt-bearing theme present in Deut 32:40-41, Ezek 36:1-7 and 44:9-14. Next, like the other instances in Ezekiel the "lifted hand" formula is continued by a finite verb; however, that verb is ידע and not נשׂא, reinforcing the difference in theme. The phrase, furthermore, is problematic in the wider context of Ezek 20 and the book as a whole. The mention of Jacob it introduces

---

78 In the first case המה כלמתם ישׂאו and in the second case נשׂאו עונם. On this formula see Baruch J. Schwartz, "The Bearing of Sin in the Priestly Literature," in *Pomegranates and Golden Bells: Studies in Biblical, Jewish, and Near Eastern Ritual, Law, and Literature in Honor of Jacob Milgrom* (eds. David P. Wright, D. N. Freedman and Avi Hurvitz; Winona Lake, Ind.: Eisenbrauns, 1995), 3-21.

is not unprecedented in the book,[79] but it goes against the negative view of the patriarchs taken elsewhere (cf. Ezek 33:23-29) and is particularly problematic because the same verse places Israel's origin in Egypt, not Canaan.[80]

The difficulties with this phrase are demonstrated by the Greek translation, which harmonizes the "lifted hand" formula with the following verb וָאוּדַע ("and became known to the seed of the house of Jacob;" καὶ ἐγνωρίσθην τῷ σπέρματι οἴκου Ιακωβ).[81] This is the only case in Ezek 20 where the translator felt the need to render נשׂא יד with that kind of harmonization. Furthermore, it is the only instance where the translator failed to specifically mention YHWH's hand (τῇ χειρί μου). These various problems suggest that the phrase וָאֶשָּׂא יָדִי לְזֶרַע בֵּית יַעֲקֹב is from a different hand than both the six occurrences of the "lifted hand" land transfer formula in the book and also the instances of this version of the formula in Ezek 36:7 and 44:12.

A precedent for this type of redaction is available in various studies that argue the redactors of the Pentateuch endeavored to connect the patriarchal and exodus traditions by inserting the patriarchs' names at key points.[82] A similar effort here would account rather neatly for this phrase.

The proposed reconstruction reads:

וְאָמַרְתָּ אֲלֵיהֶם כֹּה־אָמַר אֲדֹנָי יְהוִה
בְּיוֹם בָּחֲרִי בְיִשְׂרָאֵל
{ וָאֶשָּׂא יָדִי לְזֶרַע בֵּית יַעֲקֹב }
וָאִוָּדַע לָהֶם בְּאֶרֶץ מִצְרָיִם
וָאֶשָּׂא יָדִי לָהֶם לֵאמֹר אֲנִי יְהוָה אֱלֹהֵיכֶם

---

79 Cf. Ezek 28:25; 37:25; 39:25.

80 Zimmerli, *Ezekiel 1–24*, 407-08, attempts an explanation, but fails to persuade. Block, *Ezekiel 1–24*, 627-28, also supports this position but admits, "Why he [Ezekiel] began his history of Israel in Egypt rather than with the patriarchs is not clear."

81 Cf. Lust, "For I Lift," 163.

82 E.g. John Van Seters, "Confessional Reformulation in the Exilic Period," *VT* 22 (1972): 448-59; Thomas Römer, *Israels Väter: Untersuchungen zur Väterthematik im Deuteronomium und in der deuteronomistischen Tradition* (OBO 99; Göttingen: Vandenhoeck & Ruprecht, 1990); Thomas Römer, "Deuteronomy in Search of Origins," in *Reconsidering Israel and Judah: Recent Studies on the Deuteronomistic History* (eds. Gary N. Knoppers and J. Gordon McConville; Sources for Biblical and Theological Study 8; Winona Lake, Ind.: Eisenbrauns, 2000); Thomas Römer, "Exodus 3-4 und die aktuelle Pentateuchdiskussion," in *The Interpretation of the Exodus: Studies in Honour of Cornelius Houtman* (eds. Riemer Roukema, Bert Jan Lietaert Peerbolte, Klaas Spronk and Jan-Wim Wesselius; CBET 44; Leuven: Peeters, 2006).

and you will say to them, "Thus says the Lord Y<small>HWH</small>
on the day I choose Israel
{and I raised my hand to the seed of the house of Jacob}
and I made myself known to them in the land of Egypt
and I lifted my hand to them saying 'I am Y<small>HWH</small>, your god'"

Ezek 20:5*

This small deletion results in a smooth-reading text and removes all the difficulties this phrase presents in both Ezek 20 and the whole book. The redactor, it appears, attempted to disguise his addition by using a locution found elsewhere in the book of Ezekiel but has, by connecting that formula with unique content, actually left a trace of his presence.

All this evidence demonstrates that the shared feature of Deut 32:40-41, Ezek 36:1-7 and 44:9-14 is to address a group found guilty and to specify its punishment. The book highlights this concern by combining the "lifted hand" formula with the priestly guilt bearing formula נשׂא עוֹן. Bruce Wells has shown that in the Neo-Babylonian legal context this indicated that "the person is guilty of wrongdoing and subject to punishment, but exactly what that punishment is depends on the nature of the wrongdoing."[83] In view of this meaning, the second convention of the "lifted hand" formula serves to indicate that Y<small>HWH</small> is both the one who will determine and execute the punishment. Therefore, this formula can best be termed the *"lifted hand" punishment formula*.

Widening the perspective to consider the genre of Deut 32:40-41, Ezek 36:1-7, and 44:9-14, these passages use the "lifted hand" punishment formula in order to create a unique genre of salvation oracles (*Heilsorakel*)[84] that are typified by presenting salvation to a group of Y<small>HWH</small>'s people through the punishment of another party. In Deut 32:40 the adversaries of Israel are punished and Y<small>HWH</small> is praised because he will "cleanse the land for his people" (Deut 32:43). Immediately following the condemnation of the nations in Ezek 36:7, and explicitly because of their expulsion, Y<small>HWH</small> promises the land that it will be re-fructified, re-populated, and "[the people and the animals] will do more good to you than ever before" (Ezek 36:11). Finally, Ezek 44:9-14 not only specifies that the Levites will bear their guilt but, famously, also limits the Levites' role in the Jerusalem temple so that the Zadokites as-

---

83 Bruce Wells, *The Law of Testimony in the Pentateuchal Codes* (BZAR 4; Wiesbaden: Harrassowitz, 2004), 61.

84 Ezekiel's utilization of such a rhetorical transformation has recently been demonstrated by Lyons, *From Law to Prophecy*, 117-27. Unfortunately, Lyons does not include the עוֹן נשׂא locution among those that Ezekiel adopts and adapts from H.

cend to prominence among the priests. Therefore, even though a nar-
row view towards this punishment formula suggests a role in judgment speeches, the evidence indicates that in its wider context this
formula actually plays a role in prophetic oracles of salvation.

4. Summary

This chapter has looked in detail at the ways in which the "as I live"
and "lifted hand" formulae are employed to identify the genre of the
passages in which they appear and to determine if there is a pattern in
their usage. Several conclusions emerged.

Firstly, the "as I live" authenticating element occurs in prophetic
announcements of judgment. Only four passages—Isa 49:14-21; Ezek
18:1-32; 33:10-20; and 33:23-29—varied from this pattern. Further investigation showed that each of these four passages is a disputation
speech, and this insight required a reconsideration of the other 15 passages. Six additional passages exhibited the three constituent parts of
the disputation speech, bringing the total to 10 out of the 18 passages.
This established that the "as I live" authenticating element can introduce either the counter-thesis or argument portion of a disputation
speech. In sum, the "as I live" authenticating element is employed in
prophetic announcements of judgment, which are often constructed as
disputation speeches.

Secondly, differences in syntax and theme indicated that the "lifted
hand" formula should be considered as not one formula but as two *formulae*. The first convention, which corresponds to the Akkadian *našû-
nadānu* formula in legal documents regarding the transfer of land between parties, details Yhwh's promise to transfer land to or from his
people. This "lifted hand" land transfer formula occurs twice in an oracle of salvation (Exod 6:2-8; Ezek 47:13–48:35) and elsewhere in a genre
best called theological reflection. The second convention, associated
with the formula נשא עון, specifies the type and agent of punishment
for a guilty party. This second usage, the "lifted hand" punishment
formula, features in oracles of salvation for Yhwh's people in which
their salvation is predicated upon the punishment of their enemy or enemies. In reaching these findings, this chapter also added evidence to
the growing argument that neither convention of the "lifted hand" formula is part of a divine oath.

From a methodological point of view, the detailed analysis in this
chapter demonstrated the importance of considering the content of a
passage in making genre classifications. Content was a key indicator

that there are two conventions of the "lifted hand" formula. Noting the particular and diverse thematic concerns of the two conventions focused attention on precisely how each convention is employed and to which genre each one belongs. Indeed, the failure to make this thematic distinction and to consider the relevant cases separately is probably a contributing factor in the erroneous conclusion that the "lifted hand" formula is part of a divine oath.

Furthermore, the genre classifications made in this chapter present new options for what several of the units in question should be "read as." Here it is important to recall Knierim's point that "[t]he entirety of a text may be governed by more than one typical structure" and that it is incumbent upon the interpreter to place them into a hierarchy.[85] For instance, the frequent occurrence of the "as I live" authenticating element in disputation speeches encourages placing that "typical structure" at the top of the hierarchy for Ezek 20:1-31: the *Unheilsgeschichte* is not primarily to be "read as" a historical survey but first and foremost as a disputation between YHWH and the elders of the exilic community. This explains, in part, why it differs so sharply from the allegorical nature of Ezek 16 and 23, the book's two historical surveys. By contrast, Ezek 20:1-31 foregrounds the mistaken belief of the elders and employs the historical account as a tool to convey YHWH's reasons for objecting to their inquiry. Thus it should be read not primarily as an explanation for the exile but as an apologetic for YHWH's silence. The exegetical importance of that subtle difference will be treated in due course as part of an extended argument that Ezek 20 is one instance of a disguised anti-Babylonian polemic that runs throughout the book of Ezekiel.

---

85   Knierim, "Old Testament Form Criticism Reconsidered," 462.

Chapter Four:
Social and Literary Setting of the "As I Live" and "Lifted Hand" Formulae

This chapter seeks to describe the social setting (*Sitz im Leben*) and literary setting (*Sitz in der Literatur*) of the "as I live" authenticating element and the two "lifted hand" formulae. Detailed review of the evidence for each formula demonstrates a robust correlation to a theological tradition[1] contained in the Hebrew Bible. This adds new insights about how widely and for what purposes the book of Ezekiel draws from the distinct, formulaic language of P, Dᴛʀ, and H. A precise grasp of where the book obtains these formulae from is a necessary foundation for the second part of this study, which analyzes how and why the book of Ezekiel integrates these formulae into its message.

The way in which social setting and literary setting are understood in this chapter necessitates some comment. It is an undeniable fact of biblical studies that reconstructing ancient practices remains a hypothetical endeavor. The texts give, by and large, stylized glimpses of ancient practice. Though it is methodologically justifiable to employ the biblical text as a window on actual ancient praxis, even the most ardent supporter of this work must admit the Hebrew Bible remains a very darkly shrouded window on that world. This challenge will not prevent the suggestion of a social setting (*Sitz im Leben*) for each formula, but these will be provisional and loosely-held findings at best. Rather than accepting this as the best possible outcome, this chapter will place much greater emphasis on the literary setting (*Sitz in der Literatur*) of the formulae. This focus will allow for solid conclusions to be made about the theological traditions in which these formulae were employed and from which they gained their various connotations. If this seems to create a new, previously untested, third category of theologi-

---

1   The term tradition is chosen strategically. Discussions about whether P or Dᴛʀ should be termed a "movement" (*Bewegung*), school (*Schule*), disciples or such is beyond the scope of this study. Tradition is chosen because it leaves open the questions about group size, longevity, and status of those involved in conveying the ideas that are now represented by the terms P, Dᴛʀ, and H. Tradition signifies a set of ideas that are deemed significant by one or more people and, due to this significance, passed down through one or more generations. This is a statement that should accomodate the whole range of views on what is meant by P, Dᴛʀ, and H.

cal context (*Sitz in der theologischen Tradition*) this is not the intent. Rather, the objective is to recognize and take advantage of the considerable evidence that the P, DTR, and H theological traditions constituted major parties within the ancient Israelite and Judahite elite classes, each of which engaged in debate to define legitimate ethnic, national, and religious identity. Even where actual ancient practice can be reconstructed, it is presented through the views of these theological traditions. Placing these three formulae into a theological tradition does, therefore, say something significant about their ancient context, even if that statement is different than what form criticism has traditionally sought to offer.

In order to move forward in this analysis, the book of Ezekiel will have to be placed in a subordinate position to the relevant passages found elsewhere. This move is necessitated by the strong evidence that the book adopts and adapts formulaic language from P and DTR in order to fashion its message. Thus, evidence for the theological tradition represented by the literary setting of each formula outside Ezekiel will be considered first. Only when this work has been completed will the provisional conclusions be compared with the evidence from Ezekiel to see if they are confirmed or contested.

1. Prolegomena: The Relationship between Num 13–14 and Ezekiel

Prior to investigating the relevant passages, a discussion of the relationship between Ezekiel and the spies narrative in Num 13–14 is necessary. This analysis will build a foundation for later observations about the book of Ezekiel's relationship to DTR, P, and H, the three theological traditions that have shaped the spies narrative, by demonstrating that the book of Ezekiel is familiar with the contributions of all three traditions to this story.

The preceding chapter showed the importance of Deut 32:1-43, in particular vv. 26-43, to recognizing the genre of the "as I live" authenticating element and to Ezekiel's statements about the land. While many have argued for a late exilic or post-exilic date for the Song based upon its connections with Jeremiah and Ezekiel,[2] Sanders and Mark Leuchter have presented evidence for assigning the Song a pre-exilic date.[3]

---

2   See the discussion in Driver, *Deuteronomy*, 345-47.

3   Sanders, *The Provenance of Deuteronomy 32.*; Mark Leuchter, "Why is the Song of Moses in the Book of Deuteronomy," *VT* 57 (2007): 295-317, especially pp. 315-7,

Therefore, proposing that the book of Ezekiel knew this text is relatively straightforward.[4] The situation is more complex with Num 13–14.

The "as I live" authenticating element occurs in both the non-priestly (Num 14:11-25) and priestly (Num 14:26-38) sources of the spy narrative. This indicates the possibility that Ezekiel knew one or both of those sections. Ezekiel 20:10-20 demonstrates beyond question that its author possessed a tradition of a judgment upon the first exodus generation with the transfer of the land promise to the second exodus generation. Indeed, it demonstrates this tradition was not only familiar to the author but to the exiled audience in Babylonia too. There is no doubt that Ezek 20:1-31 is highly stylized, working liberally with H's criteria as laid out in Lev 17–26[5] in order to craft its version of history, one that seeks to characterize the primary downfall of Israel as idolatry.[6] Yet, the most straightforward explanation for Ezekiel's reference to a mediated judgment announced against the first exodus generation with the "as I live" oath formula is that Num 14:11-25 was known to the author and editors of Ezekiel.

Verses 11-25 are usually assigned to a non-priestly source, frequently to a pre-exilic JE document, with the result that numerous scholars argue that this section antedates Ezekiel.[7] This argument is complicated when vv. 11b-23a are recognized as a DTR insertion into the text.[8] However, the unique characteristic of this section is Moses' intercession with YHWH, a plea that elicits YHWH's promise of restraint in judging the first exodus generation. This tradition is referenced in Ezek 5:5-17,

---

where he offers reasons to believe that the poem may have been composed as early as the tenth-century B.C.E.

4   Cf. Jason Gile, "Ezekiel 16 and the Song of Moses: A Prophetic Transformation?," *JBL* 130 (2011): 87-108.

5   Lyons, *From Law to Prophecy*, 163, suggests as many as 18 separate references to Lev 17–26 in Ezek 20:1-31. If one compares Ezek 20 with its nearest parallel, Ps 106, the emphasis becomes even more clear: Ps 106 faithfully replicates the pentateuchal account (cf. vv. 24-27), specifying that the first generation "rejected the desirable land and did not trust in his [YHWH's] word" (v. 24), whereas Ezekiel suggests that they failed to obey the statutes (חקה), ordinances (משפט), and profaned the sabbath. This observation calls into question how much "history" or "tradition" even the author thought was contained in these verses.

6   Cf. Lev 26:1.

7   For instance Baruch Levine, *Numbers 1–20: A New Translation with Introduction and Commentary* (AB 4A; New York: Doubleday & Co., 1993), 91.

8   Martin Noth, *Numbers* (OTL; Chatham: SCM Press Ltd., 1968), 108-09; Ernest W. Nicholson, *The Pentateuch in the Twentieth Century: The Legacy of Julius Wellhausen* (Oxford: Oxford University Press, 1998.), 180; Boorer, *The Promise of the Land*, 331, note 7.

where it is adapted to the changed circumstances of the exiles' post-597 B.C.E. life in order to explain YHWH's prior decision not to restrain from punishing Jerusalem any longer. The same passage combines the notion of YHWH's restraint with terms and images from Lev 26 in a first person speech by YHWH. These textual features constitute three of Carr's six criteria for determining the direction of dependence,[9] suggesting that the assignment of this text to DTR does not preclude its knowledge by the book of Ezekiel.

The priestly version (Num 14:26-28) is almost universally assigned to P, variously dated, but now usually placed in the late sixth century or, more often, the fifth century B.C.E. The notable exception is Israel Knohl, who assigns this passage to H and dates it to the reign of Hezekiah.[10] Even though the evidence Knohl uses to date H to the reign of Hezekiah is debatable,[11] there are features distinctive of H's influence in these verses. For instance, the unique contribution of this section is to portray YHWH's judgment as a *lex talionis* punishment, symbolically relating the 40 years of wandering to the 40 days of reconnaissance (Num 14:33-34). This logic is replicated elsewhere only in Ezek 4:4-8, where it symbolizes the length of the exile. The relative complexity of Ezek 4—containing two specified periods of time for different issues[12]—compared to the bare symbolism in Num 14 suggests that Ezekiel is developing and expanding the ideas found there.

Another indication that Ezekiel knows Num 14:26-38 is that Ezek 20:1-31 is the only other passage in the Hebrew Bible that contains both the "as I live" and "lifted hand" land transfer formulae. In Ezek 20, the author uses the "lifted hand" formula to evoke the exodus events and the "as I live" formula to designate the disputation speech genre of this passage. It is unlikely that a later author would add the "as I live" oath

9   Carr,"Genesis," 126; cf. Molly M. Zahn, "Reexamaning Empirical Models: The Case of Exodus 13," in *Das Deuteronomium zwischen Pentateuch und deuteronomistischem Geschichtswerk* (eds. E. Otto and R. Achenbach; Frlant 206; Göttingen: Vandenhoeck & Ruprecht, 2004).

10   Israel Knohl, *The Sanctuary of Silence: The Priestly Torah and the Holiness School* (Minneapolis, Minn.: Fortress, 1995), 90-2, 107-8; cf. Milgrom, *Leviticus 17–22*, 1439-43. Knohl's key arguments are discussed further in §2.b of this chapter.

11   Knohl, *Sanctuary of Silence*, 204-14; for details see §3 on the social setting of the "lifted hand" land transfer formula. Cf. Milgrom Jacob Milgrom, *Leviticus 23–27: A New Translation with Introduction and Commentary* (AB 3B; New York: Doubleday, 2000), 2363-65.

12   Greenberg, *Ezekiel 1-20*, 118, and Block, *Ezekiel 1–24*, 178-79, argue that the 390 years refers to the rebellious deeds of the people in pre-exilic times and the 40 years, perhaps a late addition to the passage (Greenberg, *Ezekiel 1-20*, 125-26), refers to the exilic experience.

into the events of Israel's rebellion and Y<small>HWH</small>'s judgment based upon this text. More probable is the scenario in which Num 14:26-38 knew the "as I live" formula's connection to the spy narrative from Num 14:11-25 and that the book of Ezekiel, aware of the "as I live" formula's role in both those texts *and also* in other disputations, employed it in a more expansive fashion.

A final sign that Ezekiel knows the priestly spy narrative is the allusion of Ezek 36:13-15 to Num 13:32, a verse with priestly features inserted into an otherwise non-priestly section of the narrative.[13] Levine observes, "A perusal... of Ezek 36:5-12, shows the converse of a land that devours its inhabitants, for there we read of bountiful fertility, of agricultural lands worked and sown, and of towns settled and of ruins restored; of a populous nation."[14] It is more likely that Ezekiel reversed an already familiar derogatory image to make a positive statement about the future than the alternative, namely that the author of the priestly strata in Num 13–14 knew Ezekiel's application of this quote to unnamed interlocutors and, based upon that, worked it back into this evaluation of the land. The former is not only intuitively more sensible, but Michael Lyons has demonstrated that Ezek 36:1-15 does precisely this with material from Lev 26.[15]

All of this evidence shows that both the non-priestly and the priestly versions of the spy account were known by the book of Ezekiel. More specifically, the evidence indicates this awareness is already present in the earliest material within the book: 4:4-8 predicts a 40-year exile, which would be demonstrably false after ca. 557 B.C.E.; 5:5-17 predicts the total annihilation of Jerusalem's residents, which did not come to pass; 20:1-31 comes immediately after a date formula placing it to ca. 590 B.C.E., and there is little reason to push this portion of the chapter much later. Ezekiel 36:13-15 is the only text with indicators of late composition, but this does not invalidate the other evidence. Thus, it is reasonable to conclude that a text containing essentially the final form of Num 14:11-38, and perhaps other parts of the spies narrative, circulated prior to 587 B.C.E., possibly before 597 B.C.E.[16]

---

13   Levine, *Numbers 1–20*, 358.

14   Ibid.

15   Lyons, *From Law to Prophecy*, 99-100.

16   This argument applies only to Num 13–14. Although it is certainly possible that other portions of the final form of Numbers were also known to the author and editors of Ezekiel, those details are beyond the present argument. Indeed, it is possible, maybe even very likely, that Num 13–14 existed separately from the larger narrative for a substantial period of time.

Having established a rationale that Num 13–14 is an antecedent of Ezekiel, it can then be added to Deut 32 as an indicator of the DTR, P, and H language in the exodus tradition from which Ezekiel drew.

2. Social Setting of the "As I live" Authenticating Element

Owing to its more frequent use, the "as I live" authenticating element is considered first. That formula occurs 23 times in the Hebrew Bible:

Book	Citations
Numbers	14:21, 28
Deuteronomy	32:40
Isaiah	49:18
Jeremiah	22:24; 46:18
Ezekiel	5:11; 14:16, 18, 20; 16:48; 17:16, 19; 18:3; 20:3, 31, 33; 33:11, 27; 34:8; 35:6, 11
Zephaniah	2:9

Table 4.1: Occurrences of חי אני

Significant attention will be given to these passages in a moment, but first the more numerous examples of the related human authenticating element "as YHWH lives" (חי יהוה) must be considered.

(a) The Human Oath חי־יהוה and the Deuteronomistic Tradition

The phenomenal expansion of scholarship on DTR demands caution when suggesting that one has identified a previously unnoticed feature of DTR. Nonetheless, there are sufficient indications that חי יהוה is distinctive of DTR though this connection has not previously been made.[17]

---

17   In identifying the חי יהוה authenticating element to be DTR I follow the five criteria suggested by Norbert F. Lohfink, "Was There a Deuteronomistic Movement?" in *Those Elusive Deuteronomists: The Phenomenon of Pan-Deuteronomism* (eds. L. S. Schear-

The first piece of evidence is the 43 citations of the "as Yhwh lives" authenticating element that exhibit a conspicuous overlap with the Deuteronomistic History:[18] table 4.2 (p. 135) shows that each instance is a direct parallel to a DtrH pericope.

Book	Citations
Judges	8:19
1 Samuel	14:39, 45; 19:6; 20:3, 21; 25:26, 34; 26:10, 16; 28:10; 29:6
2 Samuel	4:9; 12:5; 14:11; 15:21; 22:47
1 Kings	1:29; 2:24; 17:1, 12; 18:10, 15; 22:14
2 Kings	2:2, 4, 6; 3:14; 4:30; 5:16, 20
Jeremiah	4:2; 5:2; 12:16; 16:14, 15; 23:7, 8; 38:16
Hosea	4:15
Psalms	18:47 (= 2 Sam 22:47)
Ruth	3:13
2 Chronicles	18:13 (= 1 Kgs 22:14)

Table 4.2: Occurrences of חי־יהוה

In the case of Ps 18:47 and 2 Chron 18:13 it is necessary to observe their overlap with passages inside DtrH to recognize the link. Hosea 4:15 does lie outside DtrH, but it is common to assign the verse to a later redaction, possibly under the influence of Amos' prophecies and possi-

ing and S. L. McKenzie; JSOTSup 268; Sheffield: Sheffield Academic Press, 1999), 41: (1) common contents or interests, i.e. cult centralization, veneration of Yhwh alone, observance of the Torah, of the land promised and endangered; (2) common narrative patterns, i.e. laws on the unfolding of history which leads to blessing or cursing; (3) common style, i.e. Dtr preference for series of infinitives vs. Priestly favoring of parallel sentences with finite verbs; (4) compositional devices, i.e. the framing of texts with exhortatory formulas, linking of long historical narratives through the insertion of interpretative discourses; and (5) dependence on specific Dtr texts. Minimally, the following argument shows חי יהוה meets criteria 2 and 5. Space does not allow, but a case can also be made for criterion 1 regarding oaths using Yhwh's names as a component of venerating Yhwh alone (Cf. Jer 4:2; 5:2; 12:16; Hos 4:15).

18   Hereafter, DtrH.

bly as part of a DTR reworking.[19] The opposite view—that Hosea is an ideological and linguistic precursor to DTR—once held sway, though it is not as common now. Irrespective of direction of influence, the similarities in thought and expression are clear. Perhaps Hos 4:15 cannot be the basis for asserting a DTR background to "as YHWH lives," but in the context of 42 cases that display a strong relationship to DtrH, it does not constitute a serious obstacle to the broader argument.

It is notable that the connection between חי יהוה and DTR escapes even the most extensive analyses of DTR's language. The preeminent study of this type, Moshe Weinfeld's *Deuteronomy and the Deuteronomic School*, stands out for its wide-ranging list of phrases and terms representative of DTR. Yet, throughout nearly 45 pages of references, Weinfeld does not mention חי יהוה. Perhaps his omission is not entirely surprising: to be exhaustive in such an exercise is difficult. By comparison, however, he notes the DTR character of single words like גלולים and שקוצים that appear less than 20 times.[20] Thus, the absence of a clearly formulaic phrase that appears 31 times in DtrH is noteworthy. Similarly, in over 100 pages of discussion about חי יהוה, Ziegler neither notices that it is employed only by DTR nor that it makes allusions to the DTR concepts of cult centralization, veneration of YHWH alone, observance of Torah, and the land promise.

The relationship of the "as YHWH lives" formula to DtrH requires further definition because of the complexities of DtrH's composition. The human oath formula appears in narrative blocks regarded as source material for DtrH: the history of David's rise (1 Sam 16–2 Sam 5),[21] the succession narrative (2 Sam 9–29; 1 Kgs 1–2),[22] and the Elijah-Elisha stories (portions of 1 Kgs 17–21; 2 Kgs 1–9; 13).[23] Furthermore,

---

19   On the former, see Graham I. Davies, *Hosea* (NCB; Grand Rapids, Mich.: Eerdmans, 1992), lxxi-lxxii, 127-31, and A. A. Macintosh, *A Critical and Exegetical Commentary on Hosea* (ICC; Edinburgh: T & T Clark, 1997), 162-64. On the latter, Gale A. Yee, *Composition and Tradition in the Book of Hosea: A Redaction Critical Investigation* (SBLDS 102; Atlanta, Ga.: Scholars Press, 1987).

20   Moshe Weinfeld, *Deuteronomy and the Deuteronomic School* (Oxford: Oxford University Press, 1972), 323.

21   Hereafter HDR. For a succinct overview of this source see P. Kyle McCarter, *I Samuel: A New Translation with Introduction, Notes & Commentary* (AB 8; Garden City, N.Y.: Doubleday & Co, 1980), 27-30.

22   Hereafter SN. See John Barton, "Dating the 'Succession Narrative'," in *In Search of Pre-Exilic Israel: Proceedings of the Oxford Old Testament Seminar* (ed. John Day; JSOT-Sup 406; London: T & T Clark, 2004) for a recent overview of scholarship.

23   Steven L. McKenzie, *The Trouble with Kings: The Composition of the Book of Kings in the Deuteronomistic History* (VTSup 42; Leiden: Brill, 1991), 81-100, for details on these texts.

eight instances of the "as Yhwh lives" formula appear in Jeremiah, a text that also has a complex relationship to the Dtr theological tradition.[24] In light of Richard Nelson's recent discussion of the continued importance of assessing the relationship between "sources" and DtrH, a few comments about the material relevant to this study are necessary.[25]

First, if the "as Yhwh lives" formula is not a creation of the DtrH authors and editors, the fact that it occurs in multiple DtrH sources suggests that it was not included carelessly. Note, for instance, that the central characters of each narrative use the formula: "as Yhwh lives" is heard in the speech of Saul, Jonathan, and David in HDR; the formula is found on the lips of David and Solomon in SN; and this oath features in the proclamations of Elijah, Micaiah ben Imlah, and Elisha in the prophetic narratives. Whatever might be said about the "as Yhwh lives" formula, it is not a marginal or immaterial feature of DtrH.

Ziegler's findings on the role of Saul and David's oaths using "as Yhwh lives" in the DtrH narrative confirm this point for HDR. She studies the role of the oath in biblical narrative, giving extensive attention to the use of חי יהוה in oaths by Saul and David. Her detailed work is informative and draws out many important nuances about how subtle changes in the phrasing of the oath communicate meaning. Ziegler's main conclusion, that oaths show "the underlying meaning of a narrative, revealing its internal dynamics,"[26] proves how intricately the חי יהוה authenticating element is woven into the structure of HDR. Even if HDR is only source material to DtrH, the central role of חי יהוה becomes a key feature of a foundational DtrH text by its inclusion.

Though it is difficult to say when, where, why and how such source material became part of Deuteronomy through 2 Kings, a strong case can be made that it featured in a Josianic-era version of DtrH (what some might call a proto-DtrH). Steven McKenzie, Nelson, and Römer—who represent a wide range of views about the development of DtrH—all accept that significant portions of the material in HDR was

---

24 See Thomas Römer, "Is There a Deuteronomistic Redaction in the Book of Jeremiah?," in *Israel Constructs Its History: Deuteronomistic Historiography in Recent Research* (eds. Albert de Pury, Thomas Römer and Jean-Daniel Macchi; JSOTSup 306; Sheffield: Sheffield Academic Press, 2000), for a review of scholarship on this debate; cf. Mark Leuchter, *Josiah's Reform and Jeremiah's Scroll: Historical Calamity and Prophetic Response* (Hebrew Bible Monographs 6; Sheffield: Sheffield Phoenix Press, 2006), 1-17.

25 Richard D. Nelson, "A Response to Thomas C. Römer, the So-Called Deuteronomistic History," *JHebS* 9.17 (2009): 5-14.

26 Zeigler, *Promises to Keep*, 269.

used, in one fashion or another, to support Josiah's political ambitions and religious reforms.[27] The provenance of SN is less clear, but it is hard to believe that DTrH would allow the very statement that Solomon will be David's successor on the throne to be sworn by YHWH's life if that expression somehow contradicted its theological views.[28] It is probable that significant portions of the prophetic material were added into DTrH much later—particularly the Elijah narratives in 1 Kgs 17–19—but that only reinforces the point: such material would have been carefully examined prior to its inclusion, and the prominence of the "as YHWH lives" formula in these stories suggests that DTR readily accepts this language.[29] That acceptance is easily explained if the "as YHWH lives" formula was already part of DTrH in HDR and SN. Indeed, recent research has demonstrated the rather exceptional care taken to modify or update any material with which the DTR theological tradition differed,[30] making the alternative view that this language slipped in without careful examination difficult to sustain.

Second, there is also negative evidence for identifying "as YHWH lives" as DTR: the phrase does not appear in any biblical text that is neither part of DTrH nor widely regarded as under DTR influence. Not even Ezekiel, where the correlated divine oath formula "as I live" appears so frequently, includes חי יהוה. This observation is susceptible to the dangers of any argument from silence, but it is nonetheless striking. How does one explain the absence of "as YHWH lives" outside the DTR theological tradition in the Hebrew Bible when it has not fallen out of

---

27 Thomas Römer, *The So-Called Deuteronomistic History: A Sociological, Historical and Literary Introduction* (London: T & T Clark, 2007), 96-97; McKenzie does not commit to a particular reconstruction of pre-exilic HDR texts, but does support the general point that DTR had pre-exilic sources about David and Solomon (Steven L. McKenzie, "Why Didn't David Build the Temple?: The History of a Biblical Tradition," in *Worship and the Hebrew Bible: Esays in Honour of John T. Willis* (eds. M. Patrick Graham, Rick R. Marrs and Steven L. McKenzie; JSOTSup 284; Sheffield: Sheffield Academic Press, 1999), 208-09; cf. Person, ed., *In Conversation with Thomas Römer, The So-Called Deuteronomistic History: A Sociological, Historical and Literary Introduction* (London: T. & T. Clark, 2005), 21; Richard D. Nelson, *The Double Redaction of the Deuteronomistic History* (JSOTSup 18; Sheffield: JSOT Press, 1981), 99-118.

28 On entirely different grounds, Barton, "Dating," 95-106, argues that this section of SN is pre-exilic.

29 McKenzie, *The Trouble with Kings*, 81-87; on the importance of the Elijah material for Ezekiel see Keith W. Carley, *Ezekiel Among the Prophets: A Study of Ezekiel's Place in Prophetic Tradition* (SBT 31; London: SCM, 1975), 13-47.

30 *Inter alia*, Bernard M. Levinson, *Deuteronomy and the Hermeneutics of Legal Innovation* (Oxford: OUP, 1997); idem., "The Manumission of Hermeneutics: The Slave Laws of the Pentateuch as a Challenge to Contemporary Pentateuchal Theory," in *Congress Volume: Leiden 2004* (ed. André Lemaire; Vtsup 109; Leiden: Brill, 2004).

use, which is demonstrated by its occurrence in the Lachish letters? Though there are other possible explanations, the most straightforward one is that this human oath formula was linked to DTR during the formation of the Hebrew Bible in such a way that other traditions avoided using it.

In sum, the human oath formula "as YHWH lives" appears in multiple sources used in DTRH and also in two prophetic texts widely regarded as related to the DTR theological tradition; by contrast, the same formula does not appear in any text attributed to another theological tradition.

Reflection about what should and should not be called DTR language remains a necessary endeavor. It is likely to be one on which scholars continue to disagree, for the question of how to regard the relationship between originator and tradent(s) is complex. Persistent debate about what it means that the Chronicler used material from Samuel and Kings is exemplary of this issue. Be that as it may, it is hard to see how a phrase that navigated all the potential barriers to inclusion in DTRH and yet remained entirely absent from other theological traditions should be excluded from the designation DTR.

To add a third point, the link between חי יהוה and DTR goes beyond simply presence to include thematic correspondence. In an influential article about DTR,[31] Lohfink suggests five criteria that can be used for identifying DTR material. Among them he lists "common contents and interests, including the themes of cult centralization, or the veneration of YHWH alone, observance of Torah, and the land promised and endangered."[32] Although Lohfink intends this to be a representative listing, suggesting how scholars might proceed, the items are nearly a catalogue of the concerns associated with the authenticating element חי יהוה in the prophets. This is significant because Hosea and Jeremiah provide the most detailed background for how humans used this formula and illustrate its relationship to the religious practices DTR advocated.

Hosea addresses the question of cult centralization in warning Judah not to adopt the sanctuaries or worship practices of Israel:

---

31 Lohfink,"Was There," 36-66.

32 Ibid., 41.

Though you play the whore, O Israel,
>   do not let Judah become guilty.
Do not go to Gilgal;
>   Do not go up to Beth-aven,
and do not swear, "As Yʜᴡʜ lives."

Hos 4:15

The vitriol of this passage for Israel's sin of worshiping at Gilgal and Beth-Aven is manifest and goes so far as to term Israel "a stubborn heifer" (Hos 4:16).

Regarding the veneration of Yʜᴡʜ alone, two of Jeremiah's oracles reveal the deep connection between allegiance to Yʜᴡʜ and the form of the oath. The first of these two passages deals with the repentance God desires from Israel and goes so far as to illustrate the mind of a truly faithful Yahwist by how that person swears:

If you return—declaration of Yʜᴡʜ—
>   if you return to me,
if you remove your abominations from my presence,
>   and do not waver,
and if you swear, "As Yʜᴡʜ lives!"
>   in truth, in justice, and in righteousness,
then nations shall be blessed by him,
>   and by him they will boast.

Jer 4:1-2[33]

Jer 12 goes even further to suggest that Yʜᴡʜ presents a choice to those nations surrounding Judah: they may either reap punishment for their opposition to God's design or they may change course and be rewarded by Yʜᴡʜ. Such repentance is exemplified by the form of swearing: "if they will diligently learn the ways of my people, to swear by my name, 'As Yʜᴡʜ lives,' as they taught my people to swear by Baal, then they shall be built up in the midst of my people" (Jer 12:16).

Concerning Torah observance, Jeremiah again evinces a pronounced relationship between this Dᴛʀ concept and the human oath with חי יהוה. Already Jer 4:1-2 and Jer 12:16 have been mentioned; those passages relate to the commands against idols (Deut 7:26),[34] fol-

---

33 Cf. Ps 24:4.

34 Weinfeld, *Deuteronomy and the Deuteronomic School*, 323.

lowing in the ways of my people (דרכי עמי; Cf. Deut 8:6; 10:12),[35] and living "in truth, in justice, and in righteousness" (באמת במשפט ובצדקה; Cf. Deut 4:1; 5, 8, 45; 24:13 and *passim*). Jer 5:1-2 adds to this list a particularly sharp contrast wherein the one faithful person on whose account Yнwн would spare Jerusalem is the antithesis of those that, "even though they say 'as Yнwн lives,' they swear falsely" (Jer 5:2). This comparison is certainly extraordinary, but it points to the pivotal role oaths played in the Dтr conception of Yahwistic faith.

Finally, in relation to the land promised and endangered, Jer 16:14-15 and 23:7-8 testify that, by the exilic period, the ideological background of the authenticating element חי יהוה was tied up with the exodus from Egypt and the promised return from exile.[36]

> Therefore, the days are coming—declaration of Yнwн—when they will no longer say,[37] "As Yнwн lives who brought the people of Israel up from the land of Egypt," but "As Yнwн lives who brought the people of Israel up from the land of the north and from all the lands where he had driven them." I will bring them back to their land, which I gave to their ancestors."
>
> Jer 16:14-15

> Therefore, the days are surely coming—declaration of Yнwн—when they will no longer say "As Yнwн lives who brought the people of Israel up from the land of Egypt," but "As Yнwн lives who brought up and led in the seed of the house of Israel from the land of the north and from all the lands where he had driven them[38] so that they will dwell in their own land."
>
> Jer 23:7-8

These two passages indicate that the tradition of Yнwн's mighty acts on behalf of Israel in the exodus from Egypt was the original ideological background for the "as Yнwн lives" authenticating element. As a means of describing the magnitude of returning from exile, the book of Jeremiah reconceives the "as Yнwн lives" authenticating element by

---

35 Ibid., 333, for further references.

36 Since these two passages are nearly identical, scholars tend to believe one of them is an editorial addition copying the other, generally favoring 23:7-8 as the earlier of the two. For an overview of research see Geoffrey H. Parke-Taylor, *The Formation of the Book of Jeremiah: Doublets and Recurring Phrases* (SBLMS 51; Atlanta, Ga.: Society of Biblical Literature, 2000), 72-78; cf. Jean-Daniel Macchi, "Les doublets dans le livre de Jérémie," in *The Book of Jeremiah and Its Reception* (eds. A. W. H. Curtis and Thomas Römer; BETL 128; Leuven: Peeters, 1997), 131-33.

37 Reading יאמרו based upon evidence from LXX, Tg, and Jer 23:7.

38 Reading הדיחם based upon evidence from LXX and Jer 16:15.

suggesting that Y<small>HWH</small>'s mighty acts in the so-called second exodus
would so far surpass those of the first exodus that even this most
solemn of statements would have to be modified. Regarding D<small>TR</small>, these
two passages confirm the promise and endangerment of Israel's possession of the land is interwoven with the חי יהוה authenticating element. Coupled with various other arguments for the D<small>TR</small> character of
Jer 16:1-15,[39] this constitutes strong evidence for a thematic connection
of חי יהוה to D<small>TR</small>.

This section has demonstrated that the "as Y<small>HWH</small> lives" human authenticating element is a unique feature of numerous strands of D<small>TR</small>H
source material and D<small>TR</small> influenced prophetic texts. Therefore, it can be
termed D<small>TR</small> language, even though it may not be an original creation of
the Deuteronomists.

(b) The "As I Live" Authenticating Element and the
Deuteronomistic Tradition

It is clear that the divine oath with חי אני corresponds to the human
oath with חי יהוה.[40] The connection between the "as Y<small>HWH</small> lives" authenticating element and D<small>TR</small> was demonstrated through its appearances in D<small>TR</small> passages, common content, and a shared narrative pattern
where the unfolding of history leads to the blessing or cursing of Israel.
A simplistic transference of these qualities from "as Y<small>HWH</small> lives" to "as I
live" is not assured, but retracing these analytical steps demonstrates
an analogous relationship.

First off, there is a similar *prima facie* occurrence of the "as I live"
authenticating element in D<small>TR</small> passages. Looking again at table 4.1 (p.
134), Deut 32:40 obviously has a connection to D<small>TR</small>. Deuteronomy 32,
long noted as a distinct unit within the book of Deuteronomy, has been
variously dated. In his monograph *The Provenance of Deuteronomy 32*,
Sanders makes a strong case for a pre-exilic date, with the ninth or early eighth century as the most attractive options.[41] If Sanders is correct,

---

39 Louis Stulman, *The Prose Sermons of the Book of Jeremiah: A Redescription of the Corre-
    spondences with the Deuteronomistic Literature in the Light of Recent Text-Critical Re-
    search* (SBLDS 83; Atlanta, Ga.: Scholars Press, 1986), 69-70.

40 Manfred R. Lehmann, "Biblical Oaths," *ZAW* 81 (1969): 83-85; Greenberg, "The He-
    brew Oath Particle," 38; Hugh C. White, "The Divine Oath in Genesis," *JBL* (1973):
    173-74.

41 Sanders, *The Provenance of Deuteronomy 32.*; see specifically, pp. 433-6. With different
    arguments, Leuchter, "Why is the Song of Moses in the Book of Deuteronomy,"
    295-317, places the Song of Moses in a pre-exilic, Josianic context.

then Deut 32 may be the source from which all the other occurrences of "as I live" draw. The current argument does not necessitate such an early dating of Deut 32, but the possibility that it is the basis for later usage does merit further study.

Deuteronomy 32, however, elicits the same questions about the relationship of DTR to its source material addressed in the previous section. It is not necessary to rehearse the arguments for a Josianic-era edition of DTRH given above, but it is vital to mention that Mark Leuchter has gathered substantial evidence that Deut 32 was part of that text.[42] Should his argument be disregarded, the later inclusion of the Song of Moses would remain analogous to the earlier discussion concerning the later inclusion of the Elijah-Elisha material. That is to say, given the Deuteronomists' willingness to modify problematic source material, permitting the "as I live" divine oath to remain in the climactic section of the Song of Moses amounts to an implicit acceptance of it.

The two occurrences of "as I live" in Jeremiah (Jer 22:24; 46:18) also have a connection to DTR,[43] but this link requires clarification. Among the various approaches to this issue,[44] Leuchter's model for an evolving relationship between the historical prophet, the first and subsequent editions of his scroll, Josiah, and the DTR theological tradition supports a reciprocal relationship in which Jeremiah embraced DTR's program in his own distinct but interrelated way.[45] For instance, the critique of kingship found in Jer 22:24 and of foreign nations present in 46:18 matches important themes in Deuteronomy and DTRH. Though there are justifiable reasons to differ with parts of Leuchter's reconstruction, the thematic similarity between the critique of kingship in Jer 21:1–23:8, especially the section introduced by the divine oath in Jer 22:24-27, and the DTR views expressed in the summary speeches of 2 Kgs 17 and 25 shows there is more than an incidental link between these texts and adds to the case for identifying the "as I live" formula as DTR.

---

42   Ibid.

43   On the DTR influence in Jeremiah, see Louis Stulman, *The Prose Sermons of the Book of Jeremiah: A Redescription of the Correspondences with Deuteronomistic Literature in the Light of Recent Text-Critical Research* (SBLDS 83; Atlanta, Ga.: Scholars Press, 1986), esp. 7-55, 119-46..

44   In addition to Stulman, the commentaries by McKane, *Jeremiah*, 1:xlvii-cvii and Holladay, *Jeremiah: A Commentary on the Book of the Prophet Jeremiah*, 2:10-80 contain differing but influential views on the issue.

45   This argument is laid out in whole in two monographs: Leuchter, *Josiah's Reform* and Mark Leuchter, *The Polemics of Exile in Jeremiah 26–45* (Cambridge: Cambridge University Press, 2008).

What, then, can be said of the remaining instances in Num 14:21, 28, Isa 49:18, and Zeph 2:9? Issues relating to the redaction of Num 13–14 were covered at the open of this chapter, which explained the presence of DTR, P, and H in the spies narrative. The first case of YHWH swearing is among verses widely regarded as Yahwistic (Num 14:11-25), but with a major DTR insertion (Num 14:11b-23a).[46] Thus, one can arguably label the "as I live" authenticating element in Num 14:21 as DTR. The second case, Num 14:28, is almost unanimously allocated to the P section spanning vv. 26-38. Though there is independent evidence that significant portions of this passage antedate P and were adopted by it,[47] the more convincing position is Knohl's argument that Num 14:26-35 is an editorial addition by H, which edited the entire spy narrative in Num 13–14.

Further attention will be given to Knohl's thesis in section three of this chapter, but an evaluation of his position on Num 14 is necessary now. Knohl argues that there are three characteristics indicative of H in Num 14:26-35: the use of first-person speech by YHWH after Exod 7, similarities to Ezekiel, and that "the editorial level of HS combines Priestly traditions with JE ones by borrowing JE expressions and combining them with Priestly expression and linguistic forms unique to HS."[48] Knohl, unfortunately, does not specify the "JE expressions" he identifies in Num 14:26-35, but the reappearance of the "as I live" formula is likely to be one of them. Although a recognition of this relationship would be accurate, the attribution to JE would have to be contested and changed to DTR. Even so, Knohl's logic is sound and there is arguably a DTR background even for the use of the "as I live" formula in this P or H passage.

---

46 This observation originally belongs to Noth, *Numbers*, 108-09, but is now followed by many commentators: Philip J. Budd, *Numbers* (WBC 5; Waco, Tex.: Word Books, 1984), 152-53; Eryl W. Davies, *Numbers* (NCB; Grand Rapids, Mich.: Eerdmans, 1995), 142-45; Dennis Olson notes that de Vaux, Beltz, Flanagan and Miller all "follow Noth's division with minor exceptions, and that even Gray's work, which precedes Noth, largely agrees with this position (Dennis T. Olson, *The Death of the Old and the Birth of the New: The Framework of the Book of Numbers and the Pentateuch* [BJS 71; Chico, Calif.: Scholars Press, 1985], 224, note 1); Levine, *Numbers 1–20*, 348, appears open to this source analysis, but falls short of advocating it; see also Jean-Louis Ska, *Introduction to Reading the Pentateuch* (Translated by Sr. Pascale Dominique. Winona Lake, Ind.: Eisenbrauns, 2006), 94.

47 Sean E. McEvenue, "The Source-Critical Problem in Num 14,26-38," *Bib* 51 (1969): 462-63.

48 Knohl, *Sanctuary of Silence*, 92.

Concerning Isa 49:18, the question of its relationship to Dᴛʀ remains open. On the one hand, Joseph Blenkinsopp[49] and Walter Brueggemann[50] have argued for a strong affinity between Isa 40–55 and Dᴛʀ. They are supported by a growing number of scholars for whom Deut 32 provides important background to the message and language of Deutero-Isaiah.[51] On the other hand, Albertz represents the contrasting viewpoint that Deutero-Isaiah speaks "a prophetic language neither Deuteronomistic nor priestly, but strongly influenced by the Psalms."[52] Notwithstanding Albertz's legitimate challenge,[53] the resonance of Deut 32 in Isa 49:14-21 is determinative for the current question. For instance, beyond Yʜᴡʜ's oath with the "as I live" authenticating element (cf. Deut 32:40), White observes that the profession of Deut 32:39 comes close to the eschatological hymn of praise in Isa 49:13.[54] This evidence is further supported by the thematic similarity between Isa 49:14-21, a passage that deals with the future inhabitants of the land, and all the other uses of the "as I live" formula. This final argument moves beyond the present point, but it will arise again shortly. Together, these points support the conclusion that Deutero-Isaiah is aware of the Dᴛʀ background for this formulae.

Zephaniah presents a unique set of issues because of its placement in the Book of the Twelve. Recent efforts to detail the redaction and collection of individual books into partial collections and ultimately into the various forms of the Book of the Twelve propose a range of

49   Joseph Blenkinsopp, *Isaiah 40–55: A New Translation with Introduction and Commentary* (AB 19A; New York: Doubleday, 2002), 51-54.

50   Walter Brueggemann, "Isaiah 55 and Deuteronomic Theology," *ZAW* 80 (1968): 191-203. Although the article focuses on Isa 55, Brueggemann makes clear he feels this position is evidence of a wider relationship in Isa 40–55.

51   White, "The Divine Oath in Genesis," 173; Thomas A. Keiser, "The Song of Moses a Basis for Isaiah's Prophecy," *VT* 55 (2005): 486-500; Ronald Bergey, "The Song of Moses (Deuteronomy 32.1-43) and Isaianic Prophecies: A Case of Early Intertextuality," *JSOT* 28 (2003): 33-54.

52   Rainer Albertz, *Die Exilszeit: 6. Jahrhundert v. Chr* (Biblische Enzyklopädie, 7; Stuttgart: Kohlhammer, 2001), 284; ET Rainer Albertz, *Israel in Exile: The History and Literature of the Sixth Century B.C.E.* (Studies in Biblical Literature 3; Translated by Green, David. Atlanta, Ga.: Society of Biblical Literature, 2003), 379.

53   For instance, even if argument were to conclude Isa 40–55 does not fall within the Dᴛʀ theological tradition, it is quite possible to argue that the Deutero-Isaiah knows the חי אני authenticating element from an earlier source shared with Dᴛʀ. One plausible scenario is that the cultic uses of this formula (as alluded to by Hos 4:15; Amos 8:14) formed that common source. This proposal would rest on the line of argument that identifies Deutero-Isaiah as a cultic singer or singers, which goes back as far as Westermann, *Isaiah 40-66*, 8.

54   White, "The Divine Oath in Genesis," 173-74.

views on DTR influence. This is certainly not the place to debate those issues, but a few of the findings are instructive.[55] First, the superscription (Zeph 1:1), no matter its historical authenticity nor its date of inclusion, undeniably suggests DTR connection by associating the prophet's words with the reign of Josiah.[56] Second, the hypothesis that a Book of the Four (Amos, Hosea, Micah, and Zephaniah) once circulated as a collection, and that this collection was a DTR corpus, is predicated on the many shared phrases and, more importantly, shared ideas in these books.[57] Schart's reserved judgment is probably the most one can assert at this time:

> Some have used the concept "deuteronomistic" to characterize those redactors. This seems unwise, since typical Deuteronomistic language can only rarely be identified... To be more cautious, one may speak of a redaction which inserted some passages in addition to the superscriptions, passages which come close to Deuteronomistic thoughts.[58]

Zephaniah is, as a result, not an assured witness for the DTR character of the "as I live" authenticating element; rather, it contributes to a cumulative argument that Num 14:21, 28, Isa 49:18, and Zeph 2:9 share enough DTR phrases, and lack any evidence for connecting the formula with another theological tradition, to aid in demonstrating a link between "as I live" and DTR.

The evidence for connecting חי אני to the DTRH is not as definitive as with חי יהוה, but it nevertheless maintains a correlation between the "as I live" authenticating element and DTR.[59]

---

55   For further details on the question see James Nogalski and Marvin A. Sweeney, eds. *Reading and Hearing the Book of the Twelve* (SBLSymS 15. Atlanta, Ga.: Society of Biblical Literature, 2000).

56   Sweeney, *Zephaniah*, 46-47.

57   Adele Berlin, *Zephaniah: A New Translation with Introduction and Commentary* (AB 25A; New York: Doubleday, 1994), 14-15.

58   Aaron Schart, "Redactional Models: Comparisons, Contrasts, Agreements, Disagreements," in *SBL Seminar Papers 1998* (Society of Biblical Literature 1998 2; Orlando, Fl.: Scholars Press, 1998), 903; See also Aaron Schart, "Reconstructing the Redaction History of the Twelve Prophets: Problems and Models," in *Reading and Hearing the Book of the Twelve* (eds. James D. Nogalski and Marvin A. Sweeney; SBLSyms 15; Atlanta, Ga.: Society of Biblical Literature, 2000), 34-48; Aaron Schart, *Die Enstehung des Zwölfprophetenbuchs* (BZAW 260; Berlin: Walter de Gruyter, 1998), 31-46, 204-18. For another view on Zepheniah's development, see Ehud Ben Zvi, *A Historical-Critical Study of the Book of Zephaniah* (BZAW 198; Berlin: Walter de Gruyter, 1991).

59   One wonders if Levitt Kohn would have included חי אני in her list of D/DTR phrases if the DTR features of the human authenticating element חי יהוה were known to her.

Secondly, there is also a connection between the "as I live" authenticating element and the theological expansion of the divine name יהוה צבאות. This title is most closely associated with the Zion tradition, but it also appears ten times in DtrH (1 Sam 1:3, 11; 4:4; 15:2; 17:45; 2 Sam 6:2, 18; 7:8, 26-27). It is notable that five of those instances are in 2 Sam 6–7, the DtrH account of Yhwh's promise of a royal line to David. This conspicuous title also appears in human speech: the prophets Elijah and Elisha both swear with the expanded authenticating element "as Yhwh Sabaoth lives" (חי יהוה צבאות; 1 Kgs 18:15; 2 Kgs 3:14), further substantiating the connection to DtrH. The issue of DtrH's relation to its source material is again pertinent here. So too are arguments already presented: note the presence of יהוה צבאות in HDR[60] and the Elijah-Elisha cycle; recall too that HDR is likely part of a Josianic-era version of DtrH. Indeed, the five instances of יהוה צבאות in 2 Sam 6–7 aid in tying these foundational chapters together.[61]

In the prophetic texts, the expanded title is found in divine speech, such as Yhwh's oath to judge Egypt in the book of Jeremiah:

As I live—declaration of the King,[62]
　　whose name is Yhwh of hosts—
one is coming
　　like Tabor among the mountains,
　　and like Carmel by the sea.
Pack your bags for exile,
　　you who dwell in Egypt!
For Memphis will become a waste,
　　it will be a ruin, without inhabitant.

　　　　　　　　　　　　　　　　　　　　　　　Jer 46:18-19

60　For detailed analysis of 2 Sam 6–7, a central passage to DtrH, see McKenzie, "Why Didn't," 204-16; Römer, *The So-Called Deuteronomistic History*, 91-97; and P. Kyle McCarter, *II Samuel: A New Translation with Introduction, Notes and Commentary* (AB 9; Garden City, NY: Doubleday, 1984), 161-231.

61　Frank Moore Cross, *Canaanite Myth and Hebrew Epic: Essays in the History of the Religion of Israel* (Cambridge, Mass.: Harvard University Press, 1973), 274-89, especially pp. 281-5; see also Nelson, *Double Redaction*, 99-118.

62　The kingship of Yhwh, a motif common to Jeremiah (8:19; 10:7, 10; 48:15; 51:57), is not as prominent elsewhere in Dtr, although it does occur in the tribal blessings of Deuteronomy (Deut 33:5).

This passage corresponds well with the use of יהוה צבאות elsewhere in Jeremiah, where fully one-third of its appearances are in the prose passages often linked to a DTR redaction.[63] Finally, the same expanded title appears in YHWH's oath in the book of Zephaniah:

> Therefore, as I live—declaration of YHWH of hosts, the God of Israel—
> Moab shall become like Sodom
>   and the Ammonites like Gomorrah,
> a land possessed by nettles and salt pits,
>   and a desolation forever.
> The remnant of my people shall plunder them,
>   and the survivors of my nation[64] will inherit them.
> This will be their lot in return for their pride,
>   because they scoffed and boasted
>   against the people of YHWH of hosts.
>
> Zeph 2:9-10

Third and finally, when Lohfink's five criteria are considered for the "as I live" authenticating element several further points can be made. Lohfink noted particular topical interests as one of his criteria, listing among them "the land promised and endangered."[65] This topic was addressed in the previous chapter, but it is worth mentioning once more that every instance of the "as I live" authenticating element occurs in a passage concerning the land in some fashion. Numbers 14 announces the first exodus generation's prohibition from entering the land; Deut 32 describes how YHWH will cleanse the land and prepare it for his people; Isa 49 portrays the restored land as too small for the burgeoning community of returnees; in Jer 22 YHWH swears that Zedekiah will never again see Jerusalem or Judah; and, finally, all 16 instances in Ezekiel address who will inhabit the land. One other topic Lohfink identifies is concern for the veneration of YHWH alone. The clearest passage in this regard is Deut 32:40: "See now that I, even I, am he; there is no god beside me" (Deut 32:39a). Furthermore, Deut 32:40, situated within the Song of Moses, must certainly come under Lohfink's idea of

---

63   Jer 7:3, 21; 8:3; 16:9; 19:3, 15; 25:8, 27:4, 18-19, 21; 29:4, 8, 17, 21, 25; 32:14-15, 18; 33:11-12; 35:13, 18-19; 39:16; 44:2, 11. This allocation of 27 of 77 total instances of יהוה צבאות to the so-called "C corpus" of Jeremiah is based upon Stulman's listing of passages commonly associated to this stratum (Stulman, *The Prose Sermons*, 56-118).

64   Reading with the *qere*.

65   Lohfink, "Was There," 41.

common narrative pattern, "such as the laws on the unfolding of history which lead to blessing or curse,"[66] a description that could also be easily applied to various passages in Ezekiel such as 5:5-17 and 20:1-44.

The evidence presented in this section confirms the initial impression given by the relationship between the "as Yhwh lives" human authenticating element and the "as I live" divine authenticating element that both formulae are characteristic of Dtr. The convergence of its appearance only in DtrH and prophetic texts linked to Dtr, coupled with its absence from other theological traditions, and the presence of key Dtr themes in the passages where it appears support its classification as Dtr language. Perhaps the Deuteornomists did not create this formula, but they accepted it into their lexicon.

Although this evidence is substantial enough to stand on its own, it is further strengthened when the Dtr use of the divine oath with the verbal root שבע is addressed. This additional evidence demonstrates that Dtr used the "as I live" authenticating element and the divine oath with שבע as a complementary pair of expressions.

(c) The Divine Oath with שבע and the Deuteronomistic Tradition

The divine oath using the verbal root שבע is the most frequent form in the Hebrew Bible, occurring 67 times.[67] Despite the logical expectation that the verb שבע would introduce statements including other authenticating elements (i.e. Jer 4:2; 5:2), this is never the case in the divine oath.[68] Another possible way of dividing up this large group of data for analysis is to distinguish between those places where the text records Yhwh swearing[69] and those where it recounts a time Yhwh has previ-

---

66 Ibid.

67 Gen 22:16; 24:7; 26:3; 50:24; Exod 13:5, 11; 32:13, 33:1; Num 11:12; 14:16, 23; 32:10, 11; Deut 1:8, 34, 35; 2:14; 4:21; 6:10, 18, 23; 7:13; 8:1; 9:5; 10:11; 11:9, 21; 13:18; 19:8; 26:3, 15; 28:9, 11; 29:12 [ET 13]; 30:20; 31:7, 20, 21, 23; 34:4; Joshua 1:6; 5:6; 21:43, 44; Judges 2:1; 1 Sam 3:14; 2 Sam 3:9; Isa 14:24; 45:23; 54:9; 62:8; Jer 11:5; 22:5; 32:22; 44:26; 49:13; 51:14; Amos 4:2; 6:8; 8:7; Mic 7:20; Pss 89:4 [ET 3]; 36 [ET 35]; 50 [ET 49]; 95:11; 110:4; 132:11.

68 In Jer 44:26 the two appear together, but the verb שבע does not introduce Yhwh's oath. Rather, it describes a human action that is to be prohibited by Yhwh in the future.

69 There are 14 instances of this: Gen 22:16; 26:3; 1 Sam 3:14; Isa 14:24; 45:23; 54:9; 62:8; Jer 22:5; 44:26; 49:13; 51:14; Amos 4:2; 6:8; 8:7.

ously sworn.[70] Still, the most helpful categorization of these passages is
by their content. Horst also used this criterion,[71] breaking the instances
into those concerning Yhwh's promise of the land, the Davidic
dynasty,[72] and prophetic salvation or judgment speeches.[73]

The first category, those instances of the divine oath dealing with
the land, is the largest and most relevant to the present discussion:

Book	Citation
Genesis	22:16, 24:7, 26:3, 50:24
Exodus	13:5, 11, 32:13, 33:1
Numbers	11:12, 14:16, 23, 32:10, 11
Deuteronomy	1:8, 34, 35, 2:14, 4:21, 6:10, 18, 23, 7:13, 8:1, 18, 9:5, 10:11, 11:9, 11:21, 19:8, 26:3, 26:15, 28:11, 30:20, 31:7, 20, 21, 23, 34:4
Joshua	1:6, 5:6, 21:43
Judges	2:1
Jeremiah	11:5, 32:22

Table 4.3: The Verbal Root שבע and Yhwh's Promise of the Land

Again, a brief review of these citations reveals a strong correlation to
Dtr. Horst noted this relationship and observed, "[t]he oath sworn to
the fathers belongs, therefore, to the specifics of the Deuteronomistic
theology, it was important to it and was recited relentlessly by it."[74]
More recently and far more extensively, Thomas Römer has studied the
divine oath in the book of Deuteronomy, confirming what Horst noted.

---

70 There are 53 instances of this: Gen 24:7; 50:24; Exod 13:5, 11; 32:13; 33:1; Num 11:12;
    14:16, 23; 32:10, 11; Deut 1:8, 34, 35; 2:14; 4:21; 6:10, 18, 23; 7:13; 8:1; 9:5; 10:11; 11:9, 21;
    13:18; 19:8; 26:3, 15; 28:9, 11; 29:12 [ET 13]; 30:20; 31:7, 20, 21, 23; 34:4; Joshua 1:6; 5:6;
    21:43, 44; Judges 2:1; 2 Sam 3:9; Jer 11:5; 32:22; Mic 7:20; Pss 89:4 [ET 3], 36 [ET 35], 50
    [ET 49]; 95:11; 110:4; 132:11.

71 Horst, "Der Eid," 298-99.

72 2 Sam 3:9; Jer 22:5; Pss 89:4 [ET 3], 36 [ET 35], 50 [ET 49]; 110:4; 132:11.

73 Isa 14:24; 45:23; 54:9; 62:8; Jer 11:5; 44:26; 49:13; 51:14; Amos 4:2; 6:8; 8:7; Mic 7:20.

74 Ibid., 298. "Der den Vätern geschworene Eid gehört also zu den Specifica deutero-
    nomischer Theologie, die ihr wichtig sind und darum unermüdlich von ihr vorgetra-
    gen werden." Cf. Seely,"Raised Hand," 413.

Römer's significant contribution is to observe that the patriarchal triad—Abraham, Isaac, and Jacob—occurs in Deuteronomy in close connection with Y<small>HWH</small>'s sworn promise to give Israel the land.[75] This phenomenon corresponds to six of the 23 instances of Y<small>HWH</small>'s oath,[76] where the patriarchal triad is appended asyndetically. The other 17 cases identify the recipients of Y<small>HWH</small>'s oath simply as Israel's ancestors (אבות), a group that originates in Egypt. From this evidence, and the near total absence of the patriarchs in the remainder of D<small>TR</small>H,[77] Römer concludes that "[t]he identification of the fathers of Dtn with the patriarchs is to be attributed to the 'final redaction' of the Pentateuch, with the aim to stress and to underline its 'unity.'"[78] Römer maintains the disunity that needed to be overcome was an ongoing rift between the Judahites exiled to Babylonia and those left in Judah after 586 B.C.E.:

> The patriarchs, by contrast, seem in the same period to have represented an origin myth that might be called "autochthonous," in the sense that they were apparently popular among the nonexiled population (in Ezek 33:24, those who remained in Palestine laid claim to the land by appealing to Abraham). These patriarchs, of whom the Deuteronomists were not terribly fond, nonetheless found their way into Deuteronomy.[79]

---

75 Römer, *Israels Väter.* See also Römer, "Deuteronomy," 112-38; this is translated from the original French entitled, "Le Deutéronome à la quête des origines," in *Le Pentateuque: Débats et recherches* (ed. P. Haudebert; Lectio Divina, 151; Paris: Cerf, 1992 [65-98]).

76 The triad appears seven times in total (Deut 1:8; 6:10; 9:5, 27; 29:12; 30:20; 34:4), which Römer argues is no accident (Römer, *Israels Väter*, 269-70). Deuteronomy 9:27 is the only instance where the patriarchal triad appears without the divine oath.

77 Römer works from the belief that Deuteronomy originates with a seventh century Josianic core (that is nearly impossible to delimitate) and that "several decades later, Deuteronomy emerged totally transformed, after being considerably enlarged, and was inserted into the Deuteronomistic History. The work of the deuteronomistic redaction gave Deuteronomy, *grosso modo*, its current form and structure. This *deuteronomistic* edition of Deuteronomy, then, is what I take as the starting-point of my inquiry" (Römer, "Deuteronomy," 115). For earlier support of this view, and commentary on the book as a whole, see Mayes, *Deuteronomy.*

78 Römer, *Israels Väter*, 269. "Die Identifikation der Väter des Dtn mit den Erzvätern ist der 'Endredaktion' des Pentateuchs zuzuscheiben, mit dem Bestreben, seine "Einheit" zu betonen und zu unterstreichen."

79 Römer, "Deuteronomy," 135; cf. Pohlmann, *Ezechielstudien* and Pohlmann, *Ezechiel 1–19*, who argues Ezekiel (and Jeremiah, for that matter) demonstrates a similar debate between those exiled to Babylon in 597 B.C.E. and those left in Judah. Greenberg has also wondered if Ezekiel's avoidance of the patriarchs is "perhaps deliberate" (Greenberg, *Ezekiel 1-20*, 364; cf. Block, *Ezekiel 1–24*, 627-28).

And how is it that the patriarchal triad encroached into Deuteronomy? Römer persuasively argues that their presence is evidence that:

> for the deuteronomistic editors of Deuteronomy the fathers evoke Egypt, the insertion of the names of the patriarchs at certain points must be attributed to a *post*deuteronomistic redaction. The identification "fathers = patriarchs" is facilitated from the moment Deuteronomy no longer functions as a prologue to the Deuteronomistic History, but as a conclusion to the Pentateuch.[80]

Although Römer deals extensively with the passages where the divine oath appears, he directs his attention only towards the identity of the ancestors. His resulting conclusion that the final redaction of the Pentateuch is motivated by a need to resolve tension between those appealing to the patriarchs and those appealing to the ancestors in Egypt as the legitimate source of Israel's identity will be especially important in the following chapter. But, it overlooks something crucial for the present study: the divine oath with שׁבע in DTR is used to promise the land. That is to say, simply, that DTR uses the divine oath with שׁבע to indicate blessing. This assertion must be balanced by three exceptions in Deuteronomy. The first two are a pair: Deut 1:35 recalls YHWH's oath to prohibit the first exodus generation from entering the land and Deut 2:14 affirms that this oath was fulfilled during the wilderness wandering (cf. Josh 5:6). The third exception is Deut 4:21, where YHWH swears that Moses will not enter the land. However, those three occasions should not overshadow the uniformity that prevails in the other 22 instances in Deuteronomy, and also in five further instances found in DTRH and Jeremiah, where this form of the divine oath describes YHWH's promise to give Israel the land. The consistency of this distinction across various books and genres indicates that it is not incidental.

The genre analysis in the previous chapter demonstrated that the "as I live" authenticating element is used only in YHWH's sworn pronouncements of judgment. The most plausible explanation for these new observations is that the two formulae constituted a correlated pair. When DTR wanted to speak of YHWH swearing to bless Israel it used the divine oath with שׁבע and, alternatively, when it wanted to speak of YHWH swearing to judge or curse Israel it employed the divine oath with the "as I live" authenticating element. This distinction is maintained in the book of Ezekiel, supporting the argument that this

80 Römer, "Deuteronomy," 130; cf. Römer, *Israels Väter*, 269.

prophetic text was fully aware of the DTR context for the "as I live" formula and intentionally employed it in service of its message.

Pausing for a moment to consider the possible social setting from which DTR adopted the "as I live" authenticating element, its role in announcing YHWH's judgment described in military terms appears significant. Five passages (Num 14:11b-23a, 26-38; Deut 32:26-42; Jer 46:18-26; Zeph 2:8-11) deal with YHWH's role in war between nations. Of these passages, Deut 32:1-43 and Zeph 2:8-11 would generally be considered the earliest. Sanders' extensive study of the Song of Moses suggests the poem is related to a pre-exilic hostile invasion. If he is correct, then YHWH's oath characterizes how God deals with Israel's enemies in that historical situation. Zephaniah 2:8-11 expresses a similar view, which Sweeney notes "clearly presupposes some threat against Moab and Ammon that would be understood as an action by YHWH."[81] Sweeney argues the larger purpose of the oracle is to motivate the audience to faith in YHWH who, through military action, will restore to Judah territory formerly held by the northern kingdom.[82] All this evidence suggests the original setting for the formula could be prophetic assurances offered prior to battle: these "war oracles," once obtained by divination, maintain the purpose of encouraging the king and army prior to battle; but, in the Hebrew Bible, the oracle is an unsolicited message of YHWH delivered through the prophet. Indeed, Duane Christensen has argued that Zeph 2 is one place where the transformation from the older divinatory social setting to the literary setting of DTR prophetic writings has taken place.[83]

---

81 Sweeney, *Zephaniah*, 135.

82 Ibid., 106-09.

83 Duane L. Christensen, *Transformations of the War Oracle in Old Testament Prophecy* (Missoula, Mont.: Scholars Press, 1975); cf. Duane L. Christensen, "Zephaniah 2:4-15: A Theological Basis for Josiah's Program of Political Expansion," *CBQ* 46 (1984): 669-82. Deuteronomy 20 suggests that this sort of practice was known in Israel and Judah, but basing a historical reconstruction on a speech that is undeniably stylized to serve Deuteronomy's theological program is problematic.

Martti Nissinen has demonstrated a similar dynamic for the social and literary setting of the "fear not" formula ("Fear Not: A Study on an Ancient Near Eastern Phrase," in *The Changing Face of Form Criticism for the Twenty-First Century* [eds. Marvin A. Sweeney and Ehud Ben Zvi; Grand Rapids, Mich.: Eerdmans, 2003]).

3. Social Setting of the "Lifted Hand" Land Transfer Formula

In the previous chapter, evidence indicated that the "lifted hand" formula is used in two separate conventions. The first of those two conventions, the "lifted hand" land transfer formula, will be considered in this section. Recall that there are eleven instances of this usage, which are summarized in table 4.4 (p. 155). There is a strong consensus that this formula is typical of P. In her extended study of words and phrases shared by the book of Ezekiel, P and D/DTR, Risa Levitt Kohn categorizes this formula as one of 97 shared by P and Ezekiel. Most major commentators on Ezekiel make the same attribution, finding it unnecessary to argue the case in any sustained way.[84] Even Johan Lust, in his detailed argument against accepting the formula as an oath, adopts the same perspective.[85] This consensus may overstate the clarity of the case. The broadest foundation for this attribution is the seven-fold usage of the formula in Ezek 20. However, scholars have increasingly noted the mix of P and DTR influences in this chapter. Thus, Ezek 20 should not be the basis for such an argument, but rather a text that may be used to confirm observations made elsewhere.

Putting Ezek 20 aside for a moment, there remain eight instances of the "lifted hand" land transfer formula: Exod 6:8, Num 14:30, Deut 32:40, Ezek 36:7, 44:12, 47:14, Ps 106:26, and Neh 9:15. Among this group Deut 32:40 is undoubtedly in a DTR passage. The evidence for Num 14:11b-23a also being DTR was reviewed earlier. Ps 106:26, Pons has argued, also evinces a DTR scheme of history.[86] Numbers 14:30 occurs in a passage that Noth thought to be "not so much of 'continuous sources' as of an unsystematic collection of innumerable pieces of tradition..."[87]; Levine and Jacob Milgrom attribute this passage to an early

---

84   Zimmerli comments that Ezekiel's choice of יד נשא "opposes placing Ezek 20 too close to Deuteronomy. The linguistic contacts much more strongly... place Ezek 20 close to the language of the Priestly Document (in particular Ex 6)" (Zimmerli, *Ezekiel 1–24*, 406-08); cf. Greenberg, *Ezekiel 1-20*, 363-64, and Block, *Ezekiel 1–24*, 626-28, especially note 63 where Block states, "Ezekiel's avoidance of *nišbaʿ*, 'to swear,' may also reflect an anti-Deuteronomist polemic..."

85   Lust, "For I Lift," 162.

86   Pons, , 214-33.

87   Noth, *Numbers*, 4.

Citation	Infinitive Construct	Verbal Root
Exodus 6:8	לָתֵת	נתן
Numbers 14:30	לְשַׁכֵּן	שׁכן
Ezekiel 20:5b	לֵאמֹר	אמר
Ezekiel 20:6	לְהוֹצִיאָם	יצא
Ezekiel 20:15	הָבִיא	בוא
Ezekiel 20:23	לְהָפִיץ	פוץ
Ezekiel 20:28	לָתֵת	נתן
Ezekiel 20:42	לָתֵת	נתן
Ezekiel 47:14	לְתִתָּהּ	נתן
Psalm 106:26	לְהַפִּיל	נפל
Nehemiah 9:15	לָתֵת	נתן

Table 4.4: נשׂא יד Land Transfer Formula

Priestly source,[88] while others have suggested various sources[89] including the Yahwistic or non-P source,[90] post-P^g additions,[91] and even a Dᴛʀ hand.[92] Indeed, the evidence may not be as uniform as the consensus suggests it to be.

Perhaps the most significant challenge to the consensus that the "lifted hand" land transfer formula is typical of P is the increasing evidence for activity by H in passages generally attributed to P. The leading voice here is Israel Knohl. In his monograph *The Sanctuary of Silence*, Knohl argues that even Exod 6:2-8, 7:1-6, what many have seen as

---

88   Levine, *Numbers 1–20*, 364-69, assigns Num 14:11-25 to JE and Num 14:26-39a to P, deducing a date for the extant passage during or after the exile. Milgrom argues for a unified, chiastic structure in this pericope (*Numbers: The Traditional Hebrew Text with the New JPS Translation* [JPS Torah; Philadelphia: Jewish Publication Society, 1990], 387-88). On redaction he says: "the entire text of Num 13–14 is reflected in Deut 1:19-46... Since the Deuteronomic account gives no indication of having been edited later to harmonize with Num 13–14, it must be concluded that the present, composite text of Numbers is old and, more importantly, that both traditions preceded the writing of Deut." He divides the passage into 14:20-25 and 14:26-35, "two traditions... artfully woven together... but each contains vital information, and this made it impossible for the redactor to keep one and omit the other" (Ibid., 390). See also Jacob Milgrom, "The Structures of Numbers: Chapters 11–12 and 13–14 and Their Redaction. Preliminary Gropings, in Honor of Robert Gordis," in *Judaic Perspectives on Ancient Israel* (eds. Jacob Neusner, Baruch Levine and Ernest S. Frerichs; Philadelphia: Fortress, 1987), 58.

89   For instance, Philip Jenson's summary chart shows that Noth, Elliger, Lohfink, and Weimar place it outside P^g (Philip P. Jenson, *Graded Holiness: A Key to the Priestly Conception of the World* (JSOTSup 106; Sheffield: Sheffield Academic Press, 1992), 223).

90   McEvenue, "The Source-Critical Problem in Num 14,26-38."; Sean E. McEvenue, *The Narrative Style of the Priestly Writer* (AnBib 50; Rome: Biblical Institute Press, 1971), 90-96

91   Noth, *Numbers*, 110-11.

92   David Frankel, *The Murmuring Stories of the Priestly School: A Retrieval of Ancient Sacerdotal Lore* (VTSup 89; Leiden: Brill, 2002), 316-17. Frankel argues for a complex diachronic development from two separate, pre-exilic sources: a non-P and a P murmuring story that are combined into an "original editorial version." This text is incorporated in a "post-editorial addition" which Frankel assigns to a Dᴛʀ hand. He summarizes: "to a large extent, the P murmuring tradition, like its non P counterpart, is earlier than Ez 20, developed independently of the Sinai tradition, and was not significantly influenced by the DᴛʀH. This evidence tends to support our contention that the bulk of the P murmuring traditions are essentially pre-exilic and, at root, quite early."

the very crux of P, is actually a product of H.[93] There are many potential reasons to differ with Knohl, but even the possibility that he is right
adds to the evidence that the situation must be assessed carefully.

A passage by passage review of the evidence for the theological tradition behind each of these instances of the "lifted hand" land transfer
formula is necessary. In particular, this review will have to heed the arguments of Knohl,[94] and the related work of Milgrom,[95] Christophe Nihan,[96] and Jeffrey Stackert:[97] H can and should be distinguished from P.
This review will provide a tentative answer to the question of literary
setting for the "lifted hand" land transfer formula that can then be compared with the evidence in Ezekiel.

(a) A Reevaluation of the Literary Setting for the "Lifted
Hand" Land Transfer Formula

Prior to reviewing the passages in question, it is necessary to give a
more comprehensive summary of Knohl's argument. He begins with a
detailed study of the sabbath and festival legislation in Leviticus, focusing in particular on how H incorporates P's legislation while simultaneously departing from it. Based upon this study, he concludes that H is
later than P and consciously attempts to make changes to its program.
Knohl's findings on the relationship between the legal material in P
and H and their relative dating has largely been confirmed in the work

---

93 Knohl uses the sigla HS, for Holiness School, and PT, for Priestly Torah. For ease, in
this study those sigla will be simplified to H and P in order to match the more generally accepted symbols.

94 Knohl's work, to a certain extent, is anticipated by Alfred Cholewiński, *Heiligkeitsgesetz und Deuteronomium: eine vergleichende Studie* (AnBib 66; Rome: Biblical Institute
Press, 1976), 338: "Unser Ergebnis: Zwei Gründe der Abfassung von Hg sind
miteinander verkoppelt: 1' ein dem Dt ähnliches und dessen Lücken ergänzendes
Gesetzeskorpus zu schaffen und 2' dieses in die Pg-Geschichte einzuschalten, um
diese neue Auffassung der Heilsgeschichte in manchen Punkten zu korrigieren."

95 Milgrom, *Leviticus 17–22*; Milgrom, *Leviticus 23–27*.

96 Nihan, *Priestly Torah*; Christophe Nihan, "The Holiness Code Between D and P:
Some Comments on the Function and Significance of Leviticus 17–26 in the Composition of the Torah," in *Das Deuteronomium Zwischen Pentateuch Und Deuteronomistischem Geschichtswerk* (eds. E. Otto and R. Achenbach; Frlant 206; Göttingen: Vandenhoeck & Ruprecht, 2004).

97 Jeffrey Stackert, *Rewriting the Torah: Literary Revision in Deuteronomy and the Holiness
Legislation* (FAT/I 52; Tübingen: Mohr Siebeck, 2007).

of Milgrom, Nihan, and Stackert. Still, Knohl has been more expansive than others in extending these findings to the narrative portions of P.[98]

Among the criteria he has used for identifying H material in narrative, the following positive and negative criteria are the most relevant.[99] First, Knohl asserts that P has no contact with the so-called JE source and that language representative of that tradition does not appear in its work. This is markedly different from H, which displays several similarities to JE. Second, H's style "contains moralizing passages and ideological justifications" like Exod 31:13, 17. Third, although first-person speech by YHWH occurs in both sources, Knohl suggests that it does not appear in P after the disclosure of the divine name to Moses. The importance of first-person speech for H has been recognized previously, for instance the eponymous refrain of Lev 17–26, "You shall be holy because I, YHWH your God, am holy" (Lev 19:2; cf. 20:26; 21:8). However, Knohl has gone farther than anyone else by suggesting that all first-person speech by YHWH after Exod 7 is indicative of H. Finally, Knohl notes the strong resemblance between the language of H and Ezekiel, a well-known observation. Rather than provide an abstract critique of these points, it will be easier to evaluate them in reference to one of the relevant passages. The obvious passage, because of its content and language, is Exod 6:2-8.

Exodus 6:2-8 narrates YHWH's revelation of his special name to Moses, who is further told that the patriarchs did not know God by the name YHWH, but as El Shaddai. The documentary hypothesis understood this as a key point in P's narrative, the so-called P^g, in which there is a three stage revelation of God's identity: as Elohim to all, as El Shaddai to Abraham, and, finally, as YHWH to Moses. The identification of Exod 6:2-8 as P is as close to settled fact as one can find in biblical studies.[100] However, a few scholars have suggested the passage may not be as unified and clearly P as is often assumed.

Lust, even if indirectly, demonstrates that vv. 3-5 sit loosely in the context of this passage.[101] Others have observed that v. 8's statement that Israel will receive the land as a "possession" (מורשה) is problematic

---

98 Knohl, *Sanctuary of Silence*, 59-110.

99 All of the following points come from Knohl (Ibid., 106-08). The points mentioned here are by no means all of Knohl's criteria, only those relevant to the subsequent analysis of the "lifted hand" land transfer formula passages.

100 Thirty-five years ago Childs could say confidently, "There has been a wide consensus for over a hundred years in assigning these verses to the Priestly source" (Brevard S. Childs, *The Book of Exodus: A Critical, Theological Commentary* [OTL; Louisville, Ky.: Westminster Press, 1974], 111).

101 Lust,"Exodus," 214-18.

because the idea that the land will belong to the people goes against P's otherwise consistent view, expressed by the term אחזה, that YHWH remains owner of the land and Israel is merely given rights to dwell on it and live off of it. Thus, Fujiko Kohata and Bernard Gosse have suggested that this verse is a late interpolation, with Kohata even arguing for DTR influence here.[102]   Knohl, for his part, is most influenced by the three-fold appearance of the recognition formula, "I am YHWH" (אני יהוה; Exod 6:2, 6, 8).[103]   He cites as support for his overall argument comments by Klostermann, Dillmann, Driver, and Haran that the passage exhibits similarities to H.[104]

Even though this evidence constitutes substantial support for continuing to inquire about the various influences behind this passage, Knohl's argument that it is the product of H fails to persaude. His dependence on the recognition formula is simply too great. It may, indeed, be more likely to appear in H, but its use in Genesis (15:7; 28:13) and Deuteronomy (29:6) means it is not exclusive to H. It is a strong argument, but it is not strong enough to bear the weight of Knohl's position alone. Further objections are leveled by Nihan, based largely upon his view of the content and message of P^g, and his summary is worth repeating: "That H develops considerably certain motifs and themes does not mean that he could not find them previously in P... the same consideration should apply here."[105]   Knohl is correct to put the question to Exod 6:2-8 about literary setting, but he needs evidence that satisfies more than one of his criteria in order to sustain his argument that this passage should be attributed to H.

The second passage to consider is Num 14:26-38, in which Knohl attributes vv. 26-35 to H. Knohl defends his position in three ways. First, he is quick to point out the language shared with Ezekiel. Given the questions about the various influences in Ezekiel, Knohl's argument must be disregarded here, as it is dangerously close to being circular. However, in this process he notes the presence of the noun זנה in Num 14:33, a term which occurs elsewhere only in the Holiness Code and Ezekiel. The connection to Lev 17–26 is notable. Second, he again emphasizes the first-person speech of YHWH. This is suggestive, but can only be part of a cumulative case. Third and finally, Knohl points out

---

102 Fujiko Kohata, *Jahwist und Priesterschrift in Exodus 3–14* (BZAW 166; Berlin: Walter de Gruyter, 1986), 28-41; Bernard Gosse, "Exode 6,8 comme réponse a Ézéchiel 33,24," *RHPR* 74 (1994): 246-47.

103 Knohl, *Sanctuary of Silence*, 17, 61.

104 Ibid., 17, note 24.

105 Nihan, *Priestly Torah*, 34-35, note 72.

the presence of "expressions typical of JE."[106] These "expressions" are never listed and must be inferred. The logical source of those phrases, however, is the directly preceding duplicate in vv. 11-25. Though Knohl regards this as JE, the DTR background of vv. 11b-23a has been discussed. Thus, one might agree with Knohl about the direction of influence but disagree on his identification of it as JE.

The strong evidence of DTR influence alongside other indicators of H is crucial. In his study of H's legal material this is precisely the dynamic that Nihan observes: "The systematic combination with the legal traditions of D is unparalleled in P, and clearly suggests a different origin for H. As in the case of Lev 26, Lev 17–25 appears to be the work of a scribe who already knows the legal traditions of both P and D, and tries to mediate between them."[107] Extending this finding into the narrative portions of the Pentateuch must be done with great caution, as it moves beyond the limits of Nihan's study. Yet, the evidence that this dynamic holds in Lev 26, surely a passage whose genre lies somewhere on a continuum between legislative and narrative text, is suggestive of its validity for narrative.[108] In view of this situation, the influence of DTR, particularly emphasized by the findings of the present study on the "as I live" authenticating element, and P, found on many fronts but none more relevant here than the presence of the "lifted hand" land transfer formula also found in Exod 6:8, is suggestive of H—not P.

This initial proposal can be further supported by another of Knohl's criteria: "ideological justifications." Milgrom has expanded the evidence for this feature, referring to it as "rationales."[109] In Num 14:26-38 the rationale for YHWH's punishing the first exodus generation with death in the wilderness is their earlier statement wishing for this fate (Num 14:2). More than constituting the presence of a justification, the *lex talionis* form of this punishment is also suggestive of H influence.[110] Then the length of the wilderness wandering is predicated upon the length of the spies reconnaissance (vv. 33-34), a logic only replicated in Ezek 4.

Taking into account the extensive first-person divine speech, DTR influence, use of rationales and, finally, *lex talionis* punishment, there is sufficient evidence that Num 14:26-38 exhibits H influence. Although it

---

106 Knohl, *Sanctuary of Silence*, 91.

107 Nihan, , 104. This is confirmed by Stackert, *Rewriting the Torah*, 224-25; cf. Milgrom, *Leviticus 17–22*, 1349-61.

108 See also Cholewiński, *Heiligkeitsgesetz und Deuteronomium*, 318.

109 Milgrom, *Leviticus 17–22*, 1371-75.

110 Ibid., 1423-25.

is possible the passage was not composed entirely by H, there seems little doubt the final form is ultimately a product of its theological tradition.   This being so, the "lifted hand" land transfer formula may be another originally P feature that was embraced by H and re-applied in the service of its own program.   But this observation must remain provisional until more evidence is considered.

The third passage to consider is Ps 106, in which vv. 6-46 comprise a confession of Israel's disobedience, and where the "lifted hand" land transfer formula appears in v. 26.   Pierre Auffret has proposed a rather complex structure for the psalm in which vv. 24-25 plus vv. 26-27 constitute the central point in an extended chiasm.[111]   This seems too intricate and the preferable option is to follow George Coats, who suggests that "this psalm shows deuteronomistic influence in constructing the events of Israel's rebellion in immediate relationship to Yahweh's forbearance and patience and in its similarity with various traditions in Deuteronomy."[112]   Psalm 106 and DTR also concur in placing Israel's origin in Egypt, not with the patriarchs in Canaan.[113]   Amidst these DTR features, the "lifted hand" land transfer formula, indicative of P or H, appears out of place.

That situation is magnified by the striking similarities between Ps 106:26-27 and Ezek 20:23, the only other passage in the Hebrew Bible that indicates that YHWH decided to scatter the people into exile even while their ancestors were still in the wilderness.   Coats adds that the account of events in vv. 28-31 corresponds not with DTR but, "with the order of events in P."[114]   This evidence leads him to conclude "that our psalm, though having much in common with Deuteronomy, is nevertheless a later stage in the development of the tradition, perhaps reflecting a point between Deuteronomy and P."[115]   This observation is reminiscent of Nihan's findings about H's distinctive use of DTR and P and suggests H's influence.   That influence is likely to be limited to the historically based confession of vv. 6-46, a text that has almost certainly been incorporated into its present setting despite originating from a

111 Pierre Auffret, ""Afin que nous rendions grâce à ton nom." Étude structurelle du Psaume 106," *SEL* 11 (1994): 75-96, especially p. 87.

112 George W Coats, *Rebellion in the Wilderness: The Murmuring Motif in the Wilderness Traditions of the Old Testament* (Nashville, Tenn.: Abingdon Press, 1968), 230; cf. Leslie C. Allen, *Psalms 101–50* (WBC 21; Nashville, Tenn.: Thomas Nelson, 2002), 66-67; Pons, , 214-33.

113 F. C. Fensham, "Neh. 9 and Pss. 105, 106, 135 and 136. Post-Exilic Historical Traditions in Poetic Form," *JNSL* 9 (1981): 39-45.

114 Coats, *Rebellion in the Wilderness*, 230.

115 Ibid., 230.

different context. The context is surely not a P literary setting as the strong influence of DTR would not be possible there. However, that literary setting could very well be H, or perhaps to be properly cautious, one should say a theological tradition familiar with and sympathetic to H.

The final passage to address is Neh 9:5b-37, another historically based confession that is recited by the Levites on behalf of the people at a national day of repentance and worship. Because of their similar genres and tone, Ps 106 and Neh 9 are often connected with one another. However, where Ps 106 treats the period from Israel's enslavement in Egypt until the exile, Neh 9 spans from creation to the exile and beyond.[116] Also similar to Ps 106, DTR influence for Neh 9 has been observed.[117] Yet, the text is a pastiche of phrases from throughout the Hebrew Bible. Hugh Williamson notes the inclusion of the P phrase "holy sabbath," the lifted hand formula, and a thematic link to Num 14:4, and he concludes "that even on the standard critical analysis of the Pentateuch the author must have known the books of Moses in substantially their present form."[118] Yet again, in Neh 9 the "lifted hand" land transfer formula appears in a passage with DTR and P features. In the same fashion as Num 14 and Ps 106, if this DTR influence precludes P as the literary setting, then the possibility for H involvement must be seriously entertained. If Williamson is correct in suggesting that Neh 9:5b-37 was composed independently from its current context within "the Judean community that was never exiled to Babylon but continued to inhabit the decimated land during the period of the exile and after," then they would have to be envisioned as a group sympathetic to H's theological program but not part of that tradition. In sum, Neh 9:5b-37 does not prove H was the literary setting for this convention of the "lifted hand" formula, but it strongly contests attributing the formula to P alone.

Summarizing the evidence to this point, it remains likely that Exod 6:2-8 derives from P. The evidence available at present is not enough to overturn the strong majority in favor of this attribution. This would indicate that P knew and used the "lifted hand" land transfer formula in at least this one instance. The influence of DTR on Num 14:26-38, on the

---

116 Fensham, "Neh. 9," 39-45.

117 Coats, *Rebellion in the Wilderness*, 247, notes in particular the recurrence of the terms ירש, ארץ and נתן.

118 H.G.M. Williamson, *Ezra, Nehemiah* (WBC 16; Waco, Tex.: Word Books, 1985), 312. See Mark J. Boda, *Praying the Tradition: The Origin and Use of Tradition in Nehemiah 9* (BZAW 277; Berlin: Walter de Gruyter, 1999) for a full treatment of the sources for Neh 9.

other hand, suggested that P's involvement may be much different than typically thought. If it is justifiable to extrapolate from the legislative to the narrative material, then such DTR features would preclude assigning these verses to P and signal the involvement of H. This move must be made with caution as it seeks to make a judgment on the development of narrative based on evidence gathered from legal material, but in Num 14:26-38 it is reinforced by other indicators of H's theological program and writing style. Thus, a tentative proposal that H adopted this P formula and adapted it to its own purposes emerges. The evidence for DTR features alongside P features in Ps 106 and Neh 9 was comparable to Num 14, strengthening the proposal for H's relationship to the "lifted hand" land transfer formula, and creating a cumulative case for this view. It remains now to evaluate this proposal against the evidence in Ezekiel.

(b) The Literary Setting in Ezekiel 20 and 47

The "lifted hand" land transfer formula appears six times in Ezek 20 and once in Ezek 47, where it is part of the preface to the reallocation of the land to the twelve tribes. The evidence for DTR influence in Ezek 47:14 is minimal, but the assertion that "this land will fall to you as an inheritance (נחלה)" is notable. This term is not exclusive to DTR, but it is DTR's preferred terminology for the land.[119] Ezekiel 20, by contrast, is the paradigmatic passage for showing the mixed influences of DTR and P on the book.[120] In Num 14 the influence of DTR and P was accompanied by signs of H's theological rationales. In this way, Ezek 20:1-31 is a close counterpart to H: the sole motivation for the *Unheilsgeschichte*— essentially a 25 verse ideological justification—is to explain YHWH's rebuff of the elders inquiry. Thus, Ezek 20 exhibits precisely the same attributes that suggested H's use of the "lifted hand" land transfer formula in the first place.

   In brief, the following can be said about the literary setting, that is the theological tradition that constructed the present *Sitz in der Literatur*, of the "lifted hand" land transfer formula. First, this formula is characteristic of the priestly writings, i.e. the larger grouping of priestly oriented texts that includes P, H, and Ezekiel. Second, there is evidence

---

119 Deut 4:20-21, 38; 9:26, 29; 10:9; 12:9, 12; 14:27, 29; 15:4; 18:1-2; 19:10, 14; 20:16; 21:23; 24:4; 25:19-26:1; 29:7; 32:9. There are numerous instance in DTRH; notable are Josh 11:23; 24:28; Judg 18:1; 21:23; 1 Sam 10:1; 2 Sam 20:1; 1 Kgs 8:36.

120 Levitt Kohn, *A New Heart and a New Soul*, 96-104.

from Exod 6 that P did know and use this formula. Third, there is evidence from Num 14:26-38, Ps 106, and Neh 9:5b-37 that H knew and used this formula. It is probable that H adopted the language from P but adapted it to advance its own theological program, which is also true of Ezek 20, as is discussed further in the next chapter.[121]

Before leaving this topic for now, a few comments on the possible social setting (*Sitz im Leben*) for the "lifted hand" land transfer formula are in order. The combination of evidence from the ancient Near Eastern survey and genre analysis indicate the formula's origin is in legal procedures. Outside of Israel and Judah this legal process was under royal purview; it is possible this was also true in those two states, but there is no evidence for that practice. By contrast, in the Hebrew Bible this formula has a literary setting (*Sitz in der Literatur*) characterized by priestly and cultic concerns. How and why was this formula adopted by a group or groups so heavily influenced by the priesthood and temple? One possibility is that in the development of legal practice in ancient Israel and Judah the jurisdiction over land transfers moved from the royal to the priestly domain. Another, less speculative possibility is that P, H, and Ezekiel adopted the formula in order to challenge a royal function. Whereas the monarchy has a strong presence in DTR and prerogative over every domain of the state, the king is largely missing from P, H, and Ezekiel. Indeed, Milgrom has argued that H intentionally replaced the human monarchy with YHWH as king.[122] As a result of this shift, H makes YHWH the subject of the land transfer formula and, thus, the royal agent who authorizes or prohibits the transfer of land. Because YHWH occupies the position typically reserved for the human monarch, the priests then step in to serve as YHWH's envoys, announcing the legal decision that has been made.[123]

---

121 See ch. 5, §2a.

122 Milgrom, *Leviticus 17–22*, 1414-16.

123 For further evidence that Ezekiel transforms Judah's traditional offices in this manner, see C. L. Crouch and C. A. Strine, "YHWH's Battle Against Chaos in Ezekiel: The Transformation of Judahite Mythology for a New Situation," *JBL* Forthcoming (2013).

4. Social Setting of the "Lifted Hand" Punishment Formula

The second convention of the "lifted hand" formula, associated with the bearing of guilt, appears only four times in the Hebrew Bible (see table 4.5 on p. 165). Evidence was advanced earlier that Ezek 20:5a is a late insertion and that, even though it is similar in syntax to this convention of the "lifted hand" formula, its conspicuously different subject matter places it at some remove from the other three instances.[124] This leaves three cases that exhibit topical consistency. Deuteronomy 32:40, Ezek 36:7, and 44:12 each describe YHWH holding a group responsible for its misdeeds by executing punishment upon it. In each case, the misdeed involves some form of human presumption about YHWH's lack of power. Further, in each case YHWH's judgment results in blessing for YHWH's people, a dynamic shown in the previous chapter.

Citation	Prepositional Phrase	Finite Verb(s)	Verbal Root(s)
Deuteronomy 32:40	אֶל־שָׁמַיִם	אֲשַׁלֵּם, אָשִׁיב	שׁלם, שׁוב
Ezekiel 20:5a	לְזֶרַע בֵּית יַעֲקֹב	וָאִוָּדַע	ידע
Ezekiel 36:7	—	יִשָּׂאוּ	נשׂא
Ezekiel 44:12	עֲלֵיהֶם	וְנָשְׂאוּ	נשׂא

Table 4.5: נָשָׂא יד Guilt Bearing Formula

Despite this correspondence, a subtle yet important difference is evident between Deuteronomy and Ezekiel's use of the formula. In Ezek 36:7 the "lifted hand" guilt bearing formula is paired with the idiom נָשָׂא כְּלִמָּה[125] and in Ezek 44:12 with the phrase נָשָׂא עָוֹן.[126] Baruch Schwartz observes that in P and H these phrases are a metaphor "for guilt and not punishment,"[127] and Zimmerli saw it as "characteristic of punishment formulae in sacral law."[128] There is evidence to confirm

---

124 See ch. 3, §3.

125 This formula occurs at Ezek 16:52, 54; 32:24-25, 30; 34:29; 36:6-7, 15; 39:26; 44:13.

126 This formula occurs at Ezek 4:4, 5, 6; 14:10; 18:19, 20; 44:10, 12.

127 Schwartz, "Bearing of Sin," 12. On the relationship between the two phrases see pp. 10-11, note 27.

128 Zimmerli, *Ezekiel 1–24*, 452.

these remarks from Neo-Babylonian legal practice, where, according to Bruce Wells, "for someone to bear sin means that the person has failed to comply with the instructions of administrative superiors and that the person is now subject to punishment."[129] He also observes that "this expression does not indicate a particular kind of punishment. It indicates that the person is guilty of wrongdoing and subject to punishment, but exactly what that punishment is depends on the nature of the wrongdoing... The punishment is not always death, however."[130] Wells proceeds to demonstrate the relevance of this Babyolnian background for the Hebrew Bible in a study of Lev 5:1, a casuistic passage on giving testimony.[131] By corollary, his findings suggest that Ezekiel employs the נשא עון formula to indicate the guilty group is subject to punishment and the "lifted hand" formula specifies that Yнwн will determine its form and implement it.

By combining the guilt bearing formula, found in P and H, and the "lifted hand" formula found in Deut 32:40, the book of Ezekiel has created something new and unique. Since this combination is exclusive to Ezekiel, the logical conclusion is that this book alone constitutes its literary setting (*Sitz in der Literatur*). Still, this expression, like numerous others in Ezekiel, exhibits a link to Dᴛʀ, P, and H.

Seeking to move beyond the literary setting to the social setting (*Sitz im Leben*), there are more conflicting signals. The "lifted hand" formula as used in Deut 32:40 implies a military background, perhaps the so-called war oracle if such a genre was a feature of ancient military practice.[132] The connection to the guilt bearing formula suggest both a legal and cultic derivation, precisely the same settings that shaped the "lifted hand" land transfer formula. Thus, it is inviting to suggest this is another place where the priestly class cleverly usurped an otherwise royal prerogative, but this remains only conjecture.

5. Implications for Ezekiel's Relationship to the Holiness Code

As the first part of this study nears its end, it is appropriate to evaluate what the new insights gathered here offer for contemporary scholars who have frequently used Ezekiel's formulaic language as a guide to

---

129 Wells, *The Law of Testimony*, 73.

130 Ibid., 61.

131 Ibid., 78-82.

132 On this see Christensen, *Transformations of the War Oracle*.

the diachronic relationship between it and other biblical texts, in particular Dᴛʀ, P, and H.

Commentators by and large describe Ezekiel as closely related to P, perhaps even the bridge between P and H. Even so, scholars struggle to explain important aspects of the relationship between Ezekiel and P. For instance, in her extensive treatment of Dᴛʀ and P language in Ezekiel, Levitt Kohn observes "[s]cholars attempting to determine the relationship between Ezekiel and P continually wrestle with the fact that Ezekiel neither wholeheartedly adopts nor rejects P's language or content. Most find it impossible to imagine that Ezekiel could have disregarded any part of P had the source existed in his day."[133]

The number of links between Ezekiel and Dᴛʀ are not insubstantial either, but an explanation for them has also remained elusive. Noting the influence of Dᴛʀ on Ezekiel, Zimmerli still felt it necessary to remark that "[o]verall the smallness of the contact of Ezekiel with the language and ideas of the well-defined world of Deuteronomy is striking."[134] Joyce has gone much further than Zimmerli in recognizing a Dᴛʀ influence upon Ezekiel, but even he remains hesitant to draw them too closely together, attributing their similarities to "the deuteronomistic influences that eddied around [Ezekiel] both in Jerusalem and in Babylonia."[135] A new and more satisfactory explanation for Ezekiel's similarities and differences to these texts is now possible.

The preceding study has shown that the "as I live" authenticating element is a feature of Dᴛʀ and that the "lifted hand" land transfer formula, though likely used by P in Exod 6:2-8, has strong links to H in Num 14:26-38 and Ps 106. Other similarities between Ezekiel and H include the pollution and personification of the land, *lex talionis* punishments, a proclivity for first-person speech by Yʜᴡʜ,[136] support for Yʜᴡʜ's unmediated kingship as the way forward,[137] and usage of the terms נחלה and אחזה,[138] respectively shared with Dᴛʀ and H,[139] in its positive description of the land. The conclusion is obvious. Ezekiel

---

133 Levitt Kohn, *A New Heart and a New Soul*, 112.

134 Zimmerli, *Ezekiel 1–24*, 46.

135 Joyce, *Ezekiel*, 38.

136 Cholewiński, *Heiligkeitsgesetz und Deuteronomium*, 137; Knohl, *Sanctuary of Silence*, 107; Milgrom, *Leviticus 17–22*, 1326, item 2.

137 Cf. Ibid., 1416.

138 Ezek 44:28; 45:5-8; 46:16, 18; 48:20-22.

139 Dᴛʀ: Deut 4:20-21, 38; 9:26, 29; 10:9; 12:9, 12; 14:27, 29; 15:4; 18:1-2; 19:10, 14; 20:16; 21:23; 24:4; 25:19-26:1; 29:7; 32:9; cf. Josh 11:23; 24:28; Judg 18:1; 21:23; 1 Sam 10:1; 2 Sam 20:1; 1 Kgs 8:36. H: Lev 25:10, 13, 24-25, 27-28, 32-34, 41, 45-46; 27:16, 21-22, 24, 28.

employs language from DTR and P in the service of a theological program distinct from either the DTR or P tradition.[140] This technique
makes it a counterpart to H. Perhaps even more important, the theological program this language supports agrees with H at nearly every
point.

Levitt Kohn attempts to explain this situation by arguing Ezekiel is
unique in fusing of P and DTR material in this way, though it was subsequently imitated by the redactor of the Pentateuch.[141] Her proposal is
problematic for several reasons.[142] Above all else, her model neither accounts for H's style nor for Ezekiel's similarities to H. Instead, it is necessary to place Ezekiel in the same theological tradition as H, a family
of writers with priestly concerns who accept large parts of both DTR
and P theology but, differing from each one in significant ways, adopt
and adapt the formulaic language found in the traditions in order to
advocate their own theological program.

Among those who have presented evidence that H works in this
way, only Knohl has suggested that H's efforts extend to the narrative
portions of the Pentateuch. Nihan has persuasively challenged Knohl's
wide-ranging list of H narrative material.[143] Knohl is just too ambi-
tious. Recognizing that the book of Ezekiel does employ the method
Knohl identifies in quasi-legal texts (the "test cases" of Ezek 14:12-23;
18:1-32; 33:10-20), narrative (Ezek 20:1-31), riddles and allegories (Ezek
16; 17), and even its eschatological vision (Ezek 47:13–48:35), does indicate that his proposal needs further consideration, albeit with proper
caution.

As an illustration, this study offered additional evidence to support
Knohl's suggestion that Num 14:25-38, or at least a considerable portion of it, comes from H and not P. The presence of the DTR "as I live"
authenticating element, in particular, is not indicative of P although it
is characteristic of H.[144] Resolving the question in even this one passage
requires further work to develop the methodological controls used so

---

140 For a similar conclusion reached on different methods, see Lyons, *From Law to Prophecy*.

141 Levitt Kohn, *A New Heart and a New Soul*, 110-18.

142 For a critique of her proposal see Joyce, *Ezekiel*, 38; cf. below, ch. 7, section 2(a)ii.

143 Nihan, *Priestly Torah*, 34-35, note 72. Cf. Christophe Nihan, "The Priestly Covenant,
Its Reinterpretations, and the Composition of "P"," in *The Strata of the Priestly Writ-
ings: Contemporary Debate and Future Directions* (eds. Sarah Shectman and Joel S.
Baden; Athant 95; Zurich: Theologischer Verlag Zürich, 2009), 94-97.
Milgrom, *Leviticus 17–22*, 1332-44, who generally follows Knohl closely on issues re-
garding P and H, also departs from his model in this case.

144 Nihan, "Holiness Code," 104.

effectively on the legal material of the Pentateuch. There is good reason to believe such work can and will produce new insights about the composition of the narrative portions of the Pentateuch.

6. Summary

The stated goal of this chapter was to to describe the literary setting (*Sitz in der Literatur*) of the "as I live" and "lifted hand" formulae and to offer, where possible, some findings on the social setting (*Sitz im Leben*) from which they emerged. The "as I live" authenticating element—on the strength of its analogy to the "as YHWH lives" authenticating element, Lohfink's criteria for DTR writing, and its complementary role to the divine oath with שבע —has its literary setting in the writings of the DTR theological tradition. Though evidence for a particular social setting is sparse, there are some indications the "as I live" formula may come from the prophetic announcements that preceded battles.

The "lifted hand" land transfer formula is considered a feature of P by scholarly consensus. The simplicity of this attribution was challenged for two reasons: first, the evidence of Ezek 20, which is nearly a compendium of DTR and P language, cannot be as determinative as often asserted; second, in view of changing perceptions about the extent of P and H, each of the passages where this formula appears merited reevaluation before presuming composition by P. Upon further review, the presence of DTR influence, justifying rationales, and theological concepts distinctive of H, not P, meant that only Exod 6:2-8 remained as a clear indication that P is the literary setting of the "lifted hand" land transfer formula. On balance, the evidence indicates H adopted the formula from P and adapted it to serve its own theological program. The role of the formula in Ezek 20 and 47 did not disprove this in any way, but their relationship to H demands further consideration, which will be given in the next chapter. The likely social setting of this formula, as clearly exhibited by its use in Mesopotamia, is royal endorsement of legal agreements for land transfer. As a mediating step, it seems that P and H replaced the human king with YHWH, the divine king, in an effort to either usurp or polemicize a royal prerogative.

Finally, the second convention of the "lifted hand" formula demonstrated close links to the priestly guilt bearing formula in Ezekiel. The combination of these two formulae created a new expression that is unique to Ezekiel based on existing evidence. Thus, its literary setting is the Ezekiel tradition. This combined formula possesses links to military practice and sacral law, perhaps indicating another place where the priestly writings transfered language with an originally royal social setting to the cultic sphere.

The second part of this study will apply these findings to the interpretation of various passages, primarily in Ezekiel but also beyond it. The exegesis of Ezekiel will proceed with the conviction that certainly the literary setting, and possibly the social setting, of the "as I live" and "lifted hand" formulae was known to the composer and editors of that text. This belief is based upon various studies that show the book is consciously and artfully employing language from other sources to craft its message and advance its theological program. There is too much evidence that each one of the three formula possessed recognizable and distinguishable connotations to presume a text as sophisticated as the book of Ezekiel used them haphazardly.

Excursus Two: The Meaning of the "Lifted Hand" Formula

The evidence presented to this point concerning the "lifted hand" formula can now be drawn together in order to reach a conclusion on the question of whether it is or is not an authenticating element for the divine oath. In short, the evidence indicates that Biblical Hebrew נשׂא יד is not an idiom for swearing predicated upon a symbolic gesture of raising a hand while stating an oath.

1. Summary of Evidence

Excursus one demonstrated that there are considerable barriers to this interpretation within the Hebrew Bible. Psalm 10:12, where the psalmist implores YHWH to raise his hand in order to defeat the psalmist's enemies, was one plain example that YHWH does not raise his hand to swear. Among those passages where YHWH is said to raise a hand, evidence previously offered by Lust showed that the gesture relates to YHWH's judgment, not to the divine oath authenticated by YHWH's life. The lack of any attempt to translate the phrase as an oath in the LXX supports this line of argument and cautions against assuming that this gesture characterized oath swearing in antiquity. The absence of a corresponding human oath formula, a feature the other two divine oaths exhibited, added evidence against interpreting נשׂא יד as an authenticating element.

However, Excursus 1 did more than criticize the consensus viewpoint: it provided positive evidence for an alternative meaning. First, a rationale for substituting non-synonymous language was introduced: P, H, and Ezekiel intentionally avoid certain formulae and technical terms because of their theological connotations. In particular, the evidence of a connection between the divine oath and DTR's land theology, epitomized by the expressions with the verbal root ירשׁ, motivated P, H, and Ezekiel to deviate from the DTR language. This deviation necessitated an expression that was parallel to but not synonymous with DTR's divine oath with the verbal root שׁבע. So, P, H, and Ezekiel selected the "lifted hand" land transfer formula: this formula corresponds to the Akkadian *našû-nadānu* formula attested in royal deeds at Ugarit and Hatti, a background that allowed these authors to emphasize that YHWH is the royal authority who remains the owner of all land even when he tenders it to an individual or group of his choosing. Far from being a trivial issue, this land theology is consistent with P, H, and Ezekiel's use of the terms אחזה or נחלה for the land, and thus indicative of a sustained attempt to distinguish its land theology.

Although the "lifted hand" land transfer formula is not unmodified in its biblical usage, there are logical explanations for its variances that place it on a historical continuum that accords with both its antecedents and its descendants. The present proposal for why the Biblical Hebrew idiom adapts the hand imagery would benefit from more evidence about how well the scribes at Ras Shamra understood that image, when and why the Biblical Hebrew adaptation emerges, and when and why the hand imagery falls into disuse. However, this lacuna is mitigated by at least two points. First, this study offered a theological rationale for the adaptation that agrees with earlier and unrelated studies: the phrase נשאתי את־ידי לתת foregrounds Yhwh as the active agent in the land transfer and reinforces that Yhwh gives tenure, and not inalienable possession, of the land to Israel. Second, though there are places where the adaptation cannot be fully explained, these lacunae are less problematic than other options. For instance, the ambiguity in how the hand imagery is transformed is by no means a greater difficulty than the lack of any extant textual precedent for reading נשא יד as an authenticating element. And, that ambiguity is still less difficult than the total absence of evidence for what the hand gesture might mean if the "lifted hand" formula were related to swearing. On balance, the likelihood that an integral component of the already existing našû-nadānu formula was adapted to accommodate a well-documented theological concern of P, H, and Ezekiel makes more sense than an otherwise undocumented hand gesture that has as many as five possible explanations and no parallel outside the Hebrew Bible.

The "lifted hand" land transfer meaning does not account for all the instances where Yhwh is said to lift his hand. The genre analysis in chapter three pointed out that there are two distinct contexts in which נשא יד appears: the majority of cases concern Yhwh's promise of land to Israel, but in a minority of cases (Deut 32:40; Ezek 36:7; 44:12) the formula specifies who will execute judgment on a guilty party. Lust argued for this interpretation already, stating that the "lifted hand" formula is a metonymy for an active intervention of one party against another. However, because Lust did not account for the differences produced by the two distinct conventions, he applied this meaning to all the instances of נשא יד without discretion. By recognizing the two contexts, limiting Lust's findings to only the three instances of the "lifted hand" punishment formula, and showing the background for this meaning in Neo-Babylonian legal language, this study borrows the strongest parts of Lust's proposal while mitigating its weaknesses.

2. Summary of Findings

Therefore, it is preferable to understand Biblical Hebrew נשׂא יד in two distinct conventions, neither of which expresses a symbolic action for swearing. The first convention, referred to here as the "lifted hand" land transfer formula, has its ancient Near Eastern counterpart in the Akkadian idiom *našû-nadānu*. P, H, and Ezekiel substitute this formula for DTR's favored expression, the divine oath with the verbal root שׁבע plus נתן. Contrary to the consensus view, this is not a synonymous interchange: rather, P, H, and Ezekiel select a phrase that is parallel to the DTR language but omits implications that are unacceptable. The "lifted hand" land transfer formula may be called a parallel to DTR's divine oath of blessing, but not its synonym.

The second convention, called the "lifted hand" punishment formula, has non-biblical parallels throughout the ancient Near East where the hand is an image of power utilized in active interventions. This formula is used in the Hebrew Bible to specify that YHWH will execute punishment upon a guilty party or parties.

Because this view challenges the consensus and draws on evidence from a number of sources, there are certain to be challenges to its adoption. Therefore, it is important to note at this juncture that the argument of section two incorporates but is not wholly dependent upon this particular point. Rather, the central arguments and claims in part two rely more directly upon the preceding observations about genre and literary setting that contribute to this conclusion. Thus, even should one differ with the strong evidence against reading נשׂא יד as an authenticating element for the divine oath the subsequent argument of this book may still be accepted.

Part Two: The Function of the "As I Live" and "Lifted Hand" Formulae

Part two of this study will explore how the book of Ezekiel employs the "as I live" authenticating element and the two "lifted hand" formulae. These formulae structure numerous passages in the book that contain an explicit, public condemnation of the non-exiled Judahites and a disguised discourse of resistance against the exiles' Babylonian captors.

When Ezekiel deals with the Judahites remaining in the land, it denies the theological foundations that support their appeals to a combined Abraham-Jacob tradition that would establish the non-exiled community as the rightful heirs to YHWH's land. Instead, the book argues explicitly that true Judahite nationalists trace their origin to the ancestors in Egypt whom YHWH redeemed in the first exodus. Just as a faithful remnant of that community was redeemed from under foreign oppression to manifest YHWH's glory to the world, so again in this age a faithful remnant living outside the land and under foreign oppression will be redeemed in order to demonstrate YHWH's glory.

The Babylonians receive a similar critique, but this discourse lies just below the surface of Ezekiel's statements. In particular, the book uses the prominent affiliations of the "as I live" and "lifted hand" formulae to the exodus tradition in order to disguise its subversive message that YHWH, not Marduk, is the divine sovereign that controls kings, nations, and history. The events of 597 and 587 B.C.E. are not indicators that Marduk had defeated and disempowered YHWH, but reveal that YHWH orchestrates history in order to purify the land, to identify a community of faithful Yahwists, and to show that Judah's divine patron remains worthy of the peoples' undivided allegiance.

Different as these two polemics may be in form, they share a single objective, namely to define the boundaries of legitimate Judahite nationalism and faithful Yahwism. YHWH's people are those that identify their lineage with the ancestors in Egypt, reject all forms of image-based worship, interpret both history and contemporary events through the lens of the exodus tradition, and remain convinced that YHWH chooses a faithful community outside the land and under foreign oppression to illustrate his sovereignty over nations, history, and other deities.

Chapter Five: The Intra-Judahite Polemics of Exile

The former territory of Israel and Judah exhibits an undeniable importance in the book of Ezekiel. Leslie Allen is correct to observe that in the book "[l]ife is repeatedly defined in terms of returning to the land."[1] The exiles' potential return to Judah is not, however, universally popular—not even among all those who worship Yʜwʜ. The question "Who shall possess the land in the future?" is perhaps the most contentious in Ezekiel, pitting the community of Judahites living in the Babylonian exile against the community that remained in the land. The contentious nature of the issue is illustrated above all by the argumentative tone of Ezek 33:23-29, a disputation speech centered on the non-exiles' claim: "Abraham was only one man, yet he got possession of the land; but we are many; the land is surely given to us to possess" (Ezek 33:24). On the surface this quote appears harmless, but Ezekiel's vitriolic reaction to this claim that portrays the non-exiles as defiled, rebellious, and soon to be destroyed by Yʜwʜ, demonstrates the contentious nature of both the future of the land and also the figure of Abraham for the exiles. The former is widely accepted, but it remains debatable whether Ezekiel rejected Abraham's role as an esteemed patriarch of this community. Focusing on the "as I live" authenticating element and its allusions to the exodus tradition in Ezek 5:5-17, 33:23-29, 20:32-44, and 11:14-21, this chapter shows that Ezekiel denied that Abraham should be regarded as an honored ancestor.

By contrast to Abraham, the figure of Jacob in Ezekiel has remained largely absent from contemporary analysis of the land dispute between the two Judahite communities. This situation is due, in large part, to the positive role Jacob plays when he is explicitly mentioned in the book (Ezek 20:5; 28:25; 37:25; 39:25). Yet there are problems with this assessment of Jacob in Ezekiel. By applying the new insights gained in part one of this study, this chapter will demonstrate that the book of Ezekiel contains a sustained polemic against a combined Abraham and Jacob tradition. These two figures comprise the foundation of the non-exiles' claims to possess the land, and both come under attack in the book of Ezekiel. This attack is spearheaded by the divine oath with the "as I live" authenticating element and supported by the "lifted hand"

---

1   Leslie C. Allen, *Ezekiel 20–48* (WBC 29; Dallas, Tex.: Word Books, 1990), xxiv.

land transfer formula. In particular, the connotations of the "as I live" authenticating element indicate that Ezek 35:1–36:15 is directed against the non-exiles, not a foreign nation, and the "lifted hand" punishment formula supports the argument that the future inhabitants of YHWH's land will be a community that returns from the Babylonian exile in a second exodus.

Finally, this chapter contextualizes the vitriolic rhetoric as part of a larger effort in which the book of Ezekiel is engaged, namely to assert that the Judahite community in exile remains the authority on social, political, and religious issues. Ezekiel, mouthpiece for part of the exilic community that is comprised of the elites of Jerusalem deported in 597 B.C.E., speaks as though it represents the dominant group on such issues in an attempt to maintain the perception that it *actually is* the dominant group. In other words, the form of its dispute with the non-exiles is as much a weapon in its fight for power as is the content of those disputations.

1. The End of YHWH's Restraint: Ezek 5:5-17

Following the call of the prophet Ezekiel and a series of sign actions, Ezek 5:5-17 possesses a key *Sitz in der Literatur*: as the first explication of the prophet's message,[2] it introduces the magnitude and extraordinary nature of the judgment that will come upon Jerusalem. This sets the stage for all that follows in chs. 6–24, and even for a great deal of what is found in Ezek 33:23–48:35. The address to Jerusalem follows on logically from the preceding sign acts that are directed at the same city. It is notable that Jerusalem is located in the midst of the nations (בתוך הגוים) and surrounded by countries (סביבותיה ארצות): this is the site of Mt Zion. Though it remains debatable whether Ezekiel endorses the election of Jerusalem as told by the Zion tradition, the positive portrayal of the renewed Jerusalem in Ezek 20 as "my holy mountain" (הר-קדשי, Ezek 20:40) suggests a positive, albeit somewhat distant, relationship to the Zion tradition.[3]

---

2   Margaret S. Odell, *Ezekiel* (Smith & Helwys Bible Commentary; Macon, Ga.: Smith & Helwys, 2005), 41, is correct that Ezek 5:5-7:27 are part of the interaction between just the prophet and YHWH that initiates Ezekiel into his role as watchman. There is, therefore, no public audience in view yet.

3   Zimmerli, *Ezekiel 1–24*, 41; Block, *Ezekiel 1–24*, 197-99; Thomas Renz, "The Use of the Zion Tradition in the Book of Ezekiel," in *Zion, City of Our God* (eds. Richard S. Hess and Gordon J. Wenham; Grand Rapids, Mich.: Eerdmans, 1999), 77-103.

Thus, it is fitting that Ezek 5:9 describes Yhwh's judgment of Jerusalem as something "Yhwh has never done and will never do again." Perhaps the intent of the statement is only to communicate the extraordinary scale of Yhwh's action, but the formulation of Ezek 5:9 invites the audience to compare the coming devastation of Zion with its knowledge of Yhwh's prior acts of judgment. It is noteworthy, then, that vv. 13-16 detail the particulars of this unprecedented judgment in language that alludes to the exodus tradition. Scholars regularly note that these verses recall Lev 26,[4] but there are also crucial links with Num 14 and Deut 32.

Greenberg and Block both discuss the connections between Ezek 5 and Deut 32—Greenberg suggesting that 5:5-17 has "embellishments, toward the end, from Deut 32"[5]—but neither scholar, nor any other, has noted how Ezek 5:14-15 reverses Yhwh's restraint in judgment described in Num 14:13-16 and Deut 32:26-27. These passages are not normally connected to one another, but the first part of this study showed the consistency with which Numbers, Deuteronomy, and Ezekiel employ the "as I live" divine oath formula to introduce judgment against Yhwh's people. An allusion to Num 14 and Deut 32 in Ezek 5 is, therefore, reasonable.

In Ezek 5:14, for instance, the judgment is said to make Jerusalem an object of mocking (לְחֶרְפָּה) in "the nations that surround you" (בַּגּוֹיִם אֲשֶׁר סְבִיבוֹתָיִךְ; cf. Ezek 5:8). This outcome will reverse the premise for Yhwh's restraint in Num 14:13-16, where Moses pleads that Yhwh not destroy the first exodus generation all at once (וַיִּשְׁחַט בַּמִּדְבָּר) because of what the Egyptians will conclude about God's power (מִבִּלְתִּי יְכֹלֶת יְהוָה לְהָבִיא אֶת־הָעָם הַזֶּה). The same rationale appears in Deut 32:26-27, where Yhwh refrains from destroying (אַפְאֵיהֶם)[6] the people because his adversaries would conclude this was the result of their own strength. The stark contrast between Yhwh's previous forbearance and current action is underscored by the ominous declaration "my eye will show no pity; nor will I show mercy."[7]

---

4   Zimmerli, *Ezekiel 1–24*, 175-76; Greenberg, *Ezekiel 1-20*, 124-28; Block, *Ezekiel 1–24*, 204; Levitt Kohn, *A New Heart and a New Soul*, 43-75.

5   Greenberg, *Ezekiel 1-20*, 127; cf. Block, *Ezekiel 1–24*, 203-4, 212-6.

6   On the difficulties in translating this *hapax legomenon* see Sanders, *The Provenance of Deuteronomy 32*, 202-03. Sanders is probably correct to translate as "destroy," based on the parallel in the second half of the verse and against the evidence of LXX that gives διασπερῶ αὐτούς "I shall scatter them." However, it is certainly noteworthy that when faced with this rare word the LXX translator opted for interpreting this as a threat reminiscent of the exile.

7   See Block, *Ezekiel 1–24*, 205, for details on this translation.

One way of interpreting YHWH's change of attitude is to conclude that the sins of the people have grown so great, have tested God's restraint so many times, that they can no longer be tolerated. However, one might equally conclude that the lack of restraint is determined by the identity of those living in Jerusalem, namely that for Ezekiel those remaining in Jerusalem and Judah are not YHWH's people. The accuracy of that inference from Ezek 5:5–7:27 is confirmed by the immediately following section, Ezek 8–11, in which YHWH returns from Babylon to destroy Jerusalem.[8] YHWH's people are in exile. By appearing (e.g. Ezek 1) and residing (i.e. Ezek 11:14-21) in Babylonia, YHWH indicates as much. The text draws an analogy between the Judahite community in exile and the ancestors who came out of Egypt in the first exodus community: in both cases, this is the group to whom YHWH's promise of restraint belongs. Because the non-exiles lie outside that community they are not protected by YHWH's promise of restraint and are subject to total destruction.

To introduce an observation that will repeat throughout this chapter, this rhetoric also serves to characterize the Judahite exiles as the dominant social group who, by virtue of this role, believe they can define the content of the public transcript. Ezekiel 5 is simply the first case where the book of Ezekiel seeks "to affirm and naturalize the power of dominant elites,"[9] specifically the Judahites in Babylon. In this case, the intent is to stigmatize the non-exiles by depicting their sinfulness as not only the peak of Jerusalem's rebellion against YHWH but as even worse than the nations around Judah (5:7). This is surely not what those living in Jerusalem thought, evidence of which is the description of its prophets proclaiming peace and safety for the city and its royalty after 597 B.C.E. (cf. Jer 23:13-17; 26:1-11; 27:1–28:11).

Scott characterizes this sort of rhetoric memorably: "the power to call a cabbage a rose and to make it stick in the public sphere implies the power to do the opposite, to stigmatize activities or persons that seem to call into question official realities."[10] He notes the common labeling of revolutionaries as bandits, criminals, or hooligans as a thinly veiled effort to disparage those groups and "attempts to divert attention from their political claims."[11] So it is in Ezek 5:5-17, the first of several cases where the Judahite non-exiles are depicted as rebellious,

---

8   William A. Tooman, "Ezekiel's Radcal Challenge to Inviolability," *ZAW* 121 (2009): 498-514.

9   Scott, *Domination*, 18.

10   Ibid., 55.

11   Ibid.

utterly incapable of living according to Y<small>HWH</small>'s commands. Character-
izing them as reprobates is one way in which the book marginalizes
their claim to be the community with whom Y<small>HWH</small> is present and with
whom Y<small>HWH</small> will reside in the future.

2. This Land is Our Land

In 1972 John Van Seters framed the issues raised by Ezekiel's hostility
to the non-exiled population's Abraham-based land claims:

> what is noteworthy is the fact that the theme of the promise to the patri-
> arch and his descendants is not used. Furthermore, Ezekiel repudiates an
> appeal to Abraham as a claim to the land because for him possession of the
> land is entirely conditional upon obedience to the law. For him the law and
> the promise were two aspects of the oath or covenant with the fathers of
> the exodus-wilderness generation.[12]

Van Seters was neither the first nor the last to recognize the close
connection between the exodus tradition and the book of Ezekiel, but
he was the first to suggest Ezekiel could illuminate the process by
which the patriarchal and exodus traditions were integrated: the failure
to use the patriarchs in this passage, argues Van Seters, reflects a situation in which the patriarchal tradition and the exodus tradition were
not yet united.[13]

Four decades later this point remains in debate.[14] Some agree with
Van Seters' basic idea that Ezek 33:23-29 indicates that early in the
sixth-century B.C.E. there did not yet exist a connection between the tradition of Y<small>HWH</small>'s land promise to the patriarchs as recorded in Gen 12–
35 and the exodus tradition.[15] Moreover, some take the mention of
Abraham by himself as evidence that the Abraham and Jacob traditions

---

12   Van Seters, "Confessional Reformulation," 449.

13   Ibid., 451-54.

14   More recently, Schmid, *Erzväter und Exodus*, 87, remarks that Ezekiel is second only
     to Hos 12 among the prophetic texts in its importance for determining the relation-
     ship between the patriarchs and the exodus tradition.

15   For further development of this argument, see John Van Seters, *Abraham in History
     and Tradition* (New Haven, Conn.: Yale University Press, 1975) and *Prologue to Histo-
     ry: The Yahwist as Historian in Genesis* (Zürich: Theologischer Verlag Zürich, 1992).
     This line of argument is expanded and augmented by Römer, *Israels Väter*. See also
     Matthias Köckert, "Die Geschichte Der Abrahamüberlieferung," in *Congress Volume
     Leiden 2004* (ed. André Lemaire; VTSup 109; Leiden: Brill, 2006), 106.

had not yet been integrated.[16] Some interpreters disagree entirely and continue to believe that Ezek 33:23-29 is entirely compatible with a pre-exilic combination of the Abraham and Jacob traditions,[17] limiting Ezekiel's objection to just the behavior of the non-exiles. So, the question persists: does the book of Ezekiel dispute the idea of a land promise to Abraham? And what of Jacob's role in the book?

This section shall argue that a re-evaluation of Ezek 33:23-29, 20:1-44, and 35:1–36:15 in light of the new evidence for the meaning of the "as I live" authenticating element and the "lifted hand" land transfer formula demonstrates that the book of Ezekiel disputes the validity of a combined Abraham-Jacob tradition that is being used by the non-exiles—a situation that indicates that the two patriarchs' traditions had been linked, probably in some written form, by circa 585 B.C.E. To show this to be the case, the passages dealing with Abraham are treated first, after which an extended discussion of Ezek 35:1–36:15 considers the evidence for the anti-Jacob polemic.

The tenor of Ezekiel's statements in these passages will support a larger point: Ezekiel's polemic against the combined Abraham-Jacob tradition is indicative of its effort to stigmatize the Judahites that remain in Judah. Ezekiel's derogatory tone presents its ideas as the authoritative public transcript, the discourse that the dominant class deems appropriate for open interaction between the powerful and powerless. The sharp tone that the book of Ezekiel takes vis-à-vis the Judahites regarding which community will possess the land in the future reflects a community that knows its power has ebbed, perhaps totally dissipated, and will use the only tools available to it in order to keep their crumbling facade of power from completely collapsing.

To begin, then, it is best to attend to Ezekiel's explicit dispute with the non-exiles' appeal to the Abraham tradition in Ezek 33:23-29.

---

16   On the independence of the Jacob narrative from the Abraham narrative, see: Erhard Blum, *Die Komposition der Vätergeschichte* (WMANT 57; Neukirchen-Vluyn: Neukirchener Verlag, 1984); David M. Carr, *Reading the Fractures of Genesis: Historical and Literary Approaches* (Louisville, Ky.: Westminster John Knox, 1996). Thomas Römer, "Recherches Actuelles Sur Le Cycle D'Abraham," in *Studies in the Book of Genesis: Literature, Redaction and History* (ed. A. Wénin; Betl 160; Leuven: Peeters, 2001), 192, also suggests this possibility.

17   Greenberg, *Ezekiel 21-37*, 687-90; Block, *Ezekiel 25–48*, 258-61.

(a) Abraham Was One Man: Ezek 33:23-29

A major shift in the book of Ezekiel comes at 33:21-22, with the report of Jerusalem's destruction.[18] Most interpret this message as the fulfillment of the judgment against Israel discussed in chs. 1–24, from which it is separated by the oracles against the nations in chs. 25–32, and as the event that allows for the following oracles of salvation. This three-fold division of the book has its merits, but it obscures the fact that Ezekiel's message from 33:23 to the end of the book remains tinged with judgment.[19]

Ezekiel 33:23-29 is a disputation speech that follows the book's habit of recounting the interlocutor's words as preface to giving YHWH's counterargument. Indeed, it was this passage that initially suggested a link between the "as I live" authenticating element and the disputation speech. That link, furthermore, pointed to the correlation between the disputation speech format and the contentious question of the land: of the five passages that address the topic (11:14-21; 20:1-31; 20:32-44; 33:23-39; 35:10-15),[20] all incorporate this genre in some way (only Ezek 11:14-21 lacks the "as I live" formula, an exclusion explained in due course).

The specific, *a fortiori* logic of the non-exiles' thesis in Ezek 33:24 is clear:[21] "Abraham was one man and he possessed the land; but we are numerous: to us the land is given as a possession." On the surface, the logic of the prophet's response is equally transparent: the non-exiles have defiled themselves by their conduct and, thus, they will die in YHWH's judgment. If they perish they most certainly cannot possess the land. The indictment goes beyond just this behavioral component and challenges the underlying premises upon which the non-exiles' claims are founded. Though the quotation itself is some evidence of this feature, there is other evidence in the passage that shows the true depth and breadth of Ezekiel's objections.

The "as I live" authenticating element (v. 27) is preceded by a series of six indictments and is followed by a series of six punishments, placing it at the critical pivot between the motivation for YHWH's judgment

---

18 Zimmerli, *Ezekiel 25–48*, 193-94; Greenberg, *Ezekiel 21-37*, 681-82; Block, *Ezekiel 25–48*, 234-35.

19 Contrary to this traditional three-fold understanding of judgment against Israel, judgment against the nations, and salvation for Israel, see Sweeney, "The Assertion of Divine Power," 156-72, and Mayfield, *Literary Structure.*

20 One might add Ezek 34:1-16 and ch. 37 to this list, although this is debatable.

21 Greenberg, *Ezekiel 21-37*, 684.

and the specification of it.[22] The six indictments show strong connections to Lev 26 (see table 5.1 on p. 184),[23] as the the six punishments do
as well (see table 5.2 on p. 185). Michael Lyons, in his recent study on
the use of H by Ezekiel, demonstrates that "[t]his technique, wherein
the author draws on different prohibitions in H, changes them into ac-
cusations, and combines them" occurs throughout Ezekiel.[24]

Still, the depth of congruence between Ezekiel and H's theology regarding the land is rarely perceived. Note the distinction between the
object of the first three and the last three punishments: the sword, wild
beast, and pestilence (v. 27) will fall upon the people left in the land,
namely those who are quoted at the outset of this disputation speech;
the remaining three judgments, by contrast, are addressed to the land

Action	Ezekiel	Holiness Code
Eating meat with blood	33:25	Lev 17:10-16; 19:26
Worship gillulim	33:25	Lev 26:30
Shed blood	33:25	Lev 17:4?
Depend on their sword	33:26	Lev 17:4[25]
Commit abominations	33:26	Lev 18:22, 26, 27, 29, 30; 20:13
Defile their neighbor's wife	33:26	Lev 18:20; 20:10

Table 5.1: Parallels to H in the Indictment of Ezek 33:23-29

---

22   Block, *Ezekiel 25–48*, 258, mentions that vv. 24-29 are a remarkable hybrid of the
     prophetic proof oracle and the classic disputation. This is achieved, in part, by the
     way the "as I live" formula functions.

23   Michael Fishbane, *Biblical Interpretation in Ancient Israel* (Oxford: Clarendon Press,
     1985), 294, notes, "In fact, the language of these punishments echoes the punish-
     ments for covenantal malfeasance listed in Lev. 26:19, 25, 30-33, and thus under-
     scores the fact that the delicts noted in Ezek 33:25 refer to acts of covenantal malfea-
     sance found in Lev. 17–18."

24   Lyons, *From Law to Prophecy*, 95.

25   Greenberg, *Ezekiel 21-37*, 685, connects this to the previous wrongdoing in "shedding
     blood."

Judgment	Ezekiel	Holiness Code
Fall by sword	33:27	Lev 26:25
Devoured by animals	33:27	Lev 26:22
Die by pestilence	33:27	Lev 26:25
Desolate and devastate the land	33:28	Lev 26:33
End the land's proud might	33:28	Lev 26:19
None will pass through	33:28	–

Table 5.2: Parallels to H in the Judgment of Ezek 33:23-29

(הארץ) itself, specified as the mountains of Israel (הרי ישׂראל) in v. 28b. This subtle shift indicates that the defiling behavior of the non-exiles caused both them *and the land* to be impure.[26] That idea is otherwise unique to H.[27] Christophe Nihan remarks:

---

26 Milgrom, *Leviticus 17–22*, 1404-05; Joosten, *People and Land*, 169-92, particularly 178-80; Nihan, *Priestly Torah*, 395-575. Kutsko, *Between Heaven and Earth*, 126-27, note 110, anticipates this point.

Julie Galambush has argued for a distinction between Ezekiel and Leviticus on this point ("God's Land and Mine: Creation as Property in the Book of Ezekiel," in *Ezekiel's Hierarchical World: Wrestling With a Tiered Reality* (eds. Stephen L. Cook and Corrine L. Patton; SBLSyms 31; Atlanta, Ga.: Society of Biblical Literature, 2004), 98-102). However, the distinction she attempts to draw between the land as merely victim in Leviticus (and Jeremiah for that matter) and guilty of its own sins in Ezekiel (highlighting Ezek 6; 7; 14:12-23) is overstated. This is demonstrated by Lev 18:25, wherein the land is punished for its iniquity (ואפקד עונה עליה). The relationship between people and land for H and Ezekiel is so close that the land (under its various titles) can be a metonymy for the people when desired.

27 Even if one accepts the argument in Milgrom, *Leviticus 17–22*, 1575, that the concept of land pollution is "stated (or implied) by every pentateuchal source (e.g., Gen 4:11-12 [JE]; Num 25:33-34 [P]; Deut 21:4 [D])," it is important to note that even he qualifies this by observing that "H has taken the ubiquitous notion that homicide pollutes the land... and applied it to other violations" (Ibid., 1579). Because Ezekiel specifies that the defiling actions go far beyond homicide, and even beyond the "sexual violations" that Milgrom identifies in D (Ibid., 1404), this passage should be correlated to H and not to a more commonly held concept, even if such a general outlook did prevail.

More generally, disobedience to the law is now repeatedly conceived of as leading to the pollution not only of the sanctuary (Lev 20:2, 4), as in P (Lev 4; 16), but of the entire land (Lev 18:24-30; 20:22ff; and 26:34-35!), a notion unparalleled elsewhere in the Torah although here again it is reminiscent in some respects of the theology of the book of Ezekiel where a similar view is found with regard to the city of Jerusalem (see, e.g., Ez 22).[28]

In addition to Nihan's link with Ezek 22, others connect the idea with Ezek 36:25.[29] These connections make the presence of the same idea in Ezek 33 unsurprising. However, Nihan's assertion that this idea occurs nowhere else in the Torah needs refinement because it is present in Deut 32:39-43, a key parallel passage. Those verses, the final strophe of the poem, assert that YHWH "will repay those who hate him, and cleanse the land for his people" (Deut 32:43bβ), using the "as I live" authenticating element to introduce this purifying judgment.[30] This thematic overlap is unlikely to be a coincidence.

How does this particular conception, shared by Ezekiel, H, and the Song of Moses, contribute to a polemic against the Abraham tradition? The answer lies in the related terminology of the non-exiles claim: "Abraham was one man and he *possessed* (ויירש) the land. And we are many: to us the land is given as a *possession* (למורשה)" (Ezek 33:24). The noun מורשה is rare, and especially so outside of Ezekiel, where it only refers to the land once.[31] However, Rendtorff has demonstrated that the related verbal form is central for Gen 15,[32] the quintessential statement of the land promise to Abraham.[33] Whereas Gen 15 uses ירש in an overwhelmingly positive sense, all seven instances of מורשה in Ezekiel are negative.[34] Five times it refers to one nation being conquered by another (Ezek 25:4, 10; 36:2, 3, 5) and the two other instances (Ezek 11:15; 33:24) appear in the non-exiles' land claims that Ezekiel rejects. When Ezekiel does intend to speak positively about the people's con-

28 Nihan, *Priestly Torah*, 559.

29 Milgrom, *Leviticus 17–22*, 1574, discusses this interpretation at Qumran.

30 Driver, *Deuteronomy*, 380-81.

31 Exod 6:8. Deut 33:4 refers to the torah of Deuteronomy.

32 Rolf Rendtorff, "Genesis 15 im Rahmen der theologischen Bearbeitung der Vätergeschichten," in *Werden und Wirken des Alten Testaments: Festschrift für Claus Westermann* (eds. R. Albertz and et al.; Göttingen: Vandenhoeck & Ruprecht, 1980), 74-81. See also Block, *Gods of the Nations*, 79-81.

33 One might further note that another four occurrences of verbal forms from ירש occur in the the patriarchal narratives and build connections to both Isaac and Jacob. Cf. Gen 21:10; 22:17; 24:60 (where it is applied to Rebekah); 28:4 (where it is referred to as "the blessing of Abraham" [ברכת אברהם]).

34 Ezek 11:15; 25:4, 10; 33:24; 36:2, 3, 5.

trol of the land it selects either אחזה,[35] the term used in Lev 17–26, or
נחלה, a word favored in Deuteronomy and DtrH.[36]

Each of these three terms possesses a particular ideological slant.
Habel explains the nuance of מורשה, as used positively in Gen 15:
"Here Abraham, progenitor of the people of Israel and the representative of the ancestral households of Israel, is promised the land uncondi-
tionally and given control (*yaraš*) over that land for the people."[37] This
differs from אחזה, H's preferred term, which refers to those "who possess their land as property (*ʾaḥuzzah*) held in tenure under divine ownership."[38] One might further clarify this with reference to Gillis Gerleman's detailed study on אחזה and נחלה, where he observes that "[a]s
אחזה, the land is not described as a belonging, but as arable land of Israel that is granted as an allocation and for usufruct."[39] Thus, אחזה
emphasizes that Yʜᴡʜ remains the true owner of the land and offers Israel only conditional residence whereas מורשה signifies a permanent,
unconditional right to the land, possibly even implying that true ownership has passed from Yʜᴡʜ to the human residents.[40]

---

35 Ezek 44:28; 45:5-8; 46:16, 18; 48:20-22.

36 Ezek 35:15; 36:12; 44:28; 45:1; 46:16-18; 47:14, 19, 22-23; 48:28-29. Cf. Deut 4:20-21, 38;
9:26, 29; 10:9; 12:9, 12; 14:27, 29; 15:4; 18:1-2; 19:10, 14; 20:16; 21:23; 24:4; 25:19-26:1;
29:7; 32:9. At the risk of being repetitive, one might again note how Ezekiel combines terms from Dᴛʀ and H here.

It should be noted that Dᴛʀ does use ירש. However, Lohfink points out that this is
solely related to the manner by which the land is taken (military conquest) and
comes in the context of a "total system" that portrays Yʜᴡʜ as the true owner of the
land (N. Lohfink, "יָרַשׁ," *TDOT* 6:368-96, especially p. 385).

37 Habel, *The Land is Mine*, 125.

38 Ibid., 110; Block, *Gods of the Nations*, 81-84.

39 "Als אחזה wird das Land nicht als Eigentum, sondern als Anbaugebiet Israels beze-
ichnet, das zur Verfügung und Nutzung eingeräumt wird" (Gillis Gerleman,
"Nutzrecht und Wohnrecht: zur Bedeutung von אחזה und נחלה," *ZAW* 89 (1977):
318). Although Habel, *The Land is Mine*, 99, stresses the differences between אחזה
and נחלה, Gerleman correctly draws them closer together. He argues, "Die Er-
klärung dieser vieldiskutierten Erscheinung ist einfach und ergibt sich von selbst,
wenn man sieht, daß hljn nicht »Eigentum«, sondern »Wohnsitz« meint" (Gerleman,
"Nutzrecht Und Wohnrecht," 320). Cf. Block, *Gods of the Nations*, 76-79.

40 One might further support this distinction by looking at the different terms used in
Gen 15 and 17 for the land promise. In Gen 15, the tradition closest to the non-exiles' claim, the verb ירש is used five times. Genesis 17 instead chooses to specify the
land as לאחזת עולם (Gen 17:8). One might read in this the security of Yʜᴡʜ's
promise, e.g. the promise continues indefinitely. However, one might just as readily
stress that עולם modifies, and thus qualifies, אחזה and indicates that the land will always be held in tenure and remain owned by Yʜᴡʜ, presumably to utilize different-
ly if so preferred. This would indicate that a similar difference of opinion about the
land is present even within in the non-P and P sections of Genesis.

The book of Ezekiel selects its words carefully, in order to simultaneously indict the behavior of the non-exiles and refute the very
premise of their appeal to Abraham, namely the descendants of Abraham cannot possess (ירש) the land because YHWH will not allow any
group this form of control over the land. This two-pronged rebuttal
demonstrates that Ezek 33:23-29 is a polemic against the Abraham tradition and its claims to possess the land. The allusions to Lev 17–26
and Deut 32:39-43 identify Ezekiel's counter-thesis with the exodus tradition, reinforcing the idea that those two origin narratives were in conflict when this passage was composed.

Further support for this view comes from Ezek 11:14-21. This passage includes a claim strikingly similar to the inhabitants of Jerusalem
in Ezek 33:23-29: "They have gone far from YHWH; to us this land is giv-
en for a possession (למורשה; Ezek 11:15)."[41] Despite lacking an explicit
reference to the Abraham tradition, the recurrence of enmity between
the non-exiles and the exiles and the claim that the land has become a
מורשה for the former plainly connects the two. Ezekiel 33:23-29 and
11:14-21 also employ the same polemical logic. For instance, the distinctive idea that the land has become defiled lies behind Ezek 11:18:
"when [the exiles] return to it they will remove all its detestable things
and all its abominations from it." The abominable behavior of the non-
exiles, detailed at length in Ezek 8, polluted the land such that the returning community must cleanse it just as in Ezek 33.

This concept also colors the notoriously difficult phrase in v. 16:
"Therefore say: 'Thus says the Lord YHWH: Though I removed them far
away among the nations, and though I scattered them among the countries, yet I have been a sanctuary to them for a little while (מקדש מעט)
in the countries where they have gone.'" The difficulties in translating
the phrase מקדש מעט are well known but,[42] though its interpretation re-

---

41 Zimmerli, *Ezechiel 25–48*, 198; Greenberg, *Ezekiel 21-37*, 688; Block, *Ezekiel 25–48*, 258;
    Joyce, *Ezekiel*, 193.

42 Good overviews are provided in Block, *Ezekiel 1–24*, 349-50, and Joyce, *Ezekiel*,
    112-14. Joyce indicates there are two reasons to prefer the degree interpretation: (1)
    vv. 16 and 17 should be read separately, not linked, and (2) usage elsewhere permits
    this translation. The second is indisputable; the degree interpretation is possible
    based on other occurrences. However, the first places a harder break between the
    two verses than necessary. They are separate, but are both responses to the non-ex-
    iles' contention and can be read in parallel. Verse 16 addresses the present tense re-
    sponse of YHWH—what God is doing. Verse 17 addresses the future response of
    YHWH—what God will do. This evidence for the temporal interpretation is further
    supported by the sign act in Ezek 4:4-9 (cf. Greenberg, *Ezekiel 1-20*, 104-05) and, in
    due course, by the way Ezekiel manipulates the themes of the Babylonian *akītu*
    festival.

mains debatable, there is sufficient evidence for the temporal under-standing adopted here. This is based partially on Joosten's description of the nexus between land and people in H:

> One of the theological axioms of H—in fact, the most fundamental of its theological axioms—is that YHWH is present in the midst of his people, in the camp and, later, in the land. YHWH's holy presence radiates outward from the sanctuary throughout the entire land and imposes its demands on all the inhabitants. This fundamental axiom explains the notions of YHWH's ownership and lordship over the land. The land occupied by the Israelites is his because he dwells there in his sanctuary.[43]

YHWH's presence, or conversely in Ezek 11 YHWH's absence, demon-strates the invalidity of the Jerusalemites' logic: because YHWH had ac-tually abandoned the non-exiles their claims are unsubstantiated. Ezekiel 33:23-29 indicates that Ezekiel shares this theological view, sup-porting the argument that its two-fold dynamic—the land belongs to Is-rael because YHWH dwells there and YHWH's demands are relevant be-cause of his presence—underlies all of Ezek 11:16-21. The further step to relocate YHWH's presence among the exiles emulates the way that the divine presence accompanied the exodus generations when they were outside the land. YHWH's presence with the exiles also creates the re-quired circumstances for the ongoing relevance of the commandments (חקה) and decrees (משפט) upon the exiles (11:20). Taken together, these two themes declare unmistakably that it is from the exiles that the fu-ture inhabitants of the land will emerge.

The quotations from the non-exiles, accurately represented or not, historically accurate or not, reflect that the authors and tradents of the book of Ezekiel believed the non-exiles were using language character-istic of the public transcript. The appeal to Abraham affirms the posi-tion of the non-exiles, who believe that by the sheer size of their com-munity in the land they are greater than the esteemed patriarch. This is even more evident in the quotation at 11:15, where the accusation is that the Judahites in exile are the ones who have moved away from YHWH. This accusation seeks to stigmatize the behavior of the exilic community and, by this very action, to enshrine the non-exiles as the dominant social group.

Ezekiel retaliates by stigmatizing both claims. The argument of Ezek 33:25-29 impugns both the moral character of those making the claims and undercuts the logic upon which the claim is founded. The bald reversal of logic is even clearer in Ezek 11: the non-exiles claim

---

43 Joosten, *People and Land*, 176-77.

that Yʜᴡʜ is with them is countered directly by the assertion that Yʜᴡʜ resides with the exiles in the temporary sanctuary. This point is underscored by the narrative of Ezek 8–11, where the extended denunciation of the Jerusalemites deeds (Ezek 8), requires a complete purge of that city (Ezek 9), after which the כבוד יהוה moves eastward towards the exiles in Babylonia. Yʜᴡʜ's oath with "as I live" in Ezek 11 and 33 underscores the disputational tone of both passages and is part of a thoroughgoing dependence on the exodus tradition, a choice that shows the discord between it and the Abraham tradition. When considered together, these two passages demonstrate that there was an intense thrust and parry between the two Judahite communities over the content of the public transcript.

(b) The Land of Sojourn: Ezek 20

Perhaps the best known discussion of the land in Ezekiel is ch. 20, which, despite its prominence, continues to produce problems for interpreters. Chapters three and four of this study brought clarity to how vv. 1-31 employ the "lifted hand" land transfer formula: by portraying Yʜᴡʜ as the royal figure who authorizes the transfer of all land, it explains that the numerous changes in Israel's relationship to the land have all been under Yʜᴡʜ's control. The idea is carried forward in vv. 32-44, which describe the exiles' return as a second exodus at the end of which Yʜᴡʜ will once again allow them to inhabit the land.

The consensus view that the "lifted hand" formula is a divine oath obscures its real importance in Ezek 20. As a result of that common interpretation, many scholars suggest that נשא יד functions as a synonym for Yʜᴡʜ's oath with the verbal root שבע, which is common in Deuteronomy. For instance, Thomas Römer, in his thorough analysis of the oath of the land, writes:

> This phrase [נשא יד] ... indicates, in my opinion, the clear parallelism to the Dtr נשבע texts and [supports] the retention of the usual translation "he raised the hand (to swear)" (cf. the parallel of חי אנכ(י) and נשא יד in Ezek 20 and Deut 32:40).[44]

---

44 Römer, *Israels Väter*, 492-93. "diesem Ausdruck ... spricht m. E. der eindeutige Parallelismus zu den dtr נשבע-Texten für die Beibehaltung der üblichen Übersetzung 'die Hande (zum Schwur) erheben' (vgl. auch das Nebeneinander von חי אנכ(י) und נשא יד in Ez 20 und Dtn 32,40)."

Pons previously proposed the same dynamic: "Initially, Ezekiel moves intentionally away from Deuteronomy: it uses נשא יד for 'to render an oath,' instead of שבע as is habitual in Deuteronomy."[45] For Pons, this was one of many indications that Ezek 20 is actually a polemic against DTR. Seely, as another example, remarks that "Ezekiel prefers *nśʾ yd* while the Deuteronomic material is full of *nšbʿ*. This may show an archaizing tendency in Ezekiel, or simply that he prefers other traditions to Deuteronomy."[46] These examples could be multiplied,[47] but the point is clear.

Albeit correct to note the subtle yet important avoidance of the characteristically DTR שבע, these scholars are wrong about the rationale. Ezekiel is not opposed to the DTR use of the divine oath, as demonstrated by Ezek 20's use of the DTR "as I live" authenticating element. Rather, Ezekiel does not use שבע because that term connotes a singular, permanent promise of blessing that was sworn to the ancestors in Egypt. To express the numerous changes in status that YHWH decrees for Israel vis-à-vis the land, Ezekiel must choose the "lifted hand" land transfer formula. In doing so, the book also draws on its broader connotation in the ancient Near East, especially the notion emphasized by Labuschagne's study of the land transfer formula, which indicates that "[t]he documents... picture [the king] as administrator and controller of the land and estates, in fact *as the real owner of land*... He takes property away from the one and gives it to the other... that is, he 'transfers' property from one to the other."[48] The unbroken ownership of the land by the royal figure, for Ezekiel a divine king, is the concept invoked in Ezek 33:23-29 and 11:14-21 in order to refute the non-exiles' claims. Its fourfold appearance in Ezek 20:1-31 reinforces its importance for Ezekiel.

Focusing on Ezek 20:32-44 one sees that this disputation portrays YHWH's intention to gather the people out of exile, to purify them in the desert by judging those continuing in rebellion and, finally, to restore them to the land of Israel with worship in Jerusalem. These steps can be summarized as a second exodus,[49] a motif previously associated

---

45   Pons, "Le vocabulaire," 218-19. "Éz s'éloigne d'abord délibérément de Dt il utilise נשא יד pour «prêter serment», au lieu de שבע si habituel au Dt."

46   Seely, "Raised Hand," 420.

47   Zimmerli, *Ezekiel 1–24*, 407-08; Block, *Ezekiel 1–24*, 626, especially note 63; Allen, *Ezekiel 20–48*, 9-10.

48   Labuschagne, "našû-nadānu," 177. Emphasis added.

49   Levitt Kohn, *A New Heart and a New Soul*, 107-10; Corrine Patton, ""I Myself Gave Them Laws That Were Not Good": Ezekiel 20 and the Exodus Traditions," *JSOT* 69 (1996): 73-90; Block, *Ezekiel 1–24*, 651; Joyce, *Ezekiel*, 153.

with Ezek 20:32-44. Recent studies have shown that this theme is constructed with a mix of terms from D<small>TR</small>, P, and H.[50] The most detailed is Risa Levitt Kohn's monograph *A New Heart and a New Soul*.[51]

Notwithstanding the thorough nature of her study, Levitt Kohn fails to recognize the connections between the "as I live" formula, divine judgment in the D<small>TR</small> tradition, and the exodus motif demonstrated in chapters three and four of this study. The interplay of these features in Ezek 20:32-44 magnifies the importance of the exodus theme. Tellingly, the very first words in Y<small>HWH</small>'s speech are "as I live," which evoke the divine judgment announced in D<small>TR</small> exodus tradition (Num 14:21; Deut 32:40). Verse 33 pairs the "as I live" formula with the D<small>TR</small> phrases "a mighty hand and an outstretched arm" and "with wrath poured out," making the allusion to D<small>TR</small> unmistakable. Y<small>HWH</small>'s speech climaxes with the "lifted hand" land transfer formula (v. 42); this language evokes the priestly tradition's account (cf. Num 14:26-38) of the same exodus events detailed in Deut 32, which is further confirmation of the earlier observation that Ezek 20 positively adopts D<small>TR</small>, P, and H language in order to express its theology. Moreover, by presenting the return from exile as yet another change in the people's status with relationship to the land effected by Y<small>HWH</small>, Ezek 20:32-44 implicitly denies the non-exiles' claims based upon the Abraham tradition.

In view of these emphases, the rather innocuous comment that Y<small>HWH</small> will lead the exiles out "from the land of their sojourn" (מארץ מגוריהם) gains new significance. Whereas the patriarchal tradition describes Canaan as the land of sojourn in a positive sense (e.g. Gen 17:8; 21:22-34; 26:1-5; 28:4; 35:27; cf. Exod 6:4), Ezekiel transforms that image in three ways. First, the location of the peoples' sojourn is moved from Canaan to Babylon.[52] By this change, second, the land of sojourn ceases to be a desirable place that God has promised to the community and becomes a place of punishment and purification.[53] Perhaps the land of

---

50   This recognition even comes from outside studies focused directly on Ezekiel, as evidenced by Römer, *Israels Väter*, 504.

51   Levitt Kohn does not distinguish between D and D<small>TR</small> nor between P and H in this chapter or in her conclusions. The latter omission is unfortunate given the recent work by Knohl, Milgrom, and now Nihan, *Priestly Torah*, that demonstrate the important and substantial differences between P and H.

52   Despite the frequent translation of ארץ as nations, the exact parallel between Ezek 20:38, Gen 17:8; 28:4; 36:7, and especially Exod 6:4 indicates that it should be understood as a single place in which the people live as outsiders.

53   Ezek 47:13–48:35, which contains the "lifted hand" land transfer formula, is also relevant here. This passage, which concludes the book, divides up the restored land with language reminiscent of Ezek 20: the direct connection is to 20:42: "You will know that I am Y<small>HWH</small> when I bring you to the ground of Israel, to the land that I de-

sojourn need not be erased from the community's memory, but they certainly should not long for it. Third and finally, Ezek 20:38 mentions the land of sojourn in connection with those people who will not survive Yhwh's purifying judgment in the wilderness.   This analogy should not be pressed too far, but it does make such sojourners into the portion of the community unworthy of living in Yhwh's land. There is a sense of mockery and taunting about this statement, albeit a bit vague.

There is more evidence of this rhetorical tactic in Ezek 35:1–36:15. As attention turns to this oracle against Mt Seir, the present argument moves into its second section, wherein evidence will show that Ezekiel also contains an anti-Jacob polemic.

(c) Jacob and Esau: Ezek 35:1–36:15

The third passage in Ezekiel that deals with the land and its future inhabitants is Ezek 35:1–36:15. Although the ancient versions generally understood this as two separate oracles, modern scholars have recognized their connection, reinforced by the divine word formula in 35:1 that opens the section and the same formula in 36:16, indicating the opening of a new section. In between, the oracles to Mt Seir and the mountains of Israel detail the future prospects for the land. Although those basic details are not in dispute, at least one thing about this passage remains unclear: why is this the lone foreign nation oracle outside the otherwise unified collection in Ezek 25–32? What was unique about this oracle against Edom[54] that prompted this arrangement?

---

cided to transfer it to your ancestors." In parallel, Ezek 47:14 declares, "you shall receive it as a special grant, equally apportioned, which I decided to transfer it to your ancestors. This land will fall to you as a special grant." Thus, Ezek 47:13–48:35 completes the second exodus described in Ezek 20:40-44.

As further evidence of this intent, it uses variations of the verbal root נחל three times in vv. 13-14. Here, the author evokes the concept that the land remains Yhwh's property even when a tenant is given control over it, the theology Ezekiel shares with Dtr and H. As if to keep the audience from missing this, נחל appears again in 48:29, creating an inclusio around the material concerning the division of the land.

54 On the history of Edom and its role in the ancient Near East, see *inter alia*: Piotr Bienkowski, ed. *Early Edom and Moab: The Beginning of the Iron Age in Southern Jordan* (Sheffield Archaeological Monographs 7. Sheffield: J. R. Collis, 1992); Diana V. Edelman, ed. *You Shall Not Abhor an Edomtite for He Is Your Brother: Edom and Seir in History and Tradition* (Archaeology and Biblical Studies 3. Atlanta, Ga.: Scholars Press, 1995); John R. Bartlett, "The Rise and Fall of the Kingdom of Edom," *PEQ* 104 (1972): 26-37; and especially Ernst Axel Knauf, "The Cultural Impact of Secondary State Formation: The Case of the Edomites and Moabites," in *Early Edom and Moab:*

A common answer identifies the content of the oracle against Edom in chapter 35 as a particularly good thematic pair for the restoration oracle to Israel in Ezek 36:1-15. The compiler, an astute reader, placed the two oracles together in order to underscore the coming restoration of the land and resettlement of YHWH's people there. Despite the popularity of this position, there are problems with it. "Ezek. 35," remarks John Bartlett, "brings a number of charges against Edom couched in familiar and conventional terms" though "[n]ot one of them necessarily reflects any specific action of Edom's in 587 BC."[55] To his mind "Edom is but one enemy among several of whom similar charges are made."[56]

There is a slightly more sophisticated, but largely comparable, scenario that emphasizes the downfall of Edom as the basis for the blessing of Israel, or as Joyce summarizes "the 'seesaw'/'teeter-totter' phenomenon with Israel's fortunes rising as those of the nations decline."[57] This recognizes that Edom plays a symbolic role for Judah's enemies as a whole,[58] but offers little more than proximity between Judah and Edom to explain its role in Ezek 35.

Recently, Elie Assis has offered a variation on this idea by noting the particularly hostile attitude towards Edom in no less than ten separate passages.[59] Assis argues that:

> widespread historical reasons given to this phenomenon—Edom's participation in the downfall of Judah and the Edomite infiltration into Judah— are not satisfactory... Since Edom was seen as an alternative to Israel, being identified with Esau, Jacob's brother, it was thought possible that God had now chosen Edom as his people in place of Israel. The Edomite participation in Judah's destruction and especially their settlement in the promised land in their place supported their impression that Edom has replaced Israel. The anti-Edomite oracles were meant to instill into the hearts of the

The Beginning of the Iron Age in Southern Judah (Sheffield Archaeological Monographs 7; Sheffield: J. R. Collis, 1992), 47-54.

55 John R. Bartlett, "Edom and the Fall of Jerusalem, 587 B.C," *PEQ* 114 (1982): 20.

56 Ibid.

57 Joyce, *Ezekiel*, 200, offers this summary in commenting on Mathews' study of Isa 34– 35 (Claire R. Mathews, *Defending Zion: Edom's Desolation and Jacob's Restoration (Isaiah 34–35) in Context* [BZAW 236; Berlin: de Gruyter, 1995]).

58 See the extended discussion in Bert Dicou, *Edom, Israel's Brother and Antagonist: The Role of Edom in Biblical Prophecy and Story* (JSOTSup 169; Sheffield: Sheffield Academic Press, 1994).

59 Elie Assis, "Why Edom? On the Hostility Towards Jacob's Brother in Prophetic Sources," *VT* 56 (2006): 1, lists the following: Isa 21:11-12; 63:1-6; Jer 49:7-22; Ezek 25:12-14; 35; Joel 4:19-21; Amos 1:11-12; 9:13-15; Obad; Mal 1:1-5.

people that, despite the destruction, Israel is still the chosen people and the sins of Edom against Judah will not remain unpunished.[60]

The creativity of this suggestion is commendable.[61] Assis, nevertheless, can find only one text to support it: Mal 1:1-5.[62] Even though that text addresses the election of Jacob over Esau, the foundational ancestor of Edom, Mal 1:3-4 concerns the land of Edom, not Israel. Verse 5 drives home this distinction by specifying that its interest is YHWH's power to control events outside of Israel.

Assis' basic insight about Edom's role as an alternative to Israel is instructive nevertheless. Lust demonstrates that "the editors of Ezekiel sarcastically identified the inhabitants of Jerusalem with the Edomites"[63] and in Ezek 35–36 "the term [Edom] refers, not to historical-geographical Edom, but rather to Edom-Esau, the brother-enemy of Israel, and was used as a nickname for the inhabitants of Jerusalem, as opposed to 'real Israel' in exile or in the diaspora."[64] In support of this identification, Lust notes that "the quotations of Edom in Ezekiel 35–36 are almost identical with those of the inhabitants of Jerusalem in 11:15 and 33:23."[65] Lust's argument shares Assis' creativity but combines it with stronger textual evidence.

Ezekiel 33:23-29 and 20:32-44 show that the book is acutely concerned to refute the claims of the non-exiles and to stigmatize them so that they cannot be identified as the rightful inhabitants of the land. The situation is no different in Ezek 35:1–36:15: the exiles did not fear

---

60   Ibid., 19; Cf. Sweeney, "The Assertion of Divine Power," 170.

61   For instance, he is certainly correct in the approach he takes to the historicity of the Jacob and Esau tradition, building from its well-known status by the sixth century and not debating the details of how that situation came to pass (Assis, "Why Edom?" 9).

62   Assis cites as evidence texts indicating Israel's despair about its situation after 587 B.C.E.; this despair is undoubted, but that despair is always related to Israel's rejection, without any text specifying YHWH has replaced Israel. He offers two further "facts" for his position: there was Edomite participation in the destruction of Jerusalem and the Edomites colonized some land in Judah. In sum, one finds all this evidence to be less an argument for the position than circumstantial evidence that could, but certainly need not, relate to the assertion.
     With regards to Ezekiel, even if Mal 1:1-5 could sustain the argument the relevance of this passage would remain debatable because it post-dates Ezekiel.

63   Lust, "Edom—Adam," 387-401. Because this article was published the same year as Assis', it does not deal with his proposal.

64   Ibid., 400; Renz, The Rhetorical Function, 109, is less direct, but recognizes that the non-exiles are to be included in this form of address.

65   Lust, "Edom—Adam," 389.

that Yʜᴡʜ had rejected them in favor of Edom; rather, the book expresses its disdain for the non-exiles' claims to their recently lost land by mocking them.[66] To call a Judahite an Edomite, to associate them with Esau not Jacob, is a blunt insult. In this sense, Ezek 35 is the pinnacle of a series of increasingly harsh rebuttals, each of which starts with a behavioral critique, moves on to a denial of theological premises, and concludes with mockery. Thus, there is a simple explanation for the location of this oracle against "Edom" outside chs. 25–32: Ezek 35:1–36:15 is not a foreign nation oracle, but an oracle against the Judahites remaining in the land!

The taunt is not merely bombast; it selects its terms carefully to undermine the non-exiles' claim to the figure of Jacob. It is important, in this regard, to observe that Ezek 35 is the only prophetic judgment oracle that uses Seir to designate Esau/Edom. Seir is also preferred in Gen 25–36, though it remains infrequent elsewhere.[67] Bert Dicou supports this connection in his broad study of Edom's role in the Hebrew Bible, concluding "that the Genesis stories are, with regard to contents and theme, the most near to Ezekiel 35–36."[68] Genesis 25–36, not coincidentally, contains the most detailed account of the relationship between Jacob and Esau, which makes it the most reliable guide for the tradition to which the non-exiles appealed, though this relationship must be asserted with caution. Be that as it may, the terminoligcal overlap between Gen 25–36 and Ezek 35 is further evidence that Ezekiel is not making a reference to the nation of Edom but is intentionally alluding to a tradition about Jacob and Esau.

The immediate objection to this line of argument is that Jacob is mentioned positively elsewhere in Ezekiel. How could the same figure be characterized so negatively here when presented so favorably elsewhere?

Chapter four of this study demonstrated that the first mention of Jacob in the book (Ezek 20:5a) is a late insertion on two bases: first, the otherwise unparalleled usage of the "lifted hand" formula and, second, the contradictory nature of a positive mention of the patriarch in the midst of an extended oracle placing Israel's origin in Egypt. There remain three further mentions of Jacob in the book (28:25, 37:25 and 39:25) that now need examination. Analysis demonstrates that they are also later insertions.

---

66 Amos 9:12, one of the passages Assis cites in support of his argument, can also be read this way.

67 Dicou, *Edom*, 160; Mt Seir is, however, a notable geographic marker in Deut 1–2.

68 Ibid., 199

The phrase "my servant Jacob" appears in 28:25 and 37:35:[69]

וְיָשְׁבוּ עַל־אַדְמָתָם אֲשֶׁר נָתַתִּי לְעַבְדִּי לְיַעֲקֹב   28:25
וְיָשְׁבוּ עַל־הָאָרֶץ אֲשֶׁר נָתַתִּי לְעַבְדִּי לְיַעֲקֹב   37:25

Commentators have noted that Ezek 28:25-26 sits uneasily in its place, interrupts the flow of the foreign nation oracles, and is likely "a systematizing summary of Ezekiel's theology (cf. 39:21-29), possibly secondary."[70] Turning to Ezek 37:25, Jacob is not the only famed Israelite identified as the servant in vv. 24-28: there are two instances of "my servant David" (vv. 24, 25) that frame the phrase "my servant Jacob." Verse 25 also references Israel's ancestors (אבותיהם),[71] a far more common term in Ezekiel and one that makes better sense if the reference to Jacob is omitted.[72] There is also a syntactical oddity about the phrase לְעַבְדִּי לְיַעֲקֹב, an appositional construction with the preposition repeated.[73] Even though this is possible, and one must allow for the flexibility of a language, it is awkward—especially so when compared to the two instances of "my servant David" that lack the repeated preposition.[74] Finally, it is notable that the Old Greek translates with ἄρχων, suggesting the *Vorlage* contains נשיא and not the מלך that now appears in v. 25. Old Greek also lacks the phrase "they and their children and their children's children shall live there forever," showing that v. 25 has been reworked over time. On these bases, it is justifiable to conclude that the phrase "to Jacob" is an addition or gloss. The likelihood that the verse has experienced several stages of growth means it is nearly impossible to reconstruct the process by which it arrived in its final form, but confirms the suspicion that the mention of Jacob is a late redaction.[75]

---

69   Cf. Isa 44:1-2, 21; 45:4; 48:20; Jer 30:10; 46:27-28.

70   Joyce, *Ezekiel*, 180; cf. Zimmerli, *Ezechiel 25–48*, 100-01. However, compare with Greenberg, *Ezekiel 21-37*, 597-99, who gives his criteria for determining authentic material in Ezekiel.

71   See the BHS apparatus; reading, as is the consensus, with the LXX and S.

72   Ezek 2:3; 5:10; 18:2; 20:4, 18, 24, 27, 30, 36, 42; 36:28; 37:25; 47:14. Note, in particular, the importance of this term in Ezek 20.

73   Cf. Ezek 34:2; Ibid., 695.

74   Note that precisely the same construction occurs in Ezek 28:25. Although it cannot be a direct comparison, it is interesting to add that this appositional structure with the repeated preposition does not appear in Deutero-Isaiah either (Isa 41:8; 44:2; 45:4; 48:20; Cf. 44:1)

75   For instance, Emanuel Tov has argued that the MT of Ezekiel should be considered a redactional stage of Ezekiel rather than a copy of the text ("Recensional Differences Between the MT and LXX of Ezekiel," *ETL* 62 [1986]: 89-101). Lust has argued, espe-

The final occurrence of Jacob is at Ezek 39:25, part of the section from vv. 21-29 that brings to an end the famous Gog passage. This unit is also regarded as late and it too contains significant evidence of one or more stages of redaction.[76] Verse 25 contains no significant issues, but v. 26 has the challenging phrase וְנָשׂוּ אֶת־כְּלִמָּתָם. The MT as well as Old Greek understand the verb as a defective spelling of the verbal root נשׂא, reading it as an instance of the phrase נשׂא כלמה used elsewhere in Ezekiel.[77] Lust observes, however, that "[m]any modern translators and commentaries do not accept the Masoretic reading, preferring instead to read the unpunctuated text as wnšw klmh: «They shall forget their shame.»"[78] This reading fits better with the overwhelmingly positive context of the passage, matches Ezekiel's usage of other rare words,[79] and, as Joyce remarks, "provides yet another argument for the secondary nature of vv. 21-29."[80] Taking stock of the four mentions of Jacob in the book, then, in each case there is significant evidence these positive statements are late additions to the text.[81]

The strong thematic similarities between the four occurrences is further evidence that the passages are connected in some way. In each case where Jacob appears there is also a statement about the security of Israel's dwelling in the land throughout the future. Ezekiel 20:5a looks backwards and seeks to link Jacob with the original promise of the land

---

cially with reference to Ezek 34-39, that P967 testifies to an earlier version of the text (Lust, "Textual Witnesses," 7-20). Because P967 does include the reference to Jacob, the addition of this phrase must have occurred rather early. However, as will be argued later in this section, it is likely that the addition was made in the late sixth or early fifth century B.C.E.

76   Lust proposes three stages, but notes the tentative nature of that reconstruction ("The Final Text and Textual Criticism: Ez 39,28," in *Ezekiel and His Book: Textual and Literary Criticism and Their Interrelation* (ed. J. Lust; BETL 74; Leuven: Peeters, 1986), 53). Klein also assigns Ezek 39:25-29 to a redactional layer later associated with the Gog pericope (*Schriftauslegung im Ezechielbuch: Redaktionsgeschichtliche Untersuchungen zu Ez 34–39* [BZAW 391; Berlin: de Gruyter, 2008], 113). See also William A. Tooman, *Gog of Magog: Reuse of Scripture and Compositional Technique in Ezekiel 38–39* (FAT/II 52; Tübingen: Mohr Siebeck, 2011), 118-23, 188-95.

77   Ezek 16:52, 54; 32:24-25, 30; 34:29; 36:6-7; 39:26; 44:13. See Crane, *Israel's Restoration*, 192-93, for arguments supporting this interpretation.

78   Lust, "Final Text," 51.

79   For instance, Lust notes the peculiar use of כנס, a contrast to *qibbeṣ*, used elsewhere in Ezekiel in similar contexts" (Ibid., 49).

80   Joyce, *Ezekiel*, 218-19; Baruch J. Schwartz, "Ezekiel's Dim View of Israel's Restoration," in *The Book of Ezekiel: Theological and Anthropological Perspectives* (eds. Margaret S. Odell and John T. Strong; Sblsyms 9; Altanta, Ga.: Society of Biblical Literature, 2000), 53.

81   Cf. Carr, "Genesis," 289, note 50.

to Israel. Ezekiel 28:26 and 39:26 both address the future and indicate
that when Israel returns it will dwell on the land with security (בטח).
Ezekiel 37:25 is even more expansive, suggesting Israel will dwell in the
land forever (עד־עולם). Though caution remains necessary, the combination of evidence for their late dating and thematic coherence suggests these four passages are part of a coordinated redaction in the
book of Ezekiel, a possibility considered in more detail later in this
chapter.[82] It is sufficient for now to note that a precedent for that sort of
redaction has been established by Römer's detailed study of the patriarchs in Deuteronomy.[83] Given the relationship between Ezekiel and
DTR in other matters, the prospect that they underwent a similar redactional process is plausible.

Lest the larger argument be obscured, confirming that the positive
statements about Jacob are additions to Ezekiel is a first step in considering how Ezek 35:1–36:15 polemicizes the non-exiles' appeal to the Jacob tradition, a possibility suggested by Lust's observation that "the
quotations of Edom in Ezekiel 35:1–36:15 are almost identical with
those of the inhabitants of Jerusalem in 11:15 and 33:23."[84] To fully appreciate Ezekiel's response to the Jacob tradition, a systematic exegesis
of 35:1–36:15 that takes account of all the layers of meaning in the "as I
live" and "lifted hand" formulae is necessary.

(i) 35:5-9

Chapter 35 contains three sections: vv. 1-4, 5-9, and 10-15.[85] Verses 1-4,
a preamble to the rest of the chapter, contain two exodus images. First,
the familiar phrase "I stretch out my hand against you," found 13 times
in the plague narratives of Exodus, recalls YHWH's power used so that
"[t]he Egyptians shall know that I am YHWH" (Exod 7:5).[86] Second,
YHWH's declaration that Edom will be made a desolation (שממה) and its

---

82 See §3 below on the formation of the Pentateuch.
83 Römer,"Deuteronomy ", 112-38; cf. Römer, Israels Väter.
84 Lust, , 389.
85 Cf. Block, Ezekiel 25–48, 311-22.
86 Exod 7:5, 19; 8:1-2, 13; 9:22; 10:12, 21-22; 14:16, 21, 26-27; cf. Ezek 6:14; 14:9, 13; 16:27;
    25:7, 13, 16; 35:3. Of the 13 instances in Exodus, only 7:5 refers to YHWH's action; in
    the others, either Moses or Aaron is the subject of this action. Ezekiel, on the con-
    trary, ascribes this action to YHWH in every instance. Thus, whereas Exodus works to
    make Moses and Aaron the means of YHWH's actions, Ezekiel's radically theocentric
    view sees YHWH as the only active agent. Cf. Levitt Kohn, A New Heart and a New
    Soul, 33.

cities a waste (חרבה) recalls the curses of Lev 26:33.[87] These two phrases also recall the oracle against Edom in Ezek 25:12-14, perhaps an intentional effort to make the two texts sound similar. The contrast between vv. 1-4 and vv. 5-15—the latter introduces additional reasons for
judgment and new punishments not found in 25:12-14—indicates that
something more is in view in Ezek 35 despite the obvious similarities.

Verses 5-9 begin with a new charge against Mt Seir: it has cherished
an ancient enmity[88] and delivered Israel to the sword. The charge is
immediately followed by the "as I live" oath formula, used to introduce
YHWH's declaration of judgment. What is unusual in this case, if one
takes the nation of Edom as the target, is that the "as I live" formula
precedes judgment against a group of non-Israelites.[89] Indeed, of its 16
instances in Ezekiel, it is only here and later in the same passage (v. 11)
that the formula might not address Israel.[90] An argument for this shift
could be based on the move from pre-fall to post-fall material in chapters 33–38, but then one would have to explain why Ezek 34:8 immediately reverts to the norm, using the "as I live" formula to announce
judgment upon the shepherds of Israel. It is preferable, therefore, to interpret Mt Seir as an alias for the non-exiles and to draw this example
into line with every other occurrence in Ezekiel.

This is substantiated by two further indications the non-exiles are
in view. The guilt of the addressees, firstly, is described as permitting
bloodshed (v. 6b).[91] Elsewhere in Ezekiel sinful bloodshed is an indict-

---

87   Lyons, *From Law to Prophecy*, 183-84; Levitt Kohn, *A New Heart and a New Soul*, 38.

88   This charge appears in the oracles against the nations directed against the Philistines
      and not the Edomites. The meaning of עולם is ambiguous. It could mean ancient, as
      most translate, to fit with its context, where origin traditions are in question. It
      might indicate a relatively long period since the exodus, which seems to be the sense
      of Ezek 25:15. If that is the case, then it suggests that the tension between these Ju-
      dahite factions is longstanding.   Either interpretation works with the larger
      argument.

89   It does not appear that any of the major studies or commentaries note this issue, as
      they are rather uninterested in the meaning of the "as I live" formula as anything
      more than a tool for emphasizing the other content of the passages in which it
      appears.

90   There is evidence outside Ezekiel for this usage: Jer 46:18; Zeph 2:9.

91   The text of this verse is problematic. There is clearly a plus in the MT that interrupts
      the flow from the "as I live" formula to the oath particle אם־לא. Furthermore, there
      are issues in understanding the phrase דם שֵׂנֵאתָ. Although none of the proposals is
      a definitive answer to the problem, Driver's suggestion to emend the verb to נָשִׂא
      and understand it as a scribal error of metathesis is the best proposal to date (G. R.
      Driver, "Linguistic and Textual Problems: Ezekiel," *Bib* 19 [1938]: 175-87).

ment of Israel's behavior.[92]   The instances in chs. 9, 16, and 22 (which
describe this as one of Jerusalem's sins) are noteworthy, but of utmost
relevance is 33:25, where bloodshed typifies the sins of the non-exiles
who are appealing to Abraham. The outcome of YHWH's judgment, secondly, is to fill "Edom's" hills, valleys, and rivers with its slain. That
image recalls YHWH's punishment of Jerusalem in 11:6. This suggests
that another function of the "as I live" formula here is to allude to Deut
32:39-43: the authenticating element, the slain (חלל), and the sword
(חרב) each appear in Deut 32:39-43.   By invoking these images of
YHWH's consuming action in the Song of Moses (Deut 32:42-43), the author evoked its description of YHWH judging those within Israel who
"hate me" (לִמְשַׂנְאַי; v. 41),[93] yet another way of portraying the non-exiles as unworthy to live in the land.

(ii) 35:10-15

The strongest evidence yet for connecting "Edom" with the non-exiled
Judahites comes from the disputation speech in vv. 10-15. This dispute
opens with a quote that immediately evokes Ezek 11:14-21 and
33:23-29:[94] "The two nations and the two countries will be mine, and we
will take possession (ירש) of them"[95] (Ezek 35:10a; cf. 36:12). It is generally assumed that this represents a gluttonous desire by Edom to possess the land previously controlled by the now defunct northern and
southern kingdoms,[96] although some take it as a reference to Edom and
Judah.[97] Because of this view, interpreters read v. 10b (וַיהוה שם היה) as
an adversative clause, "but YHWH was there." The first difficulty with
this reading is justifying the transition from the interlocutors to a different third person subject prior to the logical transition (לכן) at the beginning of v. 11. John Olley observes the exceptional nature of such a
statement, saying it comes "unexpectedly" and that "elsewhere Lord is

---

92   Ezek 9:9; 16:38; 18:10; 22; 23:37, 45; 24:6; 33:25.

93   MacDonald, *Deuteronomy*, 176-80.

94   As noted earlier, Lust,"Edom—Adam ", 389-90, draws on this similarity in his argu-
     ment for Edom as the non-exiles.

95   Following BHS's suggestion to read a plural suffix based on the likely *Vorlage* of
     LXX, Tg, S and Vg; see Zimmerli, *Ezechiel 25–48*, 226.

96   Ibid., 235; Greenberg, *Ezekiel 21-37*, 715; Block, *Ezekiel 25–48*, 318-19; Joyce, *Ezekiel*,
     200.

97   John W. Olley, *Ezekiel: A Commentary based on Iezekiēl in Codex Vaticanus* (Septuagint
     Commentary Series; Leiden: Brill, 2009), 477; cf. John R. Bartlett, *Edom and the
     Edomites* (JSOTSup 77; Sheffield: Sheffield Academic Press, 1989), 153.

speaking in the 1st person."[98] Lust also detects the problem and comments that "[i]t is more likely that the explicit use of the past tense of the verb היה emphasizes the fact that the Lord had left Jerusalem... It may also include an allusion to the quotation in 11:15 in which the inhabitants of Jerusalem (called Edomites in chaps. 35–36) said of the Israelites, 'they have gone far from the Lord.'"[99] Lust is certainly right to draw the connection with 11:15, but he fails to carry this insight on to a more significant conclusion.

Lust later notes that "[t]he Greek translation of 35:10, 'the Lord *is* there,' incongruously anticipates the final sentence of the book."[100] But this is only incongruous if the speaker has changed. If v. 10b is read as a continuation of the interlocutors' speech, meaning it represents the non-exiles view, one can then follow the Old Greek translation by understanding this claim as an emphatic restatement of precisely the position the non-exiles' took in 11:14-21: Yhwh was with them and not the exiles. Indeed, this eliminates the peculiarity of third person divine speech identified by Olley and strengthens Lust's position.

"Edom's" desire to possess (ירש) the land indicates agreement between the Jacob and Abraham traditions. Recall that ירש was the key term in the non-exiles' claims quoted at 11:15 and, specifically in connection with the Abraham tradition, at 33:24. Regarding the latter, the importance of the term ירש for Gen 15, as demonstrated by Rendtorff, was also relevant.[101] This important term occurs in the Jacob tradition once, at Gen 28:4:

> Then Isaac called Jacob and blessed him, and commanded him, "You shall not marry one of the Canaanite women. Arise and go to Paddan-aram to the house of Bethuel, the father of your mother; take a wife from there, from the daughters of Laban, the brother of your mother. May El Shaddai bless you and make you fruitful and numerous so that you become a company of peoples. May he give to you the blessing of Abraham, to you and to your seed with you, so that you possess (לרשתך) the land of your sojourn, which God gave to Abraham."
>
> Gen 28:1-4

98　Olley, *Ezekiel*, 477.

99　Lust,"Edom—Adam," 392-93.

100　Ibid., 393, note 17. Emphasis original.

101　Rendtorff, , 74-81.

Although Gen 28:1-4 is typically linked with P's account of the Abrahamic covenant in Gen 17,[102] there is an obvious connection with Gen 15's statement of the promise that Abraham will possess the land.[103] Ezekiel's attribution of this important term to parties claiming descent from Jacob (Ezek 35:10-15), not only Abraham (Ezek 11:14-21; 33:23-29), is otherwise unprecedented. Still, this shared premise indicates that the Abraham and Jacob traditions were viewed as compatible, if not already integrated together,[104] in the first half of the sixth-century B.C.E., a possibility explored further momentarily.

Finally, Ezek 35 brings this judgment speech to a close by specifying its addressees as "Mt Seir and all Edom, all of it." Lust remarks that this phrase "is to be contrasted with 'all Israel, all of it' in 36:10. The same phrase... also occurs in 11:15, where it clearly identifies 'real

---

102 Rolf Rendtorff, *The Problem of the Process of Transmission in the Pentateuch* (JSOTSup 89; Translated by Scullion, John J. Sheffield: Sheffield Academic Press, 1990), 163-64; Carr, *Reading the Fractures*, 87.

103 Römer,"Recherches," 210.

104 There is broad support for a pre-exilic Jacob tradition, albeit in various forms. Van Seters, *Prologue*, 277-80, has called this a "pre-Yahwistic" portion of the Jacob tradition. Scholars who support an early JE source as part of the Documentary Hypothesis, for instance Nicholson, *The Pentateuch*, 239-40 and J. A. Emerton, "The Origin of the Promises to the Patriarchs in the Older Sources of the Book of Genesis," *VT* 32 (1982): 14-32, also fall in this group. Among the notable non-documentary theories of pentateuchal formation, both Blum and Carr propose a Jacob narrative that began in the northern territory and was redacted in Judah (Blum, *Die Komposition*; Carr, *Reading the Fractures*, 297-305).

By contrast, the timeframe in which the Jacob tradition was connected to the Abraham tradition remains highly debated. Scholars advocating the Documentary Hypothesis with an early JE source, of course, propose the earliest combination of this material, some retaining the pre or early monarchic context of approximately the tenth century (Nicholson, *The Pentateuch*, 239-40, 247-8). Van Seters, *Prologue*, 331-32; Blum, *Die Komposition*, 271-361 (but see his revised position in Erhard Blum, *Studien zur Komposition des Pentateuch* [BZAW 189; Berlin: de Gruyter, 1990], 214, note 35); Carr (see a brief summary of his position in Carr, *Reading the Fractures*, 305-11); and Reinhard G. Kratz, *The Composition of the Narrative Books of the Old Testament* (Translated by John Bowden. London: T & T Clark International, 2000), 272-73, approach the issue from very different angles, but converge on a date for this combination in the exilic period (cf. Albertz, *Israel in Exile*, 251-64; Ska, *Introduction*, 204-08).

Several notable scholars place the combination at the end of the exilic period or later. De Pury has defended this position in detail, arguing confidently that the combination occurred between 535-530 B.C.E. ("The Jacob Story and the Beginning of the Formation of the Pentateuch," in *A Farewell to the Yahwist: The Composition of the Pentateuch in Recent European Interpretation* (eds. Thomas B. Dozeman and Konrad Schmid; SBLSym 34; Atlanta, Ga.: Society of Bilbical Literature, 2006); cf. Albert de Pury, "Abraham: The Priestly Writer's 'Ecumenical' Ancestor," in *Rethinking Foundations: Historiography in the Ancient World and in the Bible: Essays in Honour of John Van Seters*

Israel' with the Jews living in exile or in the diaspora, excluding the real inhabitants of Jerusalem."[105] Indeed, it is yet another connection that substantiates interpreting "Edom" as an alias for the non-exiles, a sort of parting shot in this chapter to make certain the message does not go unnoticed.

It is worth mentioning, finally, that Ezek 35:1-15 shares with Ezek 11:14-21, 20:32-44, and 33:23-29 the view that the defilement of the non-exiles has polluted the land. For instance, Ezek 35 has echoes of Lev 26, especially in vv. 10-15, where Lyons has identified that the outcome of YHWH's actions, described in vv. 12, 14, and 15, is based on the program of Lev 26.[106] Like Ezek 33:28, where YHWH's judgment is directed against the land, in Ezek 35:15 Mt Seir receives punishment. Another similarity is that Ezek 35 and 33:23-29 both personify the land, additional evidence that these passages all have the non-exiles in view, even if some identify them more clearly and more readily than others.

In sum, the evidence supports reading "Mt Seir" and "Edom" in Ezek 35 as derogatory aliases for the non-exiles in Judah. The conspicuous parallels between the logic refuted in Ezek 35 and the non-exiles' appeals to the Abraham tradition elsewhere, especially in Ezek 33:23-29 and 11:14-21, indicates that the non-exiles based their claims on a land promise occurring in a combined Abraham-Jacob tradition.

Ezekiel 35 structures all this material around the DTR divine oath of judgment ("as I live"), so that one could outline Ezek 35 thus:

vv. 1-4   Original oracle against Edom
vv. 5-9   Judgment introduced with "as I live" divine oath
vv. 10-15   Dispute introduced with "as I live" divine oath

(eds. S. L. McKenzie and Thomas Römer; BZAW 294; Berlin: de Gruyter, 2000), 180; Albert de Pury, "Situer le cycle de Jacob quelques réflexions, vingt-cinq ans plus tard," in *Studies in the Book of Genesis: Literature, Redaction and History* (ed. A. Wénin; BETL 155; Leuven: Leuven University Press, 2001); and Albert de Pury, "La tradition patriarcale en Gènese 12-35," in *Le Pentateuque en question: les origines et la composition des cinq premiers livres de la Bible à la lumière des recherches récentes* (eds. Albert de Pury and Thomas Römer; Le Monde De La Bible 19; Geneva: Labor et Fides, 2002). Römer, "Recherches," 189-93 (especially p. 192), follows de Pury on most issues, but puts the combination into the post-exilic period. In his extended study on the question, Schmid, *Erzväter und Exodus*, 273, also places the combination in the post-exilic period.

105 Lust, "Edom—Adam," 393; cf. Ezek 20:40.

106 Lyons, *From Law to Prophecy*, 183-84; cf. Levitt Kohn, *A New Heart and a New Soul*, 38; Greenberg, *Ezekiel 21-37*, 724-25.

The "as I live" divine oath, the leading statement in both judgment
speeches, contributes to the larger argument of Ezek 35 in two ways:
first, recognizing that Ezekiel consistently uses this form of the divine
oath against Yhwh's people, not foreigners, signals that Mt Seir and
Edom are more than mere national designations; second, this formula
foregrounds the exodus tradition as the paradigmatic story of Yhwh
displaying power by redeeming a community of people living outside
the land and under foreign oppression.

(iii) 36:1-15

In the second panel of the larger oracle, Ezek 36:1-15, the immediate issue is establishing the text, which is in such a confused state that Block
opined it "looks like a patchwork quilt, except that quilts usually reflect
more deliberate design."[107] The chapter opens with promising clarity,
no scholar doubting that vv. 1-2 can be retained.   However, things
change abruptly with v. 3 and continue on in a disheveled state until
the end of v. 7: each of these five verses opens with the logical continuation particle לָכֵן, contains other prophetic formulae, and offers either
the opening of an assurance to Israel (v. 3, 4, 6) or of a judgment against
Edom (v. 5, 7).   Various reconstructions have been offered, with the
most widely accepted recognizing vv. 3-5 as a series of excerpts from
other oracles and the proper continuation of vv. 1-2 coming in vv. 6-7.
The road is somewhat easier to navigate from there, with only v. 10 remaining questionable and v. 12 appearing as a later transition between
vv. 8-11* and vv. 13-15.[108]

In view of the present argument, it is necessary to reevaluate this
judgment and the place of v. 5 in particular. By its inclusion of "the
rest of the nations" (שְׁאֵרִית הַגּוֹיִם) alongside "Edom, all of it," v. 5 recognizes what must have been the historical reality: even though the non-
exiles were making confident claims to the land, the actual extent of
their control must have been rather small and there is no doubt that
foreigners, including the actual Edomites, encroached on Judah's former territory. Moreover, the reappearance of the term מוֹרָשָׁה connects
v. 5 both to v. 2, which is certainly part of the original oracle, as well as
to the theme of ch. 35. To exclude it in spite of these features seems un-

---

107 Block, *Ezekiel 25–48*, 322.

108 Zimmerli, *Ezekiel 25–48*, 232-33; cf. Block, *Ezekiel 25–48*, 322-23, who argues for retaining more of the pericope as original.

wise. The end of verse 5 does appear to contain later material,[109] but there is good reason for retaining the majority of it. The proposed reconstruction of 36:1-7* is thus:

(1) וְאַתָּה בֶן־אָדָם הִנָּבֵא אֶל־הָרֵי יִשְׂרָאֵל וְאָמַרְתָּ הָרֵי יִשְׂרָאֵל

שִׁמְעוּ דְּבַר־יְהוָה (2) כֹּה אָמַר אֲדֹנָי יְהוָה

יַעַן אָמַר הָאוֹיֵב עֲלֵיכֶם הֶאָח וּבָמוֹת עוֹלָם לְמוֹרָשָׁה הָיְתָה לָּנוּ

(5) לָכֵן כֹּה־אָמַר אֲדֹנָי יְהוָה

אִם־לֹא בְּאֵשׁ קִנְאָתִי דִבַּרְתִּי עַל־שְׁאֵרִית הַגּוֹיִם וְעַל־אֱדוֹם כֻּלָּה[110]

אֲשֶׁר נָתְנוּ־אֶת־אַרְצִי לָהֶם לְמוֹרָשָׁה בְּשִׂמְחַת[111]

(6) יַעַן כְּלִמַּת גּוֹיִם נְשָׂאתֶם[112]

(7) לָכֵן אֲנִי נָשָׂאתִי אֶת־יָדִי אֶל[113] הַגּוֹיִם אֲשֶׁר לָכֶם מִסָּבִיב הֵמָּה

כְּלִמָּתָם יִשָּׂאוּ

But, you, son of man, prophesy to the mountains of Israel and you will say to the mountains of Israel: "Hear the word of YHWH: 'Thus says Lord YHWH: because the enemy said to you 'Ah' and 'the ancient heights are a possession for us.' Therefore, thus says Lord YHWH, surely with burning jealousy I have spoken against the remnant of the nations and against Edom, all of it, which took my land for themselves as a possession with joy. Because you bore the insults of the nations, therefore I myself will lift my hand against the nations that are round about you and they themselves will bear their insults.'"

---

109 כל־לֵבָב בִּשְׁאָט נֶפֶשׁ לְמַעַן מִגְרָשָׁהּ לָבַז is likely redactional.

110 Reading with BHS, including evidence from Qumran.

111 Discontinue the text of v. 5 here for three reasons: (1) the phrase כל־לֵבָב is not included in LXX and is likely to be a late MT plus (Crane, *Israel's Restoration*, 44); (2) בִּשְׁאָט נֶפֶשׁ, not only a very difficult phrase, seems in context to be an explanation for 'with wholehearted delight,' the last portion of which was just excluded on textual evidence; (3) the phrase לְמַעַן מִגְרָשָׁהּ לָבַז has no antecedent for the suffix on מִגְרָשָׁהּ and it appears to either be dittography (Elliger's suggestion in BHS) or to be a later gloss (Allen, *Ezekiel 20–48*, 168). Critically, this retains אִם־לֹא in 5a which can then serve to explain, via dittography, for the difference between MT and LXX in v. 7.

112 The majority of v. 6 is excluded because its addressee is the land (אֲדָמָה) of Israel and not the mountains, demonstrating its discontinuity. However, the final four words are included for several reasons: (1) the concluding phrase כֹּה־אָמַר אֲדֹנָי יְהוָה indicates the end of the phrase; (2) the concluding formula is followed by an obvious editorial *Wiederaufnahme*, recalling YHWH's jealousy mentioned in v. 5; (3) the final phrase is necessary for v. 7 to make sense.

113 Reading with the LXX ἐπὶ and regarding the MT as an error from dittography with v. 5.

This proposed text corresponds well with ch. 35, and thus it is unsurprising that it contains no new indicators of the Jacob tradition, albeit repeating the key term מורשה.

The new contribution of this section is to use the "lifted hand" punishment formula to specify that it is YHWH who will judge the presumptuous inhabitants of Judah. Verse 6 indicates that because the land of Israel has borne the insults (כלמה) of the nations YHWH will force those nations to endure the same fate. If any doubt remains that נשׂא יד is not an oath formula, the Old Greek translation indicates that the oath particle אם־לא in MT is a scribal error for the preposition אל, which is reflected in the above translation.[114] The phrase is actually the formula in its second convention—unique to Ezekiel—that specifies who will inflict the punishment implied in the phrase נשׂא כלמה. Consequently, it recalls YHWH's statement in 11:21 that "I will bring their deeds upon their own heads, says the Lord YHWH," emphasizing that this speech is about the conflict between the exiles and the non-exiles.

Ezekiel 36:8-15, like Ezek 35 before it, speaks about the land and its defilement with language and concepts also found in Ezek 11:14-21, 20:32-44, 33:23-29, and in their theological counterpart Lev 26. In the first place, Lyons details the connections with Lev 26:9: "I will look with favor upon you and make you fruitful and multiply you; and I will maintain my covenant with you." The emphasis on fructification and multiplication appears in vv. 9, 10, and 11 and describes an increase in both population and agricultural production. This theme is enhanced by the rare phrase הנני אליכם, also shared by Ezek 36:9 and Lev 26:9.[115] It was noted earlier that Lev 26:33 serves as background to Ezek 35; the same is true of 36:10, although here the image of wasted cities is used to describe the depths of destruction from which Israel will rise. Finally, though they lack a direct linguistic parallel, vv. 13-15 recall the description of the land in H. In both Lev 18:24-30 and 20:22-26[116] the Israelites are warned not to defile themselves as the previous inhabitants did, lest the land vomit them out (קיא). The description of the land's action in Ezekiel as devouring (אכל) and bereaving

---

114 Crane, *Israel's Restoration*, 45-46, remarks: "LXX does not reflect MT's oath formula of אם־לא ('surely')... Zimmerli (1983, p. 230) suggests that LXX's use of ἐπὶ ('against') for MT's אם־לא presupposes אל... LXX may not have understood the declarative and oath formulae used together here in MT. However, if LXX misunderstood the oath here, then why was it understood elsewhere?"

115 Zimmerli, *Ezekiel 25–48*, 238; Lyons, *From Law to Prophecy*, 180.

116 Lev 20:24a twice includes the verbal root ירשׁ, which is extraordinary in H. It is likely, however, that v. 24a is a later DTR interpolation; see the discussion in Milgrom, *Leviticus 17–22*, 1759-64, especially p. 1760.

(שכל)[117] people is somewhat different than H's, albeit not so far from it to obscure the similar conception of the land as an active agent.[118]

Finally, Ezek 36:8-15 also personifies the land. Nihan recognizes this conviction as part of H's distinct theological profile and concludes:

> In Lev 17–26 the general concern for the land's purity is further highlighted by the *personification* of the land, especially in the parenetic framework of Lev 18–20. Whereas the HB knows of a tradition of the land "devouring" its inhabitants (Num 13:32 and Ez 36:13-14), which is also taken up in Lev 17–26 (see 26:38), H goes further and introduces the conception of a land reacting to pollution caused by its inhabitants by "vomiting" them outside its boundaries (Lev 18:24-30; 20:22). The effect of such a conception is to suggest an almost *organic* relationship between the land and its inhabitants... The same conception is expressed in the final exhortation of ch. 26. The land's inability to enjoy its Sabbatical rest (26:34-35) because of the people's crimes will eventually lead to their expulsion and their dispersion among the nations."[119]

It is possible that the fundamental theological agreement between Ezekiel and H is clearest in this final section. On a literary level, these final verses round off the larger oracle in a way that reminds the audience of the critique against the non-exiles elsewhere.

The section culminates in vv. 13-15 with a brief message directed to the exiles. This material refers back to the context of the "as I live" divine oath, albeit lacking the actual formula. Greenberg has suggested a connection between 36:1-15 and Num 13–14 based on two linguistic connections in 36:3-4. Even though those verses are likely redactional,[120] his insight is not entirely nullified because he also notices the ties between the accusation leveled against the land in 36:13 and Num 13:32.[121] In light of the current argument, it is hardly surprising to find such an allusion between Ezek 35:1–36:15 and Num 13–14. But there is a finer point to be put on this too: as his final foray, the author of Ezek 36:13-15 offers hope to those in exile that they might return to the land. This hope, however, is dependent on their choice to remain faithful to

---

117 See Crane for a discussion on the textual issues and possible wordplay employed here (Crane, *Israel's Restoration*, 56-62).

118 Block, *Ezekiel 25–48*, 335, note 59; contra Nihan, *Priestly Torah*, 559-60, who sees the two ideas as distinctly different.

119 Ibid.

120 Greenberg, *Ezekiel 21-37*, 717-8, 725. It might be suggested that vv. 3-4 were added to 36:1-15 because of the connection between v. 15 and Num 13:32.

121 Ibid., 721-22; cf. Zimmerli, *Ezekiel 25–48*, 238-39; Block, *Ezekiel 25–48*, 335; Klein, *Schriftauslegung im Ezechielbuch*, 336-37.

Y<small>HWH</small> during their time outside the land and under foreign oppression. This theme, developed further in Ezek 14:12-23, 18:1-32, and 33:10-20, urges the Judahite exiles to identify themselves with the second generation of the exodus, not their parents, the first exodus generation who tested Y<small>HWH</small>, doubted the promise of military victory over the inhabitants of the land, and, therefore, met their demise in the wilderness. Those who accept this call to remain faithful to Y<small>HWH</small> will embark on a second exodus (Ezek 36:12; cf. Ezek 20:32-44) that will take them to the very land that Ezek 35:1–36:15 claims for them.[122]

(iv) The "Representational Significance" of Mt Seir and Edom

In view of this interpretation of Ezek 35:1–36:15, it is necessary to address perhaps the most likely objection: why should such a sophisticated explanation be necessary when good sense can be made of the passage based upon a straightforward reading of the terms Mt Seir and Edom? Indeed, there is evidence for the pairing of Edom's judgment and Israel's restoration elsewhere in the Hebrew Bible, namely in Isa 34–35. Those chapters, the so-called "little apocalypse," not only have in common the basic structure of judgment upon Edom and salvation for Israel, but they share the specific vision of Y<small>HWH</small>'s people returning to a re-fructified (Isa 35:6-7; Ezek 36:8-11), secure, and hospitable (Isa 35:9; Ezek 36:13-15) land. This appears to suggest a larger pattern, of which Ezek 35–36 is one example, where Edom's judgment introduces Israel's restoration.

Claire Mathews studied the composition and placement of Isa 34–35 in detail, focusing on the formation of the book of Isaiah. Along the way, she explored the similarities between Ezek 35–36 and Isa 34–35, a correspondence she sees stretching to the larger sections of Ezek 35–39 and Isa 34–39. Mathews concludes that "[t]he similarities between Isa 34–35 and Ezek 35–36 in content, structure, and placement are striking, and suggest the possibility of a literary relationship between the two."[123]

---

122 For a full treatment of these issues, see C. A. Strine, "The Role of Repentance in the Book of Ezekiel: A Second Chance for the Second Generation," *JTS* 63 (2012): 467-91.

123 Mathews, *Defending Zion*, 170.

Mathews still faces difficulties in explaining the relationship of Isa 34–35 to the story of Hezekiah's illness and recovery (Isa 36–39) and to Isa 56–66.[124] Her solution to these challenges lies in the "representational significance"[125] of Edom, a term with "bi-valent"[126] potential to point "beyond herself."[127] She remarks:

> Edom is a near neighbor of Judah whose ultimate fate serves as a contrast to hers. Yet as the descendants of Esau, *Edom may also designate those who claim Abraham as father, but who are not fit to be counted among that community that stands in proper relationship to* YHWH and can offer appropriate worship... The mention of Edom in Isa 34 thereby anticipates a theme of central import in the final stage of the book: the final, eschatological division between YHWH's servants, and His so-called enemies.[128]

Mathews conclusion about Isa 34–35, when combined with the other similarities between it and Ezek 35:1–36:15, reinforces the evidence that Mt Seir and Edom are more than plain geographic or political referents. Indeed, it is fitting that two passages that share other features would also both employ the "representational significance" of these terms. In both texts, Mt Seir and Edom are polemical aliases for a group of people who claim to be YHWH's servants but, for one reason or another, fail to conform to the definition of a faithful Yahwist as defined by the dominant group.

But, does this proposal presume a greater sophistication than the audience possessed? Two points suggest it does not. First, the Babylonian exiles were largely composed of Judah's elite class. The relatively high level of education in this group accounts for their ability to recognize the polysemy of terms and explains, at least in part, the inclusion of numerous references to non-Judahite cultures and ideas elsewhere in Ezekiel. Second, though the "representational significance" of Mt Seir and Edom in Ezek 35:1–36:15 would be difficult to identify in isolation, the structure of Ezek 33:21–39:29 alerts the audience to the possibility of such an allusion. Coming under a single date header (at 33:21), the individual units in 33:21–39:29 function as a

---

124 Cf. H.G.M. Williamson, *The Book Called Isaiah: Deutero-Isaiah's Role in Composition and Redaction* (Oxford: Clarendon Press, 1994), 211-21.

125 Mathews, *Defending Zion*, 159-61.

126 Ibid., 175.

127 Ibid., 160.

128 Ibid., 176; emphasis added. This position was previously advanced by Jacques Vermeylen, *Du prophète Isaïe à l'apocalyptique: Isaïe I-XXXV, miroir d'un demi-millénaire d'expereince religieuse en Israël* (EBib 2; Paris: Gabalda, 1977), 441-2, 489-91.

group in order to make a sustained argument, all the while retaining their individual importance and intelligibility. Sweeney demonstrated that this section is "disputational in character,"[129] a tone set by Ezek 33:23-29. That passage, which details the book of Ezekiel's opposition to the non-exiles' Abraham-based land claims, notifies the audience that the conflict with those remaining in Judah is one of its principal concerns. This notice has certainly not slipped from the audience's memory by ch. 35. There are, therefore, several indications that the "representational significance" of Mt Seir and Edom would be recognized by the audience.

In the final assessment, understanding Mt Seir and Edom as straightforward references to that land and its people remains possible. The prevalence of this view in the history of interpretation shows that, and it corresponds to the real animosity the Judahites, in Judah and Babylon, felt towards Edom. This situation does not invalidate the present argument but points to the multivalence of the text, probably an intentional feature. Indeed, it is precisely this multivalence that indicates the skill of the author: the possibility of understanding Mt Seir and Edom plainly draws the audience in and makes the subsequent identification of those groups as the non-exiles even more biting.

(d) Jerusalem's Genealogy: Ezek 16:43-58

The case of hidden identity in Ezek 35:1–36:15 invites the question, "Does the book of Ezekiel deal with Jacob in a similar way elsewhere?" To answer this question, it is necessary to look more closely at what Ezekiel knows of the Jacob tradition. The preceding analysis showed that Gen 28:4 is the key text from the Jacob tradition with respect to the non-exiles' claims to possess (ירשׁ) the land. Part of a larger section (27:46–28:9), Gen 28:4 is typically assigned to P. David Carr remarks:

> Gen 26:34-35; 27:46–28:9 presents Esau as cheating himself out of the bless-ing by marrying foreign women who upset his parents (26:34-35), and Isaac freely turning to Jacob to give him the blessing and send him forth to find a better wife (28:1-5). In the P narrative, Jacob immediately obeys (Gen 28:7), while Esau in resentment goes to Ishmael and marries Ishmael's daughter, another foreign woman (Gen 28:6, 8-9).[130]

---

129 Sweeney, "The Assertion of Divine Power," 158.

130 Carr, *Reading the Fractures*, 87; cf. Gerhard von Rad, *Genesis: A Commentary* (OTL; Translated by Marks, John H. London: SCM Press Ltd, 1961), 281-82; de Pury, "Abra-ham," 173-74.

Irrespective of the many potential questions about the redaction of this passage, it is important at present to note that the primary concern of this text is the foreign descent of Esau's wives.

Commentators have long struggled to understand why Ezek 16:3 traces Jerusalem's origins to the wrong place and the wrong parents.[131] The classification of the city as Canaanite, with an Amorite father and Hittite mother, is in tension with other biblical statements.[132] Joyce is certainly right when he observes "the intent here is to insult. Moreover, in so far as the city represents the nation, this ignores the Patriarchal tradition of origins, though this is clearly known (cf. 33:24)."[133]

Ezekiel 16 does more than ignore the patriarchal tradition: it seeks to subvert it. Esau's lineage, as given in Genesis, is Israelite through his father Isaac. His matrilineal descent links him to Bethuel the Aramean of Paddan-aram (Gen 25:19-26). Equally, in the P account Esau is ostracized by his parents because "[w]hen Esau was forty years old, he married Judith daughter of Beeri the Hittite, and Basemath daughter of Elon the Hittite; and they made life bitter for Isaac and Rebekah" (Gen 26:34-35). Therefore, the descendants of Esau are, in one manner of speaking, Arameans and Hittites. It is worth noting in this regard that the credo of Deut 26:5-11 opens, "A wandering Aramean (אֲרַמִּי) was my ancestor" (Deut 26:5), a reference to Jacob.[134] If it is possible to identify Jacob in this way, then a similar designation for Esau is plausible.

These genealogical details help to explain the identity of Ezekiel's opponent in Ezek 16:43-58: allowing for a minor scribal error, abominable Jerusalem has precisely the same lineage as Esau (v. 45). The scribal error is a metathesis of ר and מ, namely supposing the consonants הָאֲרַמִּי (Gen 25:20; cf. Ezek 16:57[135]) were accidentally transposed into הָאֱמֹרִי (Ezek 16:3, 45) by an early scribe.[136] This argument is conjec-

---

Block, *Ezekiel 1–24*, 474-75.

132 Elsewhere it is identified as a Jebusite: Josh 18:28; Judg 19:10-11; 2 Sam 24:18-25; 1 Chr 11:4-5.

133 Joyce, *Ezekiel*, 130; cf. Block, *Ezekiel 1–24*, 474-75.

134 De Pury argues that Deut 26:5-9 is a Dᴛʀ polemic against the nascent Jacob tradition necessitated by its focus on Moses (de Pury,"Jacob Story," 51-72).

135 There is some question whether the proper reading here is Aram (בְּנוֹת־אֲרָם) or, following the Syriac tradition, Edom (בְּנוֹת־אֱדֹם). See Greenberg, *Ezekiel 1-20*, 290. The difference could be either scribal error or a simple misreading by the translators.

136 This must have happened before the OG translation of Ezekiel, since no manuscript reflects such a textual variant. One must, in addition, presume that this influenced the similar identification in 16:45. This could have occurred in one of two ways: either the scribe made the same error here, in a case of extended dittography, or Ezek 16:43-58 was composed after the scribal error.

tural and, it must be admitted, there is no textual evidence for it in the ancient versions of Ezekiel. However, there is no doubt that this passage is using city names in a symbolic, probably subversive, fashion. What other explanation is there for the comparison of Jerusalem to Samaria and Sodom, each city being a metonymy for sinful behavior. Indeed, the whole point of Ezek 16:43-58 is to portray the sins of Jerusalem as worse than Samaria and Sodom and to announce the sworn divine intent to make it bear its wickedness and abominations (v. 58). This description echoes the punishment that is first announced in Ezek 5:5-17.

On the whole, the suggestion to emend האמרי to הארמי in vv. 3 and 45 adopts the strength of the prevailing insight—that this identification of Jerusalem in Ezek 16 is "sharply polemical"[137]—without having to apologize for the authors apparent error with a statement like "Ezekiel is not giving a lecture in ethnography."[138] No, Ezekiel is not an ethnographic textbook. It is an exceptionally sophisticated text that uses precise and often cleverly indirect language to make resounding arguments against dissenting views.[139]

If this is not sufficient evidence for an anti-Jacob polemic in Ezekiel, there is a further indication in the way the "as I live" formula is utilized by Isa 49:14-26, a passage which shares with Ezek 16 the metaphor of Jerusalem as YHWH's wife.[140] This passage, in which Zion opines that YHWH has forsaken her, is categorized by Graffy as a disputation speech. Nonetheless, as noted above in chapter three, it is an extraordinary example of that genre. Graffy summarizes:

---

137 Block, *Ezekiel 1–24*, 475.

138 Ibid.

139 That such a polemic is possible gains further support from the similarities between Deut 32:1-43 and Ezek 16. First, the two passages have very similar structure (Gile, "Ezekiel 16 and the Song of Moses: A Prophetic Transformation?" 87-108). Second, both Deut 32 and Ezek 16 contain an indication that YHWH will punish his rebellious people. Indeed, the polemic against Sodom and Gomorrah (Deut 32:28-33) might be the source for the introduction of Sodom as Jerusalem's wicked, smaller sister in Ezek 16:46.

140 Kathryn Pfisterer Darr, "Ezekiel's Justifications of God: Teaching Troubling Texts," *JSOT* 55 (1992): 105. Ezek 16:53-63 is likely a *Fortschreibung* to Ezek 16, possibly in two stages: vv. 53-58, 59-63. The first stage (vv. 53-58) may address the reality that the exiles were likely to return to a land still inhabited by descendants of the non-exiles who had not yet experienced the full measure of their punishment. If the present argument is correct, then the second stage (vv. 59-63) could be under the influence of Isa 49.

The disputation speech in Isa 49,14-25 shows Deutero-Isaiah's skill in adapting the genre to his own purposes. Nevertheless, he maintains the structure intact: the double refutation found in Ezekiel reappears here, and the formulae common in Ezekiel, absent in Isa 40,27-31, return in v.18 (oath formula), vv.22-25 (messenger formula) and v.23 (formula of recognition of Yahweh).[141]

Graffy helpfully notes the similarities between Ezekiel and Isa 49, but there are others besides. John Goldingay connects the two texts when commenting on 49:18: "The image of the city's finery has been a negative one, directly or indirectly... Here it becomes a positive one."[142] His comparison passages for the negative image of Jerusalem's jewelry include Ezek 16. As the sole link this would be weak, but the added presence of the "as I live" formula in v. 18 solidifies the overlap with Ezekiel. What is more, Isa 49:19 carries on YHWH's assurance by promising the restoration of Zion's waste places (חרבתיך) and desolate places (שׁממתיך), precisely the terms used to describe the land in Ezek 33:24-29 and 35:1–36:15.[143] With this range of indicators that the two passages are in dialogue with one another, it is only a small step to contend that Isa 49:14-26 is responding to the harsh polemic against the non-exiled Judahites and the Jacob tradition in Ezekiel by reversing its images.

The strongest evidence for that reversal is Deutero-Isaiah's exceptional use of the "as I live" formula: Isa 49:14-21 is the *only* passage in the Hebrew Bible where this form of the divine oath introduces salvation for Israel. Despite that inversion, it retains the usual connection with the land: Deutero-Isaiah uses it to assure Zion of its future prosperity. The exceptional use of the "as I live" authenticating element in an oracle of salvation can be explained as an effort to counter the sharp rhetoric of Ezekiel. Deutero-Isaiah's interest to portray the patriarchs positively is obvious in Isa 51:2, which points to Abraham and Sarah as progenitors of Israel.[144] Jacob plays a prominent role in Isa 40–48 gener-

---

141 Graffy, *A Prophet Confronts His People*, 98

142 Goldingay, *The Message of Isaiah 40-55*, 388.

143 In Ezek 33:23-29 it describes the dwelling places of those claiming Abrahamic descent; in Ezek 35 they describe the land after YHWH's judgment; in Ezek 36:1-15 they denote the state of the land prior to YHWH's acts to restore and resettle it.

144 Bernard Gosse, "Les traditions sur Abraham et sur le jardin d'Éden en rapport avec Is 51,2-3 et avec le livre d'Ézéchiel," in *Studies in the Book of Genesis: Literature, Redaction and History* (ed. A. Wénin; Betl 155; Leuven: Peeters, 2001), suggests that Isa 51:1-3 is unconcerned with the possession of the land, but portrays the destruction and reconstruction of Jerusalem as expulsion and re-entry into the garden of Eden. Despite the differences, Gosse's argument strengthens the relationship posited here.

ally, and in Isa 49 in particular he is esteemed through the author's designation of Yhwh as "the Mighty One of Jacob" (Isa 49:26).

3. Ezekiel and the Formation of the Pentateuch

To summarize the preceding argument, a careful review of Ezekiel's disputations about who will inhabit Yhwh's land in the future, conducted with regard for the layers of meaning in the "as I live" and "lifted hand" formulae, shows that the Judahites exiled to Babylon were engaged in a dispute with the Judahites remaining in the land, with the non-exiles appealing to a combined Abraham-Jacob tradition to support their claims to possess the land. Because there is strong evidence that these passages date to the first half of the sixth-century B.C.E.—a position that will be supported below—it is now appropriate to consider what these new findings indicate about the formation of the Pentateuch. Scholars since Julius Wellhausen have used Ezekiel in this way, hoping to verify or to invalidate models for the Pentateuch's growth, and that effort has not abated in recent scholarship.

To begin, it is necessary to revisit the evidence gathered here with respect to the date when the Abraham and Jacob traditions were combined. Ezekiel's polemic against Abraham (Ezek 33:23-29) appears immediately after the report of Jerusalem's fall, which is dated to 585 B.C.E. by the book.[145] The clearest challenge to the Jacob tradition appears in Ezek 35:1–36:15, specifically in 35:5-9 and 10-13. This section of oracles also comes under the 585 B.C.E. date heading and, in spite of the difficulties in identifying the precise date for this material, the structure of the book indicates that the editors intended to make this material roughly contemporaneous with 33:23-29.

The accusation in 35:5, that Israel was betrayed at the time of its calamity (אידם, no doubt a word play on Edom, אדום), is obviously post-587 B.C.E. But it should not be pushed too far from that date for at least three reasons. First, the dual claim that Yhwh is present with the non-exiles and that they will possess (ירש) the land is nearly identical to the pre-587 B.C.E. claim in Ezek 11:15.[146] This suggests they are not separated by a large span of time. Second, the ambitions of the non-exiles to capture the "two nations" and "two lands" (Ezek 35:10) implies a period when the nations surrounding Judah had yet to encroach on its

---

145 Greenberg, *Ezekiel 1-20*, 8; Block, *Ezekiel 1–24*, 28-29; see Zimmerli, *Ezekiel 1–24*, 10, for his argument on the "general confidence" that can be placed in these dates.

146 On this dating, see Joyce, *Ezekiel*, 110.

territory, a process that could not have taken too long to begin.[147] Third, Pohlmann uses this attitude as part of the criteria for dating texts to the so-called oldest layer of the book, the layer to which he allocates 35:10-12.[148] Given his propensity to find a later context for much of the book, this is significant. Anja Klein has also assigned a substantial portion of Ezek 35 to her so-called "der erste Fortschreibungsschub;" even though she would date this later than the sixth-century B.C.E., it is notable that she also finds reason for putting the material in the earliest stages of Ezekiel's development on different criteria.[149]

Finally, recognizing that Edom serves as a derisive reference to the non-exiles marginalizes the relevance of Edomite history for dating this passage. Indeed, recognizing the "representational significance" of Edom in Ezek 35 reinforces Bartlett's conclusion that this text does not depend upon any specific action of Edom during or subsequent to the fall of Jerusalem in 587 B.C.E.[150] That being the case, it remains possible that the Jacob-based claims could even antedate the fall of Jerusalem. There is no direct evidence for this in Ezekiel, though the somewhat more speculative argument that Jacob is also polemicized in Ezek 16 may point in this direction.[151] It seems prudent, on the whole, to conclude that both the Judahites in exile and those remaining in the land were familiar with a form of the Jacob tradition that included the land promise and was already incorporated with a form of the Abraham tradition that also contained a land promise by the first half of the sixth-century B.C.E., perhaps even before 585 B.C.E.

Moving on to consider the form of the patriarchal tradition this presupposes, the evidence points towards a version that was not yet integrated with the exodus tradition. The non-exiles' employed both the Abraham and Jacob traditions to support their possession of (ירשׁ) the land, an assertion that points towards two key texts: Gen 15 (especially vv. 7-21) and Gen 28 (especially vv. 1-4). It is, of course, possible that the tradition was combined and experienced wide currency prior to the composition of these texts, so the possibility that a patriarchal history[152] containing these verses circulated in Jerusalem prior to Ezekiel's depor-

---

147 Rainer Albertz, *A History of Israelite Religion in the Old Testament Period. Volume II: From the Exile to the Maccabees* (OTL; Translated by John Bowden. Louisville, Ky.: Westminster John Knox, 1994), 371-73.

148 Pohlmann, *Ezechiel 20–48*, 471-77; cf. Pohlmann, *Ezechielstudien*, 217-18.

149 Klein, *Schriftauslegung im Ezechielbuch*, 68-70, 309-20.

150 Bartlett, "Edom and the Fall of Jerusalem, 587 B.C," 20

151 This oracle comes under a date header placing it at 592 B.C.E. (Greenberg, *Ezekiel 1-20*, 8; Block, *Ezekiel 1–24*, 28-29).

152 Hereafter, PH.

tation must remain open.[153] That prospect would account for the so-phisticated way the book of Ezekiel uses both the verbal and the rare nominal form of the term ירשׁ in its polemics. Even if these texts were composed in the immediate aftermath of Jerusalem's destruction, then this reconstruction can help adjudicate between the various proposals for how the PH formed.

Although this evidence could support various proposals for an early dating of the first PH that adopt a documentary model, most notable among these being the concept of a pre-exilic JE source,[154] it also fits with various traditio-historical reconstructions that allow for growth by the accretion and connection of smaller sources over a long period of time. Models in both categories merit discussion.

Documentary models are problematized by the evidence that the book of Ezekiel uses the exodus tradition in its polemic against the combined Abraham-Jacob tradition. The "as I live" authenticating element is the book's preferred manner for introducing its refutations of the non-exiles' claims. And, as demonstrated earlier, the "as I live" authenticating element is one half of a coordinated pair: DTR uses it to introduce YHWH's oath of judgment, while the verbal root שׁבע announces YHWH's oath to give the land to the ancestors.[155] Supporting Römer's influential work, which demonstrates the divine oath with שׁבע is connected with the patriarchs at a late stage (in his view after the exile), it is notable that the "as I live" authenticating element is never positively connected with the patriarchs either. When these two detailed points are combined with the book of Ezekiel's general endorsement that the legitimate origin of YHWH's people must be traced to the ancestors in Egypt and the exodus tradition, all the evidence points towards the conclusion that the combined Abraham-Jacob tradition remained separate from the exodus tradition in the first half of the sixth-century B.C.E. This conclusion, of course, makes the concept of a pre-exilic document that spans Abraham, Jacob, and the exodus untenable.

Traditio-historical models fare better when evaluated against this evidence, though not all are supported by it. Among the numerous models in this category, illustrative and notable reconstructions fall

---

153 For instance, Carr remarks: "To be sure, we can not presuppose a text is only to be dated to the time when its major themes appear in other datable texts" (*Reading the Fractures*, 228; cf. Blum, *Studien zur Komposition*, 218, note 44).

154 As examples, Nicholson, *The Pentateuch.*, and Emerton, "Promises to the Patriarchs," 381-400 (for whom see also J. A. Emerton, "The Promises to the Patriarchs in Genesis," *JSOT* 39 [1988]: 381-400).

155 See above, ch. 4, §2.

into two groups: on one side, Van Seters,[156] Blum,[157] Carr,[158] and Reinhard Kratz,[159] and, on the other side, Albert de Pury, Römer, and Konrad Schmid. The proposals in the latter group share the view that the date for the first combined Abraham-Jacob narrative is in the Persian period, a view contested by the evidence from Ezekiel. Perhaps the most ardent proponent of this view is Albert de Pury, who dates this combination between 535 and 530 B.C.E. on the basis of Abraham's "ecumenical" role.[160] Römer has followed de Pury on many points, but suggests an even later Persian period date.[161] Konrad Schmid reaches the same conclusion on different grounds than either de Pury or Römer, but his model has similar issues accounting for the new evidence raised here.[162] There remain strengths in each one of these models, but they are now faced with explaining why such a large time lapse occurred between the initial joining of these two figures and the production of an integrated form of the narrative about them.

The models of Van Seters, Blum, Carr, and Kratz share the view that the Abraham and Jacob traditions were combined, in one form or another, prior to the end of the Neo-Babylonian period. Though a full scale evaluation of these models is not possible here, a brief examination of the models with respect to Ezekiel's content does allow for some important findings.

First, Blum's earlier work argued for a pre-exilic first version of the PH (»Vätergeschichte 1«).[163] He subsequently modified his view, opting to place the entire combination in an exilic version of the PH. Blum's change is motivated by issues within Genesis, and though this evidence should not be discounted, the availability of new evidence outside Gen-

---

156 Van Seters, "Confessional Reformulation," 448-59; cf. Van Seters, *Abraham*; Van Seters, *Prologue*, especially pp. 331-2. Van Seters does not appear to place any further precision on the date for a combined Abraham-Jacob composition than the "exile."

157 Blum, *Die Komposition*, 271-361 originally placed this composition in the pre-exilic period, but has later revised his position to the exilic period (Blum, *Studien zur Komposition*, 214, note 35).

158 Carr, *Reading the Fractures*, summarizes his position at pp. 305-11.

159 Kratz, *Narrative Books*, 272-73.

160 de Pury, "Abraham," 180. See also de Pury, "Jacob," 163-81; de Pury, "Situer," 213-41; and de Pury,"La tradition," 12-35.

161 Römer, "Recherches," 189-93.

162 Schmid, *Erzväter und Exodus*, 273.

163 This view, now modified, would come closest to Kratz's position, which places the PH somewhere between 722 and 587 B.C.E.

esis does warrant a reevaluation of the evidence.[164]   In particular, the
evidence that Ezekiel found it necessary to dispute claims to a combined Abraham-Jacob tradition around 580 B.C.E., perhaps earlier, suggests that Blum's original position is indeed justifiable.   The tumul-
tuous period between 597 and 587 B.C.E. emerges as a potential time to
consider.   The issue, to be sure, needs further study than is possible
here.

Second, Carr developed his argument for an exilic proto-Genesis,
the level in which he assigns the first combination of the Abraham and
Jacob traditions, by narrowing down from a range of possibilities between 722 and 560 B.C.E.[165]   As part of his argument he suggests,
"whereas almost all of the (late) references featuring Abraham and
Isaac occur in some connection with the promise theme so central to the
proto-Genesis composition, there is no such unambiguous reference to
the promise in the datable references to Jacob."[166] This latter statement
can now, it seems, be revised. The polemic against the Jacob tradition's
claim to possess (ירשׁ) the land in Ezek 35:5-9, 10-13 correlates directly
to the promise theme (cf. Gen 28:4). The observation of this new reference would allow for amending Carr's *terminus ad quem* for his proto-
Genesis upwards, potentially even to a date prior to the final conquest
of Jerusalem. Bearing in mind these potential modifications, this study
argues in favor of this sort of model for the development of the PH.[167]

As a final matter, Ezekiel's relationship to the Pentateuch offers insight into the presence of both positive and negative Jacob material in
the book as well.   While establishing the presence of the anti-Jacob
polemic in Ezekiel, the four explicit mentions of this patriarch (Ezek
20:5a; 28:25; 37:25; 39:25) were assigned to a later stage of the book's development.   Indeed, given the interest of those four passages (Ezek
20:1-31; 28:25-26; 37:15-28; 39:21-29) in the return of the people to the
land, the possibility that they arise from a coordinated redaction within

---

164 Blum, *Studien zur Komposition*, 214, note 35. The impetus for the change came from
    Matthias Köckert, *Vätergott und Väterverheißungen: Eine Auseinandersetzung mit Al-
    brecht Alt und seinem Erben* (FRLANT 142; Göttingen: Vandenhoeck & Ruprecht,
    1988), 248-55. For Blum's original work, see *Die Komposition*, 282-86.

165 Carr seems open to moving that *terminus ad quem* to an earlier date. What is more,
    the date he settles upon (560 B.C.E.) is not linked to any particular event, further im-
    plying its flexibility (Carr, *Reading the Fractures*, 227).

166 Ibid., 228.

167 Many issues regarding the diachronic growth of the patriarchal tradition are not ad-
    dressed here to be sure. For instance, careful study of the texts in Gen 12–36 gener-
    ally categorized as priestly needs new consideration in light of these new findings
    on Ezek 35:1–36:15. Otherwise unmentioned texts like Num 20 and Deut 1–2 also
    need reconsideration, but that is not possible here.

the book was introduced. Their interest in the land is, in fact, a key in explaining their relationship to the polemic against Jacob found elsewhere in the book of Ezekiel. Recall that all of the passages in which the non-exiles' claims are tied to the patriarchs deal with the future inhabitants of the land (Ezek 11:14-21; 16:43-58; 20:1-44; 33:23-29; 35:1–36:15). One logical explanation for the insertion of the positive, explicit mentions of Jacob is to harmonize the book of Ezekiel's endorsement of the exodus tradition with the patriarchal tradition. That is the same goal that Römer ascribes to the redactor who undertakes the coordinated, sevenfold insertion of the patriarchal triad alongside the divine oath promising the land to the ancestors in Deuteronomy.[168] Thus, it is possible that the process of redaction that Römer proposes integrated Deuteronomy into the Pentateuch—creating the "final form" of the first five biblical books—was mirrored by the process of redaction in the book of Ezekiel.

As for a possible setting, this is likely to have occurred after Deutero-Isaiah had gained prominence, a situation that would explain why Jacob is referred to as "my servant Jacob" (Ezek 28:25; 37:25; cf. Isa 41:8; 44:1-2; 44:21; 45:4; 48:20; Jer 30:10; 46:27). This suggests a *terminus a quo* of approximately 550 B.C.E. A *terminus ad quem* is hard to establish, but the use of the "lifted hand" land transfer formula with the patriarchal triad in Neh 9 suggests this harmonizing effort was not isolated.[169] If Williamson is correct to identify the composer of Neh 9:5b-37 as a member of the non-exiles, that would add evidence for a wider attempt to integrate the non-exiled and exiled communities and provide a timeframe for the corresponding work in Ezekiel.[170] Regardless of these uncertainties, the basic insight that the book of Ezekiel underwent a shaping process remarkably similar to the Pentateuch is noteworthy and merits consideration in future studies of the book.

---

168 Römer,"Deuteronomy," 136-38.

169 Boda, *Praying the Tradition*, 89-187, especially pp. 144-45, 165-67, 186-7.

170 H.G.M. Williamson, "Structure and Historiography in Nehemiah 9," in *Studies in Persian Period History and Historiography* (FAT/I 38; Tübingen: Mohr Siebeck, 2004), 292-93; cf. idem., *Ezra, Nehemiah*, 300-19, and idem., "The Belief System of the Book of Nehemiah," in *Studies in Persian Period History and Historiography* (FAT/I 38; Tübingen: Mohr Siebeck, 2004), 280-81.

4. Ezekiel's Fight for the Public Transcript

This chapter has demonstrated that the "as I live" and the "lifted hand" formulae figure significantly in the book of Ezekiel's effort to refute and stigmatize the non-exiles' invocation of a combined Abraham and Jacob tradition, with which the non-exiles hope to justify their claims to possess the land. The final task of the present analysis is to consider the form of Ezekiel's rhetoric, namely the explicit, harsh, often times demeaning tenor of its statements. Reflection on this issue shows that the book confronts the non-exiles' claims at three levels, each of which contributes to an effort to marginalize a group viewed as inferior. Taken together, the whole effort reflects the ways in which dominant groups seek to assert, reinforce, and maintain their power over subaltern groups.

The first feature of Ezekiel's response is to condemn the behavior of the non-exiles. Most prominent in Ezek 33:23-29, there are elements of this strategy in Ezek 5, 16, 20, and to a lesser extent in Ezek 11. Categorizing the conduct of those left in Judah as sinful and rebellious, indeed more sinful than even those nations who do not worship YHWH (Ezek 5:5-17; 16:43-58), is one way the book seeks to delegitimize the non-exiles' claim to be the rightful heirs to YHWH's land.

In his analysis of the ways in which powerful groups use public speech to impose their perspective over subordinates, Scott discusses a pair of verbal devices he calls stigmas and euphemism. These two are either side of a single coin. Euphemism is when dominant groups employ language to obscure their use of coercion, often by force; for instance, Scott cites the antiseptic term pacification to refer to an armed attack and occupation, or the politically correct capital punishment to describe state sponsored execution. Stigmatization shares this strategy, but moves in the other direction. Dominant groups select threatening or disparaging terms to portray subaltern groups as frightening and threatening; examples include labeling political enemies as bandits or hooligans, or in a religious context identifying dissenters as heretics.

It is, therefore, no accident that Ezek 33:23-29 responds to the non-exiles' appeal to Abraham for their land claim by giving a catalogue of cultic and moral failures. Denigrating their character in this way eases the way for the subsequent claim, phrased as a rhetorical question, that the non-exiles are not worthy to possess the land. This effort is not limited to the passages examined in this chapter, and space precludes a full rehearsal of the relevant texts, but other examples include the condemnation of image based worship in Ezek 8, the indictment of the

Jerusalemites' social policies in Ezek 11:2-12,[171] the invective against the non-exiles' prophets in Ezek 13, and the depiction of Jerusalem as a city of bloodshed (עיר הדמים) in Ezek 22.[172] Ezekiel's effort to stigmatize the conduct of the non-exiles is unmistakable in the disputation speeches that open with the "as I live" authenticating element and deal with the land, but it is not confined to these texts.

The second feature of Ezekiel's rejoinder is to oppose the theological bases on which the non-exiles' make their appeals. This takes a slightly different form depending on the passage in view. This chapter has observed the following: Ezek 33:23-29 and 35:1–36:15 deny the belief that the land can be possessed (ירש), maintaing instead that the land always belongs to YHWH, though the god of Israel will allow a chosen group to hold it as an אחזה or נחלה, occupying it as tenants who work the land and are granted part of its produce; Ezek 20, through its account of Israel's *Unheilsgeschichte*, denies that Abraham or Jacob represent the legitimate origin tradition of Israel; and Ezek 11:14-21 patently rejects the allegation that YHWH remains in Jerusalem and has abandoned those in the Babylonian exile.

The combined effect of these passages is to depict the community left in Jerusalem as somewhere between tragically misguided and utterly mistaken in their theological views. This is probably not unrelated to the behavioral critique; there are some indications that incorrect beliefs lead to improper conduct (e.g. Ezek 20:25-26; 44:9-14),

---

171 Odell, *Ezekiel*, 119-22.

172 Ezek 44:9-14 could also be in this list. Wellhausen famously used this passage to argue that Ezekiel degrades the Levites and mandates a "withdrawal of their right" (Julius Wellhausen, *Prolegomena zur Geschichte Israels* [5th ed. Berlin: G. Reimer, 1899], 119-20; ET Julius Wellhausen, *Prolegomena to the History of Ancient Israel* [Translated by J. Sutherland Black and W. Robertson Smith. Reprint 2008 ed. Bibliobazaar, 1885], 156). The combination of the "lifted hand" punishment formula (44:12) with the guilt-bearing formula (נשא עון; 44:10, 12) confirms what Wellhausen asserted. Bruce Wells' work on the Neo-Babylonian legal usage of the guilt-bearing formula indicates that "[t]o bear sin seems to indicate only that a person is guilty and subject to whatever punishment the court or administrative board deems necessary" (Wells, *The Law of Testimony*, 78). The "lifted hand" punishment formula, which appears between the two instances of the guilt-bearing formula (vv. 10, 12; cf. v. 13) specifies that YHWH will execute the punishment and introduces the details of the penalty—the Levitical priests shall not offer sacrifices, a special case addressed nowhere else in the legal material of the Hebrew Bible. The combined connotations of these formulae suggests the restriction from sacrifice is a punishment. By implication, then, Ezek 44:12-14 eliminates a privilege the Levites held prior to the exile. This pronouncement fits with the larger point advanced here, namely that the book of Ezekiel consistently speaks as though it is backed by the necessary social and political capital to enforce these decisions on a less powerful group of Judahites.

though this point is not foregrounded in the book. It is nevertheless true that these texts contribute to an overall characterization of the non-exiles' as inferior to the Judahite exiles. It is only Ezekiel and those Judahites in Babylonia who agree with him that are able to recognize these shortcomings. The inferiority ascribed to the non-exiles in these matters corresponds to the larger effort to classify them as socially and politically inferior.

The third and final feature of Ezekiel's endeavor is to mock the esteemed figures to whom the non-exiles' appeal for legitimacy. New ground has been broken here: this study has demonstrated that the non-exiles' appeal to Jacob in Ezek 35:1–36:15 is parodied by calling them Edomites, using the metonymy of Mt Seir for their community, and connecting their city to the descendants of Jacob's hated rival Esau. Albeit less explicit than the two prior features, this derisive engagement with opposing claims is consistent with other rhetoric in the book. It has strong precedent, furthermore, in the explicit naming of Abraham in Ezek 33:23-29 and the glaring omission of the patriarchs in Ezek 20.

This sort of taunting is squarely in the class of Scott's stigmas. "[T]he power to call a cabbage a rose and to make it stick in the public sphere" writes Scott, "implies the power to do the opposite, to stigmatize activities or persons that seem to call into question official realities."[173] Ezekiel, to borrow Scott's memorable image, uses language to make Jacob, the non-exiles' proverbial rose, into Esau, the cabbage-like figure with which they would not want to be associated. It is conceivable that the authors and tradents of Ezekiel hoped the non-exiles would learn of these disparaging remarks because they would generate anger among that group.

A similar intent probably lies behind other peculiar features of the book. For instance, the date formulae in Ezekiel uniformly refer to the reign of Jehoiachin, one of the exiles, not Zedekiah, the Babylonian-installed king over the non-exiled community. Irrespective of Ezekiel's attitude to monarchy in general,[174] this is yet another way that Ezekiel's rhetoric professes social dominance. Any question about Ezekiel's evaluation of Zedekiah is rendered moot by Ezek 12, which recalls the "futile, not to mention cowardly, attempt of Zedekiah to escape his besieged city."[175] In case any doubt remains, Ezek 17 reinforces the portrayal by depicting Zedekiah as unfaithful both to YHWH and his Baby-

173 Scott, *Domination*, 55.
174 On which, see ch. 6.
175 Odell, *Ezekiel*, 135.

lonian suzerain.   None of the community remaining in Jerusalem is
spared from Ezekiel's indictment, and portraying the non-exiles as deficient from top to bottom is yet another way to impugn any claim that
community might make for social, political, or religious authority.

Even in times when the powerful class is safely in control Scott
notes that "domination does not persist of its own momentum... and
can be sustained only by continuous efforts at reinforcement, main-
tenance, and adjustment"[176] of the public transcript.   Steven Holloway
demonstrates that the Neo-Assyrian empire, even during times of
strength, engaged in such efforts, employing political rhetoric, public
performances, and religious practice for this end.[177]

It is worth reviewing how Scott defines the public transcript:

> The public transcript is, to put it crudely, the self-portrait of dominant
> elites as they would have themselves seen. Given the usual power of dom-
> inant elites to compel performances from others, the discourse of the public
> transcript is a decidely lopsided discussion.   While it is unlikely to be
> merely a skein of lies and misrepresentations, it is, on the other hand, a
> highly partisan and partial narrative.   It is designed to be impressive, to
> affirm and naturalize the power of dominant elites, and to conceal or eu-
> phemize the dirty linen of their rule.[178]

The passages discussed in this chapter are, to be sure, highly partisan,
and the non-exiles would classify the discourse as lopsided. This tone
dominates because the book of Ezekiel is actively attempting to affirm
and naturalize the power of its community, the former Judahite elites
who are now in exile. It must pursue this goal against all external evidence to the contrary.

The immediate occasion for the passages discussed in this chapter
is a dispute about the land. Living on the land in the present and having a widely accepted claim to continue to inhabit that land in the future is, perhaps, the most tangible evidence of YHWH's favor and social
dominance for the Judahites. This is encapsulated well in the words of
Leslie Allen quoted earlier, namely that for Ezekiel "[l]ife is repeatedly
defined in terms of returning to the land."[179] Indeed, one gets the sense
in Ezekiel's tone that a life and death struggle is in progress.

---

176 Scott, *Domination*, 45.

177 Steven W. Holloway, *Aššur is king! Aššur is king!: Religion in the Exercise of Power in
the Neo-Assyrian Empire* (Culture and History of the Ancient Near East 10; Leiden:
Brill, 2001), 217-319, esp. 225-31 and 236-7.

178 Ibid., 18.

179 Allen, *Ezekiel 20–48*, xxiv.

Yet, winning an argument about the land is, for Ezekiel, a subsidiary concern, albeit emblematic of the overarching interest. The Judahite exiles are largely composed of Jerusalem's elites who were forcibly removed from those privileged positions in 597 B.C.E. Physically displaced and dislocated from the trappings of social, political, and religious power though they may be, these Judahites have not relinquished the idea that they are the rightful inhabitants of those dominant positions. Their chief desire, therefore, is not to assert their right to the land as much as it is to reassert their social dominance and to preserve what they see as their justifiable social status. Incapable of pursuing this goal by any physical or symbolic coercion because of their captivity, Ezekiel seizes the one tool of power still available to it: words. The book of Ezekiel seeks to assert power over the non-exiles by setting the parameters of the public transcript. It speaks like the powerful, not the powerless.

This attitude of superiority drives the sharply critical language used in the disputation speeches to stigmatize the views of the non-exiles. In Ezek 33:23-29 the book eviscerates the non-exiles' logic, strawman though it might be in Ezekiel's version of it. The longer metaphorical disputation in 35:1–36:15 parodies the non-exiles' appeal to Jacob, defining them as Edomites, an ethnic other that was historically inferior to Judah as a political entity. Post 597 B.C.E. Jerusalem, finally, is given the same lineage as Esau, reasserting this negative portrayal. These are the sort of things that characterize the public speech of a socially, politically, and religiously powerful community that believes it is capable of coercing agreement from dissenters.

A similar strategy appears to be at work in what Andrew Mein calls the domestication of ethics of the exilic community.[180] Having experienced the loss of Jerusalem and the autonomous realm of nationhood, he argues that "[o]nly moral actions on a more individual, domestic scale are possible."[181] Even still, "Ezekiel is not neutral about the moral behaviour open to the exiles: he clearly distinguishes what is acceptable from what is not."[182] The key comparison is in Mein's latter statement: Ezekiel speaks as the socially dominant voice, as if its determination of acceptable and unacceptable moral behavior is and will be the social norm. The book speaks as if it contains *the* public transcript, and by doing so hopes to affirm and naturalize its claim to power.

---

180 Mein, *Ezekiel and the Ethics of Exile*, 177-215.

181 Ibid., 214.

182 Ibid.

The acerbic language of Ezekiel has prompted others to recognize the animosity between the exiled and non-exiled Judahites. This study shows that this acerbic language is not just a product of the controversy but rather that the language itself is a central part of Ezekiel's effort to prevail in the fight. Commentators more often point to Ezekiel's indictment of the non-exiles' behavior as its main attack, and that should not be marginalized.[183] But, Ezekiel offers that critique with such indignation and assurance precisely because it believes that the exiles remain the dominant social party that has the social, political, and religious capital necessary to define what is and is not acceptable behavior and belief for all Judahites. With recourse to physical or legal means of imposing their dominance gone, all that remains for Ezekiel to assert this dominance is the ability to set the parameters of the public transcript. Words are its only means of displaying power. So the words it employs will have to be the strongest and most potent it can muster. The book defines and vehemently declares what counts as correct thought and rhetoric because that ability is, across time and place, the purview of the dominant. Ezekiel speaks like it represents the powerful; it hopes that doing so will make its perception reality.

5. Summary

The prominent role of the question "Who shall possess the land of Israel in the future?" for the book of Ezekiel was observed at the outset of this chapter. The contentious nature of this question, highlighted by Ezek 33:23-29, was already well-known. However, using the newly available evidence about the connotations of the "as I live" authenticating element and the "lifted hand" land transfer formula, additional clarity was given to the book of Ezekiel's objection to the non-exiles' assertion that they could possess the land, taking permanent control of it from YHWH. This view, explicitly associated with Abraham in Ezek 33, was anathema to Ezekiel, an outlook it shares with DTR and H. Therefore, the book of Ezekiel uses a combination of terms also found in DTR and H to refute it. For instance, it structured the *Unheilsgeschichte* of Ezek 20 with the DTR "as I live" authenticating element and the H "lifted hand" land transfer formula. When Ezek 33 and 20 are considered together, as was done here, the evidence shows that both the non-exiles' behavior and the theological foundations of the Abraham tradition are attacked, indicating that Ezekiel is unwilling to allow Abraham to

---

183 Renz, *The Rhetorical Function*, 49-50

function as an esteemed ancestor of the community. In short, Ezekiel sets the exodus origin tradition in opposition to the patriarchal narrative.

Next, attention turned to Ezek 35:1–36:15, which was re-examined in light of the preceding findings. Concentrating on the connotations of the "as I live" formula—namely that Ezekiel only uses it to announce judgment upon YHWH's people—exegesis demonstrated that this oracle against Mt Seir contained a subversive discourse about the Jacob tradition that was tied up with the use of Mt Seir and Edom as derogatory aliases for Jacob. As further evidence that this is the case, analysis of Ezek 35:1–36:15 revealed that it shares the logic employed to refute the non-exiles appeal to the Abraham tradition elsewhere.

All of this evidence points to the existence of a combined Abraham-Jacob tradition with a cohesive land promise during the first half of the sixth-century B.C.E. The competition between the patriarchal and exodus traditions in Ezekiel supports the conclusion that these two origin traditions remained separate from one another at this time. That result adds to much existing evidence that points away from a documentary model for the formation of the Pentateuch, though it may support numerous traditio-historical reconstructions. These findings constitute new testimony from Ezekiel about the process by which the Pentateuch reached its final form.

Finally, this chapter showed that the dispute about the land is indicative of a larger effort to stigmatize the behavior and beliefs of the non-exiles in order to reassert that the Judahites in exile are the social, political, and religious elites. The book of Ezekiel condemns the non-exiles' behavior, denies the validity of their theological positions, and mocks their honored figures. Speaking publicly in this disparaging manner is the purview of the dominant and the book of Ezekiel hopes that it can obtain dominance by speaking as if it already possesses the privileges associated with it. Form, as well and content, serves as Ezekiel's weapon in its effort to win the battle for control of the Judahite public transcript.

Chapter Six: The Inter-National Polemics of Exile

The preceding chapter demonstrated that the book of Ezekiel employs harsh, polemical, derogatory language in order to contest and condemn the Judahites that remain in the land, a community that appealed to a combined Abraham-Jacob tradition to legitimize their claims. That the book of Ezekiel, addressed to the elites deported to Babylon, should unleash its anger at this group is not hard to imagine since their assertion of social, political, and religious dominance was simultaneously a move to revoke that power from the former elites now in Babylon.

1. Whither Babylonia?

It is surprising that the book of Ezekiel never openly expresses this sort of anger or judgment against the Babylonians, the group that is actually responsible for their current predicament. As noted in the introduction, Ezekiel's failure to indict Babylon and announce its future judgment departs both from contemporaneous prophetic texts (e.g. Jer 50–51; Isa 13–14) and from Ezekiel's treatment of other foreign nations (e.g. Ezek 25–32).

Neither does Ezekiel express positive feelings towards the Babylonians. Perhaps that omission is less surprising, but it is noteworthy when compared to Jeremiah. In its so-called "letter to the exiles" (Jer 29), Jeremiah instructs the Judahites deported to Babylon to "seek the welfare of the city" (Jer 29:7), where they are to build houses, plant gardens, marry, and have children. Jeremiah also commands the people of Jerusalem not to resist the Babylonians when they come against it, but to surrender to the foreign army (i.e. Jer 21:9; 38:17-18).

Why is Babylonia effectively absent? What, if anything, explains the lack of either positive or negative rhetoric about the Babylonians in Ezekiel? Is Renz correct to conclude that Ezekiel focuses on "the enemy within" rather than those outside its community?[1]

This chapter argues that the book of Ezekiel is far from silent about Babylon, but that its criticism of its captors easily escapes detection. Indeed, the elusive nature of Ezekiel's polemic against its captors is inten-

---

1   Renz, *The Rhetorical Function*, 50

tional and fits with Scott's conclusions regarding the ways in which subaltern groups employ the "arts of resistance" to oppose their oppressors while living under the constant threat of coercive force.

Whereas the social status of the Judahite exiles allowed them to envision a dialogue with the Judahite non-exiles in which it speaks as the socially, politically, and religiously dominant class that can decide what counts as acceptable behavior and announce those verdicts publicly, it was impossible for anything like this dynamic to be imagined when the Babylonian powers that be were in view. Vis-à-vis Babylonian society, the Judahite exiles were the dominated, not the dominant. Subaltern groups, such as Ezekiel's community and audience, are compelled to act in public as the powerful group determines. "With rare, but significant, exceptions," writes Scott, "the public performance of the subordinate will, out of prudence, fear, and the desire to curry favor, be shaped to appeal to the expectations of the powerful."[2] These expectations, which Scott calls the public transcript, define the open interaction and explicit dialogue between the dominant and subaltern.

This is not, however, the only level at which language and action are working. The public transcript is complemented by a hidden transcript, Scott's term for the discourse that occurs offstage, among the subordinates when they are away from the gaze of the dominant class. The hidden transcript gives voice to the subaltern desire to resist, to assert their own dignity, and to imagine what sort of retaliatory action might be taken were it feasible. This hidden transcript, as it develops from unrefined, "raw" expressions of resistance into a sophisticated "cooked" statement of opposition, begins to find its way into the open.[3] This unveiling of the hidden transcript is rarely, and only at highly charged moments, a complete revelation; more often than not, the unveiling comprises "a partly sanitized, ambiguous, and coded version of the hidden transcript."[4] Although the hidden transcript "is always present in the public discourse of subordinate groups," it remains beyond the reach of the powerful by one of two means: either the messenger is anonymous or the message is disguised.

The following analysis of Ezek 17, 34, and 20 will demonstrate that the hidden transcript of the Judahite exiles finds its public expression in language that is ambiguous, polysemous, and often contained in elu-

---

2   Scott, *Domination*, 2. Indeed, Holloway discusses ways in which the Babylonians themselves exhibited this behavior in the immediately preceding political period when they were subordinate to the Neo-Asasyrians (*Aššur is King!*, 227-9; cf. 235-7).

3   Ibid., 119.

4   Ibid., 19.

230 The Inter-National Polemics of Exile

sive metaphors that allow for various interpretations. It is an example of the ways in which the private discourse of subaltern groups seeps into their public performance.

The relevant passages (Ezek 17:1-24; 34:1-16; 20:32-44) are united by two features: at the surface, each passage contains a critique of the non-exiles framed by a divine oath with the "as I live" authenticating element; below the surface, each passage depicts YHWH as the enduring, royal figure that leads Israel with images that are elsewhere attributed to Marduk. Because scholars tend to concentrate on what these passages indicate about Ezekiel's attitude towards the Davidic monarchy, the role of these Mesopotamian images for divine power and royal responsibility is often overlooked. Taking note of those links, however, it is evident that the book of Ezekiel adopts and adapts them in order to defend one of its central theological concepts: despite external signs that YHWH was defeated by Marduk, Judah's patron deity remained powerful, in control of his people, his land, and even foreign leaders. YHWH, therefore, remained worthy of worship.

This view, asserted in a veiled fashion because of its antipathy to the Babylonian authorized public transcript, places YHWH in direct conflict with Marduk, chief of the Babylonian pantheon and divine patron of the Babylonian monarchy. This is no accident. Divine struggle resulting in YHWH's victory is a theme of the exodus tradition, in which YHWH is victorious over the Egyptian deities and Pharaoh; Ezekiel, knowing this paradigm, re-applied it to claim that YHWH would once again conquer a foreign power and redeem an elect group of people from bondage and oppression. Thus, this chapter includes a brief exploration of how these new findings about Ezekiel can clarify the ongoing debate about the development of monotheism in ancient Judah.

2. Divine Human Cooperation: Ezek 17:1-24

Ezekiel 17, an image-rich chapter concerning the Davidic monarchy, identifies itself as a riddle (חידה) and as a proverb (משל). The chapter opens with a poetic fable (vv. 3-10), moves on to an interpretation of that tale (vv. 11-21), and finishes with an oracle about the restoration of the monarchy. Verses 3-10 will aid in contextualizing the following discussion, but vv. 11-21 are the central focus of this section. After explaining the historical events symbolized in the fable (vv. 11-15), the passage details Zedekiah's judgment on a human (vv. 16-18) and divine level (vv. 19-21). Both the human and divine judgments are introduced with the "as I live" authenticating element, a two-fold structure that reflects a broader duality that "pervades the prophecy"[5] and highlights the tight coordination of events in the human and divine realms. If focus is placed on the images used to characterize the coordinated human and divine actions, it emerges that Ezekiel implicitly denies the Babylonian imperial ideology that Yнwн had been defeated and rendered ineffective and also advances the view that Yнwн is the divine force that lies behind the Babylonian king's power.

Prior to that, it is necessary to show that the riddle itself introduces the central theme of the chapter: the connection between earthly events and activity in the divine realm.

(a) Ezek 17:1-10

The first section of Ezek 17 tells the story of two eagles who vie for the allegiance of a vine planted beside many waters (עַל מַיִם רַבִּים, 17:5). The vine is Zedekiah, the king of Judah installed by the Babylonians after the deportation of Judah's elite, including Ezekiel, in 597 B.C.E. The eagles are, respectively, the kings of Babylonia and Egypt. According to this account, the king of Babylon installed Zedekiah with the expectation that he would serve as a faithful vassal to Babylon (17:6, 13-14).[6]

This historical context has strongly influenced the way commentators interpret the phrase "many waters." Almost uniformly, scholars explain that the many waters next to which the vine resides are positive, nourishing, idyllic even, an indication of the positive character of the vine's seedbed.[7] This view, however, fails to account for both the point of the allegory and also that everywhere else in Ezekiel the image marks its referent as a force of chaos to be resisted.

Elsewhere in Ezekiel the many waters are most closely associated with Egypt, one of several ways in which this foreign nation is depicted as chaos manifest in the human realm. The treatment of Egypt as a nation and Pharaoh individually is most prominent in the oracles against the nations (Ezek 29–32), where both are persistently described with images of chaos. For instance, Egypt is called the great sea monster that dwells in the waters of the nile (הַתַּנִּים הַגָּדוֹל; Ezek 29:3), which are

---

5   Greenberg, *Ezekiel 1-20*, 317; cf. Block, *Ezekiel 1–24*, 539-48.

6   See Bernhard Lang, *Kein Aufstand in Jerusalem: Die Politik des Propheten Ezechiel* (SBB; Stuttgart: Katholisches Bibelwerk, 1978), 28-49, for discussion of the potential iconographic background to the various images and symbols.

7   Zimmerli, *Ezekiel 1–24*, 362; Greenberg, *Ezekiel 1-20*, 310; Block, *Ezekiel 1–24*, 531; Joyce, *Ezekiel*, 136.

identified as the primordial rivers (נהרות; Ezek 32:2; cf. Ezek 31:15).[8]
Egypt serves as the earthly incarnation of the chaos monster.

Margaret Odell is one of the few scholars to take note of the otherwise negative connotations of the many waters in Ezekiel and outside
of it. "[T]his is not simply a naturalistic image," she observes, but one
"elsewhere...associated with the primordial waters of chaos."[9] Bearing
in mind, then, both the negative assessment of Egypt and the chaotic
connotations of the phrase מים רבים, there is a better way of reading
Ezek 17:5 that takes account of the passage's logic, Egypt's role, and the
chaos theme.

The image plays on Zedekiah's role as a Babylonian vassal (17:5-6,
13-14): the מים רבים are the chaos waters manifest in the threatening
power of Egypt, an image repeated in Ezek 19 and 31. Zedekiah is not
planted next to many waters that will nourish him, but is installed next
to them as a political and military buffer against his suzerain's most
powerful enemy. In other words, Zedekiah is to make Judah into the
first line of Babylonian resistance against Egypt, its only military equal
in the early sixth century B.C.E. This role is evident in the key plot twist
narrated in vv. 7-8: when Zedekiah turns his allegiance to the other
great eagle he aligns himself with the very מים רבים against which he is
meant to defend (v. 8).[10] Judah is no longer a buffer against Egypt on
behalf of Babylon, but by switching its allegiance immediately becomes
the advanced front of the Egyptian threat. Verses 13-15 confirm that
this is the story the allegory means to tell, underscoring Zedekiah's in-
tentions by specifying that he turned to Egypt for horses (סוסים) and
soldiers (עם רב). Margaret Odell is correct when she remarks that although the מים רבים in Ezek 17:5, 8 "appears to be innocuous... its use
elsewhere suggests that it has a more sinister connotation."[11]

Another indication that Ezek 17 is drawing on the complex of
themes often called the *Chaoskampf* is the means by which the rebellious
vine is defeated, namely the רוח הקדים, the east wind (v. 10). A frequent image in the *Chaoskampf*, the רוח הקדים is a storm element, per-

---

8   For a detailed discussion of Egypt's role in Ezekiel, see C. L. Crouch, "Ezekiel's Ora-
     cles Against the Nations in Light of a Royal Ideology of Warfare," *JBL* (2011): 479-84

9   Odell, *Ezekiel*, 240.

10   So, read vv. 7-8 thus: 'Behold, there was another great eagle -- with great wings and
     much plumage. Look, this vine bent its roots toward him and its branches reached
     out to him so that he caused it to be nourished. In a good field, by many waters it
     was planted to grow branches and to produce fruit to be a noble vine.' Verses 9-10
     are the rhetorical question that make this clear: can it turn from its assigned role thus
     and succeed? Of course not.

11   Odell, *Ezekiel*, 240.

haps the most prominent set of divine weapons in that tradition. Though the east wind is only mentioned this one time in Ezek 17, it fits with similar descriptions of YHWH using a storm (שָׁאָה; 38:9), a storm wind (רוּחַ סְעָרוֹת; 13:11), a driving rain (גֶּשֶׁם שׁוֹטֵף; 13:11), great hail-stones (אַבְנֵי אֶלְגָּבִישׁ; 13:13), and even clouds (עָנָן; 38:9) as weapons in other passages. In the present context, it is noteworthy that the east wind is also employed to judge the rebellious queen mother who sides with Egypt in Ezek 19, a passage with numerous connections to Ezek 17.[12]

Recognizing that this fanciful imagery is drawing on a widely known ancient Near Eastern tradition about divine combat that is paralleled by human military actions is important in order to comprehend that the entirety of Ezek 17 deals with the overlap of activities in the human realm with those in the unseen, divine realm. This will come to the fore in the two-level interpretation of the narrative in vv. 16-21 that is structured by the "as I live" formula, but it is already adumbrated by the allegory.

(b) Ezek 17:11-21

Verses 11-12 open the interpretation of the fable and immediately hone in on the motivating issue: the agreement between Nebuchadrezzar and Zedekiah. Alternately called a covenant (vv. 13, 14, 15) and an oath (vv. 12, 13, 15), this probably refers to an *adê* loyalty oath imposed upon the Judahite ruler when he was placed on the throne. Nebuchadrezzar, like the Neo-Assyrian rulers before him, would have employed the *adê* loyalty oath as one of "several important steps to guarantee Zedekiah's loyalty in the future."[13] Block is correct to observe that "in a context involving covenants and oaths, Yahweh answers with an oath formula of his own: *As I live (ḥay ʾănî)*."[14] Not only does the "as I live" divine oath formula indicate the beginning of a disputation in which either an explicit or implicit view is countered but, in this context, is significant because the extant evidence suggests that the *adê* loyalty oath often involved the subjugated king swearing by his own deity,[15] likely through the *nīš X* formula invoking the life of a god or gods.

---

12 For further details, see Crouch and Strine, "YHWH's Battle Against Chaos."

13 Block, *Ezekiel 1–24*, 542; cf. Lang, *Kein Aufstand*, 50-60, esp. 54-8.

14 Ibid., 544. Emphasis orginal.

15 Cogan, *Imperialism and Religion*, 42-61; Parpola and Watanabe, *Treaties and Loyalty Oaths*, xv-xxv, xxxvii.

It remains speculative that Zedekiah swore his oath to Babylon by invoking Yhwh, yet that is the best explanation for Yhwh's statement that he will enforce his oath and his covenant (v. 19). This suggests Zedekiah swore *nīš* Yhwh, in Hebrew יהוה חי "as Yhwh lives," the prominent Dtr human authenticating element. Yhwh's response fits this proposal: the "as I live" authenticating element would provide an exact retort to Zedekiah's oath.

The interpretation proper comprises vv. 16-21, which follows the explanation of Zedekiah's rebellious appeal to Egypt. The interpretation divides into two sections, each opened by the divine oath with the "as I live" authenticating element. Verses 16-18 concern the human plane and indicate that Zedekiah's trust in Pharaoh is misguided (v. 17).[16] The resulting punishment will be enacted by his human counterpart Nebuchadrezzar (v. 16). To this point, the interpretation fits with the series of events one would anticipate based upon the standards of ancient Near Eastern international relations.

There are serious theological ramifications that follow logically on from these events, ramifications that presented a challenge to the core of Judahite theology. Evidence suggests that the Babylonians interpreted their invasion of Judah, conquest of Jerusalem, capture and deportation of its king, destruction of its temple, and deportation of the temple vessels as indicators that Marduk had defeated Yhwh.[17] It remains debatable whether the Babylonians understood such events as merely subjugation of the defeated deity or as that deity's death. Because this has some bearing on the connotation of the "as I live" authenticating element, it merits discussion.

In the immediately preceding Neo-Assyrian period, Kutsko argues that the repair of divine images, a necessary step preceding their repatriation, "is portrayed as rebirth in the house of their father (*abu*) and begetter (*zārû*), Assur, in the land of their captivity."[18] The difficulty,

---

16 There is some question about whether Pharaoh should be retained in this verse. Greenberg, *Ezekiel 1-20*, 315, against his tendency, proposes it should be omitted in this case. However, there is no evidence in the ancient versions for omitting Pharaoh and, as Block, *Ezekiel 1–24*, 545, argues, it should be retained.

17 Block, *Gods of the Nations*, 125-61; Kutsko, *Between Heaven and Earth*, 101-49.

18 Ibid., 121. This idea is found in the *mīs pî* ritual which includes recitation of "the incantation, 'Born in heaven by his own power'" (Michael B. Dick, ed. *Born in Heaven, Made on Earth: The Making of the Cult Image in the Ancient Near East* [Winona Lake, Ind.: Eisenbrauns, 1999], 79, 89). Esarhaddon also "describes more than two hundred gods 'truly born' in the Temple of Assur, and concludes with their trip to Babylon and a reference to the *pīt pî* ceremony" (Kutsko, *Between Heaven and Earth*, 121). For the connections between this ritual and Ezekiel see James M. Kennedy, "Hebrew *Pithôn Peh* in the Book of Ezekiel," *VT* 41 (1991): 233-35, and Gregory Y.

noted by Kutsko, is the absence of direct textual evidence for this practice in the Neo-Babylonian period.

Despite differences, both the Neo-Assyrian and Neo-Babylonian
texts appeal to Marduk to substantiate their military campaigns.[19] C. L.
Crouch demonstrates that the Neo-Assyrian kings connected their military efforts, especially those campaigns that maintained their authority
across the empire, to the depiction of Marduk's battle against chaos in
the *Enūma eliš*.[20] Sargon II, for instance, justifies his campaigns thus:

> Sargon is supporting his actions by simultaneously referring to *Enūma eliš*
> and identifying himself with the god of justice. This is in keeping with *the
> cosmic framework of warfare characteristic of all the Assyrian kings* as well as
> with Sargon's special interest in justice.[21]

If the Assyrian kings considered it possible and appropriate to compare
their actions to Marduk in *Enūma eliš*—an effort that required complex
explanations about the relationship of Aššur (patron god of Assyria) to
Marduk[22]—then it is reasonable to deduce that similar appeals would
have been made by Babylonian kings.

It is therefore noteworthy that *Enūma eliš* indicates that those
deities defeated by Marduk were captured and stripped of their power,
but probably not killed. Tablet IV, lines 115-128, of *Enūma eliš* describe
Marduk's successful battle against Tiamat and her cohort:

> As for the eleven creatures, the ones adorned with glories,
> And the demonic horde, which all went at her side,
> He put on lead ropes, he bound their arms.
> He trampled them under, together with their belligerence.

Glazov, *The Bridling of the Tongue and the Opening of the Mouth in Biblical Prophecy*
(JSOTSup 311; Sheffield: Sheffield Academic Press, 2001), 220-74.

A similar ritual was used in Egypt. Although Lorton has questioned its connection
to birth and birth rituals (Dick, ed., *Born in Heaven*, 165-66), Roth has presented
strong evidence for this connection (Ann Macy Roth, "The *pss-kf* and the 'Opening of
the Mouth' Ceremony: A Ritual of Birth and Rebirth," *JEA* 78 [1992]: 113-47; cf. Ann
Macy Roth, "Fingers, Stars, and the 'Opening of the Mouth': The Nature and Function of the *ntrjw*-Blades," *JEA* 79 [1993]: 57-79).

19   See David S. Vanderhooft, *The Neo-Babylonian Empire and Babylon in the Latter
     Prophets* (HSM 59; Atlanta, Ga.: Scholars Press, 1999), 34-41, on the differences.

20   C. L. Crouch, *War and Ethics in the Ancient Near East: Military Violence in Light of Cos-
     mology and History* (BZAW 407; Berlin: de Gruyter, 2009), especially pp. 119-55.

21   Ibid., 50; emphasis added.

22   Ibid., 48-52

As for Qingu, who was trying to be great among them,
He captured him and reckoned him among the doomed.
He took away from him the tablet of destinies that he had no right to,
He sealed it with a seal and affixed it to his chest.

Having captured his enemies and triumphed,
Having shown the mighty foe subservient,
Having fully achieved Anshar's victory over his enemies,
Valiant Marduk having attained what Nudimmud desired,

He made firm his hold over the captured gods,
Then turned back to Tiamat whom he had captured.[23]

Commentators disagree over how to translate the statement in line 120 (in italics above) about Qingu's fate: Philippe Talon represents one position, placing Qingu "in the number of the dead gods;"[24] Benjamin Foster, whose translation is given above, illustrates the other view that only dooms Qingu, without killing him off. The evidence favors Foster's reading, something that Alexander Heidel recognized when he noted that Tiamat, Qingu, and the other deities are described as captured, not dead, in the immediately following lines.[25] This explanation also fits with the subsequent decision to kill both Tiamat and Qingu, not to do something with their already lifeless corpses. Thus, it seems that the Neo-Babylonians understood the defeat of a deity resulted in their capture and the elimination of that deity's power, but probably not their actual death.

In view of this evidence, it is probable that the Babylonians interpreted the events of 597 and 587 B.C.E. thus: the capture and deportation of Jehoiachin in 597 B.C.E. represented Nebuchadrezzar's victory over chaos (a defiant, foreign society)[26] in the model of Marduk's victory over Tiamat; the installation of Zedekiah and the imposition of the loyalty oath upon him denoted Nebuchadrezzar's strategy for maintaining

---

23 "The Babylonian Epic of Creation," translated by Benjamin R. Foster (*COS* 1.111: I.398), tablet IV, ll. 115-28; textual arrangement follows Philippe Talon, *The Standard Babylonian Creation Myth Enūma Eliš: Introduction, Cuneiform Text, Transliteration, and Sign List with a Translation and Glossary in French* (State Archives of Assyria Cuneiform Texts 4; Helsinki: The Neo-Assyrian Text Corpus Project, 2005), 55, 93-4.

24 Ibid., 94.

25 Alexander Heidel, *The Babylonian Genesis: The Story of Creation* (2 ed. Chicago: University of Chicago Press, 1951), 41, n. 89.

26 Crouch, *War and Ethics*, 21-22.

order; Zedekiah's subsequent rebellion suggested that chaos was creeping back into the cosmos, but that infiltration was stopped in 587 B.C.E. through the capture and deportation of Zedekiah; finally, the accompanying destruction of Jerusalem, the demolition of its temple, and the removal of its sacred equipment signified the eradication of a chaotic force; at the same time, on the cosmic plane, these events constituted Marduk's capture and imprisonment of YHWH, which neutered Judah's patron deity of all power and eviscerated any logic for Yahwistic worship.

These notions lurk just out of view when the audience hears the interpretation of the allegory on the divine plane in vv. 19-21. If vv. 16-18 contained an entirely predictable interpretation of the events, vv. 19-21 offer anything but a conventional construal. Greenberg observes about vv. 19-21:

> Just when the meaning of the fable seems to have been exhausted, *laken* (vs. 19) advises us that only now have we arrived at the consequential part of the oracle. A messenger formula announces the new message, which begins with a second oath by God. This passage appears to depict the celestial plane of the earthly events predicted in B1. As the mere agent of God, the Babylonian king has disappeared; God alone is the author of punishment, and when it occurs it will be recognized as his decree (vs. 21b).[27]

The surprising assertion about the "celestial plane" is that YHWH is not a captive; it is YHWH, not Marduk, who thwarted Zedekiah's resistance by bringing Nebuchadrezzar to Jerusalem.[28] In other words, YHWH, not Marduk, is the deity upon whom the Babylonian king's military victory is modeled. YHWH is the deity who maintains order against the forces of chaos in the cosmos.[29]

This situation is underscored by the introduction of a new image: v. 20 indicates YHWH will enact judgment by spreading out his net (ופרשתי עליו רשתי) and seizing Zedekiah within it (ונתפש במצודתי). YHWH rarely employs this weapon, and outside Ezekiel it appears only at Hos 7:12, where the northern kingdom is judged for relying upon Egypt and Assyria.[30] Inside Ezekiel, it occurs twice more in judgment

27 Greenberg, *Ezekiel 1-20*, 319.

28 In order to depict the Babylonian king as the human agent of YHWH, Ezekiel is forced to transform the role that the Judahite king traditionally played in the cosmos. For a full treatment of this topic, see Crouch and Strine, "YHWH's Battle Against Chaos."

29 Cf. Crouch, *War and Ethics*, 65-96.

30 The net, albeit rare, is one of several weapons in YHWH's arsenal associated with fishing. Elsewhere, the enemy, the sea or a sea monster, is met with רשת (12:13; 17:20;

upon Judah's king (12:13; 19:8) and once against Egypt (32:3).[31] The significance of this image follows from its role in Mesopotamia,[32] especially in *Enūma eliš*. The net is one of Marduk's weapons employed to defeat Tiamat, a victory that results in the elevation of Marduk to the head of the divine pantheon.

In Tablet IV, lines 35-44, where Marduk's preparation for battle with Tiamat is narrated, it reads:

> He made the bow, appointed it his weapon,
> He mounted the arrow, set it on the string.
> He took up the mace, held it in his right hand,
> Bow and quiver he slung on his arm.

> Thunderbolts he set before his face,
> With raging fire he covered his body.
> *Then he made a net to enclose Tiamat within,*
> He deployed the four winds that none of her might escape:

> South Wind, North Wind, East Wind, West Wind,
> Gift of his grandfather Anu; he fastened the net at his side.
> He made ill wind, whirlwind, cyclone,
> Four-ways wind, seven-ways wind, destructive wind, irresistible wind.[33]

19:8; 32:3) or חרנים (26:5, 14; 47:10), and the snare, (12:13; 17:20) מצודה or (19:4, 8) שׁחת. Even hooks, חחים (19:4, 9)—sometimes hooks applied to the opponent's jaws (38:4; 29:4) חחים בלחייך—serve as one of YHWH's weapons.

31   On YHWH's kingship in relationship to the oracles against Egypt, see Crouch, "Ezekiel's Oracles Against the Nations," 473-92.

32   Bodi, *Ezekiel and the Poem of Erra*, 162-82.

33   "The Babylonian Epic of Creation," translated by Benjamin R. Foster (*COS* 1.111: I.397), tablet IV, lines 35-44, emphasis added. Textual arrangement follows Talon, *Enūma Eliš*, 92. See also tablet VI, lines 80-4 where the net is placed with the bow in the presence of the gods as demonstration of Marduk's as evidence of his feat. Thorkild Jacobsen, *The Treasures of Darkness: A History of Mesopotamian Religion* (New Haven, Conn.: Yale University Press, 1976), 167-91, offers a succinct description of the story and of the role of the net and bow (p. 182).

A similar role is ascribed to the net ("*saparru 1b, 5b,*" *CAD* 15:161-2) of the gods in their judgment of Assurbanipal's enemies, demonstrating the applicability of this image for Ezek 17 (Maximilian Streck, *Assurbanipal und die letzten assyrischen Könige bis zum untergange Nineveh's* [Vorderasiatische Bibliothek 7.2; Leipzig: Hinrich, 1916], 37). The image is not limited to deities, as Esarhaddon claims the concept for himself in one of his inscriptions (Borger, *Inschriften Asarhaddons*, 58).

YHWH's use of this rarely mentioned weapon represents a challenge to the Babylonian ideology. The net that carried Zedekiah to Babylon does not belong to Marduk, but resides in YHWH's hand. Ezekiel subtly co-opts an attribute applied to Marduk and rehearsed to a public audience during the *akītu* element of the Babylonian new year festival in order to express YHWH's action. Greenberg is correct to remark:

> the divine oath introducing the earthly interpretaion of the fable, and expressing God's guarantee that the suzerain will vindicate his violated compact, is given a new dimension by the parallel oath introducing the divine plane of events. Events on the two planes are indeed parallel and simultaneous: for his own reasons Nebudchadnezzar will punish the Judahite rebel, but in doing so he will (all unknown to him) be executing the design of the divine architect of history upon the king responsible for violation of his covenant with Judah.[34]

He misses the larger point nonetheless, specifically that when Ezekiel asserts this is the real state of affairs he is challenging the way the dominant Babylonian powers claimed the world works. Taken seriously, Ezekiel's claim is radical. It is the sort of subversive proposal that would not be tolerated in the public transcript. However, made in this oblique fashion, it is unlikely to arouse a punitive response.

(c) Ezek 17:22-24

It is widely recognized that the climactic section of Ezek 17 offers a statement of hope for the future of Judah, but it goes essentially unnoticed that vv. 22-24 offers further evidence that Ezek 17 is consciously portraying YHWH in images typically reserved for Marduk.

Cosmological imagery is evident throughout the restoration oracle. For instance, v. 22 indicates that YHWH will take a cedar twig and plant it "on the high mountain of Israel" (בהר מרום ישראל) so that it can grow into a noble cedar (ארז אדיר; v. 23). This imagery is redolent of the "cosmic tree," a metaphor used in the ancient Near East to suggest a properly functioning, divinely ordered creation. It is likely, furthermore, that "the high mountain of Israel" means to evoke the mountaintop from where the chief deity rules. It seems the author wants to place this cedar tree on Mt Zion without saying it explicitly. Though Ezekiel's relationship to the Zion tradition is difficult to define, in this

---

34   Greenberg, *Ezekiel 1-20*, 323.

instance it appears pleased to draw on its connotations that YHWH reigns in the divine realm for its larger point.

The strongest connection to *Enūma eliš* is in v. 24. YHWH restores Judah so that "all the trees of the field," an image of foreign kings as a metonymy for their nations,[35] "shall recognize that 'I am YHWH: I make low the exalted tree and I make high the lowly tree... I am YHWH: I have spoken and I will act'" (Ezek 17:24; cf. 21:31). Note the striking similarity to Tablet IV, lines 5-8, of *Enūma eliš*:

> O Marduk, you are the most important among the great gods,
> Your destiny is unrivalled, your command is supreme!
> Henceforth your command cannot be changed,
> To raise high, to bring low, this shall be your power.[36]

Just as Ezekiel had subversive intent when it handed Marduk's net to YHWH and when it made YHWH the divine force behind Nebuchadrezzar's actions, so too here when it summarizes YHWH's power in almost verbatim terms to Marduk's. Subtle this polemic may be, but faint-hearted it is not.

It is reasonable to ask whether all these images are intentional allusions to Marduk's depiction in *Enūma eliš*. Proving that beyond any doubt is impossible. It is, however, remarkable that the two key images—YHWH's use of the net and the description of YHWH's ability to raise up and bring low—both occur in Tablet IV of *Enūma eliš*, less than 30 lines apart. Additionally, the public use of *Enūma eliš* lends itself to this sort of adoption and adaption in the hidden transcript. Scott shows that the hidden transcript "never becomes a language apart... it is in constant dialogue—more accurately, in argument—with dominant values."[37] As a central component of the annual new year celebration and probably one of its most memorable, well-attended events, the recitation of the *Enūma eliš* made it a particularly prominent component of the public transcript.[38] This prominent position makes it a likely, even obvious, source of language and images from which the hidden transcript could draw.

---

35 Ibid., 316; Block, *Ezekiel 1–24*, 552.

36 "The Babylonian Epic of Creation," Foster (*COS* 1.111: I.397), tablet IV, lines 5-8.

37 Scott, *Domination*, 135.

38 Ibid., 46 discusses the importance of official events, especially parades and royal coronations, for the affirmation of power. The recitation of the *Enūma eliš* combines those two types of events, suggesting that it was an especially important site for the dissemination of the public transcript.

(d) Hidden Transcript in Ezek 17

It is worth pausing briefly to outline the features of the hidden transcript in Ezek 17, both to clarify the argument and to lay down a few markers for the other relevant passages.

First, at the surface level Ezek 17 is a sharp critique of other Judahites. Zedekiah is the target of this passage, and it is easy to become so focused on the problems Ezekiel raises with the Judahite leadership and the Davidic monarchy that other issues fade away entirely. Perhaps this is precisely the point. Zedekiah is pointedly condemned so that attention is diverted from other issues, for instance how the images used for Yʜwʜ exhibit a striking overlap with those used for Marduk. This is not to say that Ezekiel lacks sincerity in its censure of Zedekiah, only that it took advantage of the attention it attracted in order to make another controversial point in a place where it was unlikely to stand out.

Second, Ezekiel presents its challenge to the public transcript in polysemous language. In the case of Ezek 17, the ambiguity derives from the image-rich nature of the text and the implicit statement made by its structure, in which the "as I live" authenticating element plays a critical role. The allegory (vv. 1-10) itself is open to many interpretations, evidence of which is the rhetorical question of v. 12, "Do you not know what these things mean?" The same is true of the description of events in the divine realm (v. 19-21), where the net, snare, and sword could all have multiple referents. The indication that something more pointed is being said arises from the parallel structure, in which the actions of the king of Babylon and Yʜwʜ are joined. Yet, upon scrutiny from the dominant group, the imagery could be plausibly attributed to a general knowledge of kingship metaphors and the importance of the parallel structure might quickly be attributed to chance. The polemical interpretation is accidental, one could argue, not indicative of subversive intent.

Third, it is precisely this possibility of interpreting Ezek 17 in multiple ways that makes it part of the hidden transcript. Because of the threat of coercive, penal action from the dominant class, an important trait of the "cooked" version of the hidden transcript is the ability to give it an innocuous meaning in the face of interrogation from the dominant group. Should it suit one to do so, it is easy enough to argue that Ezek 17 is consistent with the Babylonian view that Marduk is the chief deity of Babylon and that Yʜwʜ, by virtue of Jerusalem's defeat and destruction, is a vassal to him. On one side, Ezek 17 portrays the Babylonian king, Marduk's earthly representative, in positive terms. This

affirms the public transcript. On the other side, YHWH is presented as
judging the Judahite king for rebellion against Babylon, an action that
surely supports the dominant ideology. Any impression that YHWH is
presented as a challenge to, much less a replacement for Marduk, could
be denied, made out to be an unintentional consequence of depicting
YHWH as a participant in Marduk's plan.

     If this sounds like speaking out of both sides of one's mouth, that
is both true and fundamental to the argument. Scott explains that subaltern groups are characterized as cunning or deceptive across time and
place. This reputation is a result of the way in which the hidden
transcript seeps into public discourse with subtle and indirect expressions. Scott describes this as a "verbal facility" that allows the oppressed "to conduct what amounts to a veiled discourse of dignity and
self-assertion within the public transcript."[39] The modes of concealment are, he writes:

> limited only by the imaginative capacity of subordinates. The degree of
> disguise, however, that elements of the hidden transcript and their bearers
> must assume to make a successful intrusion into the public transcript will
> probably increase if the political environment is very threatening and very
> arbitrary. Here we must above all recognize that the creation of disguises
> depends on an agile, firm grasp of the codes of meaning being manipulat-
> ed. It is impossible to overestimate the subtlety of this manipulation.[40]

This is important because of the possibility that the dominant group
would interrogate the subaltern about the intent of their statements.
Then, the ambiguity of the text allows for the innocuous interpretation
to protect those who speak it against punishment. Or, as Scott writes:

> what permits subordinate groups to undercut the authorized cultural
> norms is the fact that cultural expression by virtue of its polyvalent sym-
> bolism and metaphor lends itself to disguise. By the subtle use of codes
> one can insinuate into a ritual, a pattern of dress, a song, a story, meanings
> that are accessible to one intended audience and opaque to another audi-
> ence the actors wish to exclude. Alternatively, the excluded (and in this
> case, powerful) audience may grasp the seditious message in the perfor-
> mance but find it difficult to react because that sedition is clothed in terms
> that can also lay claim to a perfectly innocent construction.[41]

---

39   Ibid., 137.
40   Ibid., 139.
41   Ibid., 159.

The book of Ezekiel qualifies, on the evidence in Ezek 17, as the sort of subaltern voice that warrants a reputation for cunning and deception. The vulnerability of the Judahite exiles to Babylonian power did not permit them "the luxury of direct confrontation."[42] In order to recognize the resistant language contained within the book of Ezekiel, it is necessary to heed Scott's guidance that "[i]f we wish to hear this side of the dialogue we shall have to learn its dialect and codes."[43] In the case of Ezek 17, that code involves a subtle yet distinct borrowing of images from Marduk's persona in *Enūma eliš* supported by a textual arrangement that employs the "as I live" formula to implicitly present the Babylonian king as Yhwh's human agent.

In sum, simultaneous with expressing a view about the guilt of the Davidic monarchy and its future prospects, Ezek 17:1-24 also asserts the enduring vitality of Yhwh despite external indications to the contrary. Thus, Block is surely correct to comment that "this oracle is not about Davidic imperialism; it is about the cosmic sovereignty and fidelity of Yahweh."[44] More pointedly, it is about attributing sovereignty in the divine realm to Yhwh against the Babylonian claim to that role for Marduk.

Ezekiel 17 is not the only place the hidden transcript surfaces, so attention shall now be given to the presentation of Yhwh as the shepherd of Israel in Ezek 34.

3. The True Shepherd: Ezek 34:1-16

Ezekiel 34 symbolizes Judah's leaders as failed shepherds whose conduct Yhwh can no longer tolerate.[45] In response, God will rescue his flock and personally take up the leadership of his people. This is described in vv. 1-16 through numerous allusions to the exodus tradition, an exemplary time in Yhwh's leadership over Israel.

In order to appreciate how the passage presents its message it is first necessary to observe the way that it evokes the exodus tradition. Like those passages discussed in the last chapter that deal with the future of Yhwh's land, Ezek 34 is heavily indebted to the language of Dᴛʀ

---

42   Ibid., 136.

43   Ibid., 138.

44   Block, *Ezekiel 1–24*, 552.

45   The identity of the failed shepherds is widely debated. Although the resolution of this question is not determinative for this study, the relationship between Ezek 34 and Jer 23:1-8 suggests they are a succession of Davidic kings.

and H. For instance, Ezek 34:4 describes the shepherds' conduct in the same way as Pharaoh is portrayed in Exodus (Exod 1:13) and with language Lev 25 uses to prohibit the treatment of fellow Israelites (Lev 25:43, 46).[46] Lemke observes, "Ezekiel's polemic is thus quite pointed. He accuses Israel's rulers of doing what their own history should have taught them to abhor and what the law of Moses expressly forbade!"[47]

Leviticus 25 is also pertinent because it specifies that such indentured service shall last only until the jubilee year. By evoking this prescription, Ezek 34 insinuates that such bondage is a fixed period that is followed by a return to YHWH's ordained order. This temporal schema is mirrored by Ezek 34's promise of restoration, which vv. 11-12 indicate comes after a time of exile that begins "on a day of cloud and gloom" (ביום ענן וערפל).

This is not the only legal instruction to which Ezek 34 makes reference, for, as Levitt Kohn notes, it also transforms the DTR command to care for a neighbors livestock. "[T]he prophet condemns the 'shepherds of Israel' for various negligent actions, including failing to restore stray sheep to the flock..., directly commanded in Deut 22.1,"[48] Levitt Kohn points out.

Finally, Ezek 34:13 describes YHWH's actions as the shepherd who finds and returns the purified flock with the verbal root נצל. It was noted earlier that this term has strong links to the exodus tradition.[49] Zimmerli found the theme so prominent that he commented, "From the point of view of its thought, this oracle [34:17-22] comes close to the oracle in 20:32ff, especially 20:35-38. There, in the context of the new exodus, reference was made also to a judgment of separation in which the godless would be weeded out."[50] In these various ways Ezek 34 uses portions of the exodus tradition to craft its polemic against the Judahite leaders.

Ezekiel 34 is also similar to Ezek 17 on the surface: it engages in an intra-Judahite polemic. It is likely this explicit objective made it appear to be of minimal consequence to the Babylonians. Indeed, the recurring indictment of the royal leaders of Judah indicates that the condemna-

---

46 Levitt Kohn, *A New Heart and a New Soul*, 67, 97; Iain M. Duguid, *Ezekiel and the Leaders of Israel* (VTSup 56; Leiden: Brill, 1994), 39.

47 Werner E. Lemke, "Life in the Present and Hope for the Future," *Int* 38 (1984): 173, note 10.

48 Levitt Kohn, *A New Heart and a New Soul*, 97.

49 Zimmerli, *Ezekiel 25–48*, 216.

50 Ibid., 217.

tion of Zedekiah in Ezek 17 is not far from view.[51] Like that passage, and those addressed in the preceding chapter, Ezek 34 is another instance where Ezekiel seeks to dictate the intra-Judahite public transcript. Fitting the pattern outlined above, Ezek 34 rebukes the behavior of the shepherds (vv. 3-4), which it connects to specific divine prescriptions (Lev 25; Deut 22) in order to imply a lack of theological knowledge, all while mocking their self-ascribed image as shepherds over the people.

Just as there was activity at more than one level in Ezek 17, there is more than one objective for the text of Ezek 34. Tracing Ezek 34's connections to both the exodus tradition and the shepherd image in the ancient Near East demonstrate that this passage also contains a hidden polemic in which YHWH, not Marduk, is the deity in control of events in the earthly realm.

Granting that the links to the exodus tradition in Ezek 34 are not as explicit as elsewhere in Ezekiel, Zimmerli is nonetheless justified to characterize it as an important part of Ezekiel's second exodus theme. It is justifiable to ask how the exodus tradition's portrayal of YHWH vis-à-vis foreign deities can inform interpretation here. YHWH's conflict with various Egyptian gods is, therefore, a pertinent parallel.

Thomas Dozeman outlines how the plague narrative and defeat of Pharaoh in Exod 7–15 implicitly depicts YHWH accomplishing those things typically attributed to key Egyptian deities.[52] For instance, the plague of frogs pits YHWH against Heket, the Egyptian goddess of life who is symbolized with a frogs head. This symbol is only one indication of the conflict, which is perhaps more pointed in relation to the life and death of children: this theme, already in view from Exod 1:15-22, pits YHWH's power against Heket's responsibility for granting children.[53] Fertility and childbirth also make Bes a probable rival to YHWH. Bes, Dozeman observes, is the Egyptian god of fertility and family protection.[54] Thus, it is relevant that the passover must be celebrated as a family (בית אב; Exod 12:3) so that the first-born child of each household might survive. When the Egyptians fail to do so, the death of their first-born children appears an indictment of Bes, who is responsible for family protection. Direct evidence that the plague narrative tradition envisions this sort of divine contest comes in Exod 8:10, where the in-

---

51   Joyce, *Ezekiel*, 196.

52   Thomas B. Dozeman, *Commentary on Exodus* (The Eerdmans Critical Commentary; Grand Rapids, Mich.: Eerdmans, 2009), 176-344.

53   Ibid., 221.

54   Ibid.

tent of the plagues is so that Pharaoh will recognize that "there is none like YHWH our god."[55] That tone is reinforced by the formula of self-recognition that carries a "polemical intent,"[56] prominent in Ezekiel but also important to Exodus. Ezek 34, like the tradition in Exod 1–15, tacitly presents YHWH as more powerful than foreign deities and committed to redeeming Israel from oppression in a foreign nation.

This concern is also an important connotation of the shepherd imagery used in Ezek 34. A prevalent ancient Near Eastern image for deities and kings,[57] there is evidence the metaphor originated in Mesopotamia,[58] a possibility for which the Sumerian King List[59] and the Code of Hammurabi provide evidence.[60] Marduk, notably, is granted this role in *Enūma eliš* (Tablet VI, line 95-108):

> Then the great gods convened,
> They made Marduk's destiny highest, they prostrated themselves.
> They laid upon themselves a curse (if they broke the oath),
> *With water and oil they swore, they touched their throats.*

---

55 תדע כי־אין כיהוה אלהינו; Exod 8:6 [ET v. 10].

56 Ibid., 197, following Zimmerli, *I Am Yahweh*, 83-87. The formula of self-introduction (I am YHWH) occurs at Exod 6:2, 6–8, 29; 7:5, 17; 8:18; 10:2; 12:12; 14:4, 18; 15:26; the recognition formula appears ten times in this section, specifically Exod 6:7; 7:5, 17; 8:6, 18; 9:14, 29; 10:2; 14:4, 18.

57 It is, indeed, a common title employed by Nebuchadrezzar; cf. Vanderhooft, *Neo-Babylonian Empire*, 34-41.

58 "Another point to be noted is its absence — as far as I know — in Ugaritic and Canaanite literature. Not even are the verbs פוץ and קבץ found in Ugaritic or in the entire West Semitic corpus. It would seem, therefore, as if the occurrence of this theme in the Old Testament is due to the direct influence of Mesopotamian civilization," Geo Widengren, "Yahweh's Gathering of the Dispersed," in *In the Shelter of Elyon: Essays on Ancient Palestinian Life and Literature in Honor of G.W. Ahlström* (eds. W. Boyd Barrick and John R. Spencer; Jsotsup 31; Sheffield: JSOT Press, 1984), 239.

59 "Dumuzid, the shepherd, ruled for 36000 years" (line 15) in J.A. Black et al., "The Electronic Text Corpus of Sumerian Literature: The Sumerian King List Translation," Cited 26 August 2010. Online: http://www-etcsl.orient.ox.ac.uk/section2/tr211.htm.

60 "I am Hammurabi, the shepherd, selected by the god Enlil, he who heaps high abundance and plenty, who perfects every possible thing for the city Nippur, (the city known as) band-of-heaven-and-earth, the pious provider of the Ekur temple; the capable king, the restorer of the city Eridu, the purifier of the rites of the Eabzu temple; the onslaught of the four regions of the world, who magnifies the reputation of the city Babylon, who gladdens the heart of his divine lord Marduk, whose days are devoted to the Esagil temple" ("The Laws of Hammurabi," translated by Martha Roth [*COS* 2.131:335-53], tablet I, line 50, to tablet II, line 12).

They granted him exercise of kingship over the gods,
They established him forever for lordship of heaven and earth.
Anshar gave him an additional name, Asalluhi,
"When he speaks, we shall all do obeisance,

At his command the gods shall pay heed.
His word shall be supreme above and below,
The son, our champion, shall be the highest.
His lordship shall be supreme, he shall have no rival,

He shall be the shepherd of the black-headed folk, his creatures.
They shall tell of his ways, without forgetting, in the future.[61]

Beyond the shepherd imagery, it is notable that this passage also portrays the other deities swearing upon their lives to install Marduk into
this position. This brings the Akkadian *nīš X* oath formula and its
connections to the "as I live" authenticating element into view. Combined with the public use of *Enūma eliš* in the new year celebrations,
this makes it a logical and readily available background for the material
in Ezek 34.

The shepherd image, popular in the late Neo-Assyrian period,[62] remains prominent through the Neo-Babylonian empire[63] and into the
Persian period. In this latter stage, it occurs in the *Cyrus Cylinder*:

*And he (Cyrus) shepherded with justice and righteousness all the black-headed
people*, over whom he (Marduk) had given him victory. Marduk, the great
lord, guardian (?) of his people, looked with gladness upon his good deeds
and upright heart. He ordered him to march to his city Babylon.

... From [Ninev]eh (?), Ashur and Susa, Agade, Eshnunna, Zamban, Metur-
nu, Der, as far as the region of Gutium, I returned the (images of) the gods
to the sacred centers [on the other side of] the Tigris whose sanctuaries had
been abandoned for a long time, and I let them dwell in eternal abodes. *I*

---

61 "The Babylonian Epic of Creation," translated by Benjamin R. Foster (*COS* 1.111:
I.401-2), tablet VI, lines 95-108. Emphasis added. Textual arrangement follows
Talon, *Enūma Eliš*, 101.

62 M. Nevader, "Exile and Institution: Monarchy in the Books of Deuteronomy and
Ezekiel" (Unpublished D.Phil Thesis, University of Oxford, 2009), 146; forthcoming
as idem., *YHWH Versus David* (OTM; Oxford: OUP, 2013).

63 See "Nebuchadnezzar II's Restoration of the Ebabbar Temple in Larsa," translated
by *Paul-Alain Beaulieu* (*COS* 2.122A:308-9) and "Nebuchadnezzar II's Restoration of
E-Urmin-Ankia, the Ziggurat of Borsippa," *idem* (*COS* 2.122B:309-10).

gathered all their inhabitants and returned (to them) their dwellings. In addition, at the command of Marduk, the great lord, I settled in their habitations, in pleasing abodes, the gods of Sumer and Akkad, whom Nabonidus, to the anger of the lord of the gods, had brought into Babylon.[64]

The *Cyrus Cylinder* demonstrates the convergence of several relevant themes. Cyrus, acting as an agent of Marduk, is depicted as the shepherd whose just rule extends to the cultic sphere, where he restores and returns captured images, presumably defiled while in Babylon, to their "eternal" homes.[65] What is more, as shepherd he is the one who gathers the dispersed inhabitants of these places and returns them to their native land. This may be the most important connotation of the image for YHWH's portrayal in Ezek 34: the shepherd as gatherer of dispersed people.

YHWH is the shepherd that will seek out his flock in the various places they have been scattered (v. 11). In a detailed analysis of this theme, Geo Widengren establishes a connection between this idea in Mesopotamia, expressed with the Akkadian *sapāḫu* (to scatter), and in the Hebrew Bible, which uses the verbal roots פוץ and זרה. Of the two Hebrew terms, פוץ is by far the more common, occurring throughout the Pentatuech (Gen 11:4, 8; Num 10:35; Deut 4:27; 28:64; 30:3; Ps 106:26-27) and frequently in Ezekiel (Ezek 11:16; 12:15; 20:23, 34, 41; 22:15; 29:12, 13; 30:23, 26; 34:5, 12, 21; 36:19; 46:18), including three times in Ezek 34. By comparison, זרה is employed this way only once in the Pentateuch (Lev 26:33), but nine times in Ezekiel (Ezek 5:2, 10; 6:5, 8; 12:14; 20:23; 22:15; 36:19; concerning Egypt, 29:12), five times in parallel with פוץ (12:14; 20:23; 22:15; 29:12; 36:19; cf. Ps 106:27). The Akkadian term for gathering, *paḫāru*,[66] corresponds to קבץ and אסף in Hebrew. The verbal root קבץ is far more prevalent in Ezekiel, where it is employed nine times in this fashion (Ezek 11:17; 20:34, 41; 28:25; 34:13; 36:24; 37:21; 39:27; concerning Egypt, 29:13). By contrast, אסף occurs this way only once (Ezek 11:17), and then it is in parallel with קבץ, suggesting it may only be selected because it is the best available synonym. Widengren summarizes the implications of the parallels in language and theme: "It is obvious that there existed in the Ancient Near East a general idea that the deity was ready to gather and restore the dispersed people (or clan or family) to its place."[67]

---

64   "Cyrus Cylinder," translated by Mordechai Cogan (*COS* 2.124: 314-16), lines 9-19.

65   See Widengren,"Yahweh's Gathering," 236.

66   *"paḫāru* 1c" *CAD* 12:27. Widengren lists it as *puḫḫuru*.

67   Widengren,"Yahweh's Gathering," 238.

Further evidence suggests these gatherings were implemented through a royal decree called the *mīšaru*-act. Widengren remarks:

> As a setting in life of such royal proclamations it would seem appropriate to suggest the promulgation of an act of justice, a *mīšaru*-act, a legislative act already existing in Old Babylonian times. The ruler promulgated such an act in order to restore a disturbed order, to re-establish *mīšaru*, 'justice', in society and in the world... He, as representative of the deity, would have carried out the gathering of the dispersed.[68]

Indeed, Widengren argues that the *Cyrus Cylinder* is indicative of a *mīšaru*-act declared upon the capture of Babylon. Yet, this theme reaches beyond the legal realm and is also invoked in the new year festival. In an *akītu* ritual written for use in Babylon, the king testifies to the success of his reign by proclaiming "I have not destroyed Babylon, not commanded its scattering."[69] Although this limited evidence must be used with care, when it is added to the strong indications that there is a connection between Ezekiel and *Enūma eliš*, especially in the related passage of Ezek 17, it is noteworthy.

Madhavi Nevader argues that these images of human kingship are relevant in Ezek 34:11-16 because "in acting as he does Yнwн is claiming to be Israel's king and only secondarily her deity. Yнwн, it would seem, is not presenting himself as Marduk, but as Hammurapi."[70] Nevader's contention, that Yнwн assumes unmediated divine kingship,[71] fits well within Ezekiel's larger theological viewpoint. Ezekiel's nearest counterpart, H, advocates precisely the same concept. Milgrom remarks on Lev 17–26: "The kingship of man is too dangerous per se. Better the kingship of Yнwн, who rewards those who obey his commandments with peace, prosperity and life."[72] Nevader stresses the human level of Yнwн's claims, and rightly so. But, the claim is also relevant on the divine level. After all, Yнwн, the divine king, adds to this

---

68 Ibid.

69 Ibid., 235; see M. Nevader, "Exile and Institution," 146, note 28, for discussion of this text.

70 Ibid., 147; cf. Vanderhooft, *Neo-Babylonian Empire*, 33-51, esp. 50-1, who shows that Nebuchadrezzar presents himself as a second Hammurapi underscores the relevance of this notion

71 "Reinstated under this new regime, Israel will flourish and the order compromised by a history of misbehaviour will be nullified through the instalment of Yнwн as king over Israel" (Ibid., 166).

72 Milgrom, *Leviticus 17–22*, 1416.

role the duties of the human king without, by any means, relinquishing divine kingship.[73]

By ascribing the roles of shepherd and gatherer of the dispersed to YHWH, the text places God in the role occupied by the kings and deities of Mesopotamia. This allows the book of Ezekiel to explain that the scattering of YHWH's people is not the result of his defeat and deportation to Babylon—the situation presumed by the *Cyrus Cylinder*—but a conscious choice of YHWH predicated upon the deficient leadership of his people.[74] Furthermore, rather than being incapacitated by his purported Babylonian captors, and as a consequence in need of a conquering liberator like Cyrus, YHWH remains fully capable of initiating the return of his presence and his people to Judah. Whether one interprets this as an outright denial of the Babylonian rhetoric (YHWH is king, therefore Marduk is not)[75] or merely a modification (Marduk may be king over Babylon and its people, but YHWH remains king over Judah and its people), it is part and parcel of Ezekiel's profession about YHWH's enduring vitality despite external indications to the contrary.

This issue—whether YHWH's power complements Marduk or supplants him—is critical to the question of monotheism and its development in ancient Israel and Judah. It is plausible to argue that the way in which Ezek 17 and 34 present YHWH as the deity who controls both the events unfolding in Judah and also determines the timing of the Judahites return from exile entails a universal control that is only compatible with a monotheistic viewpoint. On the other hand, a growing number of scholars argue that such statements of transnational control do not presume the sort of ontological claims that monotheism entails but only signify a monolatry of a "particularly potent stripe."[76] Further attention will be given to this question at the end of the chapter, but it must suffice for now to conclude that, irrespective of the position one takes on Ezekiel's relationship to monotheism, it undeniably uses the

---

73   This is not absent from the concerns of *Enūma eliš* either, which only five lines after calling Marduk shepherd of the people indicates that "[h]e shall make on earth the counterpart of what he brought to pass in heaven." "The Babylonian Epic of Creation," translated by Benjamin R. Foster (*COS* 1.111: I.402), tablet VI, line 112.

74   Block, *Gods of the Nations*, 150-61; Block, , 15-42.

75   Kutsko, for one, argues that the book of Ezekiel exhibits this sort of monotheism ("Ezekiel's Anthropology and Its Ethical Implications," in *The Book of Ezekiel: Theological and Anthropological Perspectives* [eds. Margaret S. Odell and John T. Strong; SBLSyms 9; Atlanta, Ga.: Society of Biblical Literature, 2000]).

76   Christopher R. Seitz, "The Divine Name in Christian Scripture," in *Word Without End: The Old Testament as Abiding Theological Witness* (Grand Rapids, Mich.: Eerdmans, 1998), 255.

metaphor of YHWH as shepherd to claim a far greater span of control for Judah's patron deity than the Babylonian public transcript would have allowed.

This contention corresponds with the book's radically theocentric perspective, a part of Ezek 34's message that Mein has recently emphasized:

> It may be better to understand YHWH's recovery and protection of his flock less as an expression of YHWH's love and compassion for his people (expressions which still remain absent from the text) and more as part of the demonstration of divine might that characterizes the restoration oracles more generally. The logic of the oracle is therefore of a piece with the refrain of ch. 36: 'it is not for your sake, O Israel, that I am about to do this, but for the sake of my holy name'.[77]

Mein's comments highlight the point made here: Ezek 34 is about YHWH's continued power, vitality, and ability to act in the human and divine realms. Because he arrives at this same point through a different route, Mein's conclusions reinforce the evidence raised here.

In view of all this, it is relevant to revisit the way in which the shepherd image functions in *Enūma eliš*. Marduk is presented as shepherd in order to illustrate that "his lordship shall be supreme, he shall have no rival" (Tablet VI, line 106). Transferring the image to YHWH infers transferring the ascription of divine sovereignty too. In a similar fashion to both Ezek 17 and the plague tradition in the exodus narrative, Ezek 34 has a polemical intent that it conceals in polysemous images and metaphors. The role of the "as I live" formula in this effort is limited by comparison to Ezek 17, though it contributes in two ways: first, combining with the other features noted above, it aids in evoking the exodus tradition of YHWH's victory over other deities; second, the first person form of the oath adds to the impression that YHWH remains powerful, active, and responsible for those who are obedient to him.

The remainder of the chapter, vv. 17-31, does not carry the argument forward as much as it starts "a second thought about the shepherd-flock metaphor."[78] It is notable nevertheless that Ezek 34 as a

---

77   Andrew Mein, "Profitable and Unprofitable Shepherds: Economic and Theological Perspectives on Ezekiel 34," *JSOT* 31 (2007): 502.

78   Greenberg, *Ezekiel 21-37*, 707. It seems probable that Greenberg is correct in concluding that these verses are a supplement to vv. 1-22 (Ibid.). Be this as it may, there is nothing that necessitates that they came from someone other than the author of vv. 1-22, although on the evidence available it seems that one must remain open to either option (cf. Zimmerli, *Ezekiel 25–48*, 220).

whole exhibits strong thematic similarities to Ezek 20:35-38.[79]   Consider the structural parallels:

Indictment of leaders for rebellious acts	20:1-26	34:1-6
Announcement of judgment	20:30-31	34:7-16
Description of future purifying judgment	20:32-38	34:17-22
Description of future life in the land	20:39-44	34:23-31

This resemblance points to the carefully planned arrangement often observed in the book of Ezekiel.[80]   Equally, it highlights the need to consider how Ezek 20 contributes to the book's challenge against Babylonian imperial ideology.

4. Return of the King: Ezek 20:32-44

In a similar fashion to Ezek 17 and Ezek 34, Ezek 20 presents an explicit critique of the Judahite community.   Indeed, Ezek 20 leaves no one within the history of Israel and Judah from Egypt to the fall of Jerusalem unscathed.   The tone changes little when attention turns to the present state of affairs in vv. 32-44.   Yet, there is more than just a trace of resistance against the presumed dominance of the Babylonian empire.   Ezekiel 20, in this way, fits the model identified in Ezek 17 and 34, namely in a passage that is explicitly an intra-Judahite polemic there lies just below the surface a polemic against the Babylonians.

The intent of Ezek 20:32-44 to challenge the Babylonian belief system is adumbrated in v. 23 where YHWH decides to scatter (פוץ) and disperse (זרה) Israel.   These terms are now familiar from the preceding exegesis of Ezek 34, where the evidence showed they are a way of ascribing to YHWH power attributed to Marduk (*Enūma eliš*, Tablet IV, line 106-8).   Similar language appears in Deuteronomy, which uses פוץ[81] twice to characterize YHWH's threat of judgment against the Is-

---

79   Ibid., 216; Allen, *Ezekiel 20–48*, 162-63.
80   Davis, *Swallowing the Scroll.*, gives a brief summary of her view pp. 37-9.
81   Gen 11:4, 8-9; Num 10:35; Deut 4:27; 28:64; 30:3; 1 Sam 11:11; 13:8; 14:34; 2 Sam 18:8; 20:22; 22:15; 1 Kgs 22:17; 2 Kgs 25:5; Isa 24:1; 41:16; Jer 9:15; 10:21; 13:24; 18:17; 23:1-2; 30:11; 40:15; 52:8; Ezek 11:16-17; 12:15; 20:23, 34, 41; 22:15; 28:25; 29:12-13; 30:23, 26; 34:5-6, 12, 21; 36:19; 46:18; Nah 2:2; Hab 3:14; Zeph 3:10; Zech 1:17; 13:7; Ps 18:15; 68:2; 144:6; Job 18:11; 37:11; 38:24; 40:11; Prov 5:16; Neh 1:8; 2 Chr 18:16.   Nearly half of these (21 of 49) come from DTR influenced texts: Deut 4:27; 28:64; 30:3; 1 Sam 11:11; 13:8; 14:34; 2 Sam 18:8; 20:22; 22:15; 1 Kgs 22:17; 2 Kgs 25:5; Isa 24:1; 41:16; Jer 9:15; 10:21; 13:24; 18:17; 23:1-2; 30:11; 40:15; 52:8; Zeph 3:10.

raelites (Deut 4:27; 28:64; cf. 30:3). Ezekiel, however, pairs פּוּץ with an uncommon synonym זרה,[82] which it takes from from Lev 26:33. These two terms appear together eight other times, but only twice outside Ezekiel.[83] The distinctive blend of DTR and H language is, by now, a familiar feature of Ezekiel.

The clearest indication that more than intra-Judahite issues are in view is the quotation in v. 32, which indicates a desire to be like the nations and the people of other lands (נהיה כגוים כמשפחות הארצות). YHWH's response is immediate and expressed in strongly defiant terms, a tone produced by the presence of the "as I live" authenticating element. Though this formula will not appear again in the chapter, its prominent position at the beginning of YHWH's speech indicates that it plays a crucial role in this section's message. Specifically, the "as I live" formula emphasizes that Judah's patron deity remains living and active, the same deity who accomplished the exodus from Egypt, a divine sovereign who control the exiles present situation and future experiences despite external evidence to the contrary.

The connection to Deuteronomy becomes far more important in the opening statement of Ezek 20:32-44, which condemns the idea of worshipping "wood and stone" (עץ ואבן; Deut 4:28; 28:64; Ezek 20:32). This language typifies the idol parodies in the Hebrew Bible. The polemic against image based worship is more often associated with Jeremiah (especially Jer 10) and Deutero-Isaiah (particularly Isa 44:9-22),[84] two texts that offer programmatic refutations of the practice and its foundational ritual text, the Mesopotamian mouth washing (*mīs pî*) ritual.[85] Nathaniel Levtow argues that this DTR classification of foreign divine images as wood and stone intends to assert a similar disdain for image based worship. Deuteronomy, argues Levtow, emphasizes "that, unlike Yahweh, 'the living god' (2 Kgs 19:16) who alone made heaven and

---

82 Ezek 5:2, 10, 12; 6:5, 8; 12:14-15; 20:23; 22:15; 29:12; 30:23, 26; 36:19. Deuteronomy employs the more common synonym נדח: Deut 4:19; 13:6, 11, 14; 19:5; 20:19; 22:1; 30:1, 4, 17; 2 Sam 14:13-14; 15:14; 2 Kgs 17:21; Isa 8:22; 11:12; 13:14; 16:3-4; 27:13; 56:8; Jer 8:3; 16:15; 23:2-3, 8; 24:9; 27:10, 15; 29:14, 18; 30:17; 32:37; 40:12; 43:5; 46:28; 49:5, 36; 50:17; Ezek 4:13; 34:4, 16; Joel 2:20; Mic 4:6; Zeph 3:19; Ps 5:11; 62:5; 147:2; Job 6:13; Prov 7:21; Dan 9:7; Neh 1:9; 2 Chr 13:9; 21:11.

83 Isa 41:16; Ezek 12:15; 20:23; 22:15; 29:12; 30:23, 26; 36:19. To this list should be added Ps 106:27 based upon the emendation from ולהפיל to ולהפיץ.

84 Block, *Ezekiel 1–24*, 649, note 179.

85 Dick, ed., *Born in Heaven*; Nathaniel B. Levtow, *Images of Others: Iconic Politics in Ancient Israel* (Biblical and Judaic Studies from the University of California, San Diego 11; Winona Lake, Ind.: Eisenbrauns, 2008); Blaženka Scheuer, *The Return of YHWH: The Tension between Deliverance and Repentance in Isaiah 40–55* (BZAW 377; Berlin: de Gruyter, 2008), 82-104.

earth (2 Kgs 19:15), these deities were never powerful, alive, and present in their cult images."[86]

Ezekiel 20:32-44 does not contain an explicit idol parody like its contemporaries Jeremiah and Deutero-Isaiah; rather, it presupposes that ideology and, instead of the hymnic characterization of YHWH as אלהים חיים (e.g. Deut 5:26), employs the "as I live" authenticating element to make the same point. The reference to the DTR characterization of other gods as wood and stone fits Ezekiel's comprehensive rejection of image based worship and indicates that it too endorses Deuteronomy's repeated call to abandon other gods (אלהים אחרים; esp. 28:64) and serve YHWH alone. Indeed, Ezek 20 makes the rejection of images and foreign deities the behavior necessary to demonstrate the repentance required to mark oneself out as part of the future community that will inhabit YHWH's land (Ezek 20:35-38).[87] This argument is predicated on the belief that "the Babylonian cult images are dead and powerless, whereas Yahweh is alive and powerful."[88]

Ezekiel's choice to assume the contents of the idol parody rather than to declare them openly is yet another indication that some portion of the hidden transcript is emerging in the public transcript at this point. Careful examination shows that Ezek 20:32-44 contains numerous concepts central to the idol parodies.

The first main concept is contained in the declaration that the images are merely wood and stone, the closest Ezekiel comes to openly voicing the polemic. Another indication that Ezek 20:32-44 is shaped by the idol parodies is the reference to YHWH's kingship. Commentators have long struggled for a solid explanation why the book of Ezekiel suddenly invokes divine kingship at precisely and only this point. The explicit appeal to kingship in Ezek 20:33 is entirely logical upon recognizing the text's goal to subvert the Babylonian mouth-opening ritual, in which "the ultimate goal of the *mīs pî* ritual was the enthronement"[89] of the deity. The annunciation of YHWH as king at this

---

86   Levtow, *Images of Others*, 146.

87   Cf. Strine, "Repentance in the Book of Ezekiel," 467-91.

88   Levtow, *Images of Others*, 80-85.

89   Ibid., 92. For this scheme Levtow relies upon the work of A. Berlejung, "Washing the Mouth: The Consecration of Divine Images in Mesopotamia," in *The Image and the Book: Iconic Cults, Aniconism, and the Rise of Book Religion in Israel and the Ancient Near East* (ed. K. van der Toorn; CBET 21; Leuven: Peeters, 1997).

     I note the connection, which remains unexplored at this time, between space in the *mīs pî* ritual and Ezekiel. Berlejung specifies the following locations in the *mīs pî* ritual: (1) workshop, (2) riverbank, (3) orchard, (4) temple gate, (5) Holy of Holies. The riverbank, temple gate and Holy of Holies, along with the choreographed move-point pushes that implicit point into clear view and it parallels a prominent feature in Deutero-Isaiah's idol parodies.[90]

Ambiguity remains nevertheless. Ezekiel states that YHWH reigns over the Judahites, but does not explicitly deny similar power to Marduk. The common notion of hierarchical divine pantheons in the ancient Near East, even at places in the Hebrew Bible (e.g. Deut 32:8-9; Ps 82) means that this statement is open to an interpretation in which it coincides with Babylonian hegemony. Were this the only evidence in Ezek 20 it would not be possible to conclude it is part of an implicit idol parody. In context with the other evidence, however, it does contribute to an anti-Marduk argument. Its ambiguity is a result of the asymmetric power structure that necessitates caution when voicing the hidden transcript.

To go further, Ezekiel again invokes shepherd imagery (v. 34) to specify that it is YHWH who will gather the dispersed exiles (cf. Ezek 34:11-16). Evidence for the connotations of this image in Ezekiel do not need rehearsing again, but it is worth noting that similar themes occur at important points in Deutero-Isaiah's case against image based worship (e.g. 40:10-11; cf. 45:13). Though there is evidence that vv. 32-44 were added to vv. 1-31 at some remove from their composition, in its present *Sitz in der Literatur* v. 34 works with v. 23 to indicate that YHWH effects *both* the scattering *and* the gathering of the exiles. What is more, by using the familiar DTR exodus imagery of "a mighty hand and an outstretched arm" it characterizes this act as the second exodus.[91] Thus, it is unsurprising that vv. 35-38 compare the purifying judgment in the wilderness specifically to the exodus from Egypt. Ezekiel 34 also uses this logic: subsequent to promising to gather the people (34:11-16), YHWH indicts their unjust conduct (vv. 17-19) that necessitates the judgement between the fat and lean sheep (vv. 20-22).[92] The overlap

---

ments between them, are patently similar to Ezekiel's location on the Chebar River (Ezek 1:1) and the movement of YHWH out of the Jerusalem temple (Ezek 8–11) and back into its restored form in Ezek 40–48. Furthermore, one can find similarities between the themes of the workshop and Ezekiel's visions of the כבוד־יהוה and, of course, between the role of the *āšipu* and *mašmaššu* priests and the prophet's Zadokite heritage. More detailed investigation is certainly necessary, but even such preliminary findings enhance the importance of the *mīs pî* ritual for reading and interpreting Ezekiel.

90 Levtow, *Images of Others*, 66-72; cf. Isa 52:7-10.

91 Levitt Kohn, *A New Heart and a New Soul*, 87.

92 This movement is facilitated by the introductory לכן in v. 20; for a full treatment of the issues, see Strine, "Repentance in the Book of Ezekiel," 467-91.

between these two chapters heightens the sense that they also share the objective to supplant Marduk with YHWH.

Finally, Ezek 20:40-44 presents its vision for the restored community with a concept found in the *mīs pî* ritual. At the end of the second exodus, YHWH requires the people's choice gifts and pleasing odors, a command that recalls the very purpose of the *mīs pî* ritual, as Michael Dick has observed:

> the whole essence of the ritual is contained in a single incantation, én u₄ dingir dím-ma (tablet 3; see STT 200). Here is spelled out the proposition that the statue that has not had its mouth opened does not smell incense, does not eat food, and does not drink water.[93]

The stress on the vitality of the deity, its ability to be an active agent in the divine and human realms, matches Ezekiel's concern to depict YHWH as vital and powerful. Thus, borrowing this image of worship from a familiar Mesopotamian incantation offers a sensible way to make the point in an elusive manner. That there is polemical intent in the description of this worship is suggested by its location: YHWH will receive this adoration on "my holy mountain, the mountain height of Israel," an allusion to Mt Zion and its related notions of divine enthronement and sovereignty. Finally, and a bit more speculatively, the description of Israel's attitude upon return as shameful for their past deeds recalls the attitude of the Babylonian king during day five of the *akītu* ritual, when "[t]he High Priest strikes the king's cheek, presumably to instill within the king the feeling of penitence."[94] In the larger context, this might mean that the sacrifices comprise a celebration of YHWH's, and not Marduk's, enthronement over land, temple, and people.

A brief comparison with Deutero-Isaiah illustrates what Ezek 20:32-44 achieves. Although scholars remain split on whether Deutero-Isaiah was written in Babylonia, Judah, or a combination of the two places, it is widely accepted that the text was composed around the end of the Neo-Babylonian period (ca. 539 B.C.E.). The capacity of the Babylonian dominant class to coerce subalterns to reproduce the public

---

93   Dick, ed., *Born in Heaven*, 70; Berlejung, "Washing the Mouth," 47. For STT 200, see Dick, ed., *Born in Heaven*, 96-100.

94   Mark E. Cohen, *The Cultic Calendar of the Ancient Near East* (Bethesda, Md.: CDL Press, 1993), 438. See the ritual text in Ibid., 447, and F. Thereau-Dangin, *Rituels accadien* (Paris: E. Leroux, 1921), 127-54, with the corresponding text on p. 145. On the positive role of shame in Ezek 20, see Lapsley, "Shame," 154-57.

transcript surely waned at this time. One indication of this situation is the failure of Nabonidus[95] to persuade the other members of the Babylonian elite to accept changes he wished to impose upon the religious content of the public transcript.

In that environment it was possible for subordinate groups to express more aggressive resistance in Babylon and, even more so, at its periphery. Thus, wherever Isa 40–55 originated, it had greater latitude to overtly polemicize the Babylonian public transcript, and in particular its authorization for image based worship. This liberty was so great that the text parodied Marduk and Nabu by name (Isa 46:1-2). Direct and blunt, Deutero-Isaiah's open statement of contempt is reflective of the struggle between the powerful and powerless over the public transcript. Scott remarks:

> Finally, it is clear that the frontier between the public and the hidden transcripts is a zone of constant struggle between the dominant and subordinate—not a solid wall. The capacity of dominant groups to prevail—though never totally—in defining what counts as the public transcript and what counts as offstage is, as we shall see, no small measure of their power.[96]

Deutero-Isaiah makes a statement about the diminishing or diminished power of the Neo-Bablyonians simply by demeaning Marduk and Nabu openly. That they are portrayed as captives (וְנַפְשָׁם בַּשְּׁבִי הָלָכָה; Isa 46:2) stresses the transformation in power dynamics. Deutero-Isaiah's statements are more like Ezekiel's open condemnation of the Judahite non-exiles than its disguised comments about Babylonia, illustrating the massive differences in their environments.

The extent of Neo-Babylonian control over the public transcript during the time when Ezekiel was written, by contrast, allowed some vocal resistance (e.g. it could be said that images were merely wood and stone), but far less than was possible after the emergence of Persian power. Ezekiel 20, therefore, presents an oblique message. This is what Scott predicts an oppressed community would do in the circumstances that faced the Judahite exiles during a time of Neo-Babylonian strength. It is, therefore, notable that the portrayal of YHWH as a con-

---

95   Peter Machinist, "Mesopotamian Imperialism and Israelite Religion: A Case Study From Second Isaiah," in *Symbiosis, Symbolism and Power of the Past: Canaan, Ancient Israel and Their Neighbors. Centennial Symposium of the W. F. Albright Institute of Archaeological Research and the American Schools of Oriental Research* (eds. W. G. Dever and S. Gitin; Winona Lake, Ind.: Eisenbrauns, 2003), 237-64.

96   Scott, *Domination*, 14.

trast to the images of wood and stone who, like a shepherd, gathers his people and brings them to his holy mountain in a second exodus, at which place they offer worship to Yhwh, overlaps with the message that Deutero-Isaiah expresses explicitly. The thematic overlap indicates that Ezekiel shared Deutero-Isaiah's concerns to assert Yhwh's uniqueness and eminence among the deities of the ancient Near East, but was constrained to do so in an elusive manner that did not overtly challenge the dominant Babylonian ideology. In short, Ezekiel says covertly what Deutero-Isaiah voices openly. For Ezekiel and its community, open resistance was either foolish, futile, or both. Still, Ezekiel does not abandon its traditional Judahite convictions about Yhwh and Yhwh's place in the cosmic order of things; despite having to assert its beliefs covertly, it asserts them nonetheless.

The "as I live" divine oath contributes to this disguised polemic against the Babylonians in Ezek 20:32-44 in two ways. First, it provides an elusive yet sharp contrast between lifeless cult images and the living god. Yhwh's oath serves as the opening declaration of a position that reaches its logical conclusion in v. 39, where those who reject Yhwh's claim to divine sovereignty are encouraged to continue worshipping their idols but to cease their association with Yhwh. Second, the "as I live" authenticating element evokes the exodus tradition, picking up on both the explicit historical framework of vv. 1-31 and also on its implicit, veiled assertion that Yhwh, not Marduk, is the one who brought about the exile. In Ezek 20 there is little doubt that Yhwh effected the scattering of the exiles (as does Ezek 17 before it), remains living and powerful, and, when the time is proper, will serve as their shepherd by gathering the people (as in Ezek 34). The exodus from Egypt is prominently evoked in Ezek 20 because it is the paradigmatic occasion when doubts about Yhwh's very existence provided the canvas on which to illustrate God's life and power.

5. Ezekiel and Monotheism

A common theme running though Ezek 17, 34, and 20 is the ascription to Yhwh of power and control attributed to Marduk. In particular, the preceding analysis has shown that Ezekiel claims that Yhwh controls people and events in Judah and Babylon. This theme raises a correlated question: does Yhwh's power over Judah and the nations indicate that Ezekiel includes a monotheistic theology?

The question of monotheism and its development in ancient Israel and Judah is a topic of intense debate. Not so long ago, monotheism was believed to be the defining characteristic of ancient Israelite religion, but this view gave way to a reconstruction that observed the religious practices attested in the Hebrew Bible are more frequently not monotheistic. Ancient Israel and Judah, this reconstruction contends, were monolatrous or henotheistic, essentially synonymous concepts specifying the worship of one deity without the denial of the existence of other deities. These "YHWH alone" beliefs remained a minority position until the sixth century B.C.E., when they rose to dominance as a response to the cataclysmic events of Jerusalem's destruction and the Babylonian exile.[97] Gradual theological reflection initiated in the DTR tradition reached its logical conclusion in Deutero-Isaiah, which advocates absolute monotheism in the elegant poetry of Isa 40–55. Hans Wilderberger, for one, concludes that "only in [Deutero-Isaiah] is the relevance of monotheism recognized and its consequences thought out."[98]

Hywel Clifford offers a succinct yet full account of the contours of Deutero-Isaiah's so-called monotheistic affirmation, which includes the following concepts: YHWH is the creator and sustainer of all, a direct contrast to the lifeless idols; YHWH is sovereign in history, indicated in part by his control over foreign leaders; YHWH is the only deity capable of declaring what shall be and making it so; Deutero-Isaiah makes an ontological claim when it asserts both YHWH's exclusivity and incomparability (e.g. Isa 47:8); and, finally, this combination of concepts supports a universalism that makes YHWH God, with a captial G.[99]

The book of Ezekiel does not contain all these concepts, and certainly not in the same explicit fashion as Isa 40–55, but the foregoing discussion shows that it does represent a hidden transcript that in-

---

97 Bernhard Lang, *Monotheism and the Prophetic Minority: An Essay in Biblical History and Sociology* (The Social World of Biblical Antiquity 1; Sheffield: Almond Press, 1983), 13-59; For a similar formulation see Baruch Halpern, "Brisker Pipes Than Poetry: The Devlopment of Israelite Monotheism," in *Brisker Pipes* (ed. Matthew J. Adams; Fat 63; Tübingen: Mohr Siebeck, 2009), 13-56, who argues the concepts were present long before this but that the explicit statement of the view comes only in Deutero-Isaiah. For another perspective on the development of monotheism, see Robert K. Gnuse, *No Other Gods: Emergent Monotheism in Israel* (JSOTSup 241; Sheffield: Sheffield Academic Press, 1997).

98 Hans Wilderberger, "Der Monotheismus Deuterojesajas," in *Monotheismus* (eds. H. Donner, R. Hanhart and R. Smend; Göttingen: Vandenhoeck & Ruprecht, 1977), 522.

99 Hywel Clifford, "Deutero-Isaiah and Monotheism," in *Prophecy and Prophets in Ancient Israel: Proceedings of the Oxford Old Testament Seminar* (ed. John Day; New York: T & T Clark, 2010), 267-89.

cludes strong similarities. For instance, the condemnation of images as
merely "wood and stone" (Ezek 20:32) reflects agreement with the idol
parodies.[100] The *Unheilsgeschichte* of Ezek 20 surely points to YHWH's
sovereignty in history, a theme that is also present in Ezek 17. The logic and structure of the latter passage makes the Babylonian king YHWH's
human agent for judgment and salvation, an argument that it shares
with the well-known declaration that Cyrus is YHWH's anointed (Isa
44:24-45:25). Insofar as one can infer from the presence of these two
points that Deutero-Isaiah is universalistic, then the same would be
possible for Ezekiel, though the whole argument for universalism remains fraught.[101] Finally, the declaration of the future return of YHWH's
people to the land incorporates the concept that YHWH can declare what
will happen and bring it to pass, although this is never stated directly.
The shape of the whole book, culminating with the eschatological temple vision and the indwelling of YHWH's presence there, supports this
conclusion as well.

This review indicates that Ezekiel parallels all the crucial concepts
in Deutero-Isaiah except the statements of YHWH's exclusivity. This is a
key point for the consensus interpretation, exemplified by Wilderberger, who mediates his concession that Deutero-Isaiah is "not the first evidence of monotheism in the Old Testament"[102] by suggesting that the
exclusivity formulae are evidence that Isa 40–55 is a substantial advance over all that precedes it. Clifford, meanwhile, argues that the exclusivity formulae, exemplified by "there is no other" (אֵין עוֹד), have
"an absolute sense... hence, absolute monotheism."[103] In other words,
these statements are ontological claims that YHWH is the only deity.

Recently, scholars have challenged this interpretation of the exclusivity formulae,[104] with Walter Moberly's critique standing out as the
clearest and most damaging.[105] Moberly shows, first, that the personi-

---

100 Kutsko, *Between Heaven and Earth*, 101-49; Kutsko, "Ezekiel's Anthropology," 119-41;
     cf. Sven Petry, *Die Entgrenzung JHWHs: Monalatrie, Bilderverbot und Monotheismus im
     Deuteronomium, in Deuterojesaja und im Ezechielbuch* (FAT/II 27; Tübingen: Mohr
     Siebeck, 2007).

101 Nathan MacDonald, "Monotheism and Isaiah," in *Interpreting Isaiah: Issues and Ap-
     proaches* (eds. David G. Firth and H.G. M. Williamson; Nottingham: Apollos, 2009),
     43-61.

102 Wilderberger, "Beiträge zur alttestemantlichen Theologie," 522.

103 Clifford, "Deutero-Isaiah," 275

104 MacDonald, "Monotheism," 48-52.

105 R. W. L. Moberly, "How Appropriate is 'Monotheism' as a Category for Biblical In-
     terpretation?," in *Early Jewish and Christian Monotheism* (eds. L. T. Stuckenbruck and
     W. E. S. North; JSNTSup 263; London: T & T Clark, 2004), 216-34.

fied Babylon makes the same claim that "there is no other" (Isa 47:8; cf. Zeph 2:15) though the city it is surely not the only member of an onto-logical category. The so-called exclusivity formulae, second, appear in parallel with claims "that there is none like [Yʜᴡʜ]" (Isa 46:9), which undermines the sense of exclusivity. He observes, finally, that the main point of these statements is that Yʜᴡʜ is able to create and save where other deities are powerless to do so.[106] This theme recalls Yʜᴡʜ's "tri-umph over foreign powers and deities"[107] expressed in the exodus story (e.g. Exod 6:2-8; Num 14:26-35), and underscored in Isa 45 by no less than three references to Yʜᴡʜ as savior[108] and three statements that Yʜᴡʜ redeems.[109] These points argue against reading the so-called ex-clusivity formulae as ontological statements.

If Moberly and others are correct on this issue, and the weight of evidence is currently in their favor, then it is justifiable to conclude that the hidden transcript represented by Ezekiel's disguised statements against the Babylonians contained the same theological concepts re-garding Yʜᴡʜ's exceptional role in the divine realm that are stated ex-plicitly in Deutero-Isaiah. Form, not content, distinguishes these two texts: whereas Ezekiel is inhibited in what it can say openly by the asy-metric power structure at the height of Neo-Bablyonian domination, Deutero-Isaiah is unencumbered a few decades later when Neo-Bably-onian hegemony is either crumbling or already in ruins. Ezekiel advo-cates a theological position highly consistent with Deutero-Isaiah and Jeremiah, though the latter is itself less explicit than Deutero-Isaiah. All three texts argue for Yʜᴡʜ's supremacy vis-à-vis foreign gods through a polemic against image based worship, a parody of the theology sub-stantiating such images, the claim that Yʜᴡʜ controls history, specifi-cally the actions and successes of foreign leaders, and assert that Yʜᴡʜ is the only deity that can predict the future before it comes to pass. The difference between Ezekiel and its counterparts is the visibility of its ar-gument, not the substance of it.

On this evidence, the familiar claim that Deutero-Isaiah represents a watershed moment in the development of ancient Israelite and Ju-dahite religious thought, indeed a defining moment in the history of re-ligions more broadly, is not tenable. Deutero-Isaiah is not a conceptual advance in religious thought so much as it is the first occasion on which a characteristic Judahite theological position could be stated without

---

106 Ibid., 229-31; cf. MacDonald, "Monotheism," 50.

107 Ibid., 49

108 Salvation in vv. 5-8; Yʜᴡʜ as savior in v. 21; the one who saves in v. 22.

109 Isa 45:15, 17, and 25.

fear of reprisal. Deutero-Isaiah remains innovative: there is no doubt that it contributes uniquely to the expression of the idea. But, there is far greater continuity between Deutero-Isaiah and Ezekiel than has often been recognized. Ultimately, Deutero-Isaiah's original contribution is of a rhetorical nature, in the artful poetry through which it presents the ideas.[110]

This discussion raises as many or more questions than it answers about how Ezekiel parallels Deuteronomy, Isaiah, and Jeremiah, where the debate about the development of monotheism typically occurs. It is, therefore, an indication that further study on this issue is necessary. Perhaps a call for such work in a text widely recognized as radically theocentric seems obvious, but it remains necessary.[111]

6. Ezekiel and the Arts of Resistance

It is now possible to draw together a few threads that have been running through this chapter, namely the features that Ezekiel exhibits in its partial expression of the hidden transcript that developed among the Judahite exiles during the first half of the sixth century B.C.E.

James C. Scott demonstrates that the hidden transcript may find its way into public expression through one of two techniques: "those that disguise the message and those that disguise the messenger."[112] Even though it is probable that some portion of Ezek 17, 34, and 20 are not the product of the prophet Ezekiel himself, neither anonymity nor pseudepigraphy is their primary means of disguise. Ezekiel masks its message, not its messenger. Its expression of the hidden transcript, therefore, necessarily contains portions of the public transcript and the hidden transcript side by side. "The hidden transcript," Scott shows, "never becomes a language apart," but is in "constant dialogue" with the authorized message of the dominant group.[113] Scott continues:

---

110 Mark S. Smith, *The Origins of Biblical Monotheism* (Oxford: Oxford University Press, 2001), 179-94.

111 MacDonald, *Deuteronomy*, 209-10 has also noted the need for this work.

112 Scott, *Domination*, 139.

113 Ibid., 135.

The practical modes of concealment are limited only by the imaginative capacity of subordinates... Here we must above all recognize that the creation
of disguises depends on an agile, firm grasp of the codes of meaning being
manipulated. *It is impossible to overestimate the subtlety of this manipulation.*[114]

The challenge lies in Scott's concluding statement: is it possible to
identify the subtle manipulation of language, often familiar language,
in the book of Ezekiel well enough so that our modern ears can hear the
message to which it gives voice? The difficulty of the task is suggested
by Greenberg's forewarning that "one who aspires to be an interpreter... of such a polymath... should possess a correspondingly wide
range of antiquarian knowledge."[115]
    It is inconceivable to delimit or reproduce the breadth of ancient
Near Eastern themes to which Ezekiel and its tradents made reference.
But, this is not necessary: when and where there is sufficient evidence
that the authors and tradents of this book did know know an ancient
text or tradition and made allusion to it, then it is legitimate to explore
how their adaptation of it contributes to an expression of resistance. In-
feasible as it is to identify all the glimpses of the hidden transcript that
the book of Ezekiel contains, it remains possible to recognize some of
them. Even this limited accomplishment offers significant new insight
into the book.
    To this end, this chapter has delineated three features that occur
when Ezekiel gives voice to the hidden transcript.

(a) Feature 1: Surface-level Intra-Judahite Polemic

First, Ezekiel screens its inter-national polemic from its Babylonian captors by locating it in the midst of an intra-Judahite polemic, most often
targeting Judahite leaders. Ezekiel 17 is a stinging rebuke of Zedekiah's political foolhardiness; Ezek 34 criticizes the shepherds of Israel for
their self-absorbed behavior; Ezek 20 gives quarter to no one in Israel's
history, especially the elders of Israel (Ezek 20:1). The surface-level
concern of these passages, as demonstrated in chapter five, is to seize
control of the Judahite public transcript, and that objective should not
be diminished. Yet, each one has a secondary interest in resisting Babylonian hegemony; this subsidiary position is a result of the limited free-

---

114 Ibid., 139, emphasis added.
115 Greenberg, *Ezekiel 21-37*, 395-96.

dom the author possessed more so than an indicator of the importance ascribed to this message.

(b) Feature 2: Ambiguous Imagery and Metaphors

"[W]hat permits subordinate groups to undercut the authorized cultural norms is the fact that cultural expression by virtue of its polyvalent symbolism and metaphor lends itself to disguise," writes Scott.[116] This statement could be about Ezekiel.

The second feature of its hidden transcript is to adopt and adapt prominent ancient Near Eastern symbols, images, and metaphors to ascribe to YHWH those powers and privileges the Babylonian public transcript attributed to Marduk. Ezekiel 17 hands Marduk's net to YHWH just prior to explaining that it is YHWH who raises up and makes low the nations. In this way, Ezek 17 transfers the power that Marduk wins by defeating Tiamat over to YHWH; this is all the more subversive because these events are commemorated in the pinnacle of Babylonian religious ritual, its annual new year festival. Ezekiel 34 depicts YHWH, not Marduk, as the shepherd of humanity, a role that symbolizes divine sovereignty (e.g. *Enūma eliš*, Tablet VI, line 106). Ezekiel 20, lastly, uses the shepherd imagery and adds to it the declaration that YHWH will reign, receiving worship on a high mountain. The imagery-rich and metaphorical nature of these statements imbues them with just enough imprecision so that they remain open to various interpretations. Still, by indicating that YHWH has controlled events in Egypt and Judah, was responsible for scattering the Judahites, and remains the only deity who is capable of bringing those Judahite exiles back from Babylon, Ezekiel presents YHWH as a unique, exceptionally powerful deity.

(c) Feature 3: Innocuous Interpretation

Third and finally, the indeterminate nature of each disclosure of the hidden transcript allows for an innocuous interpretation of its meaning. In each case, one can argue plausibly that the text does not challenge the Babylonian sponsored public transcript. "[I]t is the innocuous meaning—however tasteless it may be considered—that pro-

---

116 Scott, *Domination*, 158.

vides an avenue of retreat when challenged,"[117] remarks Scott, who continues:

> Alternatively, the excluded (and in this case, powerful) audience may grasp the seditious message in the performance but find it difficult to react because *that sedition is clothed in terms that can also lay claim to a perfectly innocent construction.*[118]

For Ezekiel, the first step in constructing the innocuous interpretation is to foreground the inner-Judahite polemic. There can be little doubt that these explicit critiques of Judahite leadership are equally as critical of Judah as the Bablyonians were.

The second step towards a non-confrontational interpretation is to utilize the the ambiguity in the images and metaphors. The particular ways in which Ezek 17, 34, and 20 allow for a non-hostile interpretation were detailed above, but one general point can now be added to those specific arguments: in each case, YHWH's actions might be justified by appeal to the practice of restoring and repatriating divine images. Kutsko shows that the practice of repatriating divine images captured in military operations was utilized in the Neo-Babylonian and Persian periods.[119] This practice, a classic case of *Realpolitik*, serves as a tangible indication of the imperial ruler's benevolence and seeks to curry the favor of the local population.[120]

The logical corollary of repatriating a divine image to a restored cult center was the reinstatement of worship to that deity and, to at least some extent, the power and vitality of the deity within its native land.[121] The exact nature of this is hard to define, but Cyrus' assertion that Marduk magnanimously granted him victory so he could spare the Babylonian people from their own oppressive leaders is one indication of the way in which a foreign leader might positively associate himself with the native deity. In an analogous fashion, one can envision a pro-Babylonian view in which YHWH was allowed to return to Judah, probably to a reconstructed temple in Jerusalem, and to receive worship from the people as an endorsement of the benevolence of the Babylonian

---

117 Ibid., 157.

118 Ibid., 158, emphasis added.

119 Kutsko, *Between Heaven and Earth*, 113-17.

120 See, for instance, Barbara Porter's discussion of Esarhaddon's efforts (*Images, Power, and Politics: Figurative Aspects of Esarhaddon's Babylonian Policy* [Memoirs of the American Philosophical Society; Philadelphia: American Philosophical Society, 1993], 41-76).

121 Holloway, *Aššur is King!*, 283-4.

king. This hypothetical is, perhaps, not so hypothetical at all: one can read each of the passages discussed in this chapter along these lines. Indeed, the overall shape of Ezekiel—where YHWH departs the city and brings judgment upon it, only to return in the end to a restored, idealized temple—is hospitable to this pro-Babylonian view.

Take Ezek 17 as an example. As established earlier, this chapter condemns Zedekiah, portrays Nebuchadrezzar as YHWH's agent in judging Jerusalem and its king, and ends with a general statement of YHWH's ability to prosper or punish a nation. One can argue, if and when it suits the situation, that Ezek 17 authorizes the Babylonian military action against Jerusalem, shows the Babylonian king and YHWH working in concert with one another, and envisages a Babylonian sponsored future repatriation of YHWH.[122] Its contents, furthermore, do not preclude attributing similar power to Marduk in Mesopotamia; thus, one could argue that YHWH possesses such power only in Judah, a territorial view of divine power that is stated explicitly in 2 Kings 5.

Possible readings might be multiplied for some time, but the point remains the same: a certain amount of elasticity characterizes the passages in which Ezekiel allows the hidden transcript to break into view. Though some might contend this indeterminacy weakens the argument that these texts intend to resist the Babylonians, Scott's research suggests that this is precisely the sort of ambiguity that subaltern groups are known for across time and place. What is more, all this provides an explanation for why the book of Ezekiel never comes close to expressing the scorn against its Babylonian captors that it heaps upon its fellow Judahites. Openly expressing that sort of anger would have been both futile and foolish. The book of Ezekiel, all evidence indicates, was far too shrewd to act in that manner.

(d) The Importance of Ezekiel's Neo-Babylonian Setting

A final comment on the provenance of Ezekiel is appropriate at this point. The introduction of this book reviewed the persuasive evidence that a substantial portion of the book of Ezekiel in its final form dates to the first half of the sixth-century B.C.E. and was written in Babylonia.[123] By demonstrating that significant new insights follow from attending

---

122 That a text containing this sort of propaganda might be written in advance of its actual occurrence is supported by the evidence from Esarhaddon's practices (Porter, *Images*, 43).

123 See ch. 1, section 3a.

to modes of resistance that such a subaltern community is likely to have employed, this study reaffirms the evidence that a substantial part of Ezekiel was composed in that period and place.[124]

This is not to deny that there is strong evidence that the final form of the book of Ezekiel has undergone later editing, only that texts that are often stratified into many layers might be read coherently in a Neo-Babylonian setting (e.g. Ezek 20:1-44). Thus, recent scholarship that has argued for an almost entirely post-exilic, Persian period composition of the book will need to take account of and respond to the argument laid out here.[125] The present study does not preclude some redactional activity in the Persian and even Hellenistic periods, but the sustained attempt to subvert Marduk by attributing his power to Yhwh better suits the Neo-Bablyonian period in which Marduk represented the pinnacle of social, political, and religious power. Future studies that extend the observations made here about the way Ezekiel employs imagery, metaphor, and oblique statements to express its resistance against its Babylonian captors may yield new diachronic reconstructions of the text that recognize a greater unity within it without recourse to a wholly synchronic approach.

7. Summary

This chapter began by asking why Ezekiel failed to resist its Babylonian captors when it felt comfortable speaking out against both other foreign nations and also the non-exiled Judahites. By carefully examining the way in which Ezek 17:1-24, 34:1-16, and 20:32-44 use metaphor and imagery, the study demonstrated that Ezekiel does resist Babylonian power after all, though it does so in a concealed manner. The hidden transcript of the exilic community—the discourse of resistance and retaliation it formed outside the gaze of its captors—comes into view in these three chapters. In particular, each text takes an image or metaphor used to depict Marduk as the divine sovereign and uniquely powerful deity and applies it to Yhwh. Although each passage exhibited enough ambiguity to be interpreted as non-hostile to the Babylonian's authorized public transcript, there were strong indications that Ezekiel and the exilic Judahite community understood them to be sub-

---

124 Cf. Clements, , 283-94.

125 e.g. Pohlmann, *Ezechiel 1–19*; Pohlmann, *Ezechiel 20–48*; Klein, *Schriftauslegung im Ezechielbuch*.

versive. The texts argue that YHWH, not Marduk, is more powerful than any other deity and deserves Judah's unreserved allegiance.

The relevant texts, when taken together, advocate the following view of YHWH: YHWH, the living god, is not like the lifeless, powerless cult images; YHWH is sovereign over history, including the leaders of foreign nations; and YHWH is the deity who can declare what will happen in the future before it comes to pass. This set of assertions is very similar to those made in Deuteronomy, Jeremiah, and Isaiah, where such statements are often construed as monotheistic in nature. This study did not resolve the issues in that debate, but it did show that Ezekiel needs to be an important part of it. In particular, the continuity between the concepts contained in Ezekiel and Isa 40–55 show that the latter text, for all its unique contributions, is not a sharp conceptual break with earlier prophetic texts.

Ezekiel, finally, exhibits three identifiable features in the passages where it allows the hidden transcript a modicum of public expression: the surface level concern of the passage is an inner-Judahite polemic; the primary rhetorical trait is the use of imagery and metaphor; and, finally, the passage is indeterminate enough to allow for an interpretation that is not hostile to its Babylonian captors.

Chapter Seven: Summary and Conclusion

The preceding chapters have carefully examined the "as I live" and "lifted hand" formulae in an attempt to elucidate their meaning, explore their function within the book, to discern what, if anything, the book has to say about its Babylonian captors, and to answer why Ezekiel employs these formulae so much more frequently than any other book in the Hebrew Bible. Though it was not initially obvious that these formulae contain various connotations, careful study revealed each one possesses layers of meaning, inner-biblical allusions, and a structuring role that make them far more than markers of emphasis. Noting these additional connotations provided access to the dialect and codes that characterize Ezekiel's intra-ethnic and inter-national disputes, offering a platform upon which new exegetical insights were built. The breadth of these insights, which span from Ezekiel's introductory announcement of Y<small>HWH</small>'s coming judgment upon Jerusalem to the concluding program for the redistribution of Y<small>HWH</small>'s land, show that these formulae are not incidental to the book's message, nor are they merely a convenient way of underscoring Y<small>HWH</small>'s resolve. The "as I live" and "lifted hand" formulae are creatively intertwined with the main themes and rhetorical goals of the book of Ezekiel.

Ezekiel is engaged in a two-pronged polemic, against both the Judahites left in Jerusalem who claim to be the rightful inhabitants of the promised land and also against its Babylonian captors, who maintain that their defeat of Jerusalem and the exile of its leaders illustrates that Marduk has defeated Y<small>HWH</small>. The form of both polemics is shaped by the asymmetric power relationship the Judahite exiles have with these groups: when addressing the non-exiles, the polemic is explicit, "public," and portrays the exiles as the social, political, and religious authority; when it deals with the Babylonians, the content of the polemic comes from Ezekiel's version of the "hidden" transcript that receives expression in elusive, disguised, or private language that intentionally places its views just below the surface—necessities for a subordinate group that must at least appear deferential to its overlords.

Perhaps these features are clearest in the passages where the "as I live" authenticating element appears in chapters 33–36: whereas commentators generally classify this section as oracles of salvation for Israel, the preceding study showed that the "as I live" formula marks them out as disputational in character, a disposition that this material

shares with chapters 1–24. In Ezek 33:23-29 and 35:1–36:15, the book
rejects the non-exiles claims to a combined Abraham-Jacob tradition,
mocks their esteemed ancestor Jacob, and invites the exiles to adopt the
exodus tradition as the paradigm for YHWH's action in the past, present,
and future. Meanwhile, Ezek 34:1-16 portrays YHWH as sovereign over
history, nations, and not at the mercy of Marduk or a non-Judahite
king. Using language and images redolent of the imperial rhetoric that
extolled Marduk as patron of the Babylonian king and people, chief
among all deities, and in control of foreign nations, the book frames the
Babylonian exile as a recurrence of the exodus from Egypt, the arche-
typal instance when YHWH's power was demonstrated by defeating a
foreign power and leading the people to the promised land. Ezekiel invites the exiles to construe their predicament as a repetition of those
events. On both accounts, the portrait of the future painted in Ezek
33:23–48:35 is not so much meant to prognosticate future temporal
events as it is to motivate the exiles to actions that will mark them out
as faithful to YHWH, true Judahites.

1. Summary of Findings

This study ranged widely in order to answer its guiding questions. Beginning with a comparative analysis across the ancient Near East, it
subsequently employed form criticism's process of examining structure, genre, social setting and function, finally drawing on social scientific models for the activities of subordinate groups to explain the
new insights gained along the way. A summary of the relevant findings is appropriate at this point.

After chapter one introduced the topic, chapter two cast its net
wide, looking for potential parallels to the "as I live" and "lifted hand"
formulae across the ancient Near East. Examples of deities swearing
were found in Egyptian, Akkadian, Hittite, and Ugaritic texts. The
Egyptian texts portrayed both Re and Hathor invoking Re's life by
means of the ʿnḫ authenticating element. Re's oath, a self-referential invocation of his life to swear that he will judge humanity, corresponds
with YHWH's self-referential oaths in the Hebrew Bible. This evidence
demonstrated that the book of Ezekiel is consistent with ancient Near
Eastern depictions of deities when it employs the "as I live" authenticating element in the divine oath.

Directly relevant to the book of Ezekiel's Neo-Babylonian setting
was the Akkadian nīš X authenticating element. There are four instances of deities swearing with this authenticating element, including

Ea's plan to have Ereshkigal swear by the life of the great gods. This indicated that Mesopotamian deities invoked the lives of other deities when they swore. *Enūma eliš* reinforced this point: albeit elliptical, the text describes the gods swearing to make Marduk divine sovereign by using the symbolic action of touching their throats, an act connected with invoking one's life to authenticate an oath. In the political sphere, the evidence also showed that the ubiquitous *adê* loyalty oaths were authenticated by invoking deities' lives. When Assyrian and Babylonian kings swore in the *adê*, it is likely they employed the authenticating element *nīš X*: for example, the Babylonian form "by the life of Marduk." Their vassals likely swore in a similar fashion, often if not always invoking their own patron deity. These findings were relevant to Ezek 17, which implied that Zedekiah swore an *adê* loyalty oath to Babylonia "by Yʜᴡʜ's life."

The Ugaritic evidence was less direct, but illuminating. Particularly, the *Tale of Aqhat* contained the closest cognate to the Hebrew חי אני: El authenticated his oath to provide an heir to Danel "by my life," adopting a form of the Ugartic *ḥy npš* formula. This example is peculiar, the only extant instance of a deity promising blessing upon oath outside the Hebrew Bible. Irregular as it is, this text established the possibility of such positive usage, which proved an important precedent for Deutero-Isaiah's use of the divine oath in Isa 49.

Finally, the ancient Near Eastern evidence was as significant for what it did not exhibit as for what it did. Although arguments from silence must be treated with caution, the lack of evidence for a "lifted hand" formula in divine or human oaths outside the Hebrew Bible called into question that usage in Israel and Judah. Excursus one demonstrated problems with interpreting נשא יד as an oath authenticating element internal to the Hebrew Bible: Ps 10:12, Isa 49:22, and Deut 32:40 showed that the formula referred to Yʜᴡʜ's active intervention for his people. By establishing this weakness in the consensus interpretation that the "lifted hand" formula is a symbolic gesture for swearing, a way was opened for a new approach. A new proposal emerged from evidence that connected נשא יד with the royal sanction of land transfers. Legal documents from Ugarit demonstrate that the Akkadian formula *našû-nadānu* was frequently employed in legal proceedings where the king officially sanctioned the transfer of land rights from one party to another. This three-party arrangement corresponded to the context of the "lifted hand" formula in Exod 6, Num 14, and Ezek 20. Notwithstanding slight modifications in the way these texts expressed the formula, the argument demonstrated that the "lifted

hand" formula resembled the formulae used by other ancient Near
Eastern monarchs to approve land transfers.

Chapter three analyzed the genre of each passage in the Hebrew
Bible where the "as I live" or "lifted hand" formulae appear. In the
first place, it showed that the "as I live" formula frequently occurs in
prophetic announcements of judgment with an emphasis on who will
live in YHWH's land. Four occurrences differed from this profile: Isa
49:18, Ezek 18:3, and Ezek 33:11, 27. Rather than concluding this was
anomalous, further treatment of these four passages revealed their
common context, namely the prophetic disputation speech. Subsequent review of the other passages identified six additional disputation
speeches, meaning that 10 out of the 18 passages that employed the "as
I live" authenticating element are disputations. In the second place,
this chapter showed that the "lifted hand" formula was used in two
distinct conventions. The first convention correlated to the Akkadian
našû-nadānu formula used in legal documents for the transfer of land
between parties, announcing YHWH's promise to transfer land to Israel
in a genre best called theological reflection. The second convention is
associated with the guilt bearing formula עָוֹן נָשָׂא, assigning punishment for guilt. The second convention appears, despite this meaning,
in oracles of salvation for YHWH's people that are predicated upon the
punishment of their enemy or enemies.

Chapter 4 explored the *Sitz im Leben* and *Sitz in der Literatur* for the
formulae. The limited evidence available for actual ancient practice necessitated that this question be explored in two stages. First, noting
that all the available evidence is from texts, this chapter focused on determining the literary setting (*Sitz in der Literatur*) of the formulae.
Thus, it sought to determine the theological tradition in which each formula resided. Second, and only subsequent to this first stage, did this
study attempt to determine a social setting (*Sitz im Leben*) in which the
formula was originally used. The evidence indicated that the "as I live"
divine oath is a DTR phrase used to announce YHWH's judgment against
Israel, which it did at two pivotal moments in the exodus narrative (i.e.
Num 14; Deut 32). Further evidence supporting this conclusion was
the absence of the divine oath with the verbal root שׁבע in Ezekiel. In
direct contrast to the "as I live" formula, שׁבע is the DTR expression employed when YHWH swears to bless Israel. Because Ezekiel did not
want to invoke this theme, it avoided using the verbal root שׁבע.

Earlier recognition that the "lifted hand" formula was actually *two
formulae* necessitated that analysis of it was broken into two sections.
The "lifted hand" land transfer formula received attention first.
Demonstrating difficulties with the common classification of the "lifted

hand" land transfer formula as a feature of P, careful examination showed that at least two pieces of evidence marked the "lifted hand" formula as more closely correlated to H: Y<small>HWH</small>'s first-person speech, widely agreed as typical of H, and the formula's collocation with D<small>TR</small> language, a style never exhibited by P but familiar from Lev 17–26. The second convention, the "lifted hand" punishment formula, corresponded with Neo-Babylonian legal language used to assign punishment upon guilty parties. This is a logical context for the book of Ezekiel to draw from, given its self-attested Babylonian provenance. The book of Ezekiel transferred this idiom into the divine sphere, employing it in Y<small>HWH</small>'s speeches that specify both the type of punishment to come and that Y<small>HWH</small> himself will execute that judgment (i.e. Ezek 36:7; 44:12). This is yet another example of the rhetorical sophistication and radical theocentricity of Ezekiel. As a whole, the chapter demonstrated that neither of the two "lifted hand" formulae are a synonymous substitute for the divine oath with שׁבע; on the contrary, both formulae have a distinct meaning, unrelated to the divine oath, which the book of Ezekiel utilized accordingly.

Excursus two concluded part one of the book by drawing together various lines of argument related to the "lifted hand" formula. Neither the first nor the second convention of the "lifted hand" formula is employed to authenticate an oath. The first convention, classified as the "lifted hand" land transfer formula, is a counterpart to the Akkadian idiom *našû-nadānu*. P, H, and Ezekiel substitute this parallel but non-synonymous expression for D<small>TR</small>'s favored language (the divine oath with the verbal root שׁבע plus נתן) in order to clearly distinguish their land theology from D<small>TR</small>. The second convention, termed the "lifted hand" punishment formula, draws on the ancient Near Eastern practice that uses the hand as a metonymy for power demonstrated in active interventions. Ezekiel uses this formula to specify that Y<small>HWH</small> will execute punishment upon a guilty party or parties.

Chapter five was the first of two chapters to apply these new findings in order to explore the function of the formulae in the book of Ezekiel. Specifically, this chapter addressed the role of the formulae in constructing an intra-Judahite polemic oriented around the question "Who will inhabit Y<small>HWH</small>'s land in the future?" Ezekiel's response to this contentious question marshaled all available resources against the non-exiles' appeal to a combined Abraham-Jacob patriarchal tradition. Exegesis of five passages (Ezek 5:5-17; 11:14-21; 16:43-58; 20:1-31; 33:23-29) demonstrated how the book of Ezekiel subverts the esteemed role of both Abraham and Jacob. The "as I live" divine oath contributed in three ways: one, it heightened the polemical tone because of its role in numerous disputation speeches; two, it was the clearest indicator that the oracle against Mt Seir in Ezek 35:1–36:15 does not target a foreign nation but the Judahites left in the land; three, because of its prominent role in the DTR exodus tradition (Num 14:11b-23a; Deut 32:26-43), the "as I live" formula underscored Ezekiel's argument that legitimate Judahite nationalism is bound to the exodus origin narrative.

The "lifted hand" land transfer formula aided the intra-Judahite polemic by arguing that YHWH controls every change in the peoples' status with respect to the land, including the exile to Babylonia. There is a strong relationship between this formula and the exodus tradition's theme of delivery from foreign oppression (e.g. Exod 6:8). Ezekiel used this connotation to argue that YHWH's paradigm is to redeem a community outside the land and under foreign oppression in order to manifest his glory. The polemic reaches its pinnacle in Ezek 20, where the two formulae appear a combined total of seven times. The so-called *Unheilsgeschichte* declares the book's preference for the exiles over and against the non-exiles by assembling all the possible rhetorical features at its disposal to indicate that Israel's origin is the exodus from Egypt.

The combination of these features results in an authoritative tone and a persona of power. Ezekiel speaks as if it represents the dominant class of Judah that determines legitimate social, political, and religious behavior. This is, of course, not the case: Ezekiel represented the exiles deported to Babylon, who were stripped of their former elite status and any ability to control affairs in Judah. Where others may have been driven to silence, Ezekiel was undaunted. The book gives voice to a public transcript, a form of speech that powerful groups use to define acceptable behavior and to coerce obedience to it from subordinates. Being deported to Babylon stripped the exiles of all the tools dominant groups typically employ to reproduce their power, save one: words. Ezekiel made the most of that lone remaining option.

Chapter six dealt with three texts (Ezek 17:1-24; 20:32-44; 34:1-6) that on the surface address the past failures of Judah's leaders. Close scrutiny of the images, metaphors, and language used to portray YHWH showed that Judah's leaders are not the only group under assault in these texts. The book of Ezekiel is just as disenchanted with the Babylonians, who asserted that the destruction of Jerusalem and its temple indicated YHWH's defeat. As a subordinate group living under the absolute domination of an imperial power, the Judahite exiles could not express this disenchantment openly. Like subaltern groups across time and place, the exiles resisted their oppressors in a disguised fashion intended to escape recognition and to avoid punishment from the dominant class. Their hidden transcript of resistance, developed in the relative freedom provided by a living space at some remove from the Babylonians, appeared in their public performance under disguise, a tactic accomplished through the adroit use of imagery, metaphor and polysemous language. Ezekiel 17, for instance, depicted Yhwh using using the same weapons with the same results as Marduk does in *Enūma eliš*.

The "as I live" formula is not part of the disguise per se, but the first part of this study showed that it possesses layers of meaning, inner-biblical allusions, and a structuring role that turn the seemingly innocuous oath formula into an implicit disavowal of the cult statue-induction rituals (*mīs pî* and *pīt pî*) and the *Enūma eliš*, used in the *akītu* portion of the new year festival. These two religious events epitomized the Babylonian public transcript: an authoritative discourse Babylon's elites employed to present themselves as they wished to be seen. Open, formal events like parades and rituals are one of the most common ways in which the dominant affirm their control, conceal their deficiencies, and depict their status as unanimously accepted, even inevitable. Because of their conspicuous role in these events, *Enūma eliš* and the *mīs pî* ritual texts were obvious sources for Ezekiel to adopt and adapt in its discourse of resistance.

These Babylonian texts, and others besides, contained a rationale for the worship of images and the celebration of Marduk's enthronement as divine king. All of these claims were challenged by Yhwh's oath with the "as I live" authenticating element, which asserts that, contrary to all external indications, Yhwh remains powerful and continues to rule as the divine king. First, the "as I live" formula is an explicit assertion that Yhwh is living and active, not dead. Yhwh is, furthermore, the deity who swears to do things and, in due course, makes them so. That is a stark contrast to the silence of the cultic images that are merely wood and stone (e.g. Ezek 20:32). Ezekiel shares the more explicit views of Deuteronomy, Jeremiah, and Deutero-Isaiah that cultic images are no more than lifeless wood and stone, but it can only affirm it elliptically. Second, the "as I live" formula alludes to the exodus tradition, the paradigmatic demonstration of Yhwh's power over foreign human and divine forces, namely Pharaoh and the Egyptian deities.

Ezekiel is specific in the theme it evokes from the exodus tradition, namely the "as I live" formula recalls the faithfulness of the second generation of the exodus who, unlike their parents, trusted in Yhwh's ability to cleanse the land and settle them in it (e.g. Num 14:21, 28). In precisely the same fashion, the book of Ezekiel calls the exiles to reject image based worship (Ezek 14:12-23; 18:1-32; 33:10-20) because that constitutes a boundary marker between those who accept Ezekiel's construal of events and those who it claims lack faith in Yʜᴡʜ. Those who demonstrate their faithfulness by rejecting polytheistic and syncretistic image based worship will identify themselves with the second generation of the exodus; like those ancestors, this group will survive a purifying judgment in the wilderness and re-inhabit the land (i.e Ezek 20:38)

Ezekiel's call for the Judahites in exile to exhibit absolute allegiance to Yʜᴡʜ by rejecting image based worship resembles the theology of Deuteronomy, Jeremiah, and Deutero-Isaiah. Because it is those three texts that provide the bulk of evidence for the ongoing debate about how ancient Israel and Judah arrived at monotheism, Ezekiel must be included more prominently in future discussions of this issue. The evidence, at a minimum, adds to the problems now evident in the view that Deutero-Isaiah represents a substantial conceptual advance vis-à-vis monotheism over that which precedes it.

By exposing some ways in which Ezekiel employs a disguised version of the exiles' hidden transcript this study opens up new avenues for research on Ezekiel. An initial taxonomy of Ezekiel's techniques for rhetorical disguise emerges, but it is surely not exhaustive. As others pursue this issue, the taxonomy will grow and be refined, enhancing understanding about the ways in which the exiles' expressed resistance while living under an autocratic regime.

2. The Polemics of Exile as Identity Formation

To draw this study to a close, it is sensible to reflect on its second part as a whole and to discuss what unites both sides of Ezekiel's two-pronged polemic. The intra-Judahite and inter-national disputes are two sides of the same coin, as it were, both stigmatizing non-members of Ezekiel's community and demarcating the boundaries of legitimate Judahite nationalism and faithful Yahwism. Considered as a whole, the book of Ezekiel maintains that adopting the exodus tradition as Israel's origin narrative, using that paradigm to interpret the past and envision the future, giving allegiance to Yʜᴡʜ alone, and rejecting all forms of image-based worship are the markers of Yʜᴡʜ's chosen people.

Despite stark differences in form, the two polemics work towards a single objective: defining the boundaries of the exilic community. Perhaps commentators overlook this feature because the scope of the anti-

Babylonian rhetoric was not previously appreciated, or maybe it results from a greater interest in the intra-Judahite matters.[1]

In either event, this study demonstrates that Ezekiel is just as concerned to demarcate the Judahite community from its Babylonian captors, the proximate threat to its own existence,[2] as it is to resist the more remote threat emanating from the Judahites still in the land. For Ezekiel, Judahite identity and Yahwistic faith cannot be defined with respect to either of these "others" alone but must be distinguished from both. Contrary to Renz's conclusion that the book is unconcerned to explain how the exiles should respond to the Babylonians and "their present situation in a foreign land,"[3] this study shows that Ezekiel does have a great deal to say about those issues, but its views are intentionally and artfully disguised from outsiders.

In his seminal work on ethnicity, Fredrik Barth argued that identity is constructed by the actors themselves according to the differences which they see as significant.[4] Highlighting differences produces boundaries between "us" and "them," and each boundary generates an

---

1   On the polemic against the non-exiles, the most significant studies are Pohlmann, *Ezechielstudien* and Renz, *The Rhetorical Function*. Pohlmann does not address the issue in arguing for his *golaorientierte Redaktion*, where one would expect it. Renz briefly and tangentially mentions that anti-Babylonian concerns were relevant to Ezekiel (Ibid., 234), but does not integrate them into his analysis in a substantial way.

    Ezekiel's use of Neo-Babylonian ideas is addressed by Bodi, *Ezekiel and the Poem of Erra*, Block, "Divine Abandonement," 15-42, and Kutsko, *Between Heaven and Earth*, but largely with a focus to outlining Ezekiel's theological convictions and not with attention to the formation of identity or other social issues.

2   As an example of the potential benefit of this perspective, Mein's discussion of the domestication of ethics is a notable exception to the general absence of such work (*Ezekiel and the Ethics of Exile*, 177-215). Note in particular how he describes the "[t]wo different moral worlds... one centered upon the land and politics, the other on exile and the domestic world" (p. 214). This mirrors the way Ezekiel constructs both an internal and an external polemic in two markedly different ways; a re-evaluation of Mein's argument with an eye towards the book's disguised resistance might offer additional insights into the exilic moral framework.

3   Renz, *The Rhetorical Function*, 42-55; quote from p. 55. Though it is not possible here, a re-evaluation of how Ezekiel's disguised language of resistance corresponds to the "mechanisms for survival" that Daniel L. Smith defines in *Religion of the Landless: The Social Context of the Babylonian Exile* (Bloomington, Ind.: Meyer Stone, 1989), 69-88, and Renz concludes are lacking in Ezekiel seems necessary. It is notable that in his concluding section Renz recognizes the importance of a two-pronged definition of identity over against both internal and external groups even though he relegates its role earlier in the book (*The Rhetorical Function*, 234).

4   Fredrik Barth, *Ethnic Groups and Boundaries: The Social Organization of Culture Difference* (Reissued 1998 ed. Long Grove, Ill.: Waveland, 1969).

associated boundary marker. These markers—which may be forms of speech, dress, dietary practice, or any other thing the community deems significant—distinguish the members of the community from the "other." Adherence to the boundary markers is, therefore, what perpetuates the group's existence. Identity, according to Barth's model, exists only because it is defined vis-à-vis others in the form of an "us-them" opposition.[5] Though scholars have challenged Barth's model on various fronts, it remains the guiding concept for explaining identity formation.[6]

Barth's concepts are applicable to the book of Ezekiel: legitimate Judahite nationalism and faithful Yahwism is neither based on the ideology espoused by the non-exiles nor achieved by capitulating to aspects of Neo-Babylonian culture. Those two groups—one internal and one external—constitute Ezekiel's "others." Thus, Ezekiel does not define identity in merely a binary "us-them" opposition, but in an "us-them-them" formulation.[7] And each "other" produces a set of boundaries and generates boundary markers that allow the Judahite exiles to distinguish between its members and non-members.

---

5   Cf. Dermot Anthony Nestor, *Cognitive Perspectives on Israelite Identity* (LHBOTS 519; New York: T & T Clark, 2010), 82.

6   For an illustrative evaluation of the contemporary discourse on identity and Barth's model, see, for example, Francisco J. Gil-White, "How Thick is Blood? The Plot Thickens: If Ethnic Actors Are Primordialists What Remains of the Circumstantialist/ Primordialist Controversy?," *Ethnic and Racial Studies* 22:5 (1999): 789-820 (especially pp. 790-94), Monsterrat Guibernau and John Rex, eds. *The Ethnicity Reader: Nationalism, Multiculturalism, and Migration* (Cambridge: Polity Press, 1997) (especially Eriksen's essay on pp. 33-42), and James Côté, "Identity Studies: How Close Are We to Developing a Social Science of Identity?—An Appraisal of the Field," *Identity* 6 (2006): 3-25.

     Two recent books that address the methodological issues related to identity and identity formation with respect to ancient Israel and the Hebrew Bible are Nestor, *Cognitive Perspectives*, especially pp. 77-125, and Katherine E. Southwood, *Ethnicity and the Mixed Marraige Crisis in Ezra 9–10* (Oxford Theological Monographs; Oxford: Oxford University Press, 2012), especially pp. 19-62.

7   Many argue that defining and maintaining boundaries increases in importance when a group believes its identity is under threat (Thomas Hylland Eriksen, *Ethnicity and Nationalism: Anthropological Perspectives* [Anthropology, Culture and Society; London: Pluto Press, 1993], 76; cf. Southwood, *Ezra 9–10*, 29-31, with respect to ancient Israel). If that is true, the Judahite exiles experienced it acutely. Living in the land YHWH had promised epitomized Judahite identity. The Babylonian exile not only displaced Ezekiel's community from its ancestral land, but it left another group of Judahites in it. Exile was a proverbial one-two punch to Ezekiel's identity and it would hardly be surprising that the Judahite exilic community responded vehemently to this perceived threat.

To appreciate the magnitude of the threat posed by exile for Ezekiel it is helpful to recall the factor to which Barth himself credits his major breakthrough, namely inquiring about "the anomalous persons who change their ethnic identity."[8] The Babylonian exile gave numerous reasons for the exiles to re-evaluate their allegiances. It is impossible to know what options for new identities presented themselves, but the two obvious possibilities were to accept that the Judahites remaining in the land were the exemplars of legitimate Judahite nationalism or to assimilate to the surrounding Babylonian culture. Ezekiel emphatically rejects both options. The book instead argues for a fortified Judahite nationalism that would patiently endure the exile and an unyielding allegiance to YHWH alone that defied the temptation to adopt or syncretize with foreign religious ideology.

3. Boundary Markers in Ezekiel

Ezekiel's polemic against Abraham and Jacob goes to the heart of ethnic identity. Indeed, Max Weber defined ethnic communities as those with "a subjective belief in their common descent."[9] Perhaps the quarrel about Judah's legitimate origin tradition is only symbolic of a more concrete disagreement about the land. Still, the concept of common descent plays such a strong role in defining identity that it is unsurprising Ezekiel makes it a pronounced issue[10] and that it produces a crucial boundary between the two Judahite communities.

The insulting tone that characterizes the passages in Ezekiel that address this topic is not accidental. A key contribution of this book is to demonstrate that Ezekiel uses both the content *and the form* of its disputations to advance its views. The Judahites in exile claim the forceful, authoritative language that characterizes the speech of dominant groups, denying that it belongs to those remaining in the land. This

---

8   Barth, *Ethnic Groups and Boundaries*, 6, 20-8.

9   Max Weber, "Ethnic Groups," in *Economy and Society: An Outline of Interpretive Sociology* (eds. Guenther Roth, Claus Wittich and Ephraim Fischoff; Berkeley, Calif.: University of California Press, 1978), 389-95. Here p. 389. Emphasis added.

10   The view that common descent is a "given" around which people organize themselves is often called a primordial attachment. Despite the ongoing and real debate whether primordial concepts are merely a descriptive category (e.g. Edward Shils and Clifford Geertz) or natural and fundamental to identity (e.g. Harold Isaacs or Pierre L. van den Berghe), there is no denying that communities across time and place adopt it as an important way of distinguishing members and non-members (for further discussion, see Nestor, *Cognitive Perspectives*, 84-100).

tactic seeks to create the impression that the exiles possessed the power necessary to enforce their stance, a view exemplified by the way the book of Ezekiel speaks as if it retains that authority. Even though the circumstances meant that the exiles actually held no social, political, or religious power with which they could coerce the non-exiles to act or think in a particular way, the text shows the hallmarks of a public transcript that expects, even demands, assent. Above all else, Ezekiel stigmatizes the behavior and esteemed figures of the non-exiles.

It is worth recalling here that many of the Judahite exiles were Jerusalem's pre-597 B.C.E. elites. That is to say, they were until very recently the most powerful Judahites. The ability to coerce assent in thought and action did in fact belong to them not so long ago. After 597, that power dissipated. The book of Ezekiel ignores this situation, adopting the attitude that saying it makes it so. The form of its statements—judgmental, harsh polemics—are just as much part of its argument as the content of its critiques. Stripped of all other means to assert and enforce its control over Judah, Ezekiel resorted to the only tool left at its disposal, words.[11]

But, Ezekiel could not ignore the external evidence against this view, namely that the deportation of some Judahites to Babylon indicated that YHWH had rejected them in favor of the Judahites remaining in the land. It is, therefore, notable that Barth highlights the importance of appropriating history in the definition of identity. "[W]e broke loose from the idea of history as simply the objective source and cause of ethnicity," he writes, "and approached it as a form of synchronic rhetoric—a struggle to appropriate the past, as one might say today."[12] The exodus tradition provides Ezekiel the means through which it can appropriate history in a manner that supports is position.[13] Perhaps this is not surprising; the Hebrew Bible is filled with various accounts

---

11   This description of the community suggests A. P. Cohen's conception of boundaries as collectively organized strategies for the protection of economic and political interests ("Introduction," in *Urban Ethnicity* [ed. A. P. Cohen; London: Tavistock, 1974], ix-xxiv). A full discussion of the differences between Barth's and Cohen's models is not possible here (cf. Nestor, *Cognitive Perspectives*, 92-100; Southwood, *Ezra 9–10*, 21-36). Indeed, further study of how these two models handle the evidence of Ezekiel is likely to be fruitful.

12   Barth, *Ethnic Groups and Boundaries*, 6; cf. Eriksen, *Ethnicity and Nationalism*, 71-73.

13   Recall in this respect Greenberg's assessment that "the prophet's attitude toward the traditional was wholly utilitarian: he perceived it as he needed it. He was accustomed to use the tradition to justify and explain current life and behavior... We are therefore not to look to him for an interpretation of the narratives in any objective sense... but only in such a way that would serve his cause" ("Notes on the Influence of Tradition on Ezekiel," 36).

of Israelite and Judahite history that, regardless of their historical accuracy, are appropriations of the past meant to serve various conceptions of ethnic, national, and religious identity.

Ezekiel, in particular, argued that the exodus paradigm is the pattern by which YHWH guides history and manifests his glory: just as YHWH had redeemed a community outside the land and under foreign oppression to manifest his glory in the past, so he would do again with the Judahite exiles in Babylon. This is an obvious effort to explain away tangible evidence that problematizes Ezekiel's view by interpreting its present situation through a favorable lens. But, as Barth observes, this is neither novel nor surprising.

The "as I live" and "lifted hand" formulae contribute to this historical appropriation in important ways. Although the "as I live" formula evoked YHWH's sworn judgment in the wilderness (e.g. Num 14), it simultaneously conjured up the memory of the second exodus generation that was forced to wander in the wilderness before reaching the promised land (Num 14:24, 31). The exiles, like that generation, would have to endure a period in which the community is purified, but only a temporary one. Narratives of hope—stories like the exodus—helped to make Ezekiel's position attractive. The "lifted hand" formula calls to mind YHWH's promise to bring his people into the promised land (e.g. Exod 6:2-8; Num 14:26-38). The repeated appearance of the "lifted hand" land transfer formula in Ezek 20 evokes the theme. But, it is the final two uses of the formula in the book that give it a positive aspect: in Ezek 20:42 the "lifted hand" land transfer formula presents the return from exile as a second, more permanent transfer of the land to YHWH's people; in its final occurrence at Ezek 47:13, the "lifted hand" land transfer formula introduces the allotment of the land among the tribes, Levites, priests and, indeed, YHWH himself. As a recapitulation of the first settlement, the pinnacle of the peoples' pre-exilic history, Ezekiel presents the future transfer of the land to the returning exiles as the pinnacle of future events.

Zimmerli's earlier study of Ezekiel's favored refrain, "I am YHWH, your God,"[14] is a precedent for this practice. Zimmerli demonstrated that for Ezekiel the *Selbstvorstellungsformel* indicated that "Yahweh's history with Israel is the place where the truth of his revelatory word becomes recognizable in its unfolding."[15] The "as I live" and "lifted

---

14 Ezek 5:13, 15, 17; 6:7, 10, 13-14; 7:4, 9, 27; 11:10, 12; 12:15-16, 20, 25; 13:14, 21, 23; 14:4, 7-9; 15:7; 16:62; 17:21, 24; 20:5, 7, 12, 19-20, 26, 38, 42, 44; 21:4, 10, 22, 37; 22:14, 16, 22; 24:14, 27; 25:5, 7, 11, 17; 26:6, 14; 28:22-23, 26; 29:6, 9, 21; 30:8, 12, 19, 25-26; 32:15; 33:29; 34:24, 27, 30; 35:4, 9, 12, 15; 36:11, 23, 36, 38; 37:6, 13-14, 28; 38:23; 39:6-7, 22, 28.

15 Zimmerli, *I Am Yahweh*, 11; see also his discussion in Zimmerli, *Ezekiel 1–24*, 37-38.

hand" formulae, like the *Selbstvorstellungsformel*, enable the book to explain events and cast a vision for the future in which Yhwh remains active, powerful, and willing to act for a faithful remnant of Judahites.

The more proximate threat to the Judahite exiles, namely their Babylonian captors, posed similar problems. Here, it is important to remember that identity and boundary markers rise in importance when outsiders impinge upon a community. While the Babylonians were not unknown to the Judahites prior to the deportation of 597 B.C.E., their newfound proximity and wholly transformed relationship constituted a seismic shift in their relationship to Judahite life. Ezekiel could no more define Judahite identity without reference to their Babylonian overlords than it could without reference to Yhwh.

Ezekiel employs the exodus tradition to offer hope to those who would resist assimilation into the surrounding culture. To wit, just as Yhwh guided the people out from under Pharaoh and the Egyptian deities, Yhwh could and would ultimately guide the exiles out from under the king of Babylon and his patron deity Marduk. When Ezek 17, 20, and 34 maintain that it was Yhwh who scattered the Judahites into Babylon in the first place, they do so to make a case that Yhwh can also gather them back to Judah. Coinciding with this interpretation, Ezekiel produces a boundary marker by which the community can demonstrate its adherence to this interpretation of history: the rejection of image-based worship. Allegiance to Yhwh alone, who is not like the images of wood and stone, becomes the diacritic of Judahite religious identity.[16] The absence of cult images—of Yhwh, Marduk or any other deity—marks out the Judahite exiles as a group, a unique religious community with its own identity.

Ezekiel goes further still, envisioning a future in which the threats to its conception of legitimate Judahite nationalism and faithful Yahwism are removed, perhaps even eliminated altogether.[17] For instance, Ezek 34 replaces the fallible Judahite human king with Yhwh, the reliable divine king. Yhwh, furthermore, will both cleanse the second exodus community to remove any unfaithful within it (Ezek 20:32-44; cf. Ezek 34:1-16) and use them to purge the land of any vestiges of sinful rebellion the non-exiles leave within it (Ezek 11:14-21; 35:1–36:15) so that there are no barriers to God's presence. As a result, Yhwh himself will be there in the restored land (יהוה שׁמה, Ezek 48:35). Unmediated

---

16   Ezekiel extends this idea to those remaining in Judah, a position it expresses in the harsh condemnation of image-based worship in Ezek 8.

17   Cf. Boda, *Praying the Tradition*, 195-97.

divine presence eliminates any rationale for image-based worship, ensuring that boundary marker shall never be transgressed again.

In closing, the differences between the intra-ethnic polemic and the disguised inter-national polemic can be illustrated with a warfare metaphor: the two-front battle. The terrain of the intra-ethnic battlefront allowed for an all-out, frontal assault that attacked its adversary head on. It called for overwhelming force to defeat the enemy. Thus, Ezekiel includes an explicit, public, and repeated condemnation of the non-exiles. The terrain of the second battlefront, in which Ezekiel engaged the Neo-Babylonians, was entirely different. This battlefront required "guerrilla tactics" that made it difficult if not impossible for the enemy to identify its opponent and respond to the attack. Diversion, disguise, covert tactics, and quick hitting attacks that were over nearly as soon as they had begun were required. Ezekiel, therefore, challenges the Babylonians in elusive images, subtle metaphors, and polysemous language. The book is shrewd to vary its tactics in order to achieve its unified objective.

To return to where this study began, it is now evident that the book of Ezekiel is not silent regarding its Babylonian captors. But, to hear what it has to say, one must both learn its dialect and codes and also develop an understanding of how its vocabulary operates by allusion, image, and metaphor. Therein lies the answer to another guiding question of this study: Why does Ezekiel use the "as I live" and "lifted hand" formulae so much more often than any other text? These formulae provide the book with both the elusive yet evocative language needed to disguise the inter-national polemic and also a strong allusion to the exodus tradition that supports its explicit intra-Judahite polemic. The "as I live" and "lifted hand" formulae, in short, offered Ezekiel the ability to do two things at once.

Appendix One:
A Structural Analysis of the "As I Live"
and "Lifted Hand" Passages

1. The "As I Live" Formula Passages

(a) Num 14:11b-23a

Oracle of Judgment against the First Exodus Generation (DTR)	14:11b-23a
1. YHWH's initial statement of judgment	14:11b-12
2. Moses' plea to YHWH for restraint	14:13-19
a. Because of YHWH's reputation	14:13-14
b. Because of YHWH's power	14:15-16
c. Because of YHWH's character	14:17-18
d. Moses' request	14:19
3. YHWH's moderated statement of judgment	14:20-23a
a. YHWH's restraint	14:20
b. Statement of judgment	14:21-23aα
c. YHWH's oath promising the land	14:23aβ

(b) Num 14:26-38

Oracle of Judgment Against the First Exodus Generation (P/H)	14:26-38
1. Accusation against exodus generation	14:26-27
2. Announcement of judgment against first exodus generation	14:28-30
a. YHWH's oath of judgment with "as I live"	14:28a
b. The form of YHWH's judgment	14:28b-29
c. Salvation for Caleb and Joshua	14:30
i. Fate of the first generation	14:30aα
ii. "Lifted hand" land transfer formula	14:30aβ
iii. Caleb and Joshua spared	14:30b
3. Announcement of salvation for second exodus generation	14:31
4. Further announcement of Judgment for first exodus generation	14:32
5. Second generation will bear the guilt of the first generation	14:33-34

6. Y<small>HWH</small>'s assurance of judgment   14:35
    a. Formula of self introduction   14:35aα₁
    b. Assurance formula   14:35aα₂
    c. Summary of judgment   14:35aβ₁-35b
7. Judgment on the Spies   14:36-38
    a. Judgment on the spies   14:36-37
    b. Salvation for Joshua and Caleb   14:38

(c) Deut 32:26-43

The Song of Moses: Y<small>HWH</small>'s
1. Y<small>HWH</small>'s Reason for Restraint   32:26-30
2. Y<small>HWH</small> and the other gods   32:31-33
3. Y<small>HWH</small>'s power to avenge   32:34-38
4. Y<small>HWH</small>'s announcement of punishment   32:39-42
    a. Y<small>HWH</small>'s power to judge   32:39-40a
    b. Y<small>HWH</small> swears to punish   32:40b-42
5. The call to praise   32:43

(d) Isa 49:14-21

Y<small>HWH</small>'s Answer to Zion's Lament (Disputation Format)   49:14-21
1. Zion's Lament (Thesis)   49:14
2. Y<small>HWH</small>'s Response to Zion   49:15-20
    a. Y<small>HWH</small> cannot forget Zion (argument)   49:15
    b. Y<small>HWH</small>'s care for Zion (counter-thesis)   49:16-18
       i. Y<small>HWH</small> protects Zion   49:16-17
       ii. Y<small>HWH</small> swears to glorify Zion   49:18
    c. Y<small>HWH</small> restores Zion (counter-thesis, cont.)   49:19-20
       i. Y<small>HWH</small>'s promise   49:19
       ii. The request of the children of Zion   49:20
3. Zion's response   49:21

(e) Jer 22:24-27

Y<small>HWH</small>'s Announcement of Judgment upon Jehoiachin   22:24-27
1. Y<small>HWH</small> swears to punish Jehoiachin   22:24a

2. Description of punishment upon Jehoiachin   22:24b-27
   a. Jehoiachin's deportation to Babylon   22:24b-26a
   b. Jehoiachin will die in Babylon   22:26b-27

(f) Jer 46:13-24

Oracle of Judgment upon Egypt   46:13-24
1. Command to prophesy   46:13-14a
   a. Divine word formula   46:13a
   b. Statement of the topic   46:13b
   c. Command to speak   46:14a
2. A taunt against Egypt   46:14b-17
3. Yhwh's oath of judgment upon Egypt   46:18-19
   a. Yhwh's oath with "as I live"   46:18a
   b. A description of Egypt's enemy   46:18b
   c. Command to prepare for exile   46:19
4. A description of Egypt's punishment   46:20-24
   a. Egypt the suffering heifer   46:20-21
   b. Egypt the destroyed forest   46:22-24

(g) Ezek 5:5-17

Yhwh's Programmatic Statement of Judgment against Jerusalem
1. Initial Statement of Yhwh's Reasons   5:5-7
   a. Messenger Formula   5:5aα
   b. Definition of audience: Jerusalem   5:5aβ-5b
   c. Jerusalem is worse than the nations   5:6-7
2. Statement of Punishment   5:8-10
   a. Messenger Formula / Challenge to a Duel   5:8a
   d. Extent of Yhwh's punishment   5:8b-9
   e. Description of Jerusalem's suffering   5:10
3. Statement of Reasons 2   5:11a
   a. As I Live Oath Formula   5:11aα$_1$
   b. Jerusalem's idolatry   5:11aα2-aβ
4. Manner of Punishment 1   5:11b-13
5. Jerusalem's Message to the Nations   5:14-15
6. Manner of Punishment 2   5:16-17bα

(h) Ezek 14:12-23

(i) Ezek 16:44-58

b. Restoration of Sodom, Samaria and Jerusalem	16:53-57aα₁
c. Jerusalem mocked by Aram and Philistia	16:57aα₂-57b
d. Jerusalem will bear its disgrace	16:58

(j) Ezek 17:11-22

A Dispute over the Interpretation of a Fable	17:11-21
1. Messenger formula	17:11
2. The Interpretation	17:12-15a
3. The Thesis (implied): Zedekiah's rebellion will succeed	17:15b
4. Yʜᴡʜ's First Refutation: The Human Plane of Events	17:16-18
a. Yʜᴡʜ's Counter-thesis	17:16
b. Yʜᴡʜ's argument	17:17-18
5. Yʜᴡʜ's Second Refutation: The Divine Plane of Events	17:19-21
a. Yʜᴡʜ's Counter-thesis	17:19
b. Yʜᴡʜ's argument	17:20-21

(k) Ezek 18:1-32

A Disputation about a Proverb: Whose way is proper?	18:1-32
1. Messenger formula	18:1
2. Non-exiles' Thesis	18:2
3. Yʜᴡʜ's Response	18:3-18
a. Yʜᴡʜ's Counter-thesis	18:3-4
i. Yʜᴡʜ swears the proverb is false	18:3
ii. All lives belong to Yʜᴡʜ	18:4
b. Argument	18:5-18
i. Righteous grandfather	18:5-9
ii. Unrighteous father	18:10-13
iii. Righteous son	18:14-18
5. Exiles' Thesis: generational responsibility is proper	18:19a
6. Yʜᴡʜ's Response	18:19b-20
7. The role of repentance	18:21-24
8. Exiles' Objection: Yʜᴡʜ is unfair	18:25
9. Yʜᴡʜ's Response	18:26-28
10. Exiles' Objection: Yʜᴡʜ is unfair	18:29
11. Yʜᴡʜ's Response: the principle of judgment	18:30

12. Yʜwʜ's plea to the exiles	18:31-32
a. Repent	18:31
b. Live	18:32

(l) Ezek 20:1-31

A Disputation about the Elders Inquiry of Yʜwʜ	20:1-31
1. Date Formula	20:1aa
2. Thesis: the elders can inquire of Yʜwʜ	20:1ab-1b
3. Messenger formula	20:2
4. Yʜwʜ's counter-thesis: sworn refusal of the inquiry	20:3
5. Yʜwʜ's argument: Israel's habitual sin	20:5-29
a. First exodus generation's sin in Egypt	20:5-9
b. First exodus generation's sin in the wilderness	20:10-17
c. Second exodus generation's sin in the wilderness	20:18-26
d. Israel's sins in the land	20:27-29
6. Yʜwʜ's counter-thesis: sworn refusal of the inquiry	20:30-31

(m) Ezek 20:32-44

A Dispute about Israel Worshipping Idols	20:32-44
1. Thesis: Israel's wish to worship idols	20:32
2. Yʜwʜ's counter-thesis: sworn rule over Israel	20:33
3. Yʜwʜ's Argument	20:34-38
a. Second exodus: out of exile	20:34-35a
b. Second purification: judgment in the wilderness	20:35b-38
4. Announcement of judgment	20:39
5. Oracle of salvation: the second eisodus	20:40-44
a. Restored worship in Jerusalem	20:40-42
b. Remembrance and guilt	20:43
c. Yʜwʜ's mercy	20:44

(n) Ezek 33:10-20

A Disputation about the Weight of Sin	33:10-20
1. Messenger formula	33:10aa
2. Exiles' thesis: the weight of sin is too great	33:10aβ-10b

3. Yʜᴡʜ's counter-thesis: repentance is possible   33:11-16
    a. Yʜᴡʜ swears to allow repentance   33:11
    b. The apostasy of the righteous   33:12-13
    c. The repentance of the wicked   33:14-16
4. Exiles' continued objection: Yʜᴡʜ's way is not proper   33:17a
5. Yʜᴡʜ's response to the prophet   33:17b-20
    a. Exiles' way is not proper   33:17b
    b. The principle of repentance   33:18-19
    c. Reiteration of objection and response   33:20

(o) Ezek 33:23-29

A Disputation about Who Will Inhabit the Land	33:23-29
1. Command to Prophesy	33:23
2. The Question: who will possess the land?	33:24-29
A. Non-exiles' thesis	33:24
1. Inhabitants of Judah	33:24aα
2. We are more numerous…	33:24aβ-24b
B. Ezekiel's counterthesis: the non-exiles' flawed argument	33:25-29
1. Command to speak	33:25aα_2
2. Messenger Formula	33:25aα_3
3. Indictment of non-exiles	33:25-26
C. Announcement of Punishment	33:27-28
1. Command to speak	33:27aα_1
2. Messenger Formula	33:27aα_2
3. As I Live Formula	33:27aα_3
4. Punishment against the inhabitants	33:27
5. Punishment against the land	33:28
D. Expanded Recognition Formula	33:29

(p) Ezek 34:1-22

Yʜᴡʜ Will Judge the Shepherds and the Sheep	34:1-22
1. Messenger formula	34:1
2. Command to prophesy	34:2a
3. Judgment on the shepherds	34:2b-16
a. Yʜᴡʜ's accusation against the shepherds	34:2bα_2-6
b. Announcement of punishment	34:7-10

c. Announcement of salvation	34:11-16a
i. Yнwн will seek the flock	34:11-12
ii. Yнwн will deliver the flock	34:13-16a
d. Reiteration of punishment	34:16b
4. Judgment between the sheep	34:17-22
a. Statement of intent	34:17
b. Accusation against the fat sheep	34:18-19
c. Announcement of punishment	34:20
d. Further accusations	34:21
e. Announcement of salvation to lean sheep	34:22a
f. Announcement of punishment	34:22b

(q) Ezek 35:1–36:15

Yнwн's Message to the Mountains of Israel	35:1–36:15
1. Yнwн's Judgment against "Edom"	35:1-15
a. Messenger formula	35:1
b. Command to prophesy	35:2
c. First Announcement of Judgment upon "Mt Seir"	35:3-4
i. Statement of opposition	35:3
ii. Announcement of punishment	35:4
d. Second Announcement of Judgment upon "Mt Seir"	35:5-9
i. Yнwн's accusation against "Mt Seir"	35:5
ii. Announcement of punishment	35:6-9a
iii. Recognition formula	35:9b
e. Yнwн's dispute with "Edom"	35:10-15
i. Thesis: "Edom's" claims	35:10
ii. Argument: "Edom" will bear its taunts	35:11-13
iii. Counter-thesis: "Edom's" punishment will cause joy	
	35:14-15bα
iv. Recognition formula	35:15bβ
2. Yнwн's Salvation for Israel	36:1-15
a. Command to prophesy	36:1
b. Yнwн hears Israel's plight	36:2-4
i. Yнwн has heard the taunts	36:2
ii. Yнwн's message to Israel	36:3-4
c. Yнwн will punish those who taunt Israel	36:5-7
d. Yнwн's restoration of the mountains of Israel	36:8-12
i. Refructification of Israel	36:8-11

(r) Zeph 2:8-11

2. The "Lifted Hand" Formulae Passages

(a) Exod 6:2-8

(b) Num 14:26-38

See above, section 1(b).

(c) Deut 32:26-43

See above, section 1(c).

(d) Ezek 20:1-31

See above, section 1(l).

(e) Ezek 20:32-44

See above, section 1(m).

(f) Ezek 36:1-7

See above, section 1(p).

(g) Ezek 44:9-14

Yʜwʜ's Judgment of the Levites	44:9-14
1. Messenger Formula	44:9aα
2. Restriction of the uncircumcised	44:9aβ-9b
3. Accusation	44:10
4. Announcement of punishment	44:11-14
i. Assignment of guard duty	44:11a
ii. Service to the people	44:11b
iii. Legal formula for assigning punishment	44:12
iv. Restriction from priestly duties	44:13
v. Service in the temple	44:14

(h) Ezek 47:13-14

Introduction to the Oracle about Eschatological Land Division	47:13-14
1. Messenger formula	47:13aα
2. Explanation of Oracle	47:13aβ
3. Special role of Joseph	47:13b
4. Command to divide equally	47:14

i. Stipulation of equal portions	47:14aα
ii. Transfer from ancestors to present generation	47:14aβ-b

(i) Ps 106:24-27

Yʜᴡʜ's Announcement of Punishment against the Exodus Generation	
	106:24-27
1. Lack of trust in Yʜᴡʜ	106:24-25
2. Yʜᴡʜ's announcement of punishment	106:26-27

(j) Neh 9:5b-37

A Public Prayer of Confession and Plea for Yʜᴡʜ's Help	9:5b-37
1. Praise of Yʜᴡʜ	9:5b
2. A History of Israel	9:6-37
a. Creation	9:6
b. Abraham	9:7-8
c. Egypt	9:9-12
d. Sinai	9:13-15
e. Rebellion	9:16-17a
f. Yʜᴡʜ's restraint	9:17b
g. The Wilderness Wandering	9:18-23
h. The Conquest	9:24-25
i. The Judges	9:26-28
j. The Exile	9:29-31
2. Plea for Yʜᴡʜ's Intervention	9:32-37
a. The current plight	9:32
b. Yʜᴡʜ is just	9:33
c. Israel is sinful	9:34-35
d. The current plight	9:36-37

Bibliography

Aharoni, Yohanan. *Arad Inscriptions*. JDS. Jerusalem: Israel Exploration Society, 1981.

Albertz, Rainer. *A History of Israelite Religion in the Old Testament Period. Volume II: From the Exile to the Maccabees*. OTL. Translated by John Bowden. Louisville, Ky.: Westminster John Knox, 1994.

_____. *Israel in Exile: The History and Literature of the Sixth Century B.C.E.* Studies in Biblical Literature 3. Edited by Dennis T. Olson. Translated by David Green. Atlanta, Ga.: Society of Biblical Literature, 2003.

Allen, Leslie C. *Ezekiel 20–48*. WBC 29. Dallas, Tex.: Word Books, 1990.

_____. *Psalms 101–50*. WBC 21. Nashville, Tenn.: Thomas Nelson, 2002.

Alt, Albrecht. "Ein ägyptisches Gegenstück zu Ex 3 14." *ZAW* 35 (1940): 159-60.

Amit, Yairah. *Hidden Polemics in Biblical Narrative*. Biblical Interpretation Series 25. Translated by Jonathan Chipman. Leiden: Brill, 2000.

Assis, Elie. "Why Edom? On the Hostility towards Jacob's Brother in Prophetic Sources." *VT* 56 (2006): 1-20.

Auffret, Pierre. ""Afin que nous rendions grâce à ton nom" Étude structurelle du Psaume 106." *SEL* 11 (1994): 75-96.

Barth, Fredrik. *Ethnic Groups and Boundaries: The Social Organization of Culture Difference*. Reissued 1998 ed. Long Grove, Ill.: Waveland, 1969.

Bartlett, John R. "The Rise and Fall of the Kingdom of Edom." *Palestine Exploration Quarterly* 104 (1972): 26-37.

_____. "Edom and the Fall of Jerusalem, 587 B.C." *Palestine Exploration Quarterly* 114 (1982): 13-24.

_____. *Edom and the Edomites*. JSOTSup 77. Sheffield: Sheffield Academic Press, 1989.

Barton, John. *Reading the Old Testament: Method in Biblical Study*. 2nd ed. London: Darton, Longman and Todd, 1996.

_____. "Dating the 'Succession Narrative'." Pages 95-106 in *In Search of Pre-exilic Israel: Proceedings of the Oxford Old Testament Seminar*. Edited by John Day. JSOTSup 406. London: T & T Clark, 2004.

Beckman, Gary M. and Harry A. Hoffner. *Hittite Diplomatic Texts*. 2nd ed. Atlanta, Ga.: Society of Biblical Literature, 1999.

Bedell, Ellen D. "Criminal law in the Egyptian Ramesside Period." Brandeis University, 1973.

Ben Zvi, Ehud. *A Historical-Critical Study of the Book of Zephaniah*. BZAW 198. Berlin: Walter de Gruyter, 1991.

———. "The Prophetic Book: A Key Form of Prophetic Literature." Pages 276-97 in *The Changing Face of Form Criticism for the Twenty-First Century*. Edited by Marvin A. Sweeney and Ehud Ben Zvi. Grand Rapids, Mich.: Eerdmans, 2003.

Bergey, Ronald. "The Song of Moses (Deuteronomy 32.1-43) and Isaianic Prophecies: A Case of Early Intertextuality." *JSOT* 28 (2003): 33-54.

Berlejung, A. "Washing the Mouth: The Consecration of Divine Images in Mesopotamia." Pages 45-72 in *The Image and the Book: Iconic Cults, Aniconism, and the Rise of Book Religion in Israel and the Ancient Near East*. Edited by K. van der Toorn. CBET 21. Leuven: Peeters, 1997.

Berlin, Adele. *Zephaniah: A New Translation with Introduction and Commentary*. AB 25A. New York: Doubleday, 1994.

Bienkowski, Piotr, ed. *Early Edom and Moab: The Beginning of the Iron Age in Southern Jordan*. Sheffield Archaeological Monographs 7. Sheffield: J. R. Collis, 1992.

Black, J.A., G. Cunningham, E. Fluckiger-Hawker, E. Robson, and G. Zólyomi. "The Electronic Text Corpus of Sumerian Literature: The Sumerian King List Translation." Cited 26 August 2010. Online: http://www-etcsl.orient.ox.ac.uk/section2/tr211.htm.

Blenkinsopp, Joseph. *Isaiah 40–55: A New Translation with Introduction and Commentary*. AB 19A. New York: Doubleday, 2002.

Block, Daniel I. *Gods of the Nations: Studies in Ancient Near Eastern National Theology*. Evangelical Theological Society Monograph Series 2. Jackson, Miss.: Evangelical Theological Society, 1988.

———. *The Book of Ezekiel: Chapters 1–24*. NICOT. Grand Rapids, Mich.: Eerdmans, 1997.

———. *The Book of Ezekiel: Chapters 25–48*. NICOT. Grand Rapids, Mich.: Eerdmans, 1998.

———. "Divine Abandonment: Ezekiel's Adaptation of an Ancient Near Eastern Motif." Pages 15-42 in *The Book of Ezekiel: Theological and Anthropological Perspectives*. Edited by Margaret S. Odell and John T. Strong. SBLSymS 9. Atlanta, Ga.: Society of Biblical Literature, 2000.

Blum, Erhard. *Die Komposition der Vätergeschichte*. WMANT 57. Neukirchen-Vluyn: Neukirchener Verlag, 1984.

_____. *Studien zur Komposition des Pentateuch*. BZAW 189. Berlin: Walter de Gruyter, 1990.

_____. *"Formgeschichte*—A Misleading Category? Some Critical Remarks." Pages 32-45 in *The Changing Face of Form Criticism for the Twenty-First Century*. Edited by Marvin A. Sweeney and Ehud Ben Zvi. Grand Rapids, Mich.: Eerdmans, 2003.

Boadt, Lawrence. *Ezekiel's Oracles against Egypt: A Literary and Philological Study of Ezekiel 29–32*. BibOr 37. Rome: Biblical Institute Press, 1980.

Boda, Mark J. *Praying the Tradition: The Origin and Use of Tradition in Nehemiah 9*. BZAW 277. Berlin: Walter de Gruyter, 1999.

Bodi, Daniel. *The Book of Ezekiel and the Poem of Erra*. OBO 104. Göttingen: Vandenhoeck & Ruprecht, 1991.

Boorer, Suzanne. *The Promise of the Land as Oath: A Key to the Formation of the Pentateuch*. BZAW 205. Berlin: Walter de Gruyter, 1992.

Borger, Riekele. *Die Inschriften Asarhaddons, Königs von Assyrien*. AfO 9. Graz: Im Selbstverlage des Herausgebers, 1956.

Bourdieu, Pierre. *Outline of a Theory of Practice*. Cambridge Studies in Social Anthropology 16. Translated by Richard Nice. Cambridge: Cambridge University Press, 1977.

Brueggemann, Walter. "Isaiah 55 and Deuteronomic Theology." *ZAW* 80 (1968): 191-203.

Budd, Philip J. *Numbers*. WBC 5. Waco, Tex.: Word Books, 1984.

Burney, Charles. *Historical Dictionary of the Hittites*. Historical Dictionaries of Ancient Civilizations and Historical Eras 14. Lanham, Md.: Scarecrow Press, 2004.

Cagni, Luigi. *L'Epopea di Erra*. Studi Semitici 34. Rome: Institute for the Study of the Near East, 1969.

Carley, Keith W. *Ezekiel Among the Prophets: A Study of Ezekiel's Place in Prophetic Tradition*. SBT 31. London: SCM, 1975.

Carr, David M. *Reading the Fractures of Genesis: Historical and Literary Approaches*. Louisville, Ky.: Westminster John Knox, 1996.

_____. "Genesis in Relation to the Moses Story: Diachronic and Synchronic Perspectives." Pages 273-95 in *Studies in the Book of Genesis: Literature, Redaction and History*. Edited by A. Wénin. BETL 155. Leuven: Peeters, 2001.

_____. "Method in Determination of Dependence: An Empirical Test of Criteria Applied to Exodus 34:11-26 and its Parallels." Pages 107-40 in *Gottes Volk am Sinai: Untersuchungen zu Ex 32–34 und Dt 9–10*. Edited by

Matthias Köckert and Erhard Blum. Veröffentlichungen der Wissenschaftlichen Gesellschaft für Theologie 18. Gütersloh: Kaiser Gütersloher, 2001.

_____. *Writing on the Tablet of the Heart: Origins of Scripture and Literature.* Oxford: Oxford University Press, 2005.

Childs, Brevard S. *The Book of Exodus: A Critical, Theological Commentary.* OTL. Louisville, Ky.: Westminster Press, 1974.

Cholewiński, Alfred. *Heiligkeitsgesetz und Deuteronomium: Eine vergleichende Studie.* AnBib 66. Rome: Biblical Institute Press, 1976.

Christensen, Duane L. *Transformations of the War Oracle in Old Testament Prophecy.* Missoula, Mont.: Scholars Press, 1975.

_____. "Zephaniah 2:4-15: A Theological Basis for Josiah's Program of Political Expansion." *Catholic Biblical Quarterly* 46 (1984): 669-82.

Clements, R. E. "The Chronology of Redaction in Ez 1–24." Pages 283-94 in *Ezekiel and His Book: Textual and Literary Criticism and their Interrelation.* Edited by J. Lust. BETL 74. Leuven: Peeters, 1986.

Clifford, Hywel. "Deutero-Isaiah and Monotheism." Pages 267-89 in *Prophecy and Prophets in Ancient Israel: Proceedings of the Oxford Old Testament Seminar.* Edited by John Day. New York: T & T Clark, 2010.

Coats, George W. *Rebellion in the Wilderness: The Murmuring Motif in the Wilderness Traditions of the Old Testament.* Nashville, Tenn.: Abingdon Press, 1968.

Coats, George W. *Exodus 1–18.* FOTL 2A. Grand Rapids, Mich.: Eerdmans, 1999.

Cogan, Morton. *Imperialism and Religion: Assyria, Judah, and Israel in the Eighth and Seventh Centuries B.C.E.* SBLMS 19. Missoula, Mont.: Scholars Press, 1974.

Cohen, A. P. "Introduction." Pages ix-xxiv in *Urban Ethnicity.* Edited by A. P. Cohen. London: Tavistock, 1974.

Cohen, Mark E. *The Cultic Calendar of the Ancient Near East.* Bethesda, Md.: CDL Press, 1993.

Conklin, Blane W. *Oath Formulas in Biblical Hebrew.* Linguistic Studies in Ancient West Semitic 5. Winona Lake, Ind.: Eisenbrauns, 2011.

_____. "Oath Formulae in Classical Hebrew and Other Semitic Languages." Ph.D., The University of Chicago, 2005.

＊ Côté, James. "Identity Studies: How Close Are We to Developing a Social Science of Identity?—An Appraisal of the Field." *Identity* 6 (2006): 3-25.

Craigie, Peter C. "The Poetry of Ugarit and Israel." *Tyndale Bulletin* 22 (1971): 3-31.

_____. *Psalms 1–50*. WBC 19. Waco, Tex.: Word Books, 1983.

Crane, Ashley S. *Israel's Restoration: A Textual-Comparative Exploration of Ezekiel 36–39*. VTSup 122. Leiden: Brill, 2008.

Cross, Frank Moore. *Canaanite Myth and Hebrew Epic: Essays in the History of the Religion of Israel*. Cambridge, Mass.: Harvard University Press, 1973.

Crouch, C. L. *War and Ethics in the Ancient Near East: Military Violence in Light of Cosmology and History*. BZAW 407. Berlin: Walter de Gruyter, 2009.

_____. "Ezekiel's Oracles against the Nations in Light of a Royal Ideology of Warfare." *Journal of Biblical Literature* (2011): 473-92.

Crouch, C. L. and C. A. Strine. "Yʜᴡʜ's Battle against Chaos in Ezekiel: The Transformation of Judahite Mythology for A New Situation." *Journal of Biblical Literature* Forthcoming (2013).

Curtis, Adrain. *Psalms*. Epworth Commentaries. Peterborough: Epworth, 2004.

Dalley, Stephanie. *Myths from Mesopotamia: Creation, the Flood, Gilgamesh, and Others*. Oxford: Oxford University Press, 1989.

Damrosch, David. *The Narrative Covenant: Transformations of Genre in the Growth of Biblical Literature*. San Francisco: Harper & Row, 1987.

Darr, Kathryn Pfisterer. "Ezekiel's Justifications of God: Teaching Troubling Texts." *JSOT* 55 (1992): 97-117.

Davies, Eryl W. *Numbers*. NCB. Edited by Ronald E. Clements. Grand Rapids, Mich.: Eerdmans, 1995.

Davies, Graham I. *Hosea*. NCB. Grand Rapids, Mich.: Eerdmans, 1992.

Davis, Ellen F. *Swallowing the Scroll: Textuality and the Dynamics of Discrouse in Ezekiel's Prophecy*. JSOTSup 78. Sheffield: The Almond Press, 1989.

Day, John. "The Daniel of Ugarit and Ezekiel and the Hero of the Book of Daniel." *Vetus Testamentum* 30 (1980): 174-84.

_____. *Yahweh and the Gods and Goddesses of Canaan*. JSOTSup 265. Sheffield: Sheffield Academic Press, 2000.

_____. "Why Does God 'Establish' rather than 'Cut' Covenants in the Priestly Source?" Pages 91-109 in *Covenant as Context: Essays in Honour of E. W. Nicholson*. Edited by A. D. H. Mayes and Robert B. Salters. Oxford: Oxford University Press, 2003.

de Pury, Albert. "Abraham: The Priestly Writer's 'Ecumenical' Ancestor." Pages 163-81 in *Rethinking Foundations: Historiography in the Ancient World and in the Bible: Essays in Honour of John Van Seters*. Edited by S. L. McKenzie and Thomas Römer. BZAW 294. Berlin: Walter de Gruyter, 2000.

_____. "Situer le cycle de Jacob quelques réflexions, vingt-cinq ans plus tard." Pages 213-41 in *Studies in the Book of Genesis: Literature, Redaction and*

History. Edited by A. Wénin. BETL 155. Leuven: Leuven University Press, 2001.

———. "La tradition patriarcale en Gènese 12-35." Pages 259-70 in *Le Pentateuque en Question: Les origines et la composition des cinq premiers livres de la Bible à la lumière des recherches récentes*. Edited by Albert de Pury and Thomas Römer. Le Monde de la Bible 19. Geneva: Labor et Fides, 2002.

———. "The Jacob Story and the Beginning of the Formation of the Pentateuch." Pages 51-72 in *A Farewell to the Yahwist: The Composition of the Pentateuch in Recent European Interpretation*. Edited by Thomas B. Dozeman and Konrad Schmid. SBLSymS 34. Atlanta, Ga.: Society of Bilbical Literature, 2006.

Dick, Michael B., ed. *Born in Heaven, Made on Earth: The Making of the Cult Image in the Ancient Near East*. Winona Lake, Ind.: Eisenbrauns, 1999.

Dicou, Bert. *Edom, Israel's Brother and Antagonist: The Role of Edom in Biblical Prophecy and Story*. JSOTSup 169. Sheffield: Sheffield Academic Press, 1994.

Dietrich, Manfried. *The Babylonian Correspondence of Sargon and Sennacherib*. State Archives of Assyria 17. Edited by Julian Reade. Helsinki: Helsinki University Press, 2003.

Dion, Paul-Eugène. *La langue de Ya'udi: description et classement de l'ancien parler de Zencirli dans les cadres des langues sémitiques du nord-ouest*. Waterloo: Editions SR, 1974.

Dobbs-Allsopp, F. W., J. J. M. Roberts, C.L. Seow and R. E. Whitaker. *Hebrew Inscriptions: Texts from the Biblical Period of the Monarchy with Concordance*. New Haven, Conn.: Yale University Press, 2005.

Dozeman, Thomas B. *Commentary on Exodus*. The Eerdmans Critical Commentary. Grand Rapids, Mich.: Eerdmans, 2009.

Driver, G. R. "Linguistic and Textual Problems: Ezekiel." *Biblica* 19 (1938): 175-87.

Driver, S. R. *A Critical and Exegetical Commentary on Deuteronomy*. ICC. 3d ed. Edinburgh: T & T Clark, 1902.

Duguid, Iain M. *Ezekiel and the Leaders of Israel*. VTSup 56. Leiden: Brill, 1994.

Ebeling, Erich, Bruno Meissner, Ernst F Weidner, Wolfram Von Soden and Dietz Otto Edzard. *Reallexikon der Assyriologie*. 11 vols. Berlin: Walter de Gruyter, 1928.

Edel, Elmar. *Der Vertrag zwischen Ramses II. von Ägyten und Ḫattušili III. von Ḫatti*. Wissenschaftliche Veröffentlichung der Deutschen Orient-Gesellschaft 95. Berlin: Gebr. Mann, 1997.

Edelman, Diana V., ed. *You Shall Not Abhor an Edomtite for He Is Your Brother: Edom and Seir in History and Tradition.* Archaeology and Biblical Studies 3. Atlanta, Ga.: Scholars Press, 1995.

Eissfeldt, Otto. "The Alphabetical Cuneiform Texts from Ras Shamra Published in 'Le Palais Royal d'Ugarit,' Vol. II, 1957." *JSS* 5 (1960): 1-49.

Emerton, J. A. "The Riddle of Genesis XIV." *VT* 21 (1971): 403-39.

_____. "Some False Clues in the Study of Genesis XIV." *VT* 21 (1971): 24-47.

_____. "The Origin of the Promises to the Patriarchs in the Older Sources of the Book of Genesis." *VT* 32 (1982): 14-32.

_____. "The Promises to the Patriarchs in Genesis." *JSOT* 39 (1988): 381-400.

_____. "The Site of Salem, the City of Melchizedek (Gen 14:18)." Pages 45-71 in *Studies in the Pentateuch*. VTSup 41. Leiden: Brill, 1990.

Eriksen, Thomas Hylland. *Ethnicity and Nationalism: Anthropological Perspectives.* Anthropology, Culture and Society. London: Pluto Press, 1993.

Esler, Philip. "Social-Scientific Models in Biblical Interpretation." Pages 3-14 in *Ancient Israel: The Old Testament in Its Social Context.* Philadelphia, Pa.: Fortress, 2006.

Fensham, F. C. "Neh. 9 and Pss. 105, 106, 135 and 136. Post-exilic Historical Traditions in Poetic Form." *Journal of Northwest Semitic Languages* 9 (1981): 35-51.

Fischer-Elfert, Hans-Werner. *Die satirische Streitschrift des Papyrus Anastasi I: Übersetzung und Kommentar.* Ägyptologische Abhandlungen 44. Wiesbaden: Otto Harrassowitz, 1986.

Fishbane, Michael. *Biblical Interpretation in Ancient Israel.* Oxford: Clarendon Press, 1985.

Fitzmeyer, Joseph A. *The Aramaic Inscriptions of Sefire.* BibOr 19/A. Rome: Pontifical Biblical Institute, 1995.

Foster, Benjamin R. *Before the Muses: An Anthology of Akkadian literature.* 3rd ed. Bethesda, Md.: CDL Press, 2005.

Frahm, Eckhart. *Einleitung in die Sanherib-Inschriften.* AfO 26. Edited by Hermann Hunger. Vienna: Oriental Institute University of Vienna, 1997.

Frankel, David. *The Murmuring Stories of the Priestly School: A Retrieval of Ancient Sacerdotal Lore.* VTSup 89. Leiden: Brill, 2002.

Friedrich, Johannes. *Staatsverträge des Ḫóatti-Reiches in hethitischer Sprache.* Leipzig: J.C. Hinrichs'sche, 1930.

Frymer-Kensky, Tikva. "Suprarational Legal Procedures in Elam and Nuzi." Pages 115-31 in *Studies on the Civilizations and Culture of Nuzi and the Hurrians: In Honor of Ernest R. Lacheman on his Seventy-fifth Birthday April*

21, 1981. Edited by M.A. Morrison and D.I. Owen. Winona Lake, Ind.: Eisenbrauns, 1981.

Gal, Susan. "Language and the "Arts of Resistance"." *Cultural Anthropology* 10 (1995): 407-24.

Galambush, Julie. "God's Land and Mine: Creation as Property in the Book of Ezekiel." Pages 91-108 in *Ezekiel's Hierarchical World: Wrestling with a Tiered Reality*. Edited by Stephen L. Cook and Corrine L. Patton. SBLSymS 31. Atlanta, Ga.: Society of Biblical Literature, 2004.

Garscha, Jörg. *Studien zum Ezechielbuch: eine redaktionskritische Untersuchung von 1–39*. Europäische Hochschulschriften 23. Bern: Herbert Lang, 1974.

Gelb, I.J. Review of D.J. Wiseman, *The Vassal Treaties of Esarhaddon*. *Bibliotheca orientalis* 19 (1962): 159-62.

Gelb, I.J., et al., ed. *The Assyrian Dictionary of the Oriental Institute of the University of Chicago*. 21 vols. Chicago: The Oriental Institute, 1956.

Gerleman, Gillis. "Nutzrecht und Wohnrecht: Zur Bedeutung von אחזה und נחלה." *ZAW* 89 (1977): 313-25.

Gil-White, Francisco J. "How Thick Is Blood? The Plot Thickens.: If Ethnic Actors Are Primordialists What Remains of the Circumstantialist/ Primordialist Controversy?" *Ethnic and Racial Studies* 22:5 (1999): 789-820.

Gile, Jason. "Ezekiel 16 and the Song of Moses: A Prophetic Transformation?" *JBL* 130 (2011): 87-108.

Glazov, Gregory Y. *The Bridling of the Tongue and the Opening of the Mouth in Biblical Prophecy*. JSOTSup 311. Sheffield: Sheffield Academic Press, 2001.

Gnuse, Robert K. *No Other Gods: Emergent Monotheism in Israel*. JSOTSup 241. Sheffield: Sheffield Academic Press, 1997.

Goldingay, John. *The Message of Isaiah 40–55: A Literary-Theological Commentary*. 2 vols. London: T & T Clark, 2005.

Gordon, Cyrus H. *Ugaritic Textbook: Grammar, Texts in Transliteration, Cuneiform Selections, Glossary, Indices*. AnOr 38. Rome: Pontifical Biblical Institute, 1998.

Gosse, Bernard. "Exode 6,8 comme réponse a Ézéchiel 33,24." *Revue d'histoire et de philosophie religieuses* 74 (1994): 241-47.

————. "Les traditions sur Abraham et sur le jardin d'Éden en rapport avec Is 51,2-3 et avec le livre d'Ézéchiel." Pages 421-27 in *Studies in the Book of Genesis: Literature, Redaction and History*. Edited by A. Wénin. BETL 155. Leuven: Peeters, 2001.

Gottlieb, Isaac B. "Law, Love, and Redemption: Legal Connotations in the Language of Exodus 6:6–8." *JANES* 26 (1998): 47-57.

Götze, Albrecht. *Madduwattaš.* Leipzig: J.C. Hinrichs, 1928.

Graffy, Adrian. *A Prophet Confronts His People: The Disputation Speech in the Prophets.* AnBib 104. Rome: Biblical Institute Press, 1984.

Grayson, A. K. "Akkadian Treaties of the Seventh Century B.C." *JCS* 39 (1987): 127-60.

Green, Michael A. "A Means of Discouraging Perjury." *Göttinger Miszellen* 39 (1980): 33-39.

Greenberg, Moshe. "The Hebrew Oath Particle Ḥay/Ḥē." *JBL* 76 (1957): 34-39.

_____. *Ezekiel 1–20: A New Translation with Introduction and Commentary.* AB 22. Garden City, N.Y.: Doubleday & Co., 1983.

_____. "The Design and Themes of Ezekiel's Program of Restoration." *Interpretation* 38 (1984): 181-208.

_____. "Notes on the Influence of Tradition on Ezekiel." *JANES* 22 (1993): 29-37.

_____. *Ezekiel 21–37: A New Translation with Introduction and Commentary.* AB 22A. New York: Doubleday & Co., 1997.

Greenfield, Jonas C. "*našû-nadānu* and Its Congeners." Pages 87-91 in *Essays on the Ancient Near East in Memory of Jacob Joel Finkelstein.* Edited by Maria de Jong Ellis. Memoirs of the Connecticut Academy of Arts & Sciences 19. 1977.

Gruber, M.I. *Aspects of Non-Verbal Communication in the Ancient Near East.* Rome: Biblical Institute Press, 1980.

Guibernau, Monserrat and John Rex, eds. *The Ethnicity Reader: Nationalism, Multiculturalism, and Migration.* Cambridge: Polity Press, 1997.

Güterbock, Hans Gustav. *Siegel aus Boğazköy: Erster Tiel. Die Königssiegel der Grabungen bis 1938.* AfO 5,7. Berlin: 1940.

Güterbock, Hans Gustav and Harry A. Hoffner, eds. *The Hittite Dictionary of the Oriental Institute of the University of Chicago.* 6 vols. Chicago: The Oriental Institute of the University of Chicago, 1980.

Habel, Norman C. *The Land is Mine: Six Biblical Land Ideologies.* Minneapolis, Minn.: Fortress, 1995.

Hallo, William W. "Biblical History in Its Near Eastern Setting: The Contextual Approach." Pages 1-26 in *Essays on the Comparative Method.* Edited by C.D. Evans, William W. Hallo and John B. White. PTMS 34. Pittsburgh, Pa.: Pickwick, 1980.

Halpern, Baruch. "Brisker Pipes than Poetry: The Devlopment of Israelite Monotheism." Pages 13-56 in *Brisker Pipes*. Edited by Matthew J. Adams. FAT 63. Tübingen: Mohr Siebeck, 2009.

Hals, Ronald M. *Ezekiel*. FOTL 19. Grand Rapids, Mich.: Eerdmans, 1989.

Heidel, Alexander. *The Babylonian Genesis: The Story of Creation*. 2 ed. Chicago: University of Chicago Press, 1951.

Hillers, Delbert R. *Treaty-curses and the Old Testament Prophets*. BibOr 16. Rome: Pontifical Biblical Institute, 1964.

Holladay, William. *Jeremiah: A Commentary on the Book of the Prophet Jeremiah*. 2 vols. Hermeneia. Minneapolis, Minn.: Fortress, 1989.

Holloway, Steven W. *Aššur is King! Aššur is King! Religion in the Exercise of Power in the Neo-Assyrian Empire*. Culture and History of the Ancient Near East 10. Leiden: Brill, 2001.

Hölscher, Gustav. *Hesekiel, der Dichter und das Buch: eine literarkritische Untersuchung*. BZAW 39. Giessen: Töpelmann, 1924.

Horsley, Richard A. *Jesus and Empire: The Kingdom of God and the New World Disorder*. Minneapolis, Minn.: Fortress, 2003.

———. ed. *Hidden Transcripts and the Arts of Resistance: Applying the Work of James C. Scott to Jesus and Paul*. Semeia Studies 48. Leiden: Brill, 2004.

Horsley, Richard A., ed. *Oral Performance, Popular Tradition, and Hidden Transcript in Q*. Semeia Studies 60. Leiden: Brill, 2006.

Horst, Friedrich. "Der Eid im Alten Testament." Pages 292-316 in *Gottes Recht: gesammelte Studien zum Recht im Alten Testament*. TBü 12. Munich: Kaiser, 1961.

Hoskisson, Paul. "The *Nīšum* 'Oath' in Mari." Pages 203-10 in *Mari in Retrospect: Fifty Years of Mari and Mari Studies*. Edited by Gordon D. Young. Winona Lake, Ind.: Eisenbrauns, 1992.

Hurvitz, Avi. *A Linguistic Study of the Relationship between the Priestly Source and the Book of Ezekiel: A New Approach to an Old Problem*. CahRB 20. Paris: Gabalda, 1982.

Jacobsen, Thorkild. *The Treasures of Darkness: A History of Mesopotamian Religion*. New Haven, Conn.: Yale University Press, 1976.

Jenson, Philip P. *Graded Holiness: A Key to the Priestly Conception of the World*. JSOTSup 106. Sheffield: Sheffield Academic Press, 1992.

Joosten, Jan. *People and Land in the Holiness Code: An Exegetical Study of the Ideational Framework of the Law in Leviticus 17–26*. VTSup 67. Leiden: Brill, 1996.

Joyce, Paul M. *Ezekiel: A Commentary*. LHBOTS 482. London: T & T Clark International, 2007.

Keiser, Thomas A. "The Song of Moses a Basis for Isaiah's Prophecy." *VT* 55 (2005): 486-500.

Kennedy, James M. "Hebrew *pithôn peh* in the Book of Ezekiel." *VT* 41 (1991): 233-35.

Kienast, Burkhart. "Rechtsurkunden in ugaritischer Sprache." *UF* 11 (1979): 431-52.

Kilmer, Anne D. "How Was Queen Ereshkigal Tricked? A New Interpretation of the Descent of Ishtar." *UF* 3 (1971): 299-309.

Kitts, Margo. *Sanctified Violence in Homeric society: Oath-making Rituals in the Iliad*. Cambridge: Cambridge University Press, 2005.

Klein, Anja. *Schriftauslegung im Ezechielbuch: Redaktionsgeschichtliche Untersuchungen zu Ez 34–39*. BZAW 391. Berlin: Walter de Gruyter, 2008.

Knauf, Ernst Axel. "The Cultural Impact of Secondary State Formation: The Case of the Edomites and Moabites." Pages 47-54 in *Early Edom and Moab: The Beginning of the Iron Age in Southern Judah*. Sheffield Archaeological Monographs 7. Sheffield: J. R. Collis, 1992.

Knierim, Rolf. "Old Testament Form Criticism Reconsidered." *Interpretation* 27 (1973): 435-60.

_____. "Criticism of Literary Features, Form, Tradition, and Redaction." Pages 123-65 in *The Hebrew Bible and Its Modern Interpreters*. Edited by Douglas A. Knight and Gene M. Tucker. Philadelphia: Fortress, 1985.

_____. *Text and Concept in Leviticus 1:1-9: A Case in Exegetical Method*. FAT/I 2. Tübingen: Mohr Siebeck, 1992.

Knierim, Rolf P. and George W. Coats. *Numbers*. FOTL 4. Grand Rapids, Mich.: Eerdmans, 2005.

Knohl, Israel. *The Sanctuary of Silence: The Priestly Torah and the Holiness School*. Minneapolis, Minn.: Fortress, 1995.

Köckert, Matthias. *Vätergott und Väterverheißungen: Eine Auseinandersetzung mit Albrecht Alt und seinem Erben*. FRLANT 142. Göttingen: Vandenhoeck & Ruprecht, 1988.

_____. "Die Geschichte der Abrahamüberlieferung." Pages 103-28 in *Congress Volume Leiden 2004*. Edited by André Lemaire. VTSup 109. Leiden: Brill, 2006.

Kohata, Fujiko. *Jahwist und Priesterschrift in Exodus 3–14*. BZAW 166. Berlin: Walter de Gruyter, 1986.

Korošec, Viktor. *Hethitische Staatsverträge: ein Beitrag zu ihrer juristischen Wertung*. Leipziger rechtswissenschaftliche Studien 60. Leipzig: T. Weicher, 1931.

Kramer, S. N. *The Sacred Marriage Rite: Aspects of Faith, Myth, and Ritual in Ancient Sumer*. Bloomington, Ind.: Indiana University Press, 1969.

Kratz, Reinhard G. *The Composition of the Narrative Books of the Old Testament*. Translated by John Bowden. London: T & T Clark International, 2000.

Kuhrt, Amélie. *The Ancient Near East: c.3000-330 B.C.* 2 vols. Routledge History of the Ancient World. London: Routledge, 1995.

Kutsko, John F. *Between Heaven and Earth: Divine Presence and Absence in the Book of Ezekiel*. Biblical and Judaic Studies from the University of California, San Diego 7. Winona Lake, Ind.: Eisenbrauns, 2000.

_____. "Ezekiel's Anthropology and Its Ethical Implications." Pages 119-41 in *The Book of Ezekiel: Theological and Anthropological Perspectives*. Edited by Margaret S. Odell and John T. Strong. SBLSymS 9. Atlanta, Ga.: Society of Biblical Literature, 2000.

Labuschagne, C. J. "The Song of Moses: Its Framework and Structure." Pages 85-98 in *De fructu oris sui: Essays in Honour of Adrianus van Selms*. Edited by I. H. Eybers and et al. Pretoria Oriental Series 9. Leiden: Brill, 1971.

_____. "The *našû-nadānu* Formula and Its Biblical Equivalent." Pages 176-80 in *Travels in the World of the Old Testament: Studies Presented to Professor M. A. Beek on the Occasion of His 65th Birthday*. Edited by G. Heerma van Voss, H. J. Houwink ten Cate and N. A. Van Uchelen. Assen: Van Gorcum, 1974.

Lambert, W.G. and A.R. Millard. *Atra-Ḫasis: The Babylonian Story of the Flood*. Oxford: Clarendon Press, 1969.

Lang, Bernhard. *Kein Aufstand in Jerusalem: Die Politik des Propheten Ezechiel*. Stuttgarter Biblische Beitrage. Stuttgart: Katholisches Bibelwerk, 1978.

_____. *Monotheism and the Prophetic Minority: An Essay in Biblical History and Sociology*. The Social World of Biblical Antiquity 1. Sheffield: Almond Press, 1983.

Lapsley, Jacqueline. *Can These Bones Live? The Problem of the Moral Self in the Book of Ezekiel*. BZAW 301. Berlin: Walter de Gruyter, 2000.

Lapsley, Jacqueline E. "Shame and Self-Knowledge: The Positive Role of Shame in Ezekiel's View of the Moral Self." Pages 143-73 in *The Book of Ezekiel: Theological and Anthropological Perspectives*. Edited by Margaret S. Odell and John T. Strong. SBLSymS 9. Atlanta, Ga.: Society of Biblical Literature, 2000.

Lehmann, Manfred R. "Biblical Oaths." *ZAW* 81 (1969): 74-92.

Lemke, Werner E. "Life in the Present and Hope for the Future." *Interpretation* 38 (1984): 165-80.

Leuchter, Mark. *Josiah's Reform and Jeremiah's Scroll: Historical Calamity and Prophetic Response.* Hebrew Bible Monographs 6. Sheffield: Sheffield Phoenix Press, 2006.

_____. "Why Is The Song of Moses in the Book of Deuteronomy." *VT* 57 (2007): 295-317.

_____. *The Polemics of Exile in Jeremiah 26–45.* Cambridge: Cambridge University Press, 2008.

Levine, Baruch. *Numbers 1–20: A New Translation with Introduction and Commentary.* AB 4A. New York: Doubleday & Co., 1993.

Levinson, Bernard M. *Deuteronomy and the Hermeneutics of Legal Innovation.* Oxford: OUP, 1997.

_____. "The Manumission of Hermeneutics: The Slave Laws of the Pentateuch as a Challenge to Contemporary Pentateuchal Theory." Pages 281-324 in *Congress Volume: Leiden 2004.* Edited by André Lemaire. VTSup 109. Leiden: Brill, 2004.

Levitt Kohn, Risa. *A New Heart and a New Soul: Ezekiel, the Exile and the Torah.* JSOTSup 358. London: Sheffield Academic Press, 2002.

Levtow, Nathaniel B. *Images of Others: Iconic Politics in Ancient Israel.* Biblical and Judaic Studies from the University of California, San Diego 11. Winona Lake, Ind.: Eisenbrauns, 2008.

Lichtheim, Miriam. *Ancient Egyptian Literature: A Book of Readings.* 3 vols. Berkeley, Calif.: University of California Press, 2006.

Liverani, Mario. "The Medes at Esarhaddon's Court." *JCS* 47 (1995): 57-62.

Lohfink, Norbert F. "ירשׁ." Pages 368-96 in *Theological Dictionary of the Old Testament.* Edited by G. Johannes Botterwerk and Helmer Ringgren. 6. Grand Rapids, Mich.: Eerdmans, 1990.

_____. "Was There a Deuteronomistic Movement?" Pages 36-66 in *Those Elusive Deuteronomists: The Phenomenon of Pan-Deuteronomism.* Edited by L. S. Schearing and S. L. McKenzie. JSOTSup 268. Sheffield: Sheffield Academic Press, 1999.

Longman, Tremper. *Fictional Akkadian Autobiography: A Generic and Comparative Study.* Winona Lake, Ind.: Eisenbrauns, 1991.

_____. "Israelite Genres in Their Ancient Near Eastern Context." Pages 177-95 in *The Changing Face of Form Criticism for the Twenty-First Century.* Edited by Marvin A. Sweeney and Ehud Ben Zvi. Grand Rapids, Mich.: Eerdmans, 2003.

Lorton, David. "God's Beneficent Creation: Coffin Texts Spell 1130, the Instructions for Merikare, and the Great Hymn to the Aten." *Studien zur altägzptischen Kultur* 20 (1993): 125-55.

Luckenbill, Daniel David. *The Annals of Sennacherib*. OIP 2. Edited by James Henry Breasted. Chicago: The University of Chicago Press, 1924.

_____. *Ancient Records of Assyria and Babylonia: Volume II, Historical Records of Assyria from Sargon to the End*. Ancient Records 2. Chicago: University of Chicago Press, 1927.

Lust, J. "Ez., XX, 4-26 une parodie de l'histoire religieuse d'Israel." *Ephemerides theologicae lovanienses* 43 (1967): 488-527.

_____. "The Final Text and Textual Criticism: Ez 39,28." Pages 48-54 in *Ezekiel and His Book: Textual and Literary Criticism and their Interrelation*. Edited by J. Lust. BETL 74. Leuven: Peeters, 1986.

_____. "The Use of Textual Witnesses for the Establishment of the Text. The Shorter and Longer Texts of Ezekiel." Pages 7-20 in *Ezekiel and His Book: Textual and Literary Criticism and their Interrelation*. Edited by J. Lust. BETL 74. Leuven: Peeters, 1986.

_____. "For I Lift Up My Hand to Heaven and Swear: Deut 32:40." Pages 155-64 in *Studies in Deuteronomy: In Honour of C.J. Labuschagne on the Occasion of His 65th Birthday*. VTSup 53. Leiden: Brill, 1994.

_____. "The Raised Hand of the Lord in Deut. 32:40 according to MT, 4QDeutq, and LXX." *Textus* 18 (1995): 33-45.

_____. "Exodus 6,2-8 and Ezekiel." Pages 209-24 in *Studies in the Book of Exodus: Redaction-Reception-Interpretation*. Edited by Marc Vervenne. BETL 126. Leuven: Peeters, 1996.

_____. "Edom – Adam in Ezekiel, in the MT and LXX." Pages 387-401 in *Studies in the Hebrew Bible, Qumran, and the Septuagint Presented to Eugene Ulrich*. Edited by Peter W. Flint, Emmanuel Tov and James C. VanderKam. VTSup 101. Leiden: Brill, 2006.

Lyons, Michael A. *From Law to Prophecy: Ezekiel's Use of the Holiness Code*. LHBOTS 507. New York: T & T Clark, 2009.

Macchi, Jean-Daniel. "Les doublets dans le livre de Jérémie." Pages 119-50 in *The Book of Jeremiah and its Reception*. Edited by A. W. H. Curtis and Thomas Römer. BETL 128. Leuven: Peeters, 1997.

MacDonald, Nathan. "Monotheism and Isaiah." in *Interpreting Isaiah: Issues and Approaches*. Edited by David G. Firth and H.G. M. Williamson. Nottingham: Apollos, 2009.

_____. *Deuteronomy and the Meaning of 'Monotheism'*. Forschungen zum Alten Testament 2.1. 2nd ed. Tübingen: Mohr Siebeck, 2012.

Machinist, Peter. "Mesopotamian Imperialism and Israelite Religion: A Case Study from Second Isaiah." Pages 237-64 in *Symbiosis, Symbolism and Power of the Past: Canaan, Ancient Israel and Their Neighbors. Centennial Symposium of the W. F. Albright Institute of Archaeological Research and the American Schools of Oriental Research*. Edited by W. G. Dever and S. Gitin. Winona Lake, Ind.: Eisenbrauns, 2003.

Macintosh, A. A. *A Critical and Exegetical Commentary on Hosea*. ICC. Edinburgh: T & T Clark, 1997.

Malul, Meir. *Studies in Mesopotamian Legal Symbolism*. AOAT 221. Edited by Kurt Bergerhof, Manfried Dietrich and Oswald Loretz. Kevelaer: Butzon & Bercker, 1988.

_____. *The Comparative Method in Ancient Near Eastern and Biblical Legal Studies*. AOAT 227. Neukirchen-Vluyn: Neukirchener Verlag, 1990.

Margalit, Baruch. *The Ugaritic Poem of Aqht: Text, Translation, Commentary*. BZAW 182. Berlin: Walter de Gruyter, 1989.

Márquez Rowe, Ignacio. *The Royal Deeds of Ugarit: A Study of Ancient Near Eastern Diplomatics*. AOAT 335. Munster: Ugarit-Verlag, 2006.

Mathews, Claire R. *Defending Zion: Edom's Desolation and Jacob's Restoration (Isaiah 34–35) in Context*. BZAW 236. Berlin: Walter de Gruyter, 1995.

Matties, Gordon H. *Ezekiel 18 and the Rhetoric of Moral Discourse*. SBLDS 126. Atlanta, Ga.: Scholars Press, 1990.

Mayes, A. D. H. *Deuteronomy*. NCB. Grand Rapids, Mich.: Eerdmans, 1981.

Mayfield, Tyler D. *Literary Structure and Setting in Ezekiel*. FAT II/43. Tübingen: Mohr Siebeck, 2010.

McCarter, P. Kyle. *I Samuel: A New Translation with Introduction, Notes & Commentary*. AB 8. Garden City, N.Y.: Doubleday & Co, 1980.

_____. *II Samuel: A New Translation with Introduction, Notes and Commentary*. AB 9. Garden City, NY: Doubleday, 1984.

McCarthy, Carmel. *The Tiqqune Sopherim and other Theological Corrections in the Masoretic Text of the Old Testament*. OBO 36. Göttingen: Vandehoeck & Ruprecht, 1981.

_____. *Deuteronomy*. Biblia Hebraica Quinta 5. Stuttgart: Deutsche Bibelgesellschaft, 2007.

McCarthy, Dennis J. *Treaty and Covenant: A Study in Form in the Ancient Oriental Documents and in the Old Testament*. AnBib 21. Rome: Pontifical Biblical Institute, 1963.

McConville, J. G. *Deuteronomy*. Apollos Old Testament Commentary 5. Leicester, England: Apollos, 2002.

McDowell, A.G. *Jurisdiction in the Workmen's Community of Deir El-Medîna*. Egytologische uitgaven 5. Edited by Mordechai Cogan. Leiden: Nederlands Instituut voor het Nabije Oosten, 1990.

McEvenue, Sean E. "The Source-Critical Problem in Num 14,26-38." *Biblica* 51 (1969): 453-65.

_____. *The Narrative Style of the Priestly Writer*. AnBib 50. Rome: Biblical Institute Press, 1971.

McGarry, Eugene. "The Ambidextrious Angel (Daniel 12:7 and Deuteronomy 32:40): Inner-Biblical Exegesis and Textual Criticism in Counterpoint." *JBL* 124 (2005): 211-28.

McKane, William. *A Critical and Exegetical Commentary on Jeremiah*. 2 vols. ICC. Edinburgh: T & T Clark, 1986.

McKenzie, Steven L. *The Trouble with Kings: The Composition of the Book of Kings in the Deuteronomistic History*. VTSup 42. Leiden: Brill, 1991.

_____. "Why Didn't David Build the Temple?: The History of a Biblical Tradition." Pages 204-24 in *Worship and the Hebrew Bible: Esays in Honour of John T. Willis*. Edited by M. Patrick Graham, Rick R. Marrs and Steven L. McKenzie. JSTOSup 284. Sheffield: Sheffield Academic Press, 1999.

Mein, Andrew. *Ezekiel and the Ethics of Exile*. OTM. Oxford: Oxford University Press, 2001.

_____. "Profitable and Unprofitable Shepherds: Economic and Theological Perspectives on Ezekiel 34." *JSOT* 31 (2007): 493-504.

Mendenhall, George E. *Law and Covenant in Israel and the Ancient Near East*. Pittsburgh, Pa.: The Presbyterian Board of Colportage of Western Pennsylvania, 1955.

Mercer, Samuel A. B. *The Oath in Babylonian and Assyrian Literature, with an Appendix [in Germ.] on the Goddess Esch-Ghanna*. Paris: Librarie Paul Geuthner, 1912.

_____. "The Oath in Cuneiform Inscriptions III: The Oath Since the Time of the Hammurabi Dynasty." *The American Journal of Semitic Languages and Literatures* 30 (1914): 196-211.

Milgrom, Jacob. "The Structures of Numbers: Chapters 11–12 and 13–14 and their Redaction. Preliminary Gropings, In Honor of Robert Gordis." Pages 49-61 in *Judaic Perspectives on Ancient Israel*. Edited by Jacob Neusner, Baruch Levine and Ernest S. Frerichs. Philadelphia: Fortress, 1987.

_____. *Numbers: The Traditional Hebrew Text with the New JPS Translation.* JPS Torah. Philadelphia: Jewish Publication Society, 1990.

_____. *Leviticus 17–22: A New Translation with Introduction and Commentary.* AB 3A. New York: Doubleday, 2000.

_____. *Leviticus 23–27: A New Translation with Introduction and Commentary.* AB 3B. New York: Doubleday, 2000.

Moberly, R. W. L. "How Appropriate is 'Monotheism' as a Category for Biblical Interpretation?" Pages 216-34 in *Early Jewish and Christian Monotheism.* Edited by L. T. Stuckenbruck and W. E. S. North. JSNTSup 263. London: T & T Clark, 2004.

Morschauser, Scott. "The End of the *sdf(ꜣ)-tr(yt)* "Oath"." *Journal of the American Research Center in Egypt* 25 (1988): 93-103.

_____. *Threat-formulae in Ancient Egypt: A Study of the History, Structure, and Use of Threats and Curses in Ancient Egypt.* Baltimore, Md.: Halgo, 1991.

Muilenburg, James. "Form Criticism and Beyond." *JBL* 88 (1969): 1-18.

Murray, D. F. "The Rhetoric of Disputation: Re-examination of a Prophetic Genre." *JSOT* 38 (1987): 95-121.

Nelson, Richard D. *The Double Redaction of the Deuteronomistic History.* JSOTSup 18. Sheffield: JSOT Press, 1981.

Nestor, Dermot Anthony. *Cognitive Perspectives on Israelite Identity.* LHBOTS 519. New York: T & T Clark, 2010.

Nevader, Madhavi. "Exile and Institution: Monarchy in the Books of Deuteronomy and Ezekiel." Unpublished D.Phil Thesis, University of Oxford, 2009. Forthcoming as idem. *YHWH Versus David.* OTM. Oxford: Oxford University Press, 2013.

Nicholson, Ernest W. *God and His People: Covenant and Theology in the Old Testament.* Oxford: Clarendon Press, 1986.

_____. *The Pentateuch in the Twentieth Century: The Legacy of Julius Wellhausen.* Oxford: Oxford University Press, 1998.

Niditch, Susan. *Oral World and Written Word: Orality and Literacy in Ancient Israel.* London: SPCK, 1997.

Nihan, Christophe. "The Holiness Code between D and P: Some Comments on the Function and Significance of Leviticus 17–26 in the Composition of the Torah." Pages 81-122 in *Das Deuteronomium zwischen Pentateuch und deuteronomistischem Geschichtswerk.* Edited by E. Otto and R. Achenbach. FRLANT 206. Göttingen: Vandenhoeck & Ruprecht, 2004.

_____. *From Priestly Torah to Pentateuch.* FAT II/25. Tübingen: Mohr Siebeck, 2007.

_____. "The Priestly Covenant, Its Reinterpretations, and the Composition of "P"." Pages 87-134 in *The Strata of the Priestly Writings: Contemporary Debate and Future Directions*. Edited by Sarah Shectman and Joel S. Baden. AThANT 95. Zurich: Theologischer Verlag Zürich, 2009.

Nissinen, Martti. "Fear Not: A Study on an Ancient Near Eastern Phrase." Pages 122-61 in *The Changing Face of Form Criticism for the Twenty-First Century*. Edited by Marvin A. Sweeney and Ehud Ben Zvi. Grand Rapids, Mich.: Eerdmans, 2003.

Nogalski, James and Marvin A. Sweeney, eds. *Reading and Hearing the Book of the Twelve*. Society of Biblical Literature Symposium Series 15. Atlanta, Ga.: Society of Biblical Literature, 2000.

Noth, Martin. *Überlieferungsgeschichte des Pentateuch*. Stuttgart: Kohlhammer, 1948.

_____. *Numbers*. OTL. Chatham: SCM Press Ltd., 1968.

_____. *A History of Pentateuchal Traditions*. Translated by Bernard W. Anderson. Englewood Cliffs, N. J.: Prentice Hall, 1972.

Nougayrol, Jean. *Textes Accadiens et Hourrites des archives est, ouest et centrales: Avec des études de G. Boyer et E. Laroche*. PRU 3. Paris: Imprimerie Nationale, 1955.

Odell, Margaret S. *Ezekiel*. Smith & Helwys Bible Commentary. Macon, Ga.: Smith & Helwys, 2005.

Oettinger, Norbert. *Die Militärischen Eide der Hethiter*. Studien zu den Bogazköy-Texten 22. Wiesbaden: Harrassowitz, 1976.

Olley, John W. *Ezekiel: A Commentary based on Iezekieœl in Codex Vaticanus*. Septuagint Commentary Series. Leiden: Brill, 2009.

Olson, Dennis T. *The Death of the Old and the Birth of the New: The Framework of the Book of Numbers and the Pentateuch*. BJS 71. Edited by Ernest S. Freichs. Chico, Calif.: Scholars Press, 1985.

Otten, Heinrich. "Ein hethitischer Vertrag aus dem 15./14. Jahrhundert v. Chr. (KBo XVI 47)." *Istanbuler Mitteilungen* 17 (1967): 55-62.

Pakkala, Juha. *Intolerant Monolatry in the Deuteronomistic History*. Publications of the Finnish Exegetical Society 76. Göttingen: Vandenhoeck & Ruprecht, 1999.

Palmowski, Jan. *Inventing a Socialist Nation: Heimat and the Politics of Everyday Life in the GDR, 1945-1990*. New Studies in European History. Cambridge: Cambridge University Press, 2009.

Parke-Taylor, Geoffrey H. *The Formation of the Book of Jeremiah: Doublets and Recurring Phrases*. SBLMS 51. Atlanta, Ga.: Society of Biblical Literature, 2000.

Parpola, Simo. "Neo-Assyrian Treaties from the Royal Archives of Nineveh." *JCS* 39 (1987): 161-89.

Parpola, Simo and Kazuko Watanabe. *Neo-Assyrian Treaties and Loyalty Oaths*. State Archives of Assyria 2. Helsinki: Helsinki University Press, 1988.

Patton, Corrine. ""I Myself Gave Them Laws that Were Not Good": Ezekiel 20 and the Exodus Traditions." *JSOT* 69 (1996): 73-90.

Pedersen, Johannes. *Der Eid bei den Semiten: in seinem Verhältnis zu verwandten Erscheinungen sowie die Stellung des Eides im Islam*. Strassburg: K. J. Trübner, 1914.

Perdue, Leo G. "The Testament of David and Egyptian Royal Instructions." Pages 79-96 in *Scripture in Context II: More Essays on the Comparative Method*. Edited by William W. Hallo, James C. Moyer and Leo G. Perdue. Winona Lake, Ind.: Eisenbrauns, 1983.

Person, Raymond F., Jr., ed. "In Conversation with Thomas Römer, The So-Called Deuteronomistic History: A Sociological, Historical and Literary Introduction (London: T. & T. Clark, 2005)." *JHS* 9. 2009.

Petry, Sven. *Die Entgrenzung JHWHs: Monalatrie, Bilderverbot und Monotheismus im Deuteronomium, in Deuterojesaja und im Ezechielbuch*. FAT/II 27. Tübingen: Mohr Siebeck, 2007.

Pohlmann, Karl-Friedrich. *Ezechielstudien: zur Redaktionsgeschichte des Buches und zur Frage nach den ältesten Texten*. BZAW 202. Berlin: Walter de Gruyter, 1992.

_____. *Der Prophet Hesekiel/Ezechiel Kapitel 1–19*. ATD 22.1. Göttingen: Vandenhoeck & Ruprecht, 1996.

_____. *Der Prophet Hesekiel/Ezechiel Kapitel 20–48*. ATD 22.2. Göttingen: Vandenhoeck & Ruprecht, 2001.

Pons, J. "Le vocabulaire d'Ez 20. Le prophète s'oppose à la vision deutéronomiste de l'histoire." Pages 214-33 in *Ezekiel and His Book: Textual and Literary Criticism and their Interrelation*. Edited by J. Lust. BETL 74. Leuven: Peeters, 1986.

Porten, Bezalel and Jonas C. Greenfield. *Jews of Elephantine and Arameans of Syria: Fifty Aramaic Texts with Hebrew and English Translations*. Jerusalem: Hebrew University of Jerusalem, 1984.

Porter, Barbara N. *Images, Power, and Politics: Figurative Aspects of Esarhaddon's Babylonian Policy*. Memoirs of the American Philosophical Society. Philadelphia: American Philosophical Society, 1993.

Portier-Young, Anathea. *Apocalypse Against Empire: Theologies of Resistance in Early Judaism.* Grand Rapids, Mich.: Eerdmans, 2011.

Quack, Joachim Friedrich. *Studien zur Lehre für Merikare.* Göttinger Orient-forschungen Ägypten, 23. Edited by Friedrich Junge and Wolfhart Westendorf. Wiesbaden: Harrassowitz, 1992.

Redford, Donald B. *A Study of the Story of Joseph (Genesis 37–50).* VTSup 20. Leiden: Brill, 1970.

_____. *Egypt, Canaan, and Israel in Ancient Times.* Princeton, N.J.: Princeton University Press, 1992.

Reed, David. "Rethinking John's Social Setting: Hidden Transcript, Anti-language, and the Negotiation of Empire." *Biblical Theology Bulletin* 36 (2006): 93-106.

Reiner, Erica. *Your Thwarts in Pieces, Your Mooring Rope Cut: Poetry from Babylonia and Assyria.* Michigan Studies in the Humanities 5. Ann Arbor, Mich.: Horace H. Rackham School of Graduate Studies at the University of Michigan, 1985.

Rendtorff, Rolf. "Genesis 15 im Rahmen der theologischen Bearbeitung der Vätergeschichten." Pages 74-81 in *Werden und Wirken des Alten Testaments: Festschrift für Claus Westermann.* Edited by R. Albertz and et al. Göttingen: Vandenhoeck & Ruprecht, 1980.

_____. *The Problem of the Process of Transmission in the Pentateuch.* JSOTSup 89. Translated by John J. Scullion. Sheffield: Sheffield Academic Press, 1990.

_____. *Die Bundesformel.* Stuttgart: Verlag Katholisches Bibelwerk, 1995.

_____. *The Covenant Formula: An Exegetical and Theological Investigation.* OTS. Translated by Margaret Kohl. Edinburgh: T & T Clark, 1998.

Renz, Thomas. "The Use of the Zion Tradition in the Book of Ezekiel." in *Zion, City of Our God.* Edited by Richard S. Hess and Gordon J. Wenham. Grand Rapids, Mich.: Eerdmans, 1999.

_____. *The Rhetorical Function of the Book of Ezekiel.* VTSup 76. Leiden: Brill, 2002.

Richter, Wolfgang. *Exegese als Literaturwissenschaft: Entwurf einer alttestament-lichen Literaturtheorie und Methodologie.* Göttingen: Vandenhoeck & Ruprecht, 1971.

Riemschneider, Kaspar K. "Die hethitischen Landschenkungsurkunden." *Mit-teilungen des Instituts für Orientforscung* 6 (1958): 321-81.

Rom-Shiloni, Dalit. "Ezekiel as the Voice of the Exiles and Constructor of Exilic Ideology." *Hebrew Union College Annual* 76 (2005): 1-45.

Römer, Thomas. *Israels Väter: Untersuchungen zur Väterthematik im Deutero-nomium und in der deuteronomistischen Tradition.* OBO 99. Göttingen: Vandenhoeck & Ruprecht, 1990.

_____. "Deuteronomy in Search of Origins." Pages 112-38 in *Reconsidering Israel and Judah: Recent Studies on the Deuteronomistic History.* Edited by Gary N. Knoppers and J. Gordon McConville. Sources for Biblical and Theological Study 8. Winona Lake, Ind.: Eisenbrauns, 2000.

_____. "Is There a Deuteronomistic Redaction in the Book of Jeremiah?" Pages 399-421 in *Israel Constructs its History: Deuteronomistic Historio-graphy in Recent Research.* Edited by Albert de Pury, Thomas Römer and Jean-Daniel Macchi. JSOTSup 306. Sheffield: Sheffield Academic Press, 2000.

_____. "Recherches actuelles sur le cycle d'Abraham." Pages 179-211 in *Studies in the Book of Genesis: Literature, Redaction and History.* Edited by A. Wénin. BETL 160. Leuven: Peeters, 2001.

_____. "Exodus 3-4 und die aktuelle Pentateuchdiskussion." Pages 65-79 in *The Interpretation of the Exodus: Studies in Honour of Cornelius Houtman.* Edited by Riemer Roukema, Bert Jan Lietaert Peerbolte, Klaas Spronk and Jan-Wim Wesselius. CBET 44. Leuven: Peeters, 2006.

_____. *The So-Called Deuteronomistic History: A Sociological, Historical and Literary Introduction.* London: T & T Clark, 2007.

Rooker, Mark F. *Biblical Hebrew in Transition: The Language of the Book of Ezekiel.* JSOTSup 90. Sheffield: Sheffield Academic Press, 1990.

Roth, Ann Macy. "The *psš-kf* and the 'Opening of the Mouth' Ceremony: A Ritual of Birth and Rebirth." *Journal of Egyptian Archaeology* 78 (1992): 113-47.

_____. "Fingers, Stars, and the 'Opening of the Mouth': The Nature and Function of the *nṯrjw*-Blades." *Journal of Egyptian Archaeology* 79 (1993): 57-79.

Roth, Martha T. *Babylonian Marriage Agreements 7th – 3rd Centuries B.C.* AOAT 222. Neukirchen-Vluyn: Neukirchener Verlag, 1989.

Sanders, Paul D. *The Provenance of Deuteronomy 32.* OtSt. Leiden: Brill, 1996.

Schart, Aaron. "Redactional Models: Comparisons, Contrasts, Agreements, Disagreements." Pages 893-908 in *SBL Seminar Papers 1998.* Society of Biblical Literature 1998 2. Orlando, Fl.: Scholars Press, 1998.

_____. *Die Enstehung des Zwölfprophetenbuchs.* BZAW 260. Berlin: Walter de Gruyter, 1998.

_____. "Reconstructing the Redaction History of the Twelve Prophets: Problems and Models." Pages 34-48 in *Reading and Hearing the Book of the Twelve*. Edited by James D. Nogalski and Marvin A. Sweeney. SBLSymS 15. Atlanta, Ga.: Society of Biblical Literature, 2000.

Scheuer, Blaženka. *The Return of YHWH: The Tension between Deliverance and Repentance in Isaiah 40–55*. BZAW 377. Berlin: Walter de Gruyter, 2008.

Schmid, Konrad. *Erzväter und Exodus. Untersuchungen zur doppelten Begründung der Ursprünge Israels innerhalb der Geschichtsbücher des Alten Testaments*. WMANT 81. Neukirchner-Vluyn: Neukirchner Verlag, 1999.

_____. *Genesis and the Moses Story: Israel's Dual Origins in the Hebrew Bible*. Siphrut 3. Translated by James D. Nogalski. Winona Lake, Ind.: Eisenbrauns, 2010.

Schoors, Antoon. *I Am God Your Saviour: A Form-Critical Study of the Main Genres in Is. XL-LV*. VTSup 24. Leiden: Brill, 1973.

Schwartz, Baruch J. "The Bearing of Sin in the Priestly Literature." Pages 3-21 in *Pomegranates and Golden Bells: Studies in Biblical, Jewish, and Near Eastern Ritual, Law, and Literature in Honor of Jacob Milgrom*. Edited by David P. Wright, D. N. Freedman and Avi Hurvitz. Winona Lake, Ind.: Eisenbrauns, 1995.

_____. "Ezekiel's Dim View of Israel's Restoration." Pages 43-67 in *The Book of Ezekiel: Theological and Anthropological Perspectives*. Edited by Margaret S. Odell and John T. Strong. SBLSymS 9. Altanta, Ga.: Society of Biblical Literature, 2000.

Scott, James C. *Weapons of the Weak: Everyday Forms of Peasant Resistance*. New Haven, Conn.: Yale University Press, 1985.

_____. *Domination and the Arts of Resistance: Hidden Transcripts*. New Haven, Conn.: Yale University Press, 1990.

Seely, David Rolph. "The Raised Hand of God as an Oath Gesture." Pages 411-21 in *Fortunate the Eyes that See: Essays in Honor of David Noel Freedman in Celebration of His Seventieth Birthday*. Edited by Astrid B. Beck. Grand Rapids, Mich.: Eerdmans, 1995.

Seitz, Christopher R. "The Divine Name in Christian Scripture." Pages 251-62 in *Word Without End: The Old Testament as Abiding Theological Witness*. Grand Rapids, Mich.: Eerdmans, 1998.

Singer, Itamar. "A Political History of Ugarit." Pages 603-733 in *Handbook of Ugaritic Studies*. Edited by Wilfred G.E. Watson and Nicolas Wyatt. Handbuch der Orientalistik, Nahe und der Mittlere Osten 39. Leiden: Brill, 1999.

Ska, Jean-Louis. *Introduction to Reading the Pentateuch.* Translated by Sr. Pascale Dominique. Winona Lake, Ind.: Eisenbrauns, 2006.

Skehan, Patrick W. "A Fragment of the 'Song of Moses' (Deut. 32) from Qumran." *BASOR* 136 (1954): 12-15.

———. "The Structure of the Song of Moses." Pages 156-68 in *A Song of Power and the Power of Song: Essays on the Book of Deuteronomy.* Edited by Duane L. Christensen. Winona Lake, Ind.: Eisenbrauns, 1993.

Smith, Daniel L., *Religion of the Landless: The Social Context of the Babylonian Exile.* Bloomington, Ind: Meyer Stone, 1989.

Smith, Mark S. *The Origins of Biblical Monotheism.* Oxford: Oxford University Press, 2001.

Southwood, Katherine E. *Ethnicity and the Mixed Marraige Crisis in Ezra 9–10.* Oxford Theological Monographs. Oxford: Oxford University Press, 2012.

Spalinger, Anthony J. *Aspects of the Military Documents of the Ancient Egyptians.* Yale Near Eastern Researches 9. Edited by William W. Hallo. New Haven, Conn.: Yale University Press, 1982.

Speiser, E. A. "Akkadian Documents from Ras Shamra." *Journal of the American Oriental Society* 75 (1955): 154-65.

Stackert, Jeffrey. *Rewriting the Torah: Literary Revision in Deuteronomy and the Holiness Legislation.* FAT/I 52. Tübingen: Mohr Siebeck, 2007.

Streck, Maximilian. *Assurbanipal und die letzten assyrischen Könige bis zum untergange Nineveh's.* Vorderasiatische Bibliothek 7.2. Leipzig: Hinrich, 1916.

Strine, C. A. "The Role of Repentance in the Book of Ezekiel: A Second Chance for the Second Generation." *Journal of Theological Studies* 63 (2012): 467-91.

Stulman, Louis. *The Prose Sermons of the Book of Jeremiah: A Redescription of the Correspondences with the Deuteronomistic Literature in the Light of Recent Text-Critical Research.* SBLDS 83. Atlanta, Ga.: Scholars Press, 1986.

Sweeney, Marvin A. "A Form-Critical Reassessment of the Book of Zephaniah." *CBQ* 53 (1991): 388-408.

———. "Structure, Genre, and Intent in the Book of Habakkuk." *VT* 41 (1991): 63-83.

———. "Concerning the Structure and Generic Character of the Book of Nahum." *ZAW* 104 (1992): 364-77.

———. "Formation and Form in Prophetic Literature." Pages 113-26 in *Old Testament Interpretation: Past, Present, and Future.* Edited by James Luther Mays, David L. Petersen and Kent Harold Richards. Edinburgh: T & T Clark, 1995.

_____. *Isaiah 1–39 with an Introduction to the Prophetic Literature*. FOTL 16. Grand Rapids, Mich.: Eerdmans, 1996.

_____. "A Form-Critical Reading of Hosea." *JHS* 2 (1998): 1-16.

_____. "Form Criticism." Pages 58-89 in *To Each Its Own Meaning: Biblical Criticisms and their Application*. Edited by S. L. McKenzie and S. R. Haynes. Louisville, Ky.: Westminster John Knox, 1999.

_____. *Zephaniah: A Commentary*. Hermeneia. Minneapolis, Minn.: Fortress, 2003.

_____. "The Assertion of Divine Power in Ezekiel 33:21-39:29." Pages 156-72 in *Form and Intertextuality in Prophetic and Apocalyptic Literature*. FAT 45. Tübingen: Mohr Siebeck, 2005.

Tadmor, Hayim. "Treaty and Oath in the Ancient Near East: A Historian's Approach." Pages 127-52 in *Humanizing America's Iconic Book: Society of Biblical Literature Centennial Addresses 1980*. Edited by Gene M. Tucker and Douglas A. Knight. Society of Biblical Literature Centennial Publications 6. Chico, Calif.: Scholars Press, 1982.

Talon, Philippe. *The Standard Babylonian Creation Myth Enūma Eliš: Introduction, Cuneiform Text, Transliteration, and Sign List with a Translation and Glossary in French*. State Archives of Assyria Cuneiform Texts 4. Helsinki: The Neo-Assyrian Text Corpus Project, 2005.

Thereau-Dangin, F. *Rituels accadien*. Paris: E. Leroux, 1921.

Thiessen, Matthew. "The Form and Function of the Song of Moses (Deuteronomy 32:1-43)." *JBL* 123 (2004): 401-24.

Tilly, Charles. "Domination, Resistance, Compliance. Discourse." *Sociological Forum* 6 (1991): 593-602.

Tischler, Johann. *Hethitisches Handwörterbuch*. Innsbrucker Beiträge zur Sprach-wissenschaft 102. Innsbruck: Institute for Language and Literature and the University of Innsbruck, 2001.

Tooman, William A. "Ezekiel's Radcal Challenge to Inviolability." *ZAW* 121 (2009): 498-514.

_____. *Gog of Magog: Reuse of Scripture and Compositional Technique in Ezekiel 38–39*. Forschungen zum Alten Testament 2 52. Tübingen: Mohr Siebeck, 2011.

Torrey, C. C. *Pseudo-Ezekiel and the Original Prophecy*. Yale Oriental Series 18. New Haven, Conn.: Yale University Press, 1930.

Tov, Emanuel. "Recensional Differences between the MT and LXX of Ezekiel." *Ephemerides theologicae lovanienses* 62 (1986): 89-101.

Bibliography 319

Tucker, Gene M. *Form Criticism of the Old Testament*. Guides to Biblical Scholarship: Old Testament Series. Philadelphia: Fortress, 1971.

van der Kooij, Arie. "The Ending of the Song of Moses: On the Pre-Masoretic Version of Deut 32:43." Pages 93-100 in *Studies in Deuteronomy: In Honour of C. J. Labuschange on the Occassion of His 65th Birthday*. Edited by F. García Martinez, A. Hilhorst, J.T.A.G.M. van Ruiten and A.S. van der Woude. VTSup 53. Leiden: Brill, 1994.
Van Seters, John. "Confessional Reformulation in the Exilic Period." *VT* 22 (1972): 448-59.
_____. *Abraham in History and Tradition*. New Haven, Conn.: Yale University Press, 1975.
_____. *Prologue to History: The Yahwist as Historian in Genesis*. Zürich: Theologischer Verlag Zürich, 1992.
Vermeylen, Jacques. *Du prophète Isaïe à l'apocalyptique: Isaïe I-XXXV, miroir d'un demi-millénaire d'expereince religieuse en Israël*. EBib 2. Paris: Gabalda, 1977.
Viberg, Åke. *Symbols of Law: A Contextual Analysis of Legal Symbolic Acts in the Old Testament*. Coniectanea Biblia: Old Testament Series 34. Stockholm: Almqvist & Wiksell International, 1992.
Virolleaud, Charles and Claude F-A Schaeffer. *Le Palais Royal d'Ugarit*. Mission de Ras Shamra 7. Paris: Imprimerie Nationale, 1957.
Volten, Aksel. *Zwei altägyptische politische Schriften: Die Lehre für König Merikarê (Pap. Carlsberg vi) und die Lehre des Königs Amenemhet*. AAeg 4. Copenhagen: E. Munksgaard, 1945.
von Rad, Gerhard. *Genesis: A Commentary*. OTL. Translated by John H. Marks. London: SCM Press Ltd, 1961.

Watanabe, Kazuko. *Der adê-Vereidigung anlässlich der Thronfolgereglung Asarhaddons*. Baghdader Mitteilungen 3. Berlin: Gebr. Mann Verlag, 1987.
Weber, Max. "Ethnic Groups." Pages 389-95 in *Economy and Society: An Outline of Interpretive Sociology*. Edited by Guenther Roth, Claus Wittich and Ephraim Fischoff. Berkeley, Calif.: University of California Press, 1978.
Weinfeld, Moshe. "The Covenant of Grant in the Old Testament and in the Ancient Near East." *JAOS* 90 (1970): 184-203.
_____. *Deuteronomy and the Deuteronomic School*. Oxford: Oxford University Press, 1972.
_____. "Covenant Terminology in the Ancient Near East and Its Influence on the West." *JAOS* 93 (1973): 190-99.

Wellhausen, Julius. *Prolegomena to the History of Ancient Israel.* Translated by J. Sutherland Black and W. Robertson Smith. Reprint 2008 ed. Bibliobazaar, 1885.

_____. *Prolegomena zur Geschichte Israels.* 5th ed. Berlin: G. Reimer, 1899.

Wells, Bruce. *The Law of Testimony in the Pentateuchal Codes.* BZAR 4. Wiesbaden: Harrassowitz, 2004.

West, Gerald O. "And the Dumb Do Speak: Articulating Incipient Readings of the Bible in Marginalized Communities." Pages 174-92 in *And the Dumb Do Speak: Articulating Incipient Readings of the Bible in Marginalized Communities.* Edited by John W. Rogerson, Margaret Davies and M. Daniel Carroll R. The Bible in Ethics: The Second Sheffield Colloquium. London: Continuum, 1995.

_____. "Gauging the Grain in a More Nuanced Literary Manner: A Cautionary Tale Concerning the Contribution of the Social Sciences to Biblical Interpretation." Pages 75-105 in *Gauging the Grain in a More Nuanced Literary Manner: A Cautionary Tale Concerning the Contribution of the Social Sciences to Biblical Interpretation.* Edited by M. Daniel Carroll R. Rethinking Contexts, Rereading Texts: Contributions from the Social Sciences to Biblical Interpretation. London: Continuum, 2000.

Westermann, Claus. *Isaiah 40–66.* OTL. Translated by David M.G. Stalker. Philadelphia: Westminster, 1969.

White, Hugh C. "The Divine Oath in Genesis." *JBL* (1973): 165-79.

Widengren, Geo. "Yahweh's Gathering of the Dispersed." Pages 227-45 in *In the Shelter of Elyon: Essays on Ancient Palestinian Life and Literature in Honor of G.W. Ahlström.* Edited by W. Boyd Barrick and John R. Spencer. JSOTSup 31. Sheffield: JSOT Press, 1984.

Wilderberger, Hans. "Der Monotheismus Deuterojesajas." Pages 506-30 in *Beiträge zur alttestemantlichen Theologie.* Edited by H. Donner, R. Hanhart and R. Smend. Göttingen: Vandenhoeck & Ruprecht, 1977.

Williams, Ronald J. "Egypt and Israel." Pages 257-90 in *The Legacy of Egypt.* Edited by J.R. Harris. Oxford: Oxford University Press, 1971.

Williamson, H.G.M. *Ezra, Nehemiah.* WBC 16. Waco, Tex.: Word Books, 1985.

_____. *The Book Called Isaiah: Deutero-Isaiah's Role in Composition and Redaction.* Oxford: Clarendon Press, 1994.

_____. "Structure and Historiography in Nehemiah 9." Pages 282-93 in *Studies in Persian Period History and Historiography.* FAT/I 38. Tübingen: Mohr Siebeck, 2004.

_____. "The Belief System of the Book of Nehemiah." Pages 271-81 in *Studies in Persian Period History and Historiography*. FAT 38. Tübingen: Mohr Siebeck, 2004.

Wilson, John A. "The Oath in Ancient Egypt." *JNES* 7 (1948): 129-56.

Wright, David P. *Ritual in Narrative: The Dynamics of Feasting, Mourning, and Retaliation Rites in the Ugaritic Tale of Aqhat*. Winona Lake, Ind.: Eisenbrauns, 2001.

Wyatt, Nicolas. "The Ugaritic Poem of Aqht: Text, Translation, Commentary." Pages 234-58 in *Handbook of Ugaritic Studies*. Edited by Wilfred G.E. Watson and Nicolas Wyatt. Handbuch der Orientalistik, Nahe und der Mittlere Osten 39. Leiden: Brill, 1999.

_____. *Religious Texts from Ugarit*. Biblical Seminar 53. 2nd ed. London: Sheffield Academic Press, 2002.

Yee, Gale A. *Composition and Tradition in the Book of Hosea: A Redaction Critical Investigation*. SBLDS 102. Atlanta, Ga.: Scholars Press, 1987.

Yurchak, Alexei. *Everything Was Forever, Until It Was No More: The Last Soviet Generation*. Princeton, N.J.: Princeton University Press, 2006.

Zahn, Molly M. "Reexamaning Empirical Models: The Case of Exodus 13." Pages 36-55 in *Das Deuteronomium zwischen Pentateuch und deuteronomist-ischem Geschichtswerk*. Edited by E. Otto and R. Achenbach. FRLANT 206. Göttingen: Vandenhoeck & Ruprecht, 2004.

Ziegler, Yael. ""So Shall God Do.": Variations of an Oath Formula and Its Literary Meaning." *JBL* 126 (2007): 59-81.

_____. ""As the Lord Lives and as Your Soul Lives": An Oath of Conscious Deference." *VT* 58 (2008): 117-30.

_____. *Promises to Keep: The Oath in Biblical Narrative*. VTSup 120. Leiden: Brill, 2008.

Zimmerli, Walther. "Erkenntnis Gottes nach dem Buch Ezechiel." in *Eine theologische Studie: Abhandlungen zur Theologie des Alten und Neuen Testaments*. 27. Zürich: Zwingli-Verlag, 1954.

_____. "Ich bin Yahweh." Pages 11-40 in *Gottes Offenbarung: gesammelte Aufsätze zum Alten Testament*. TBü 19. Munich: C. Kaiser, 1963.

_____. *Ezechiel 1: Ezechiel 1–24*. BKAT 13.1. Neukirchen-Vluyn: Neukirchener Verlag, 1969.

_____. *Ezechiel 2: Ezechiel 25–48*. BKAT 13.2. Nuekirchen-Vluyn: Neukirchener Verlag, 1969.

_____. *A Commentary on the Book of the Prophet Ezekiel, Chapters 1–24.* Hermeneia 1. Translated by Ronald E. Clements. Minneapolis, Minn.: Fortress, 1979.

_____. *I Am Yahweh.* Edited by Walter Brueggemann. Translated by D. Stott. Atlanta, Ga.: John Knox Press, 1982.

_____. *A Commentary on the Book of the Prophet of Ezekiel, Chapters 25–48.* Hermeneia 2. Translated by James D. Martin. Philadelphia: Fortress, 1983.

Index of Ancient Texts

1. Biblical Texts

Hebrew Bible

Genesis

2	50
4:11-12	185
9:5	74
11:4	248, 252
11:8	248
11:8-9	252
12–35	181, 219
14:22	8, 9, 74, 81, 82
14:22-23	82
15	6, 186-7, 202-3
15:7	159
15:7-21	216
15:18	6
17	187, 203
17:8	192
18:7	92
21:10	186
21:14	92
21:22-24	192
22:16	8, 149, 150
22:17	186
24:7	8, 149, 150
24:60	186
25–36	196
25:19-26	212
25:20	212
26:1-5	192
26:3	8, 149, 150
26:34-35	211-2
27:46–28:9	211
28:1-4	203, 216
28:4	192, 202, 211, 219
28:13	159

31:9	92
35:27	192
36:7	192
46:20	78
50:24	8, 13, 149, 150

Exodus

1–15	246
1:5	78
1:13	244
1:15-22	245
3:14	50
6	96, 164
6:2	119, 159, 246
6:2-8	119-23, 127, 156, 158, 162, 167, 169, 261, 281
6:3-5	158
6:4	192
6:8	9, 81, 93, 117-8, 154-5, 159, 274
6:6-8	89, 93, 120, 246
6:29	246
7	144
7–15	245
7:1-6	156
7:5	199, 246
7:17	246
7:19	199
8:1-2	199
8:6	246
8:10	245
8:13	199
8:18	246
9:14	246

Index of Authors